Those Not-So-Sweet Boys

1

YOKO NOGIRI

c o n t e n t s

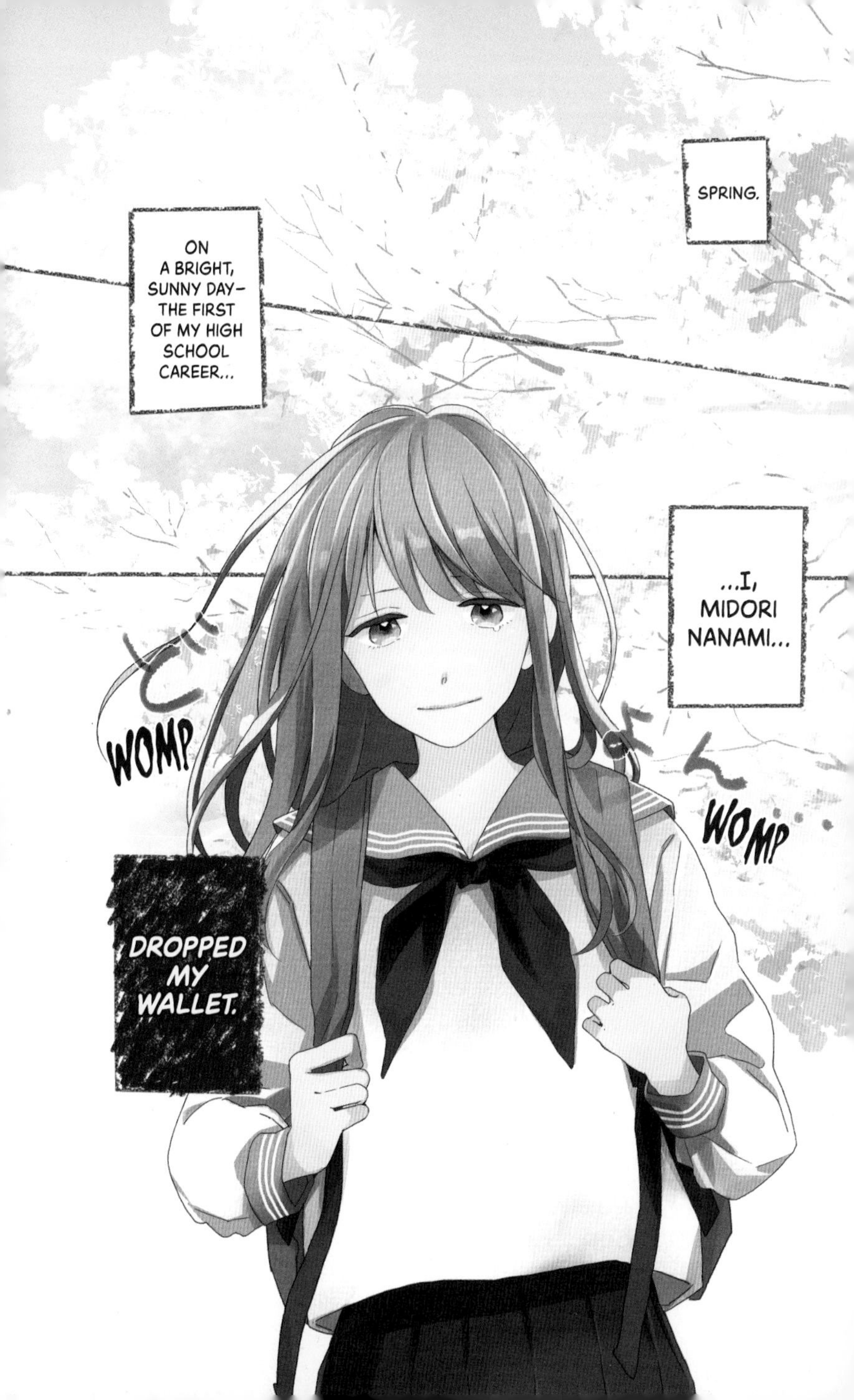
SPRING.
ON A BRIGHT, SUNNY DAY—THE FIRST OF MY HIGH SCHOOL CAREER...
...I, MIDORI NANAMI...
WOMP
WOMP
DROPPED MY WALLET.

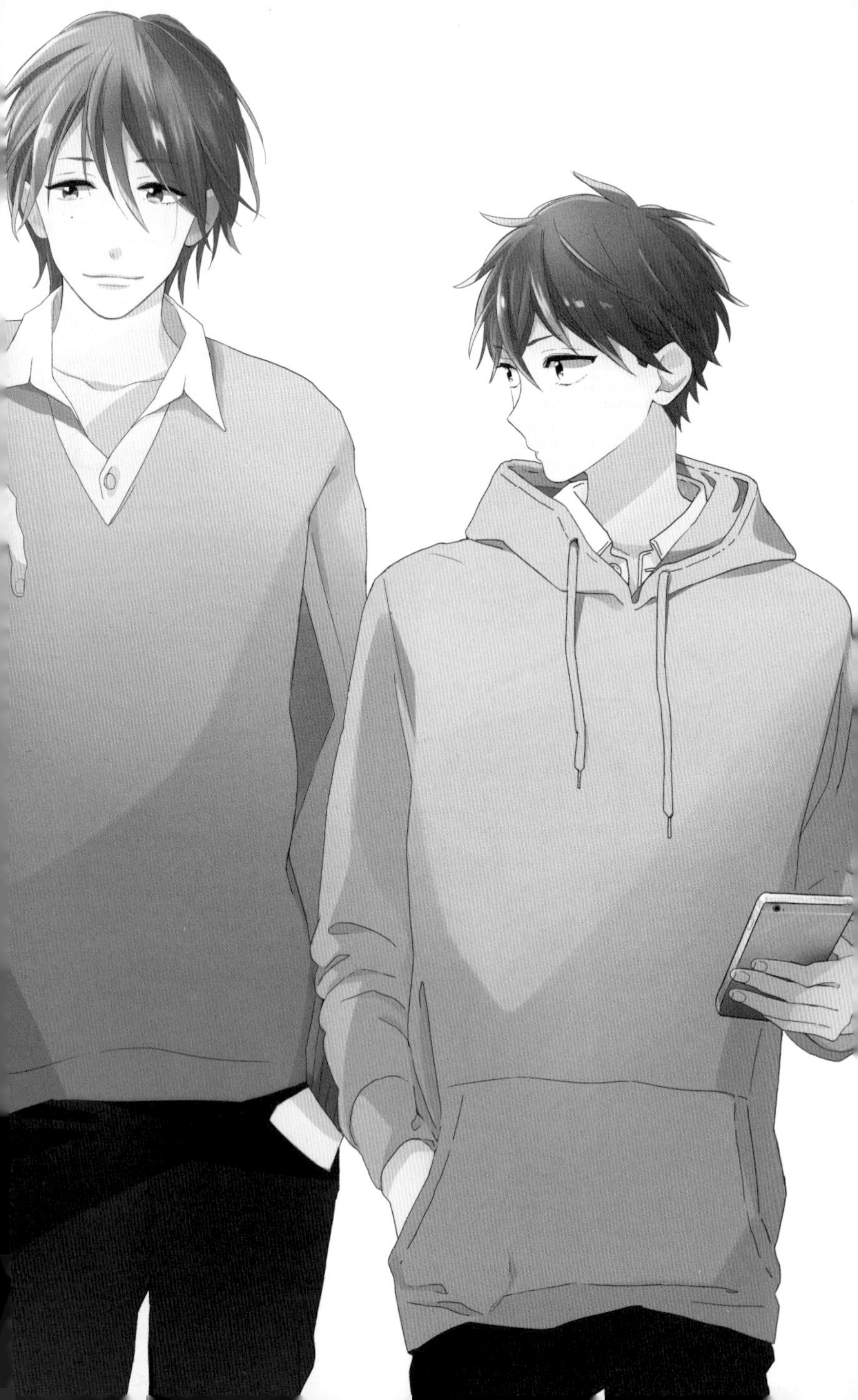

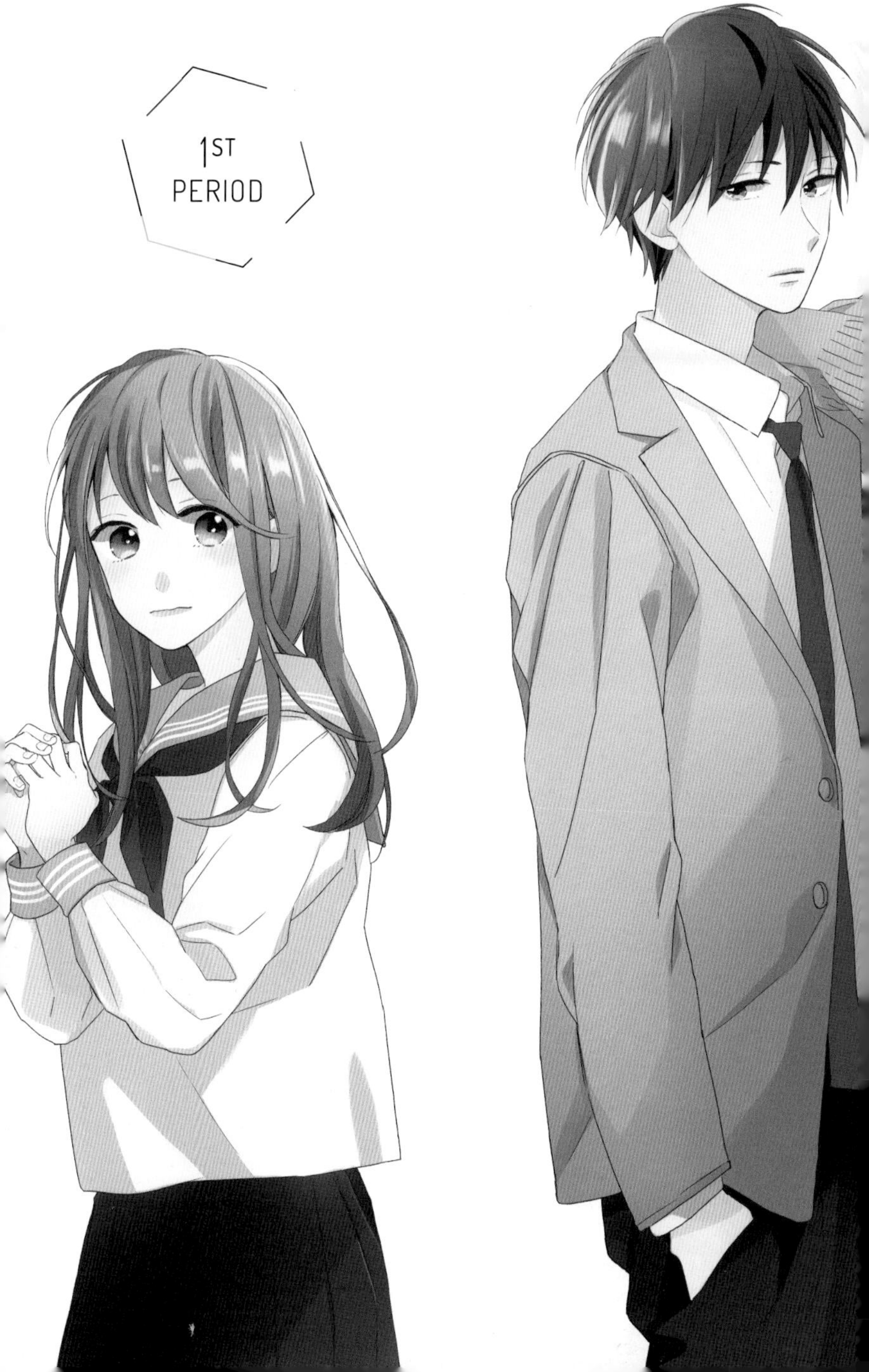
1ST
PERIOD

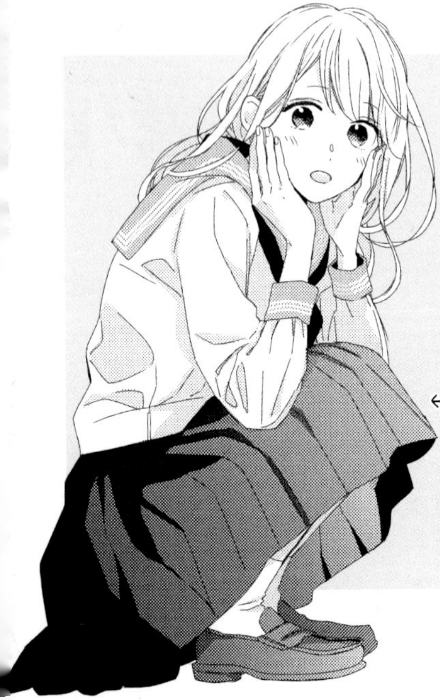

MIDORI NANAMI

HEIGHT: 157CM [5'2"], BLOOD TYPE O

BORN: DECEMBER 10, SAGITTARIUS

HOBBY: LAVISHING AFFECTION ON HER LITTLE BROTHER AND DOGS

FAVORITE SNACK: PANCAKES HER BROTHER COOKS

← HER UNIFORM IS A HAND-ME-DOWN FROM A NEIGHBOR.

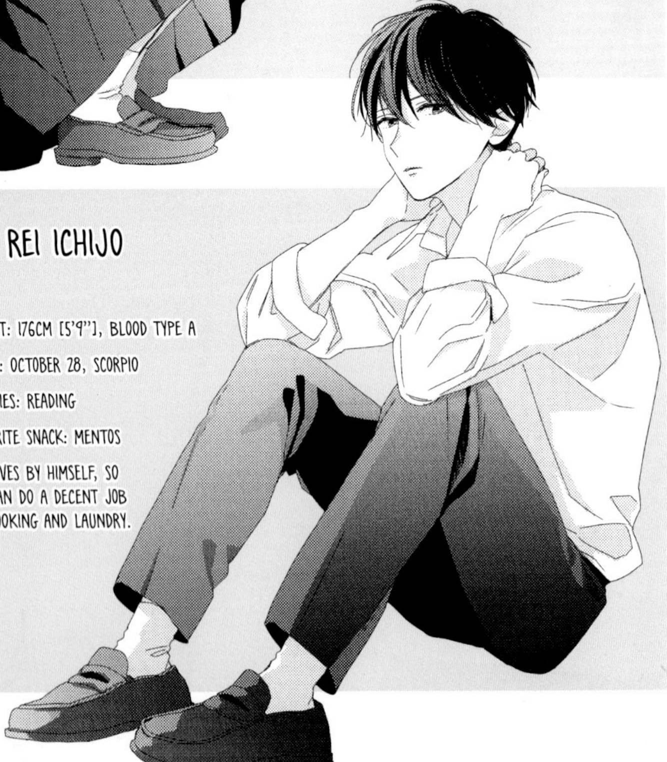

REI ICHIJO

HEIGHT: 176CM [5'9"], BLOOD TYPE A

BORN: OCTOBER 28, SCORPIO

HOBBIES: READING

FAVORITE SNACK: MENTOS

HE LIVES BY HIMSELF, SO HE CAN DO A DECENT JOB AT COOKING AND LAUNDRY.

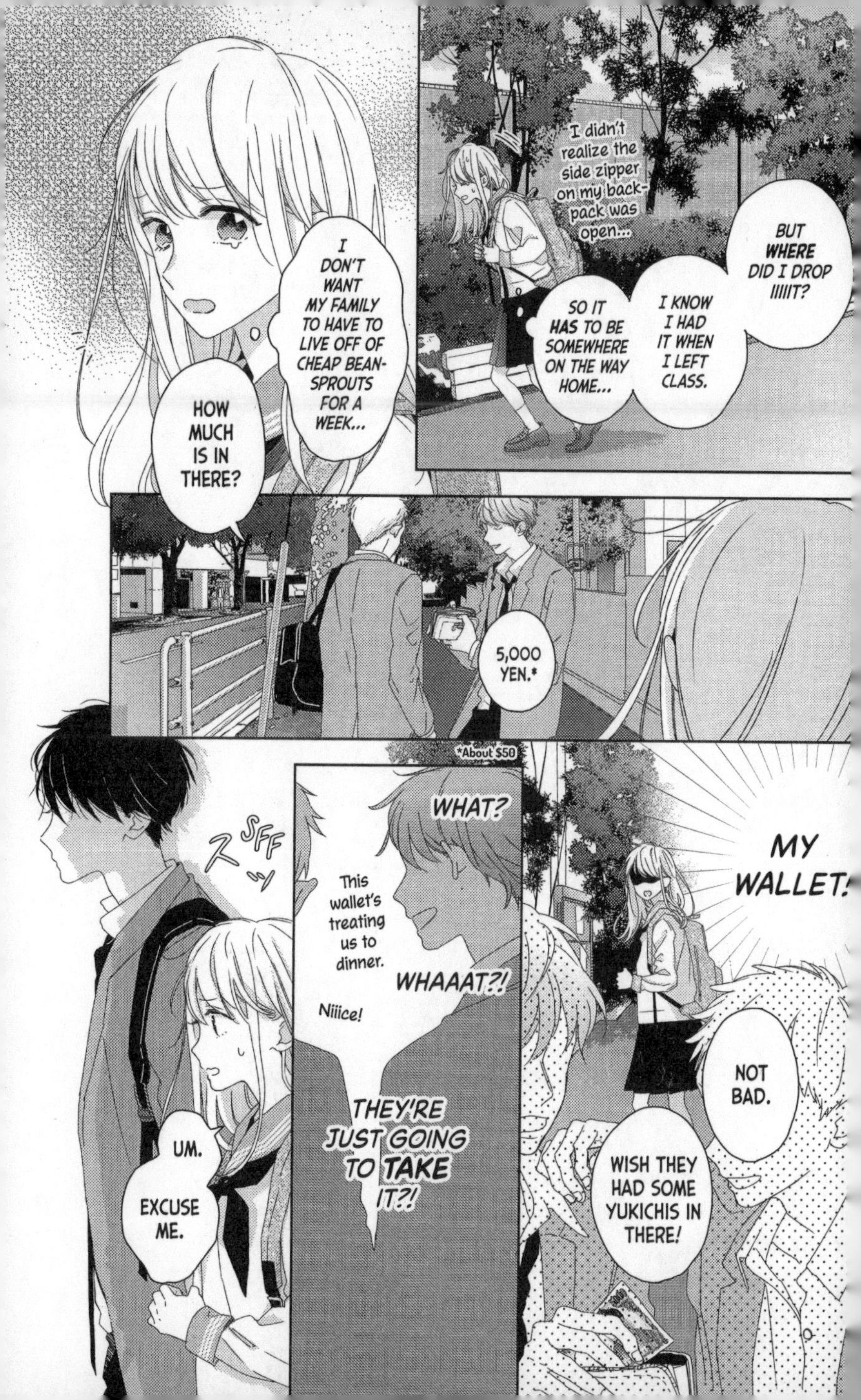
I didn't realize the side zipper on my back-pack was open...
BUT WHERE DID I DROP IIIIIT?
I KNOW I HAD IT WHEN I LEFT CLASS.
SO IT HAS TO BE SOMEWHERE ON THE WAY HOME...
I DON'T WANT MY FAMILY TO HAVE TO LIVE OFF OF CHEAP BEAN-SPROUTS FOR A WEEK...
HOW MUCH IS IN THERE?
5,000 YEN.*
*About $50
MY WALLET!
NOT BAD.
WISH THEY HAD SOME YUKICHIS IN THERE!
WHAT?
This wallet's treating us to dinner.
WHAAAT?!
Niiice!
THEY'RE JUST GOING TO TAKE IT?!
スッ
SFF
UM.
EXCUSE ME.

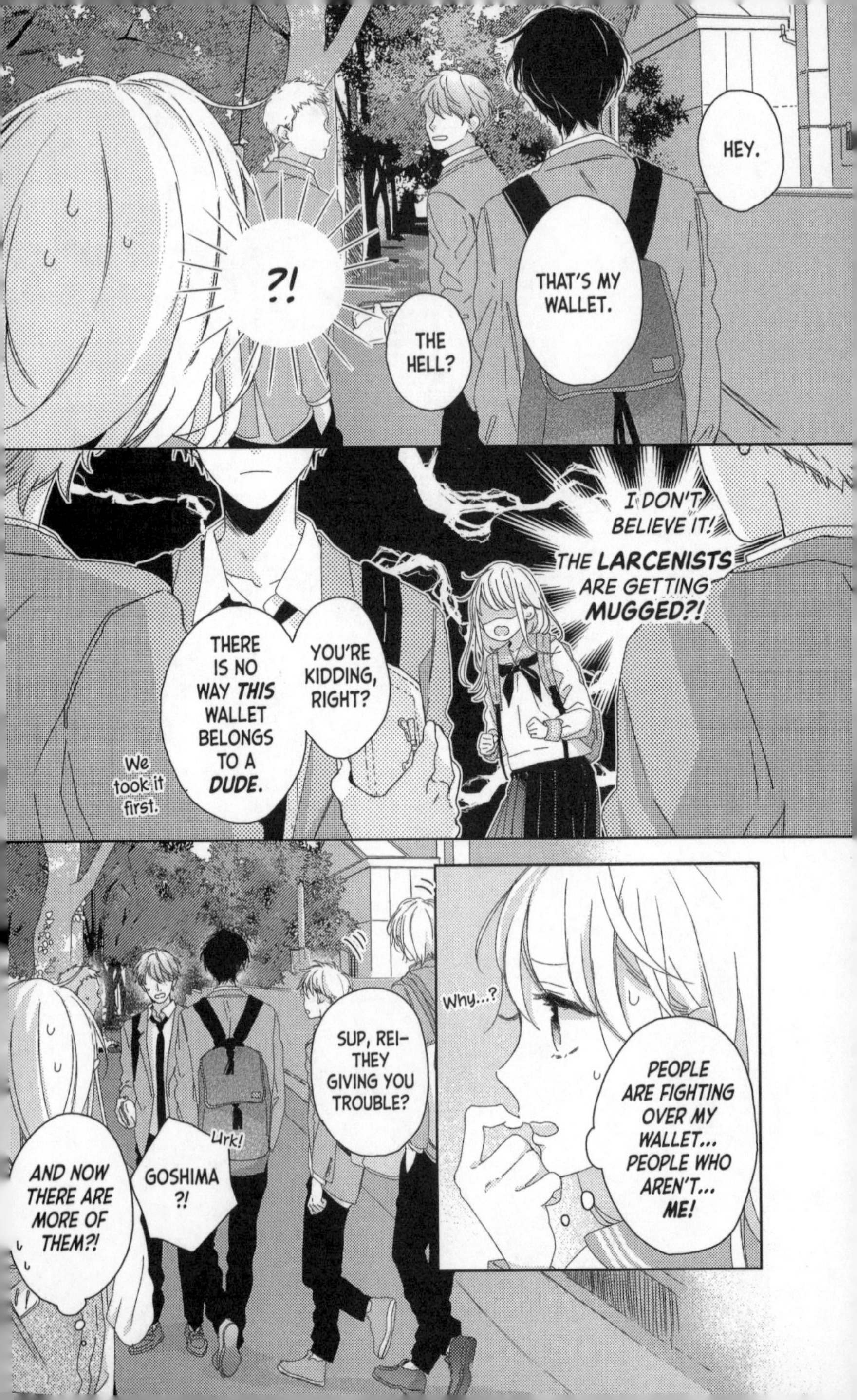
HEY.
THAT'S MY WALLET.
THE HELL?
?!
I DON'T BELIEVE IT! THE LARCENISTS ARE GETTING MUGGED?!
YOU'RE KIDDING, RIGHT?
THERE IS NO WAY THIS WALLET BELONGS TO A DUDE.
We took it first.
Why...?
PEOPLE ARE FIGHTING OVER MY WALLET... PEOPLE WHO AREN'T... ME!
SUP, REI— THEY GIVING YOU TROUBLE?
Urk!
GOSHIMA?!
AND NOW THERE ARE MORE OF THEM?!

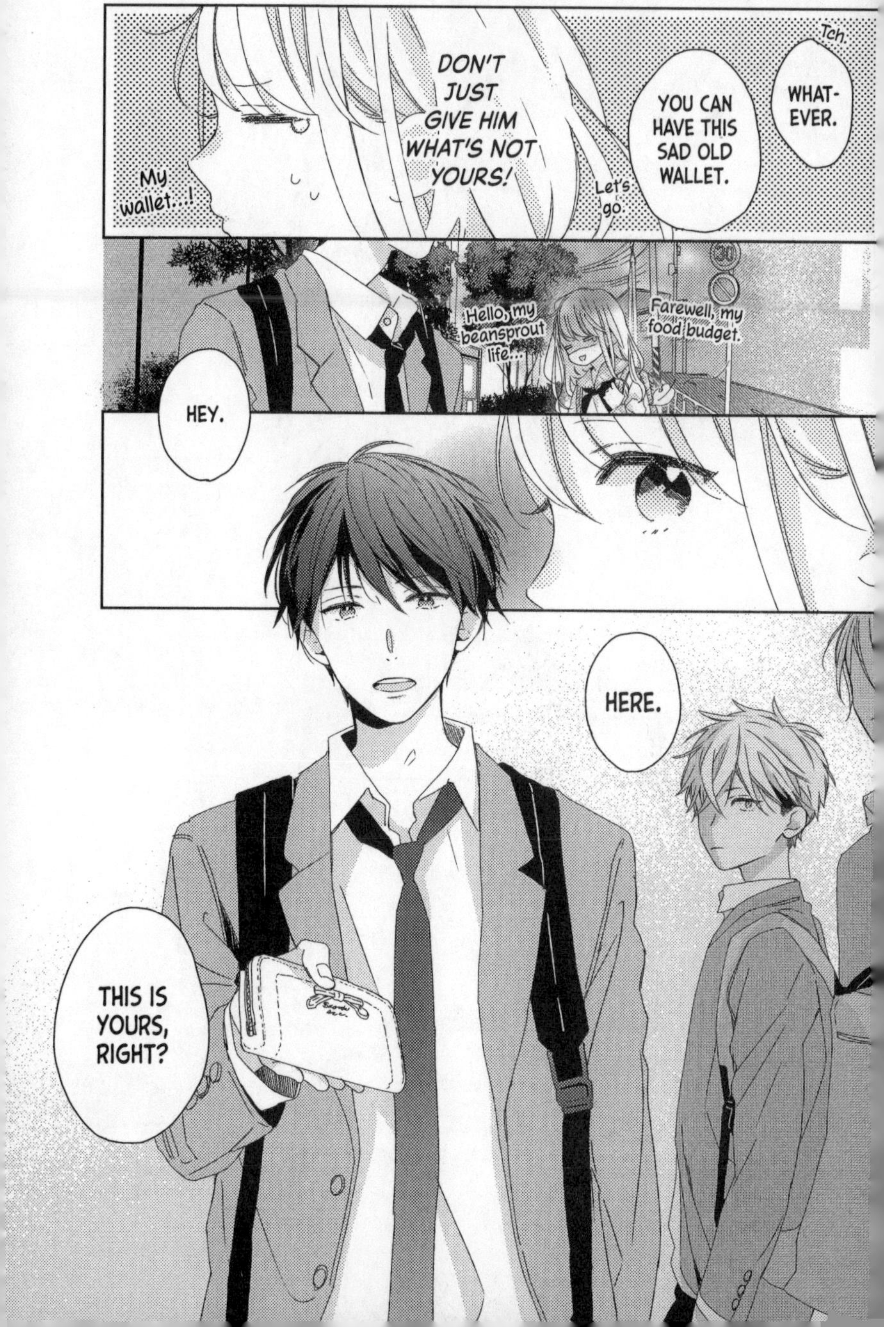
Tch.
WHAT-EVER.
YOU CAN HAVE THIS SAD OLD WALLET.
Let's go.
DON'T JUST GIVE HIM WHAT'S NOT YOURS!
My wallet...!
Farewell, my food budget.
Hello, my beansprout life...
HEY.
HERE.
THIS IS YOURS, RIGHT?

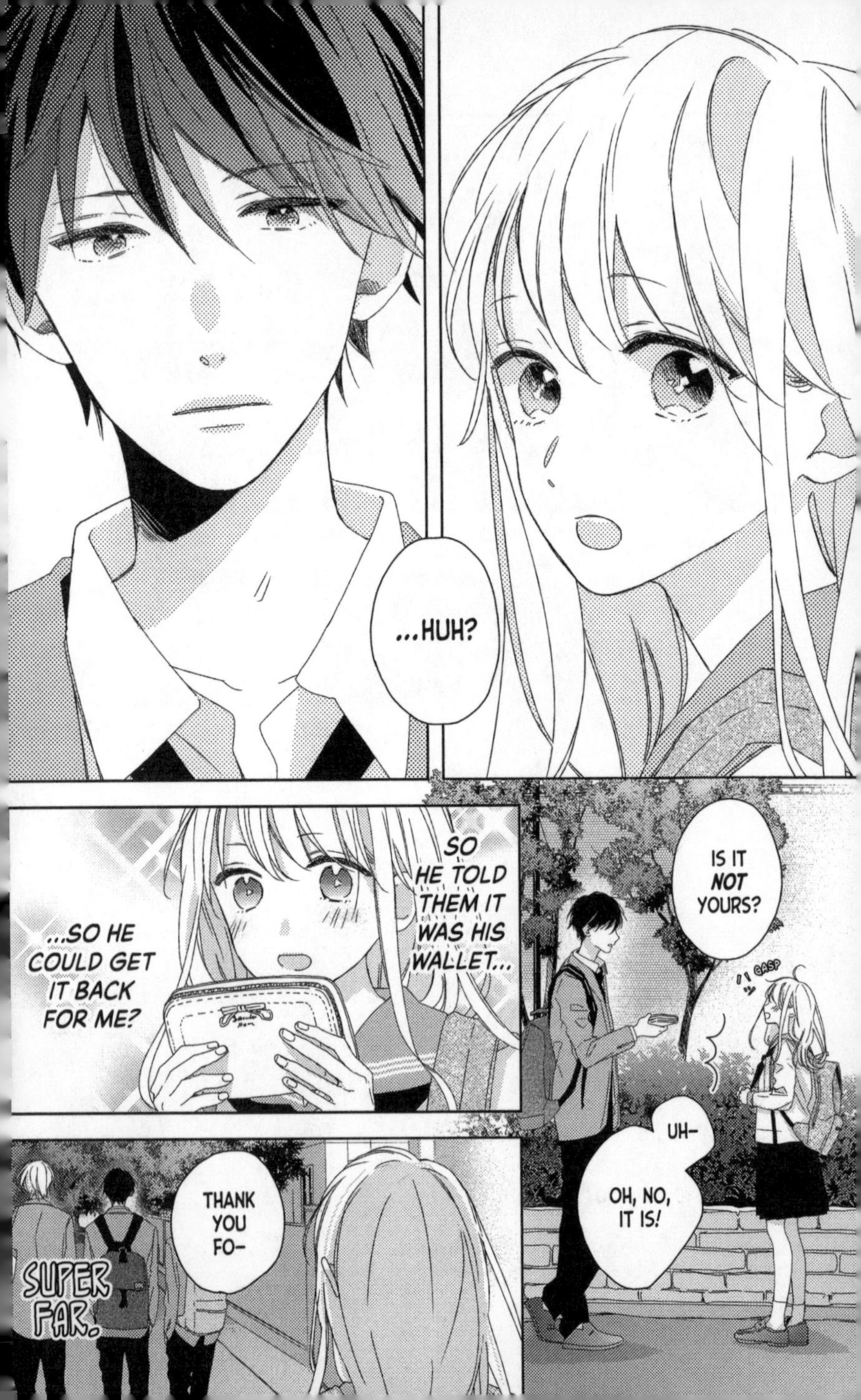
...HUH?
IS IT NOT YOURS?
GASP
UH–
OH, NO, IT IS!
SO HE TOLD THEM IT WAS HIS WALLET...
...SO HE COULD GET IT BACK FOR ME?
THANK YOU FO–
SUPER FAR.

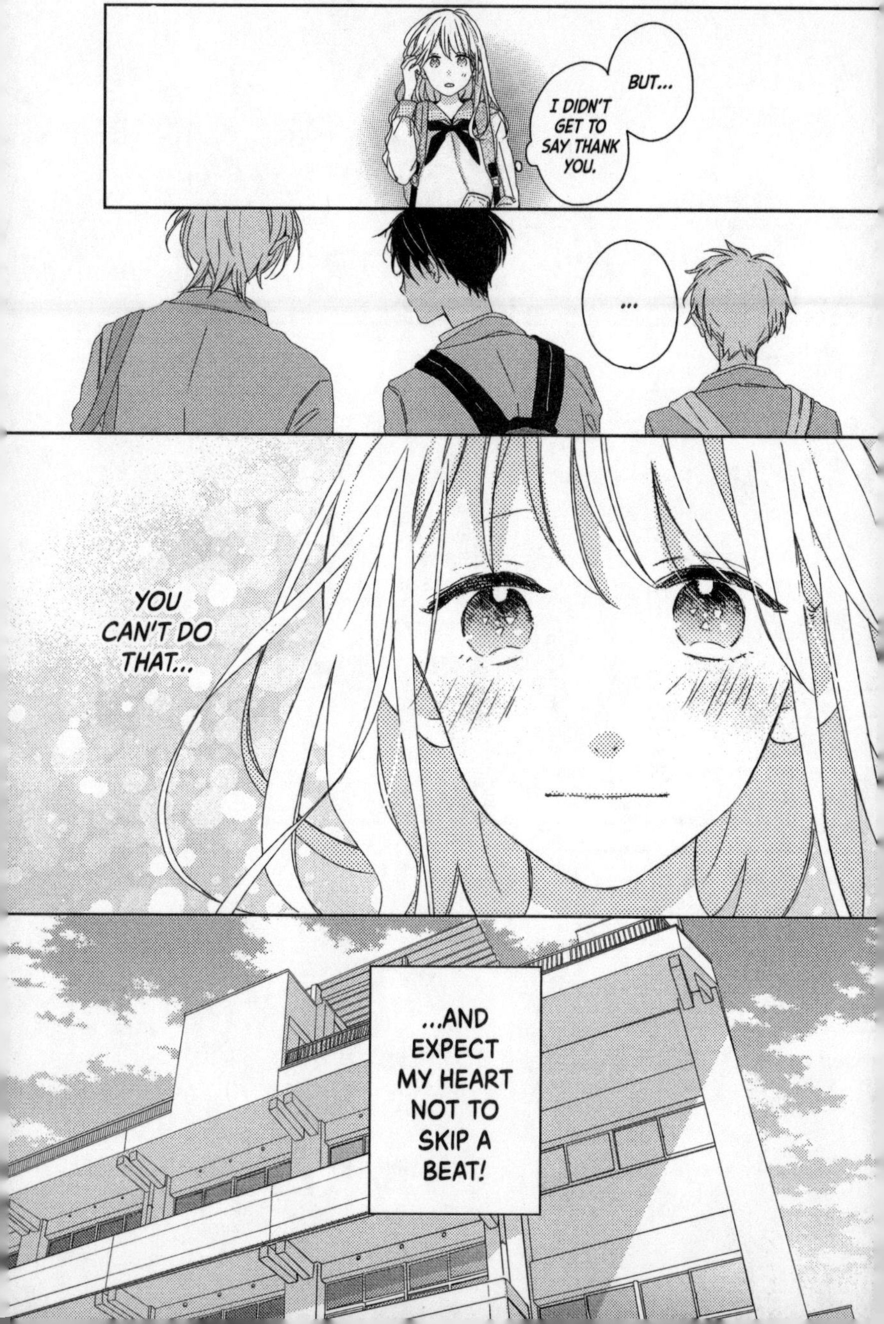
BUT... I DIDN'T GET TO SAY THANK YOU.
...
YOU CAN'T DO THAT...
...AND EXPECT MY HEART NOT TO SKIP A BEAT!

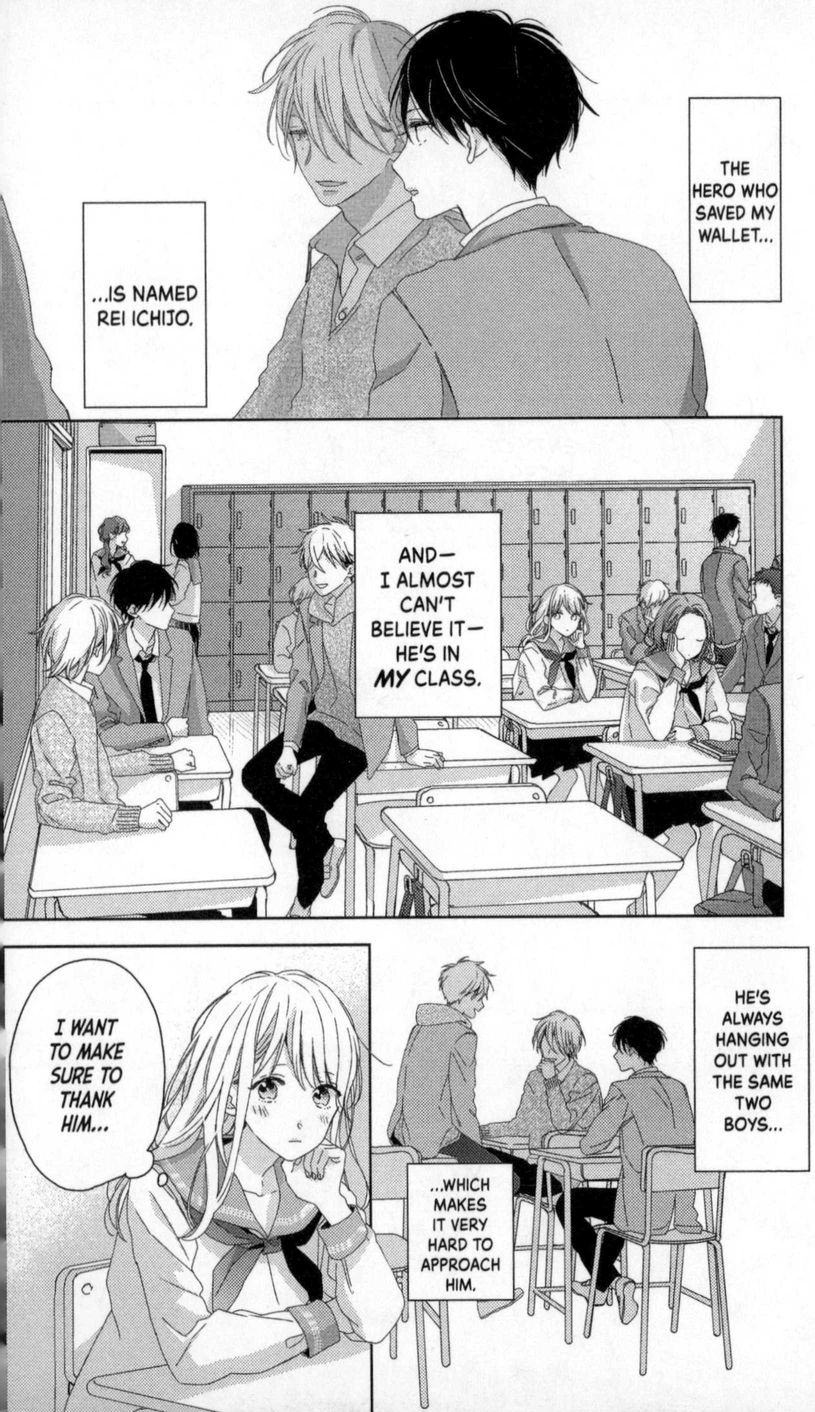
THE HERO WHO SAVED MY WALLET...
...IS NAMED REI ICHIJO.
AND— I ALMOST CAN'T BELIEVE IT— HE'S IN *MY* CLASS.
HE'S ALWAYS HANGING OUT WITH THE SAME TWO BOYS...
...WHICH MAKES IT VERY HARD TO APPROACH HIM.
I WANT TO MAKE SURE TO THANK HIM...

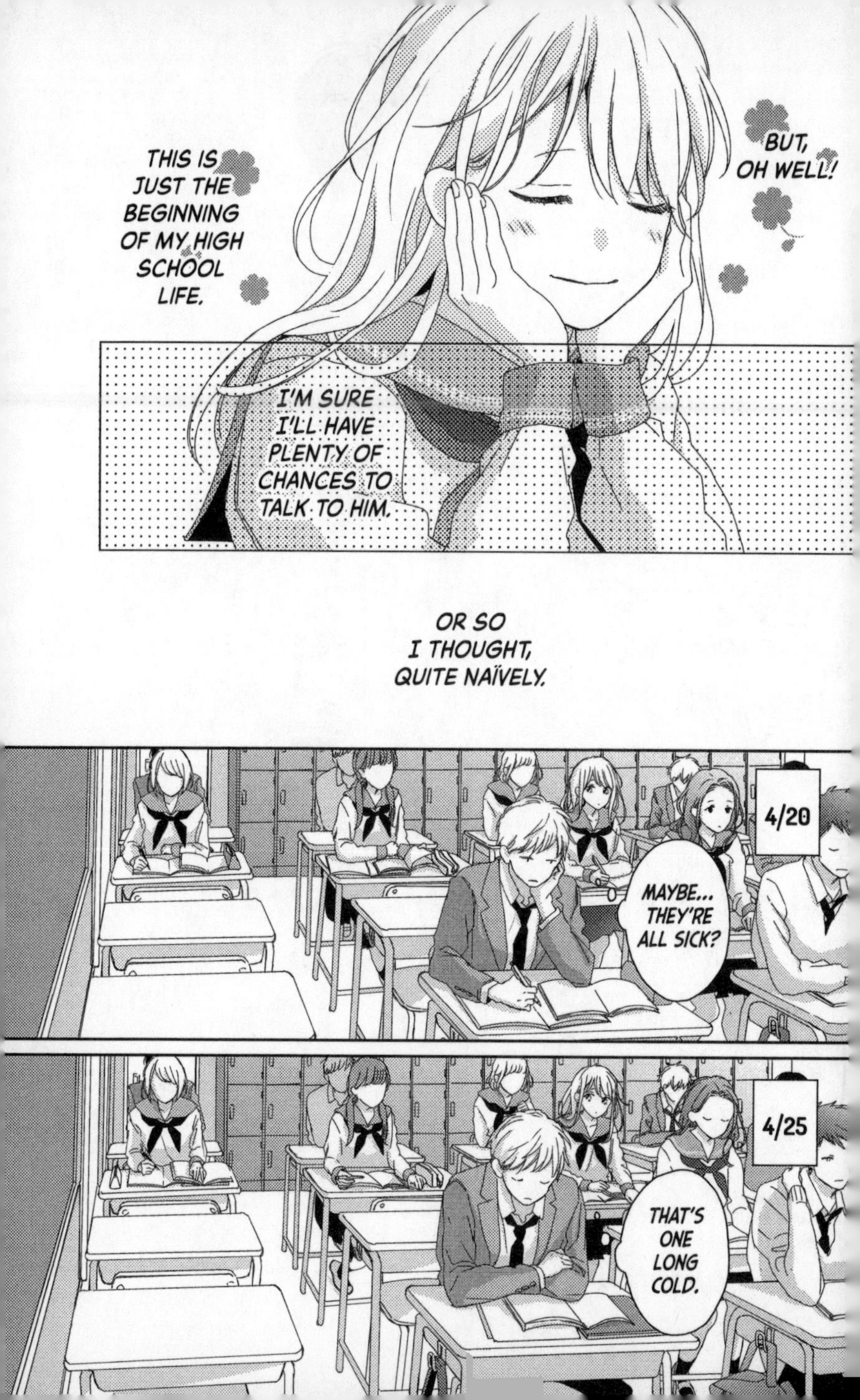
BUT, OH WELL!
THIS IS JUST THE BEGINNING OF MY HIGH SCHOOL LIFE.
I'M SURE I'LL HAVE PLENTY OF CHANCES TO TALK TO HIM.
OR SO I THOUGHT, QUITE NAÏVELY.
4/20
MAYBE... THEY'RE ALL SICK?
4/25
THAT'S ONE LONG COLD.

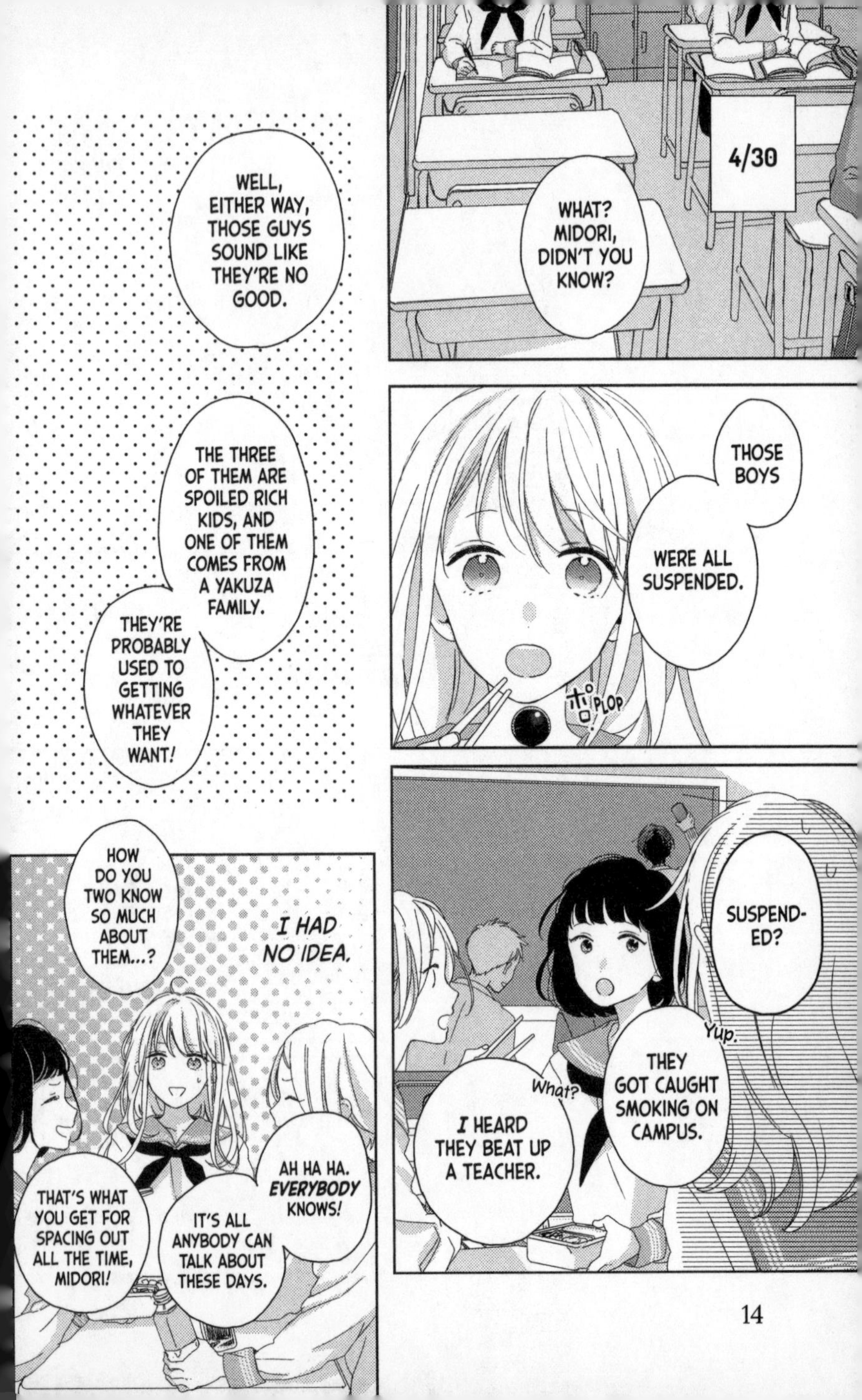
4/30
WHAT? MIDORI, DIDN'T YOU KNOW?
THOSE BOYS
WERE ALL SUSPENDED.
PLOP
SUSPEND-ED?
Yup.
THEY GOT CAUGHT SMOKING ON CAMPUS.
What?
I HEARD THEY BEAT UP A TEACHER.
WELL, EITHER WAY, THOSE GUYS SOUND LIKE THEY'RE NO GOOD.
THE THREE OF THEM ARE SPOILED RICH KIDS, AND ONE OF THEM COMES FROM A YAKUZA FAMILY.
THEY'RE PROBABLY USED TO GETTING WHATEVER THEY WANT!
HOW DO YOU TWO KNOW SO MUCH ABOUT THEM...?
I HAD NO IDEA.
AH HA HA. EVERYBODY KNOWS!
IT'S ALL ANYBODY CAN TALK ABOUT THESE DAYS.
THAT'S WHAT YOU GET FOR SPACING OUT ALL THE TIME, MIDORI!

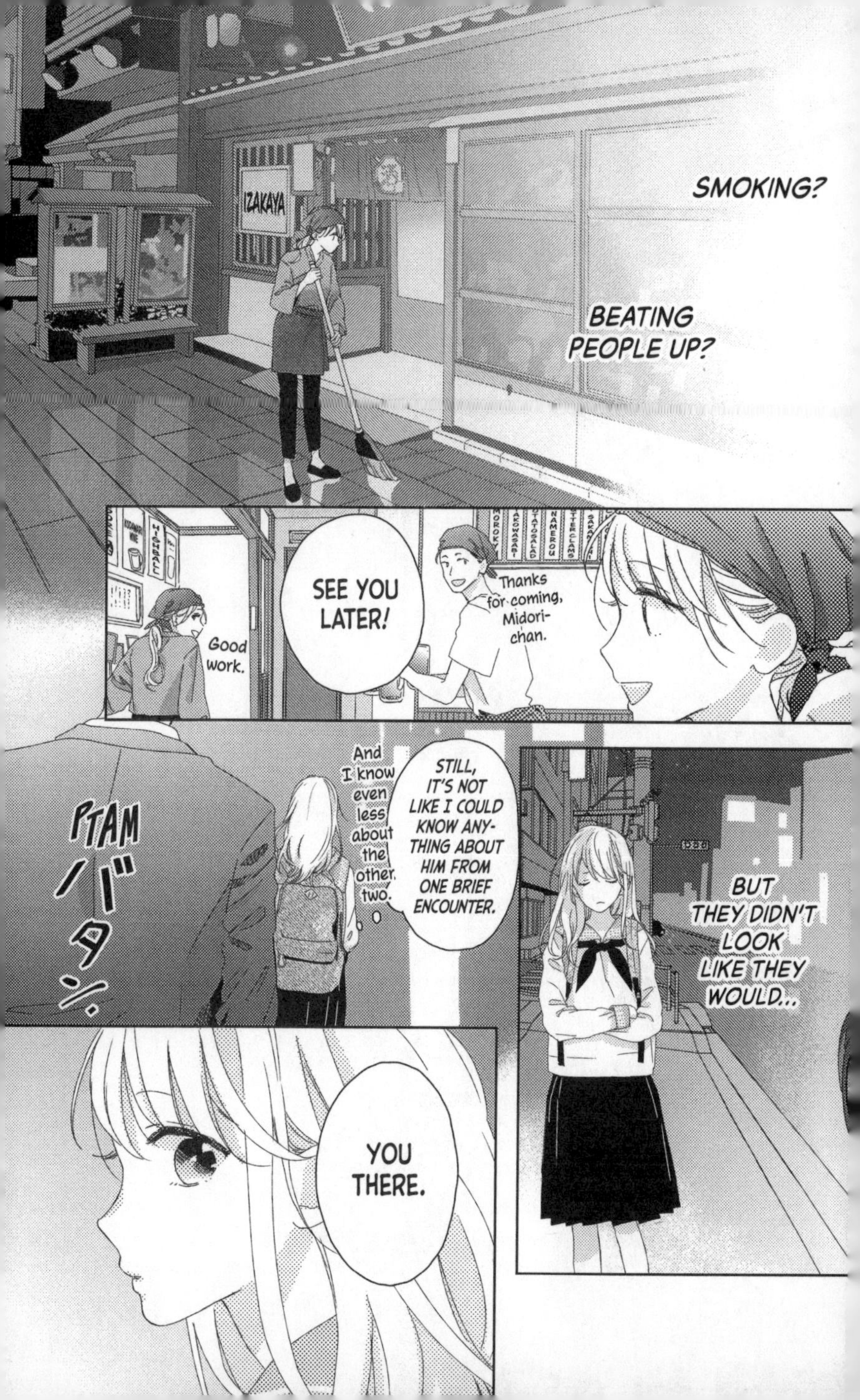
IZAKAYA
SMOKING?
BEATING PEOPLE UP?
Thanks for coming, Midori-chan.
SEE YOU LATER!
Good work.
BUT THEY DIDN'T LOOK LIKE THEY WOULD...
STILL, IT'S NOT LIKE I COULD KNOW ANY-THING ABOUT HIM FROM ONE BRIEF ENCOUNTER.
And I know even less about the other two.
PTAM
バタン
YOU THERE.

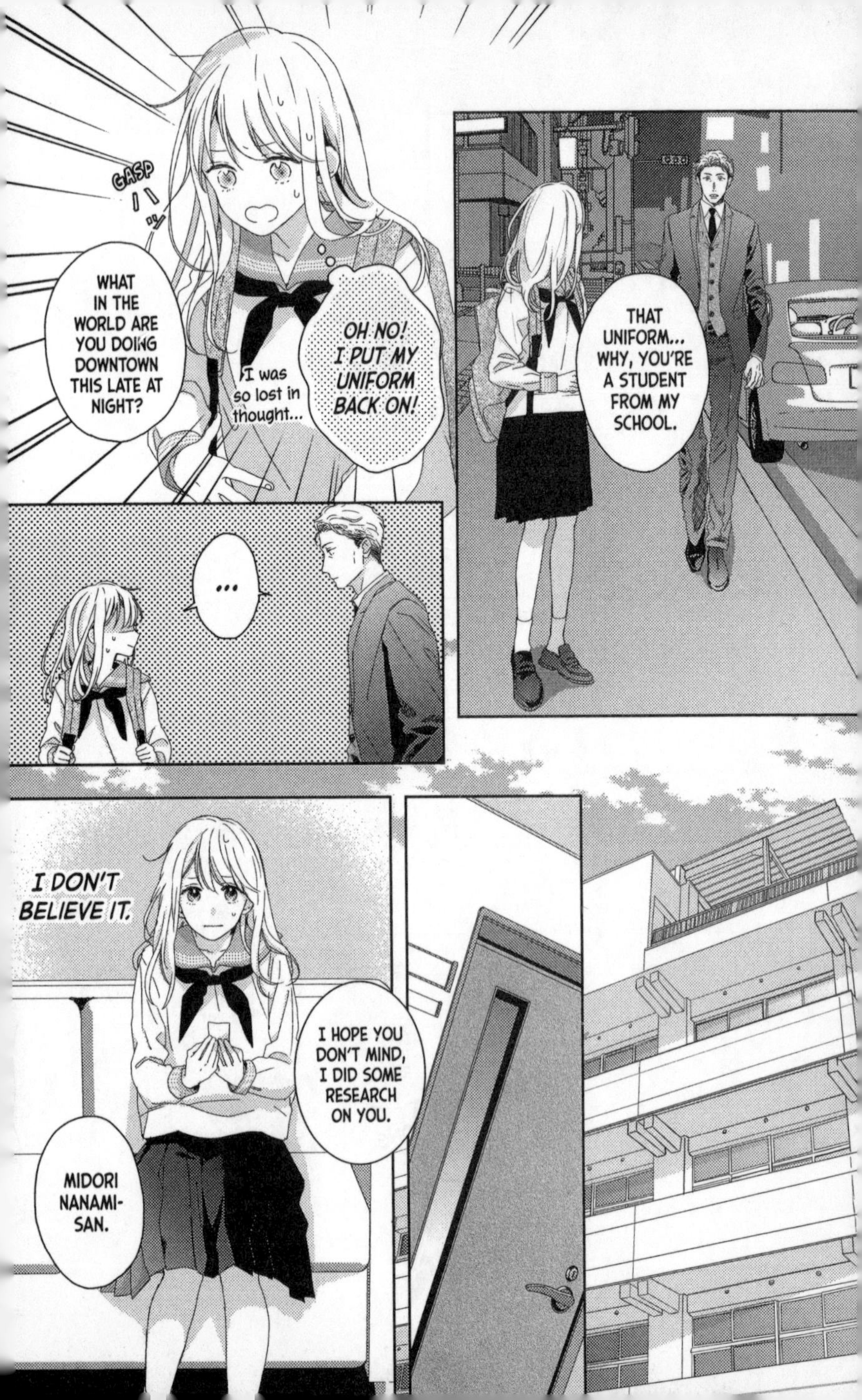
THAT UNIFORM... WHY, YOU'RE A STUDENT FROM MY SCHOOL.
GASP
WHAT IN THE WORLD ARE YOU DOING DOWNTOWN THIS LATE AT NIGHT?
OH NO! I PUT MY UNIFORM BACK ON!
I was so lost in thought...
...
I HOPE YOU DON'T MIND, I DID SOME RESEARCH ON YOU.
MIDORI NANAMI-SAN.
I DON'T BELIEVE IT.

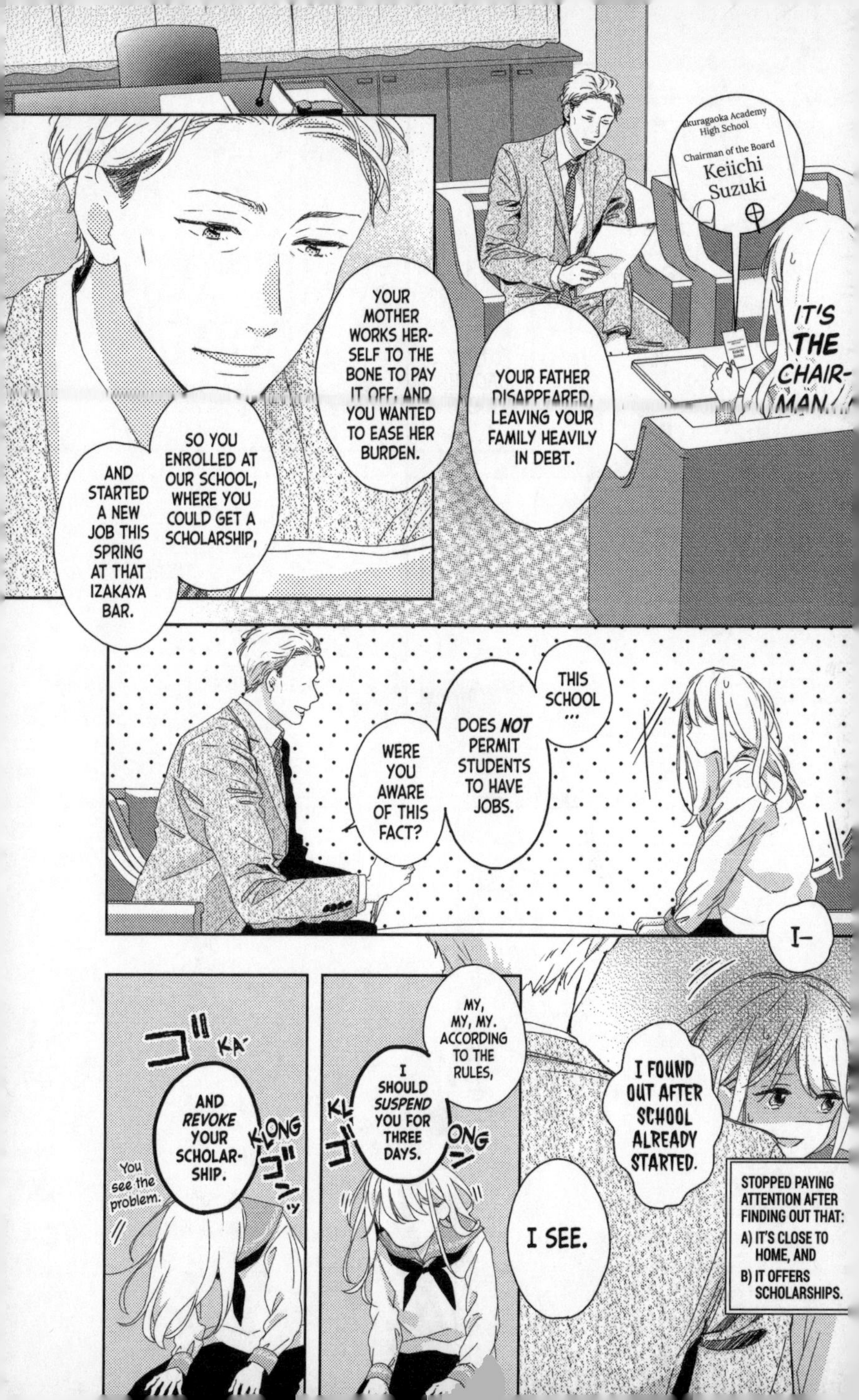
kuragaoka Academy High School
Chairman of the Board
Keiichi Suzuki
IT'S THE CHAIRMAN.
YOUR FATHER DISAPPEARED, LEAVING YOUR FAMILY HEAVILY IN DEBT.
YOUR MOTHER WORKS HERSELF TO THE BONE TO PAY IT OFF, AND YOU WANTED TO EASE HER BURDEN.
SO YOU ENROLLED AT OUR SCHOOL, WHERE YOU COULD GET A SCHOLARSHIP,
AND STARTED A NEW JOB THIS SPRING AT THAT IZAKAYA BAR.
THIS SCHOOL...
DOES *NOT* PERMIT STUDENTS TO HAVE JOBS.
WERE YOU AWARE OF THIS FACT?
I—
I FOUND OUT AFTER SCHOOL ALREADY STARTED.
STOPPED PAYING ATTENTION AFTER FINDING OUT THAT:
A) IT'S CLOSE TO HOME, AND
B) IT OFFERS SCHOLARSHIPS.
I SEE.
MY, MY, MY. ACCORDING TO THE RULES,
I SHOULD *SUSPEND* YOU FOR THREE DAYS.
KLONG
AND *REVOKE* YOUR SCHOLARSHIP.
KA-
KLONG
You see the problem.

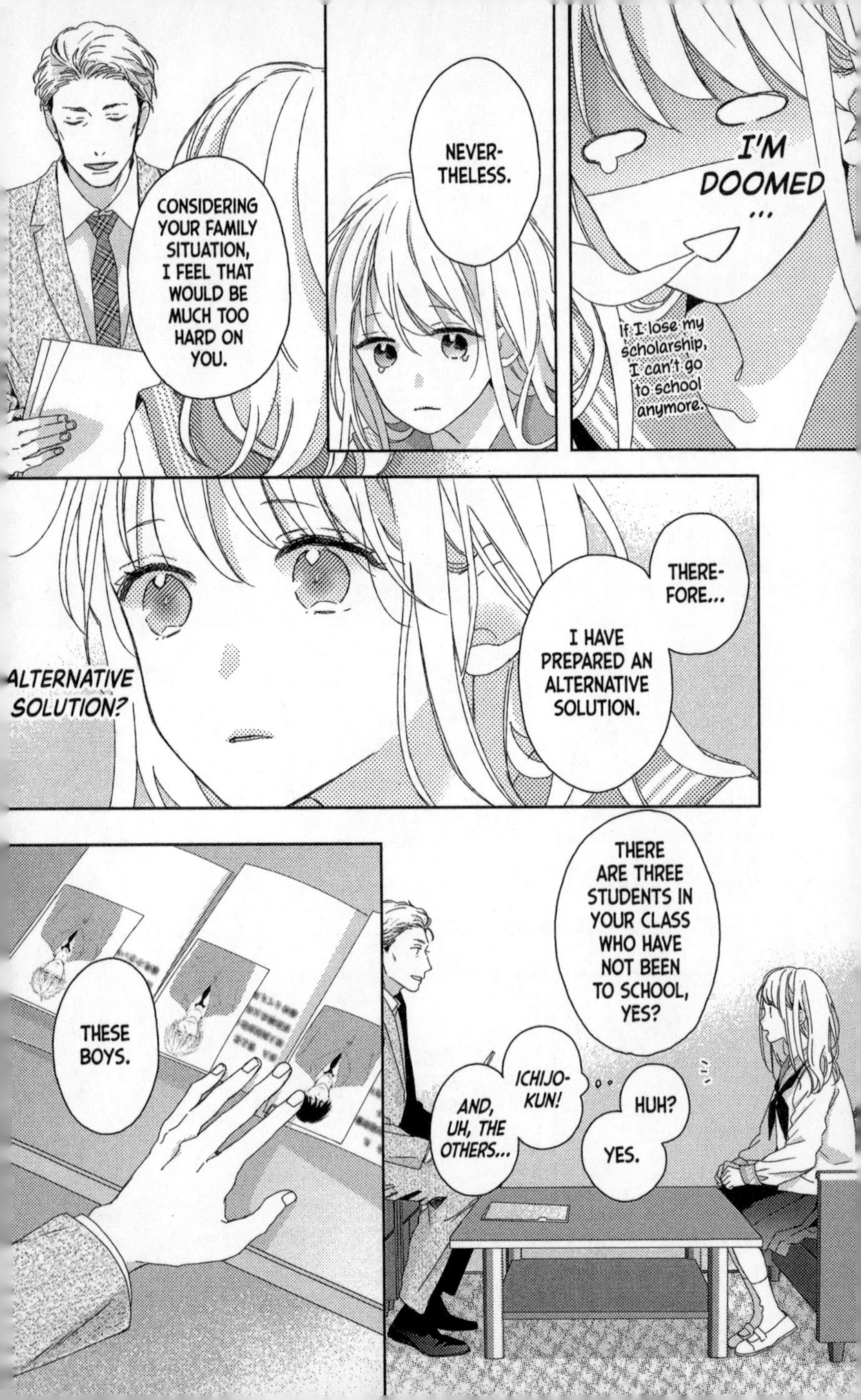
I'M DOOMED...
If I lose my scholarship, I can't go to school anymore.
NEVER-THELESS.
CONSIDERING YOUR FAMILY SITUATION, I FEEL THAT WOULD BE MUCH TOO HARD ON YOU.
THERE-FORE...
I HAVE PREPARED AN ALTERNATIVE SOLUTION.
ALTERNATIVE SOLUTION?
THERE ARE THREE STUDENTS IN YOUR CLASS WHO HAVE NOT BEEN TO SCHOOL, YES?
HUH?
YES.
ICHIJO-KUN!
AND, UH, THE OTHERS...
THESE BOYS.

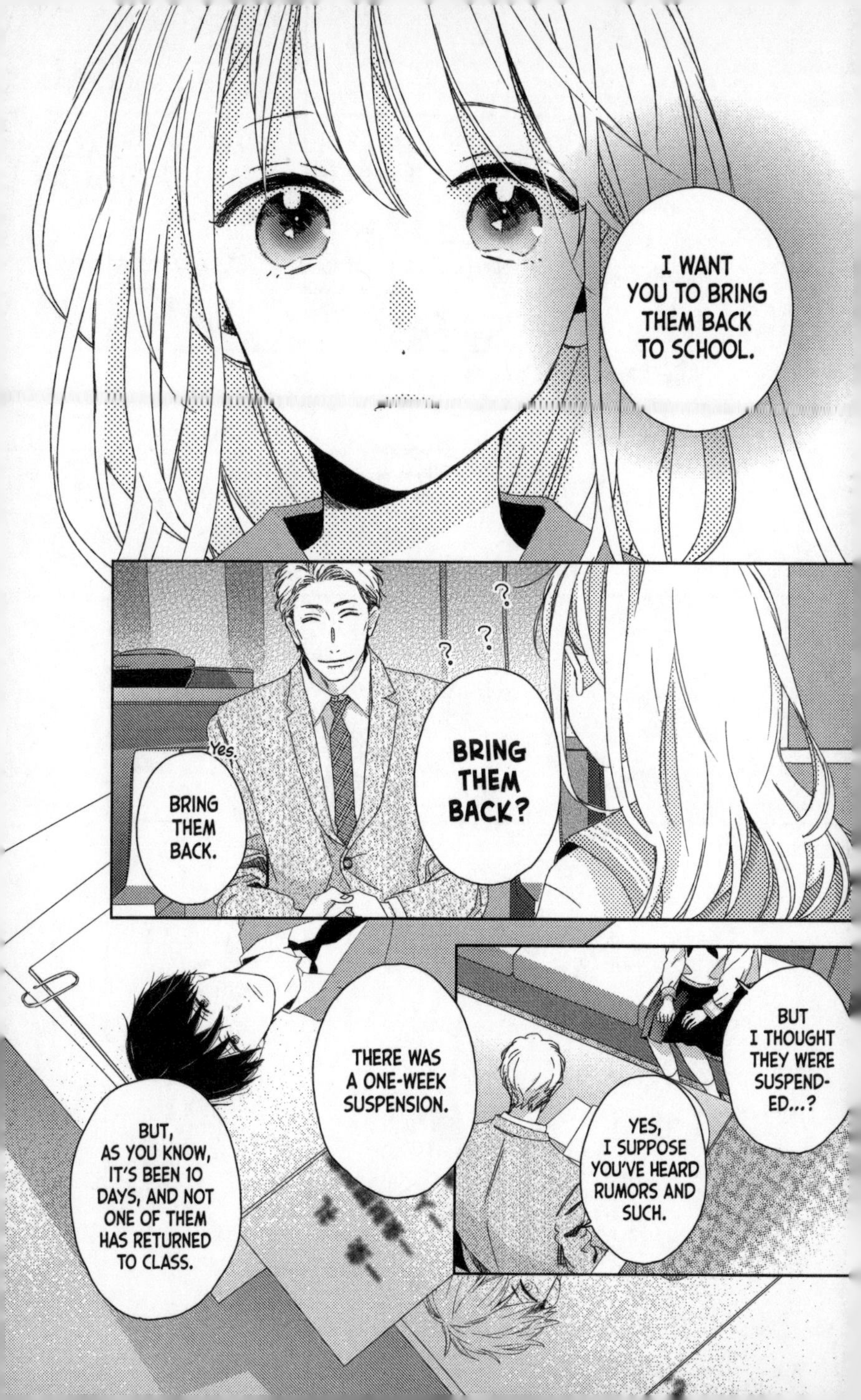
I WANT YOU TO BRING THEM BACK TO SCHOOL.
BRING THEM BACK?
Yes.
BRING THEM BACK.
BUT I THOUGHT THEY WERE SUSPEND-ED...?
YES, I SUPPOSE YOU'VE HEARD RUMORS AND SUCH.
THERE WAS A ONE-WEEK SUSPENSION.
BUT, AS YOU KNOW, IT'S BEEN 10 DAYS, AND NOT ONE OF THEM HAS RETURNED TO CLASS.

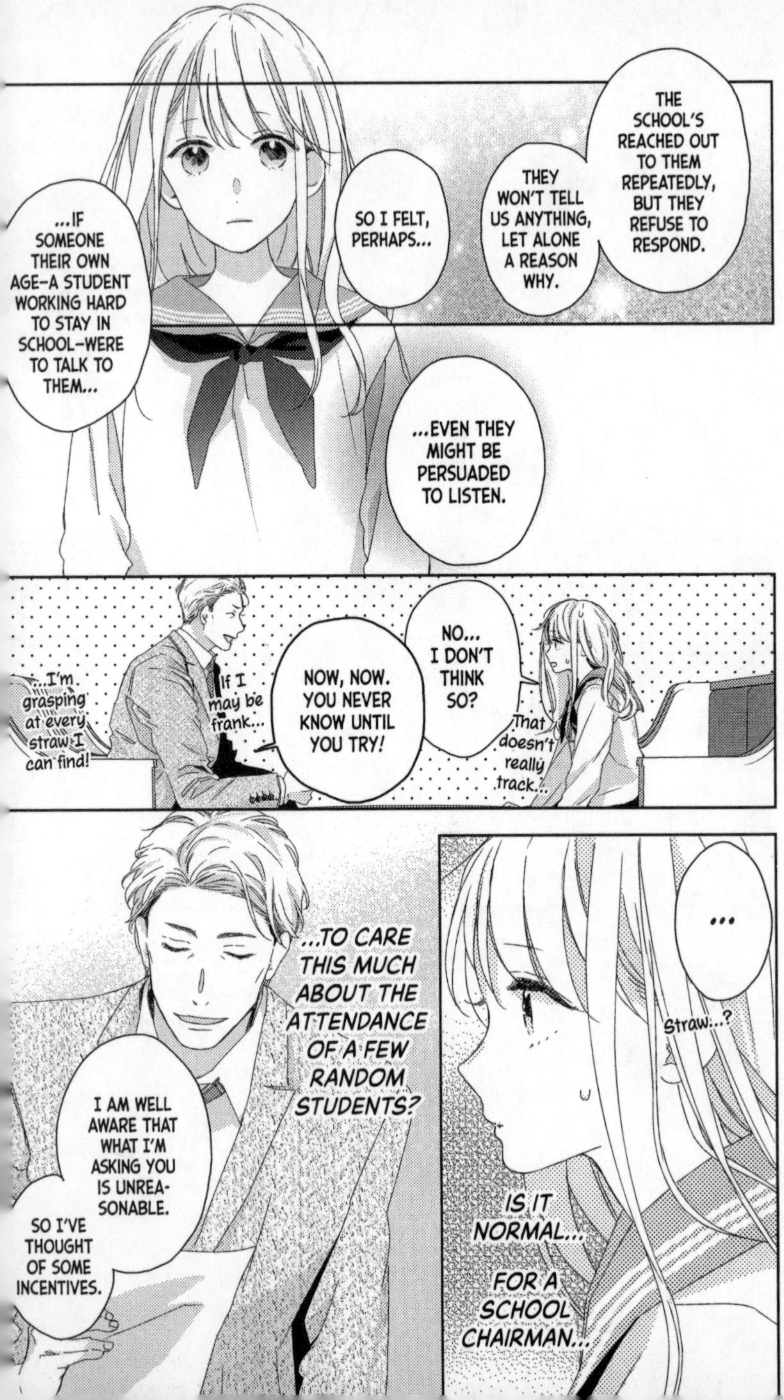
THE SCHOOL'S REACHED OUT TO THEM REPEATEDLY, BUT THEY REFUSE TO RESPOND.
THEY WON'T TELL US ANYTHING, LET ALONE A REASON WHY.
SO I FELT, PERHAPS...
...IF SOMEONE THEIR OWN AGE—A STUDENT WORKING HARD TO STAY IN SCHOOL—WERE TO TALK TO THEM...
...EVEN THEY MIGHT BE PERSUADED TO LISTEN.
That doesn't really track...
NO... I DON'T THINK SO?
NOW, NOW. YOU NEVER KNOW UNTIL YOU TRY!
If I may be frank...
...I'm grasping at every straw I can find!
...
Straw...?
IS IT NORMAL...
FOR A SCHOOL CHAIRMAN...
...TO CARE THIS MUCH ABOUT THE ATTENDANCE OF A FEW RANDOM STUDENTS?
I AM WELL AWARE THAT WHAT I'M ASKING YOU IS UNREA-SONABLE.
SO I'VE THOUGHT OF SOME INCENTIVES.

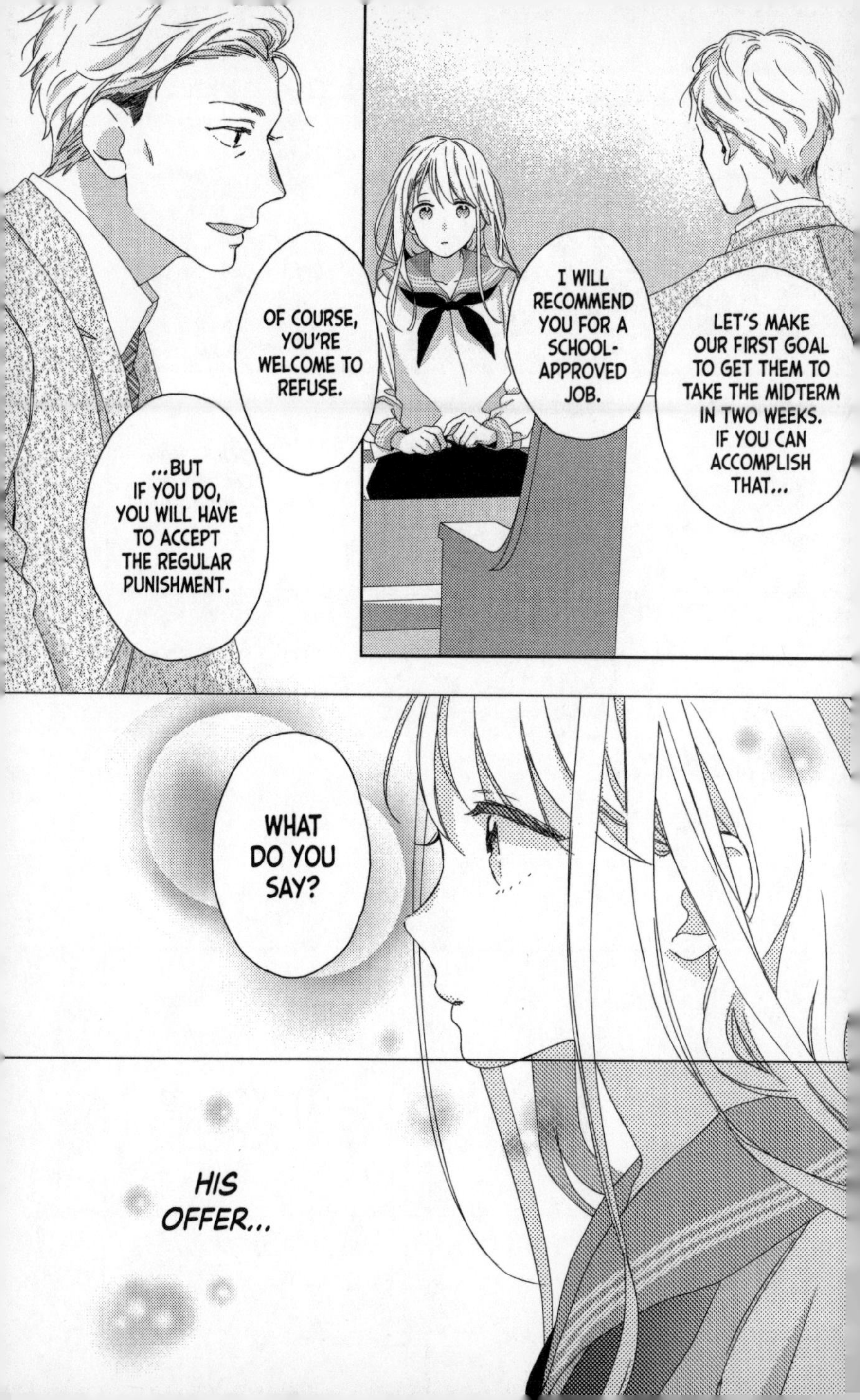
LET'S MAKE OUR FIRST GOAL TO GET THEM TO TAKE THE MIDTERM IN TWO WEEKS. IF YOU CAN ACCOMPLISH THAT...
I WILL RECOMMEND YOU FOR A SCHOOL-APPROVED JOB.
OF COURSE, YOU'RE WELCOME TO REFUSE.
...BUT IF YOU DO, YOU WILL HAVE TO ACCEPT THE REGULAR PUNISHMENT.
WHAT DO YOU SAY?
HIS OFFER...

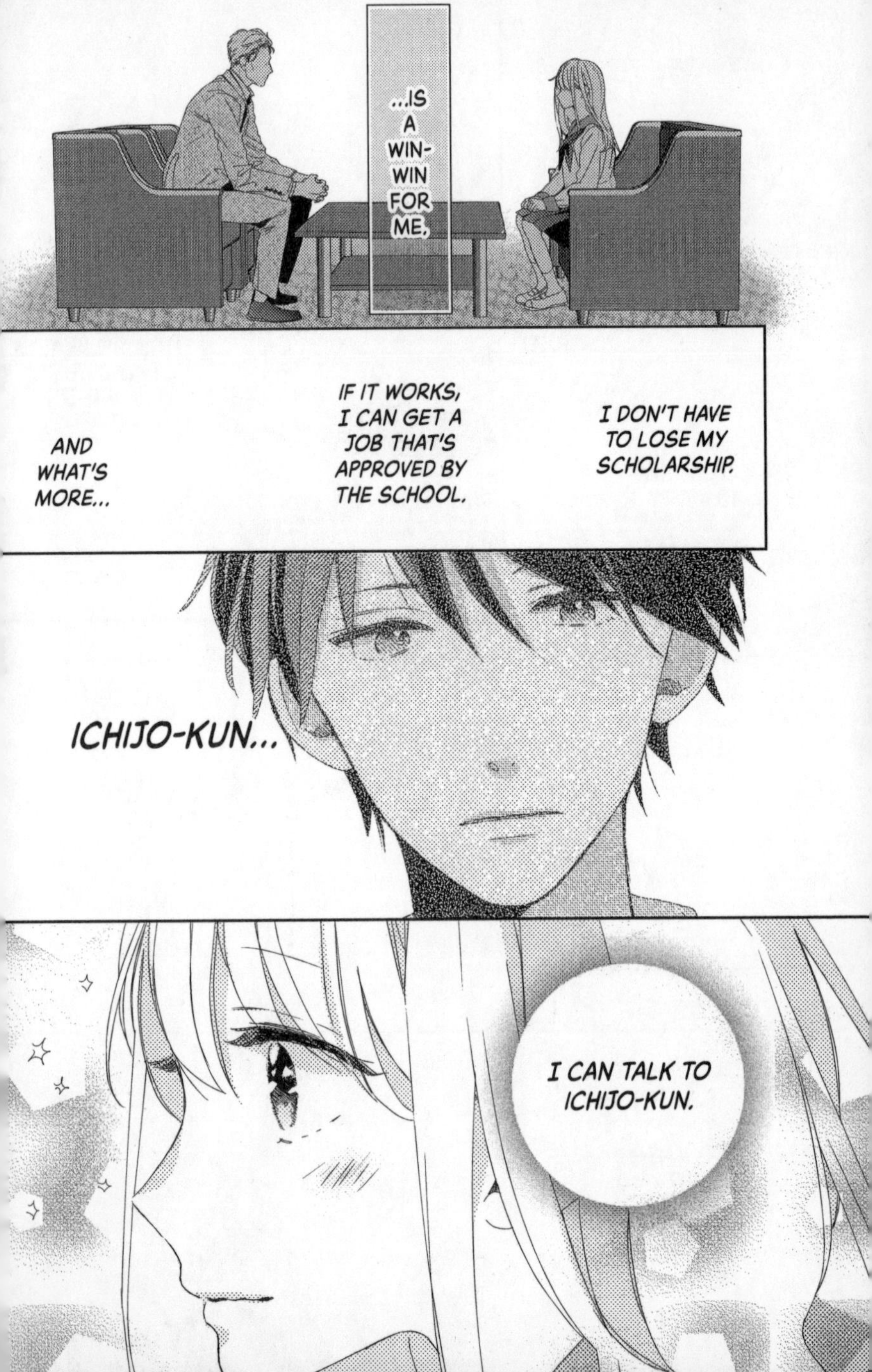
...IS A WIN-WIN FOR ME.
I DON'T HAVE TO LOSE MY SCHOLARSHIP.
IF IT WORKS, I CAN GET A JOB THAT'S APPROVED BY THE SCHOOL.
AND WHAT'S MORE...
ICHIJO-KUN...
I CAN TALK TO ICHIJO-KUN.

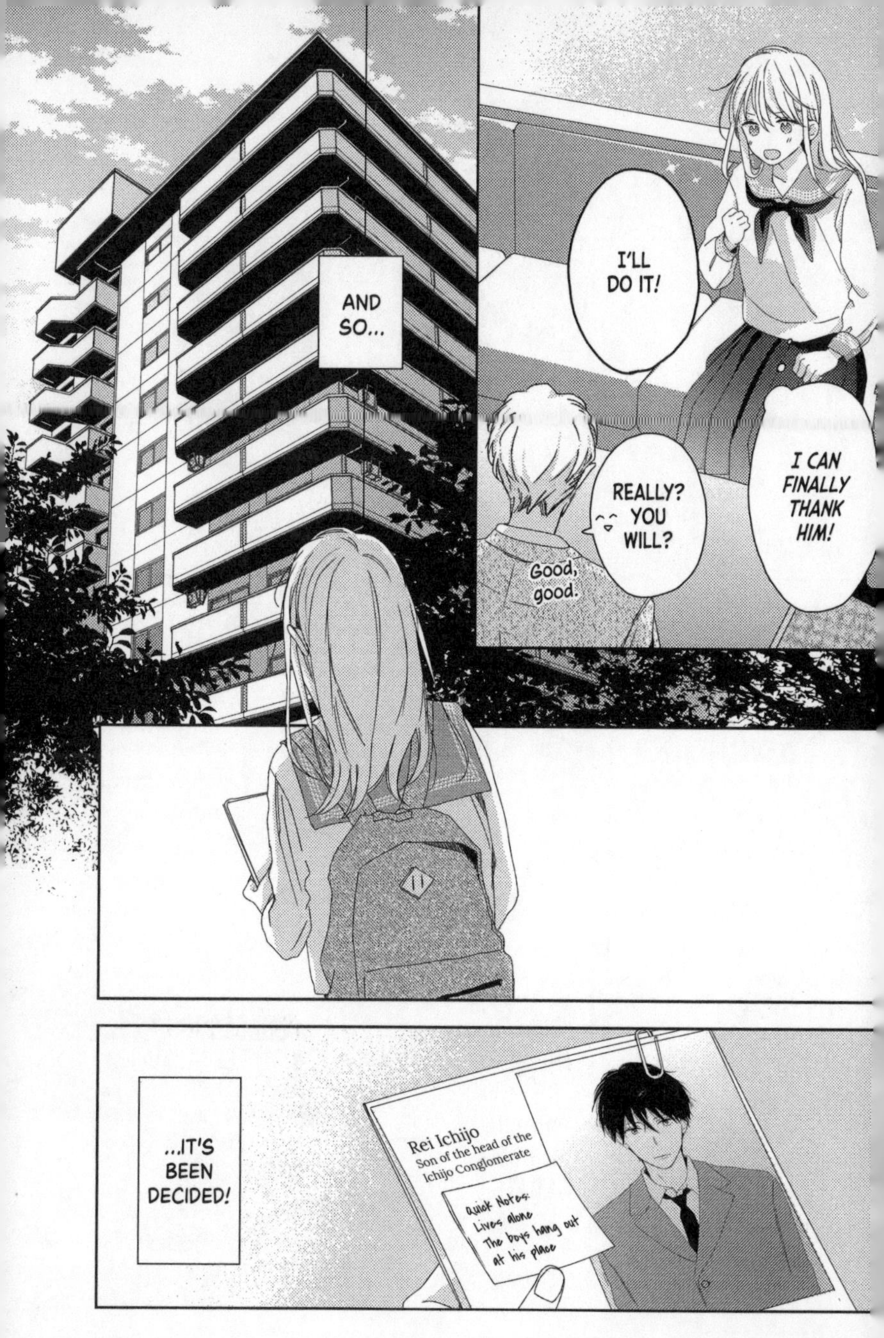
I'LL DO IT!
I CAN FINALLY THANK HIM!
REALLY? YOU WILL?
Good, good.
AND SO...
Rei Ichijo
Son of the head of the Ichijo Conglomerate
Quick Notes:
Lives alone
The boys hang out at his place
...IT'S BEEN DECIDED!

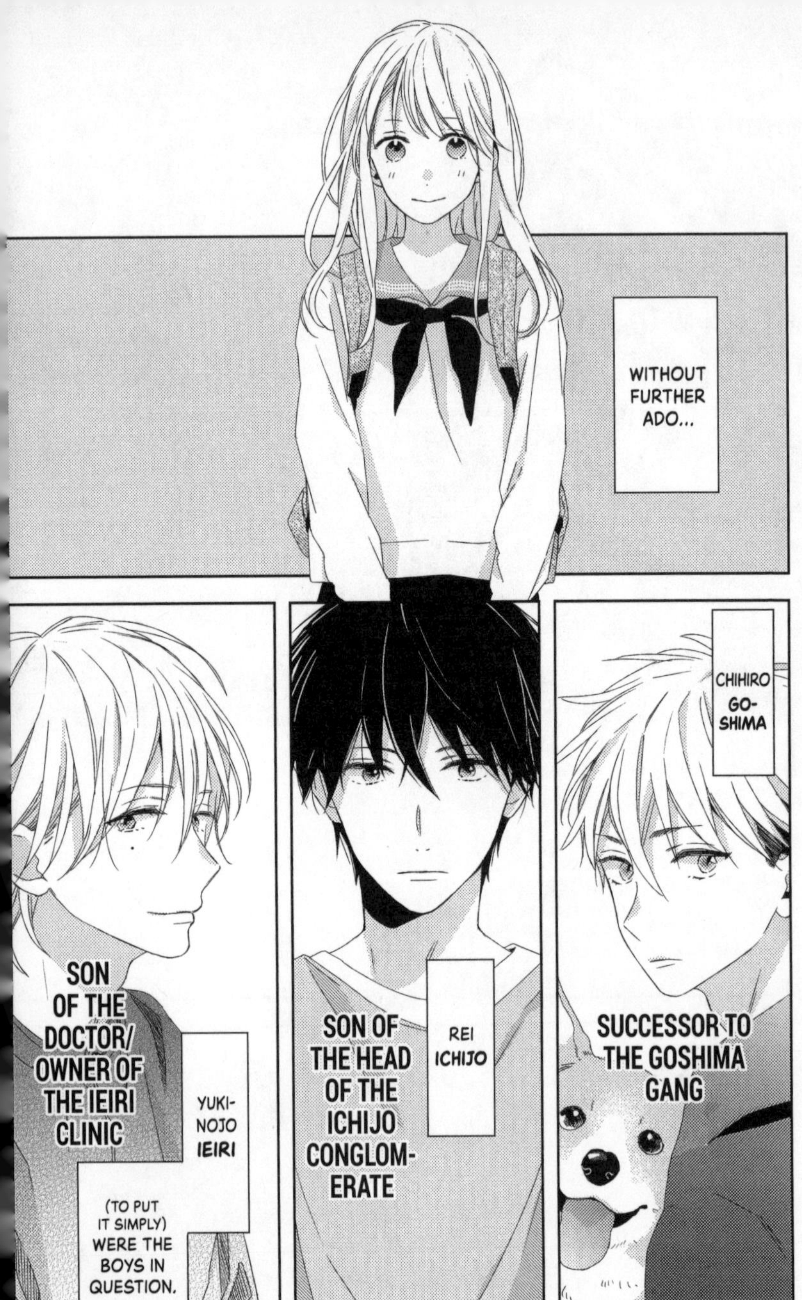
WITHOUT FURTHER ADO...
CHIHIRO GO-SHIMA
SUCCESSOR TO THE GOSHIMA GANG
REI ICHIJO
SON OF THE HEAD OF THE ICHIJO CONGLOM-ERATE
YUKI-NOJO IEIRI
SON OF THE DOCTOR/ OWNER OF THE IEIRI CLINIC
(TO PUT IT SIMPLY) WERE THE BOYS IN QUESTION.

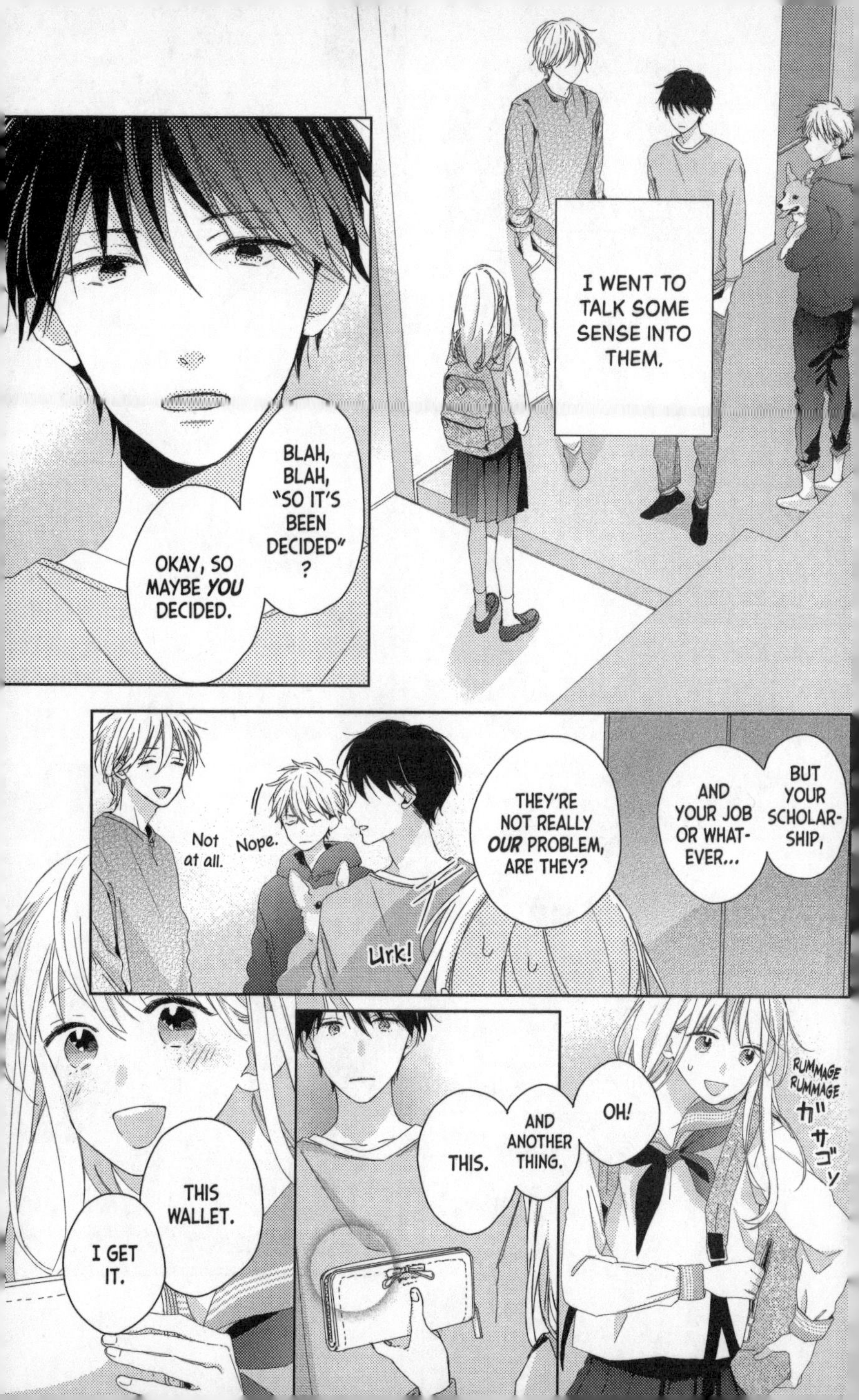
I WENT TO TALK SOME SENSE INTO THEM.
BLAH, BLAH, "SO IT'S BEEN DECIDED"?
OKAY, SO MAYBE *YOU* DECIDED.
BUT YOUR SCHOLARSHIP,
AND YOUR JOB OR WHATEVER...
THEY'RE NOT REALLY *OUR* PROBLEM, ARE THEY?
Nope.
Not at all.
Urk!
RUMMAGE RUMMAGE
ガサゴソ
OH!
AND ANOTHER THING.
THIS.
THIS WALLET.
I GET IT.

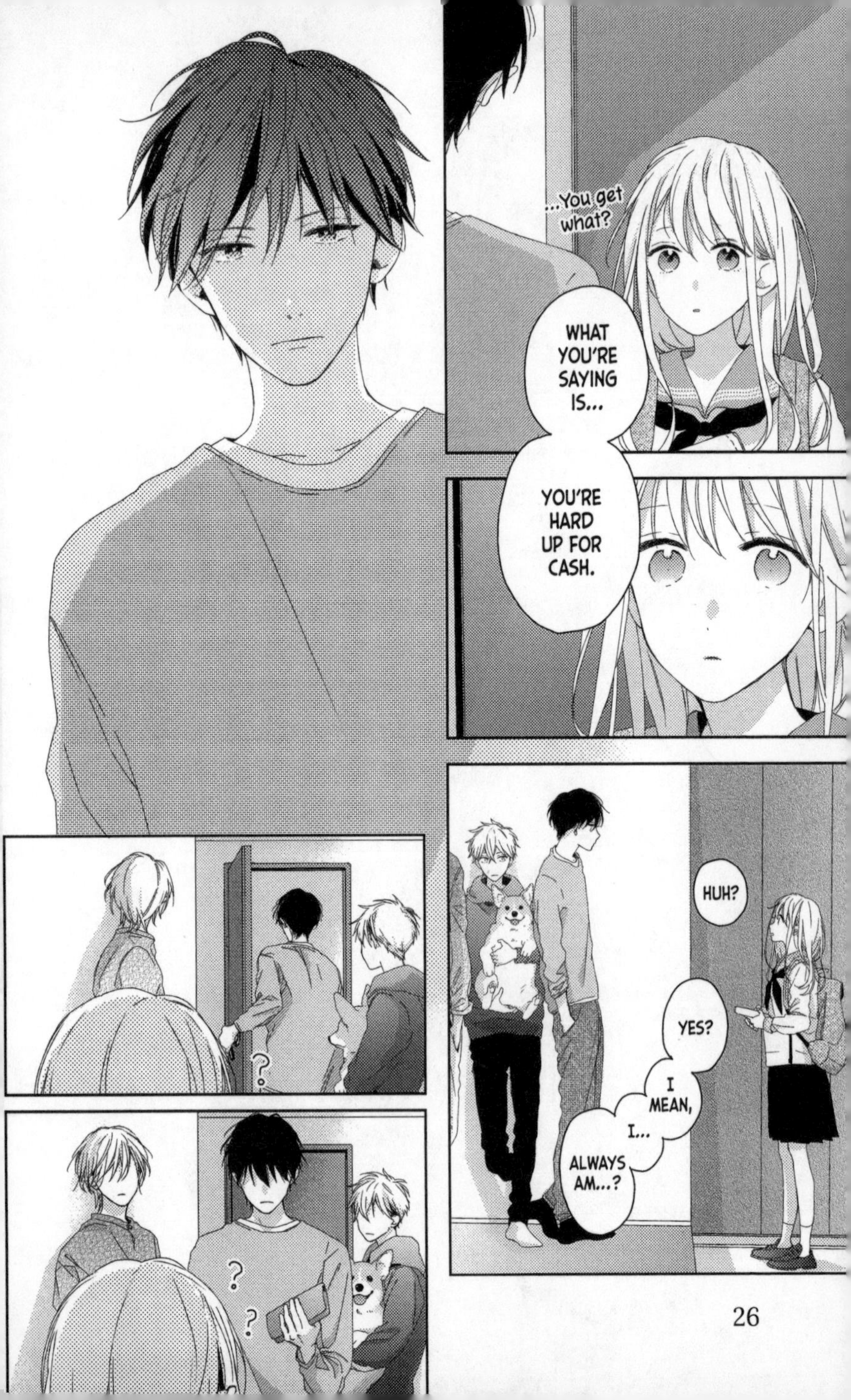
...You get what?
WHAT YOU'RE SAYING IS...
YOU'RE HARD UP FOR CASH.
HUH?
YES?
I MEAN, I... ALWAYS AM...?
?
?
?

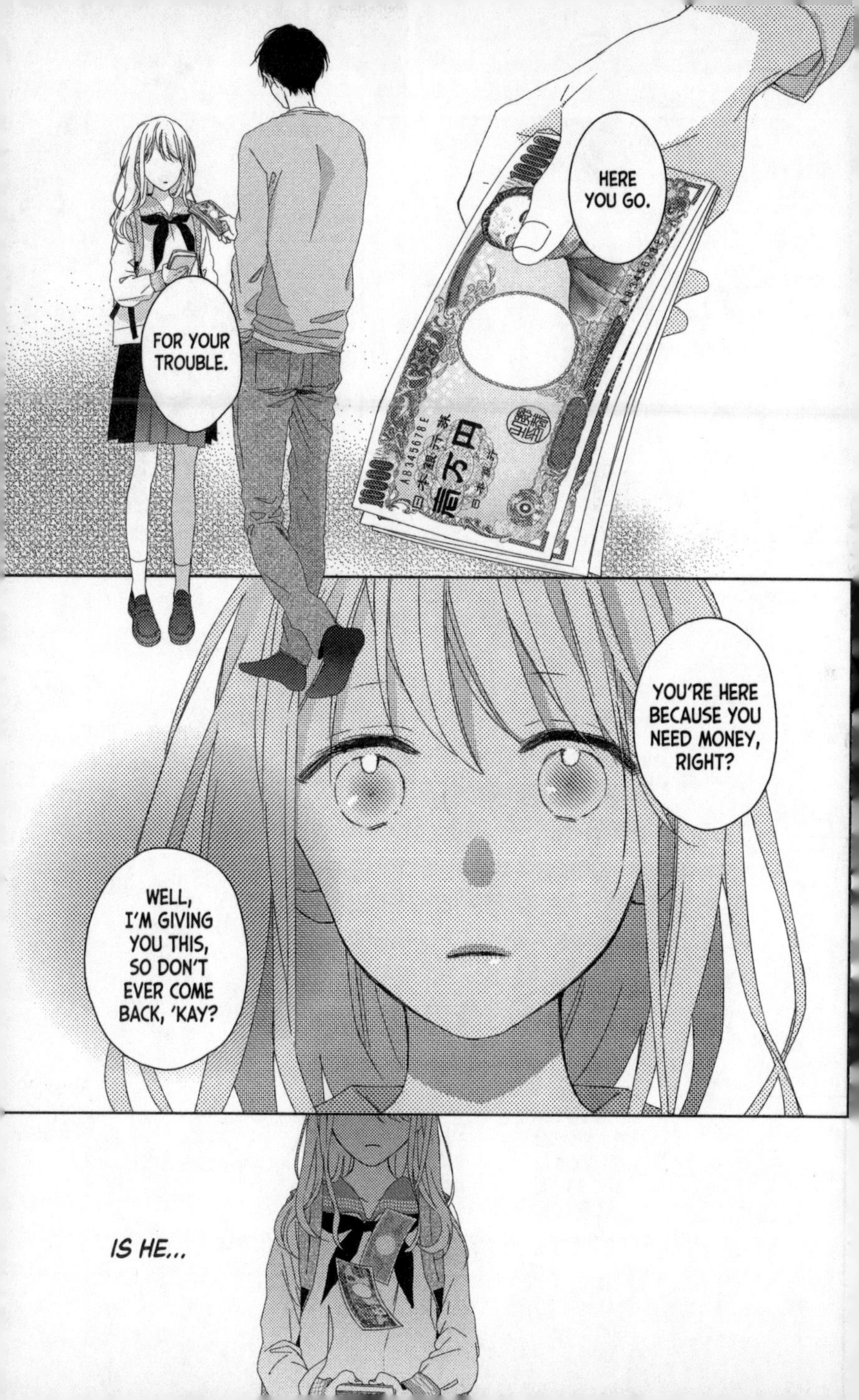
HERE YOU GO.
FOR YOUR TROUBLE.
YOU'RE HERE BECAUSE YOU NEED MONEY, RIGHT?
WELL, I'M GIVING YOU THIS, SO DON'T EVER COME BACK, 'KAY?
IS HE...

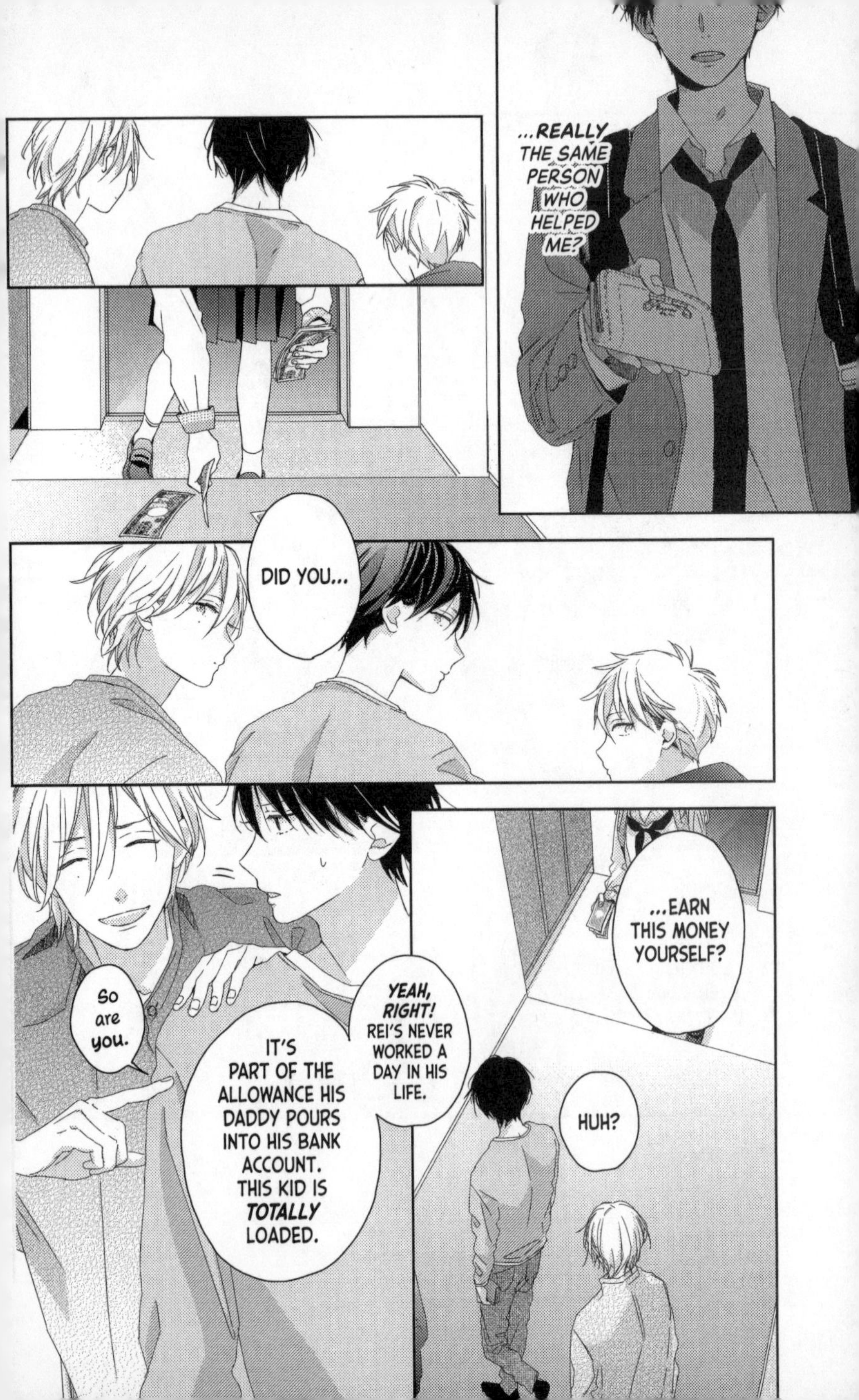
...REALLY THE SAME PERSON WHO HELPED ME?
DID YOU...
...EARN THIS MONEY YOURSELF?
HUH?
YEAH, RIGHT! REI'S NEVER WORKED A DAY IN HIS LIFE.
IT'S PART OF THE ALLOWANCE HIS DADDY POURS INTO HIS BANK ACCOUNT. THIS KID IS TOTALLY LOADED.
So are you.

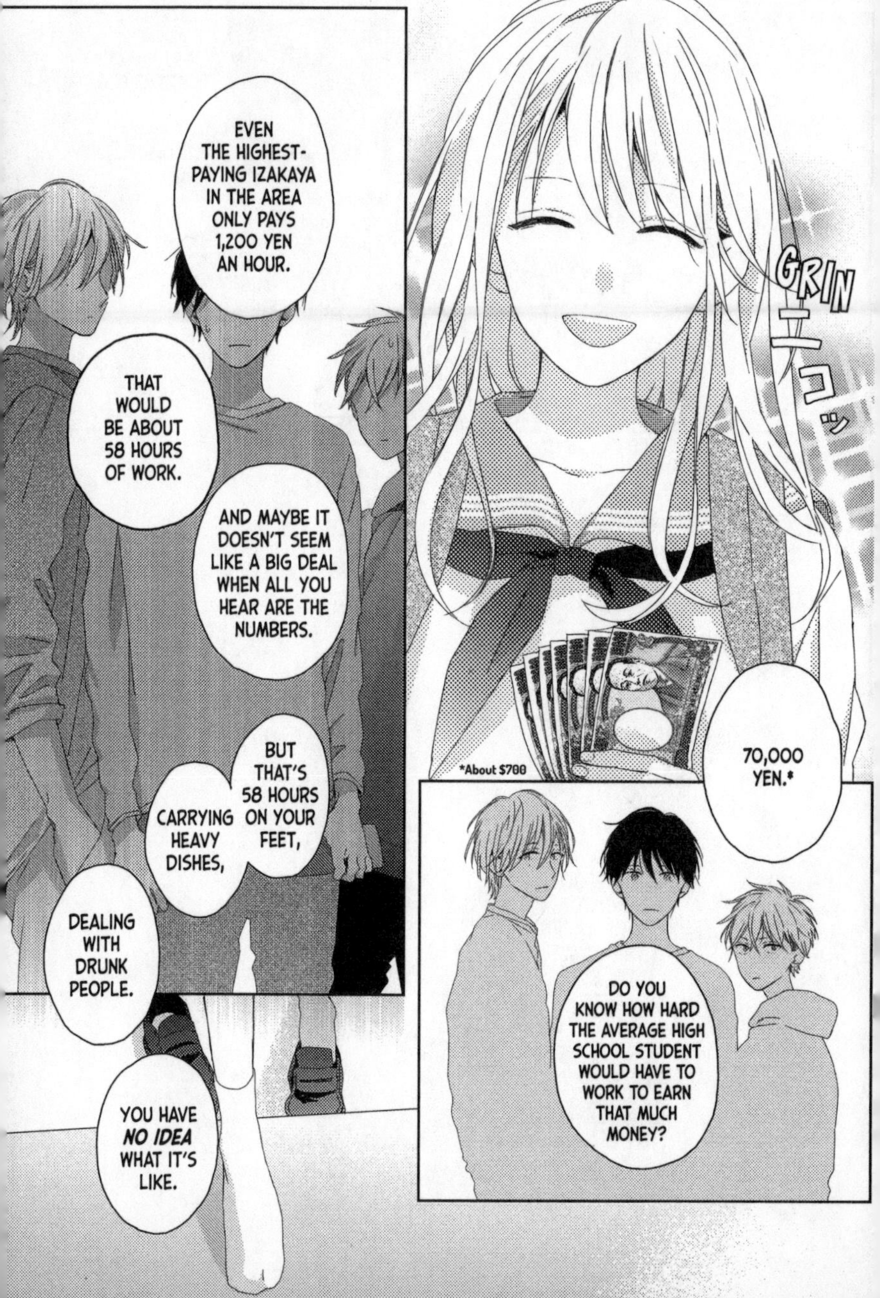
GRIN
ニコッ
70,000 YEN.*
*About $700
DO YOU KNOW HOW HARD THE AVERAGE HIGH SCHOOL STUDENT WOULD HAVE TO WORK TO EARN THAT MUCH MONEY?
EVEN THE HIGHEST-PAYING IZAKAYA IN THE AREA ONLY PAYS 1,200 YEN AN HOUR.
THAT WOULD BE ABOUT 58 HOURS OF WORK.
AND MAYBE IT DOESN'T SEEM LIKE A BIG DEAL WHEN ALL YOU HEAR ARE THE NUMBERS.
BUT THAT'S 58 HOURS ON YOUR FEET,
CARRYING HEAVY DISHES,
DEALING WITH DRUNK PEOPLE.
YOU HAVE *NO IDEA* WHAT IT'S LIKE.

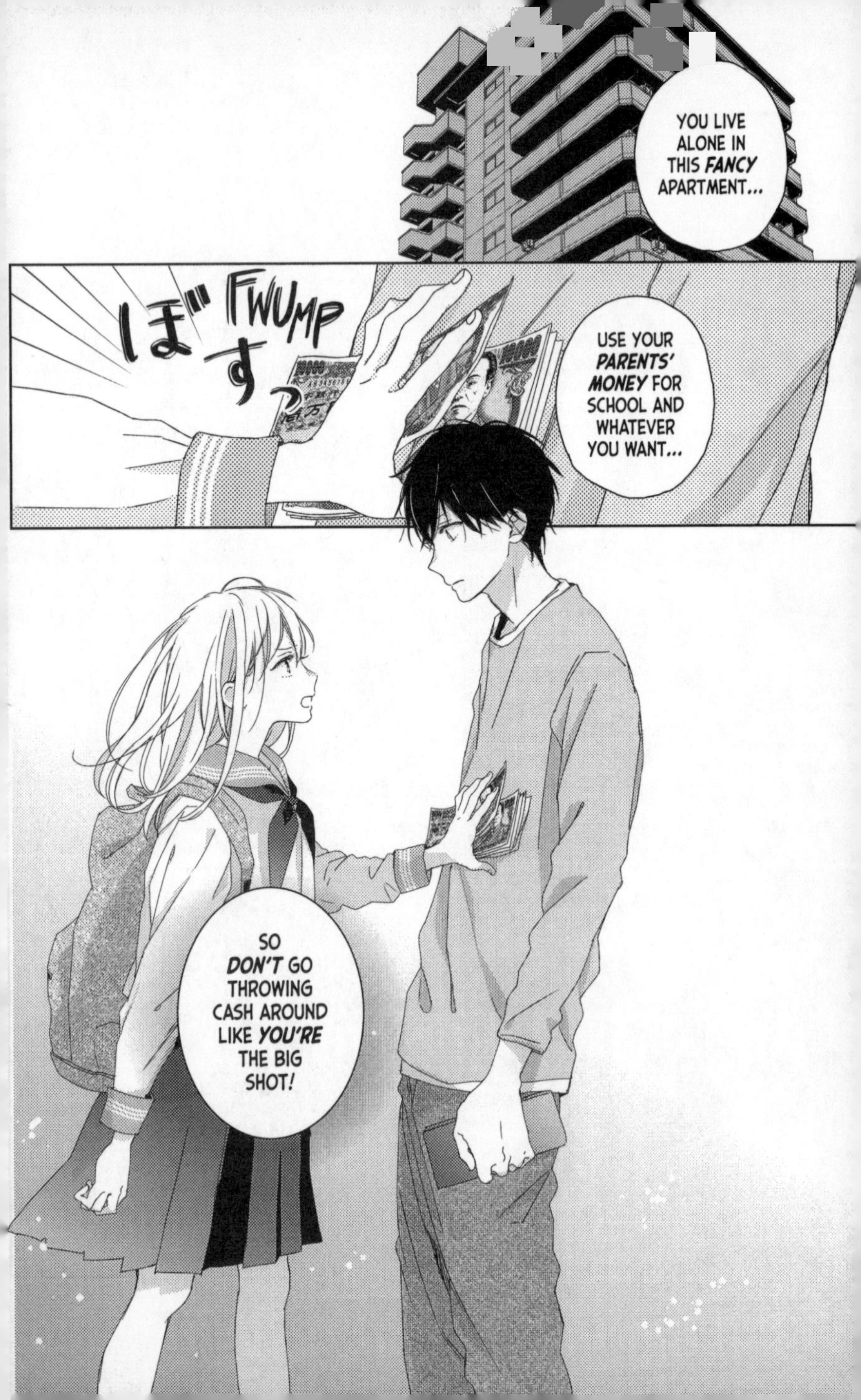
YOU LIVE ALONE IN THIS *FANCY* APARTMENT...
USE YOUR ***PARENTS' MONEY*** FOR SCHOOL AND WHATEVER YOU WANT...
ぼ
FWUMP
すっ
SO ***DON'T*** GO THROWING CASH AROUND LIKE ***YOU'RE*** THE BIG SHOT!

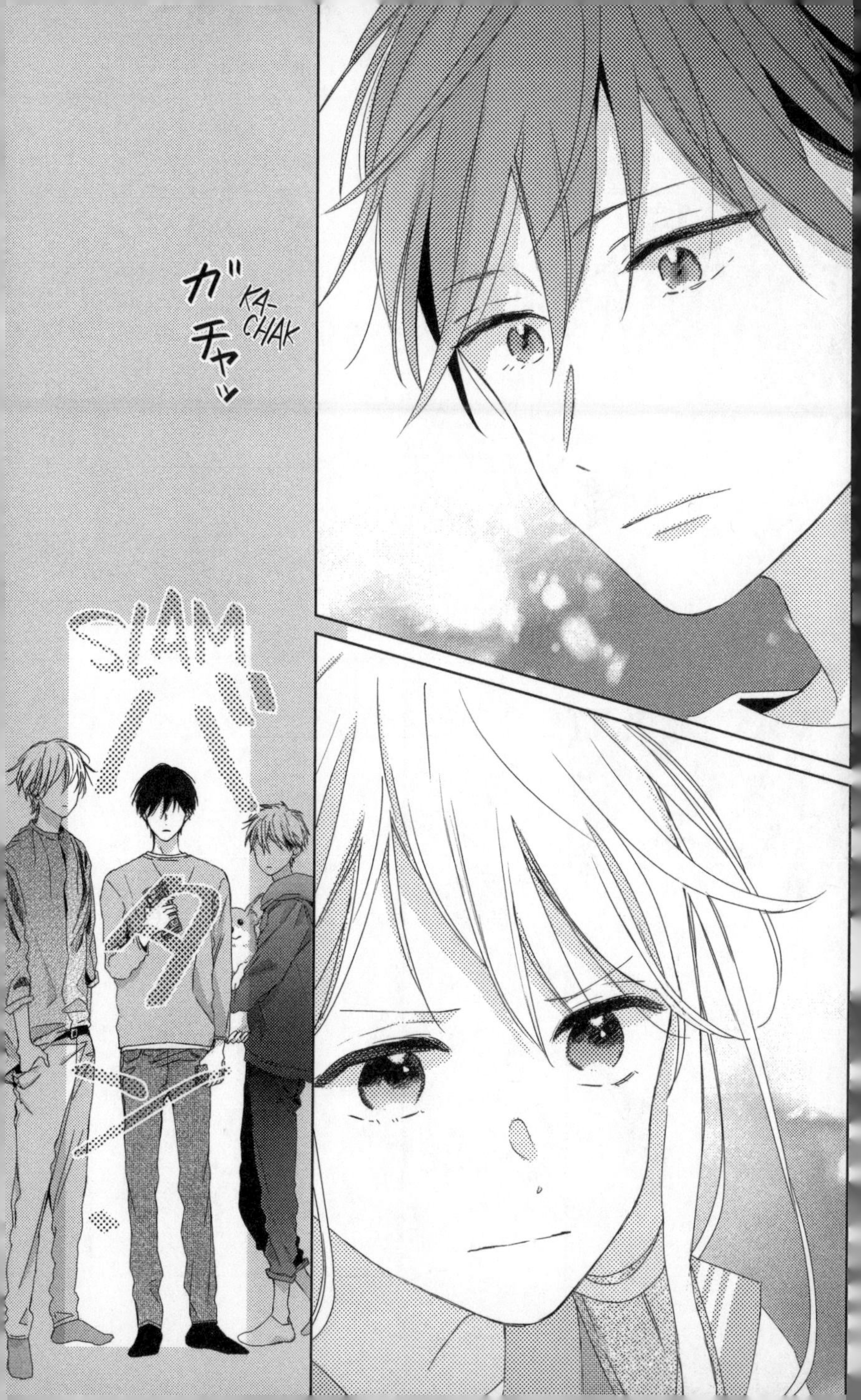
ガチャッ
KA-CHAK
SLAM
バタン

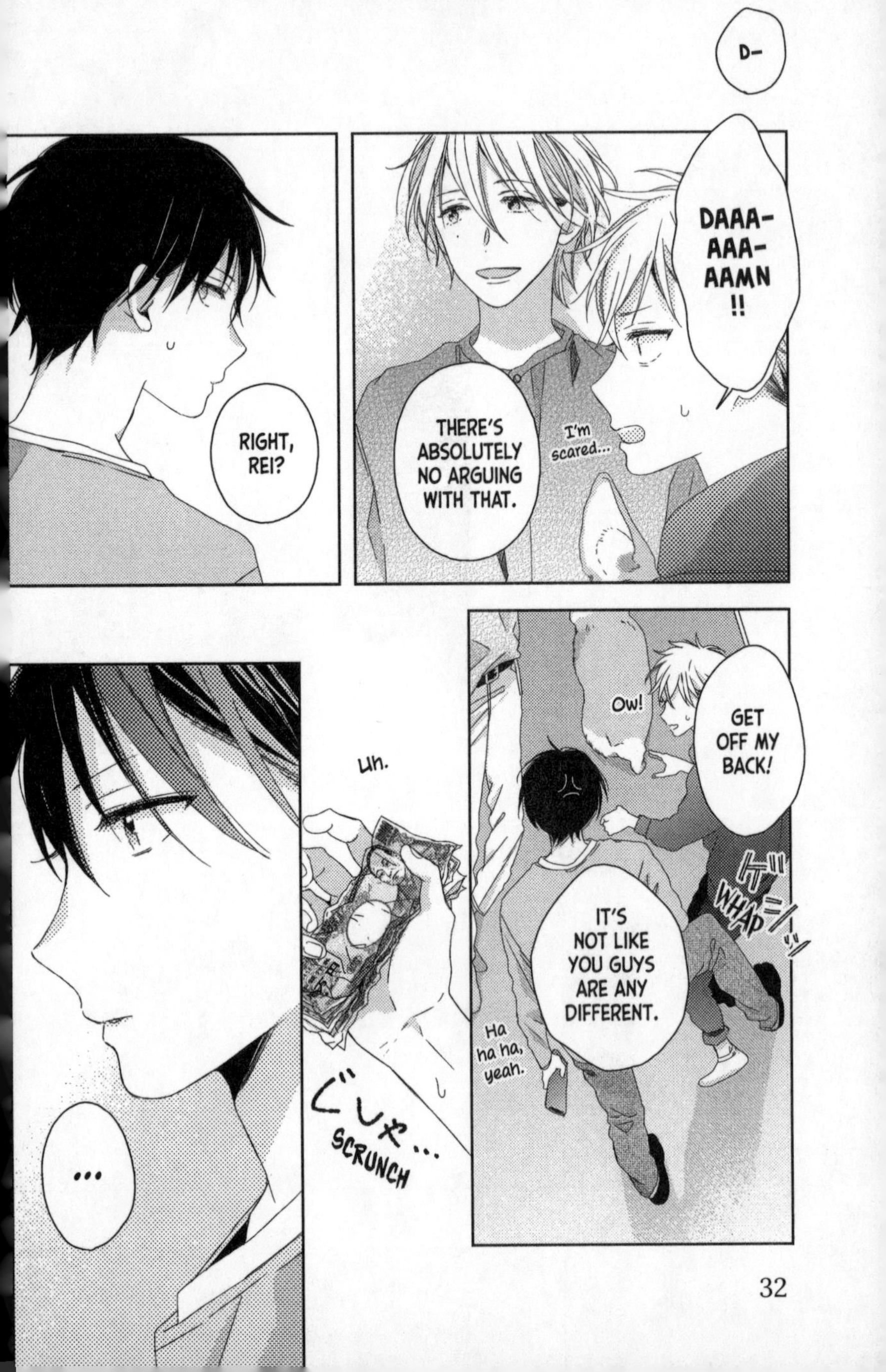
D-
DAAA-AAA-AAMN!!
THERE'S ABSOLUTELY NO ARGUING WITH THAT.
I'm scared...
RIGHT, REI?
GET OFF MY BACK!
Ow!
WHAP
IT'S NOT LIKE YOU GUYS ARE ANY DIFFERENT.
Ha ha ha, yeah.
Uh.
ぐしゃ...
SCRUNCH
...

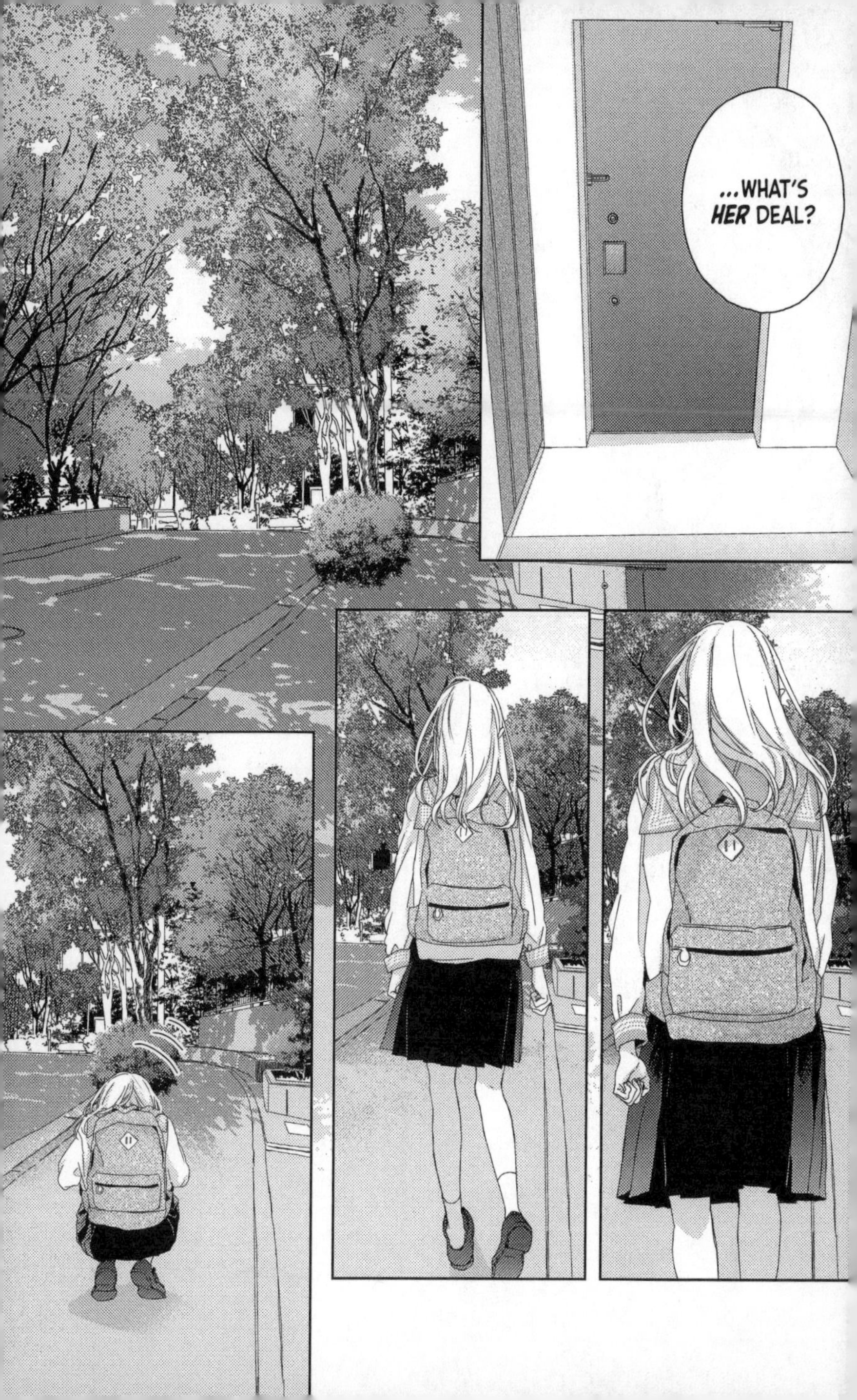
...WHAT'S *HER* DEAL?

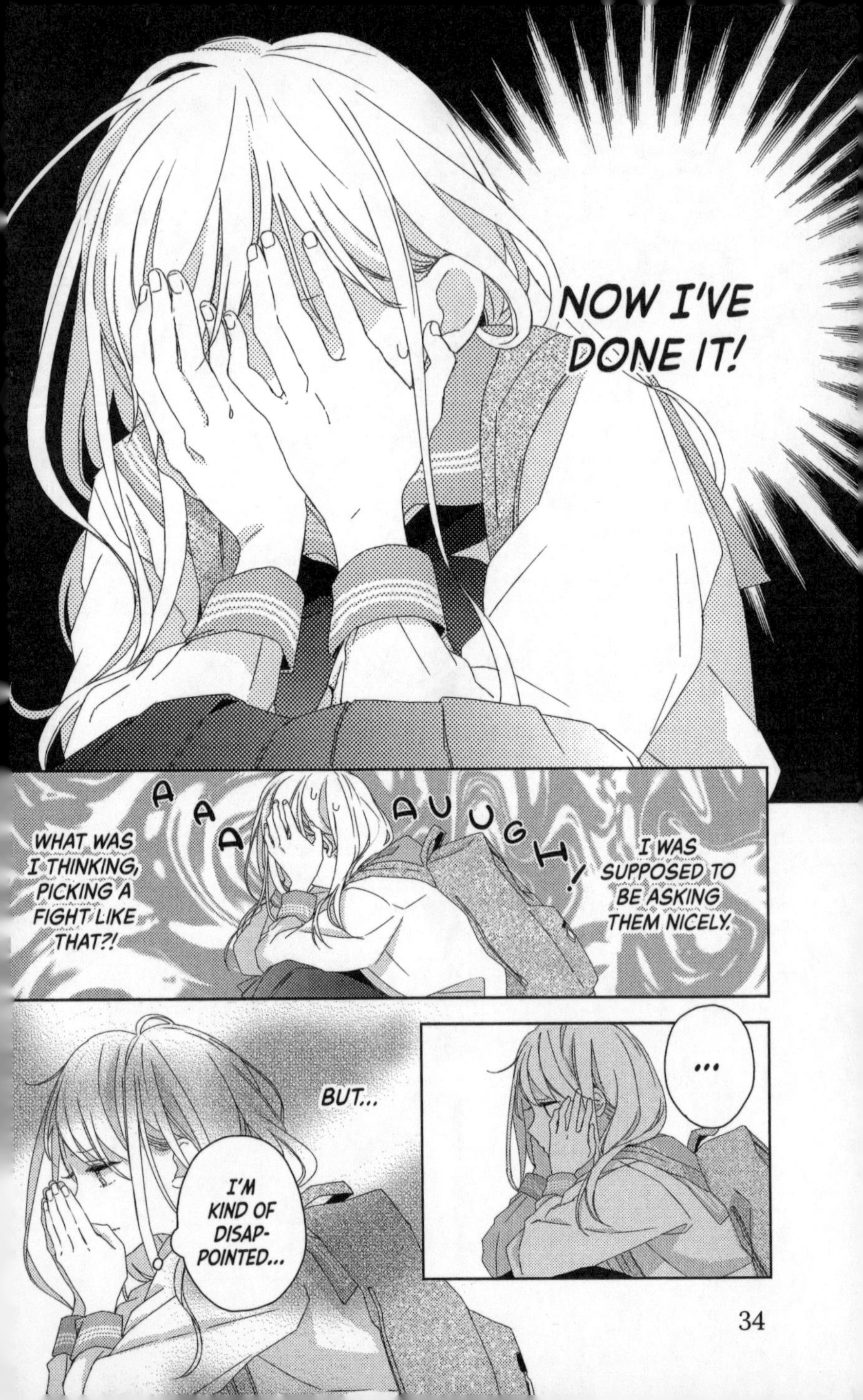
NOW I'VE DONE IT!
I WAS SUPPOSED TO BE ASKING THEM NICELY.
AAAAUUGH!
WHAT WAS I THINKING, PICKING A FIGHT LIKE THAT?!
...
BUT...
I'M KIND OF DISAP-POINTED...

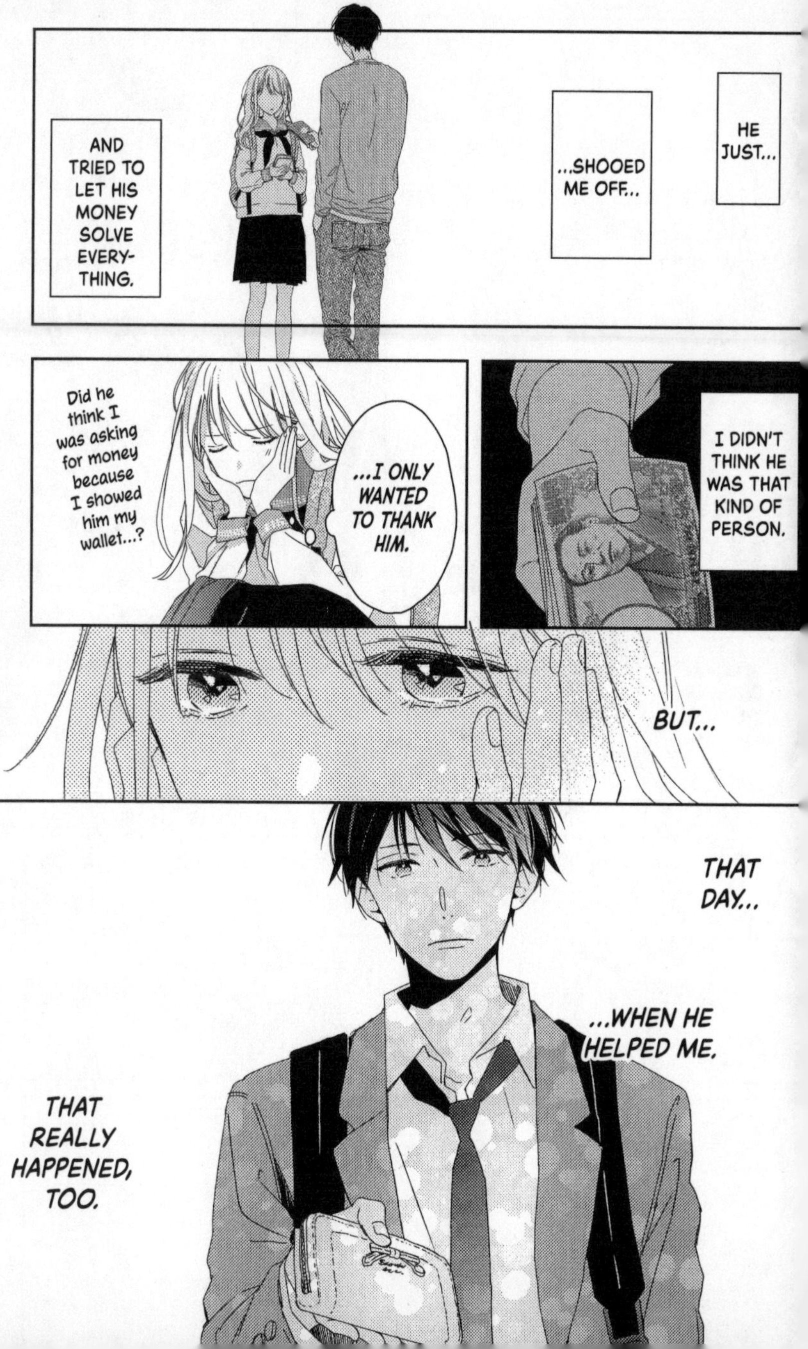
HE JUST...
...SHOOED ME OFF...
AND TRIED TO LET HIS MONEY SOLVE EVERY-THING.
I DIDN'T THINK HE WAS THAT KIND OF PERSON.
...I ONLY WANTED TO THANK HIM.
Did he think I was asking for money because I showed him my wallet...?
BUT...
THAT DAY...
...WHEN HE HELPED ME.
THAT REALLY HAPPENED, TOO.

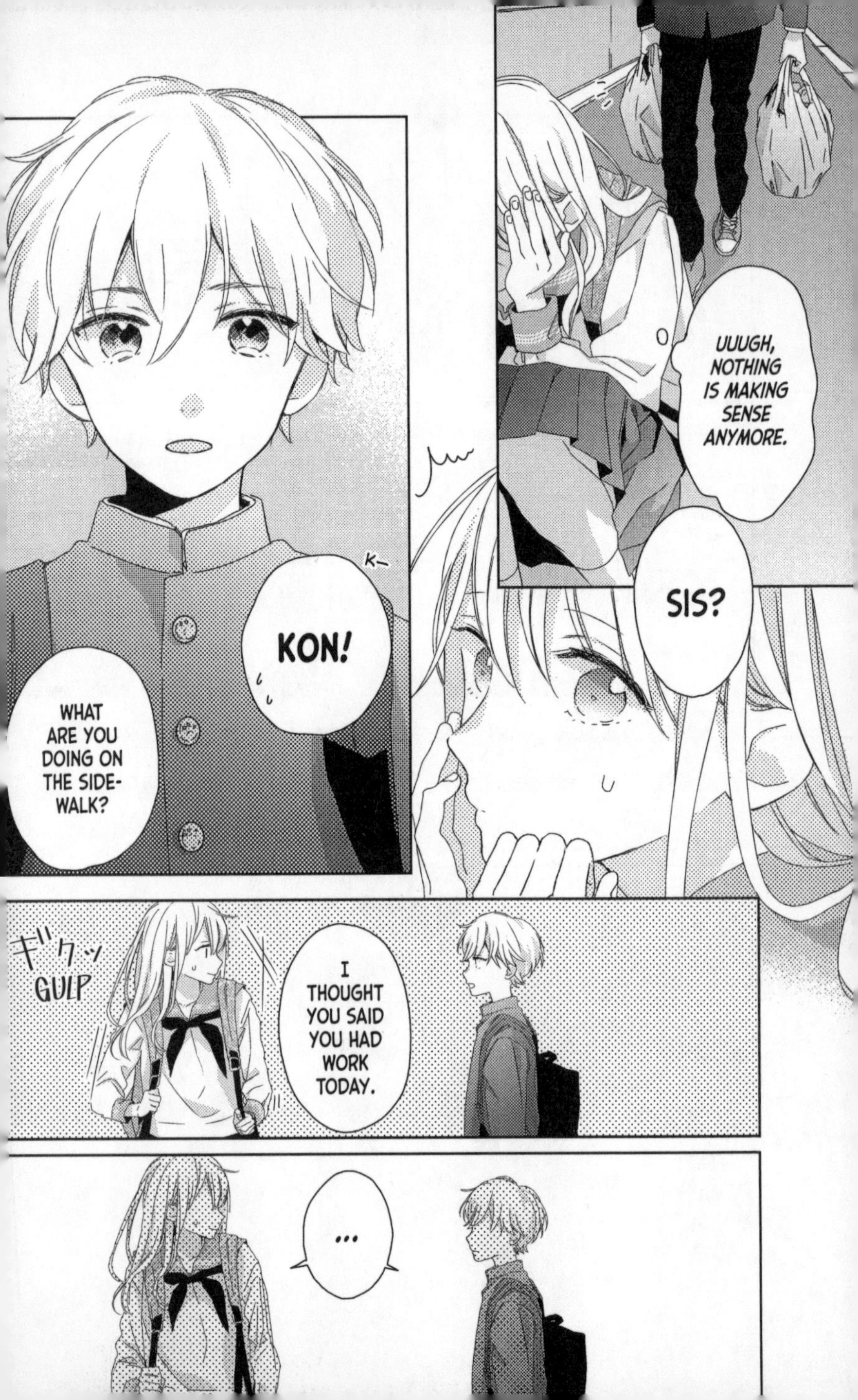
UUUGH, NOTHING IS MAKING SENSE ANYMORE.
SIS?
K—
KON!
WHAT ARE YOU DOING ON THE SIDE-WALK?
I THOUGHT YOU SAID YOU HAD WORK TODAY.
ギクッ
GULP
...

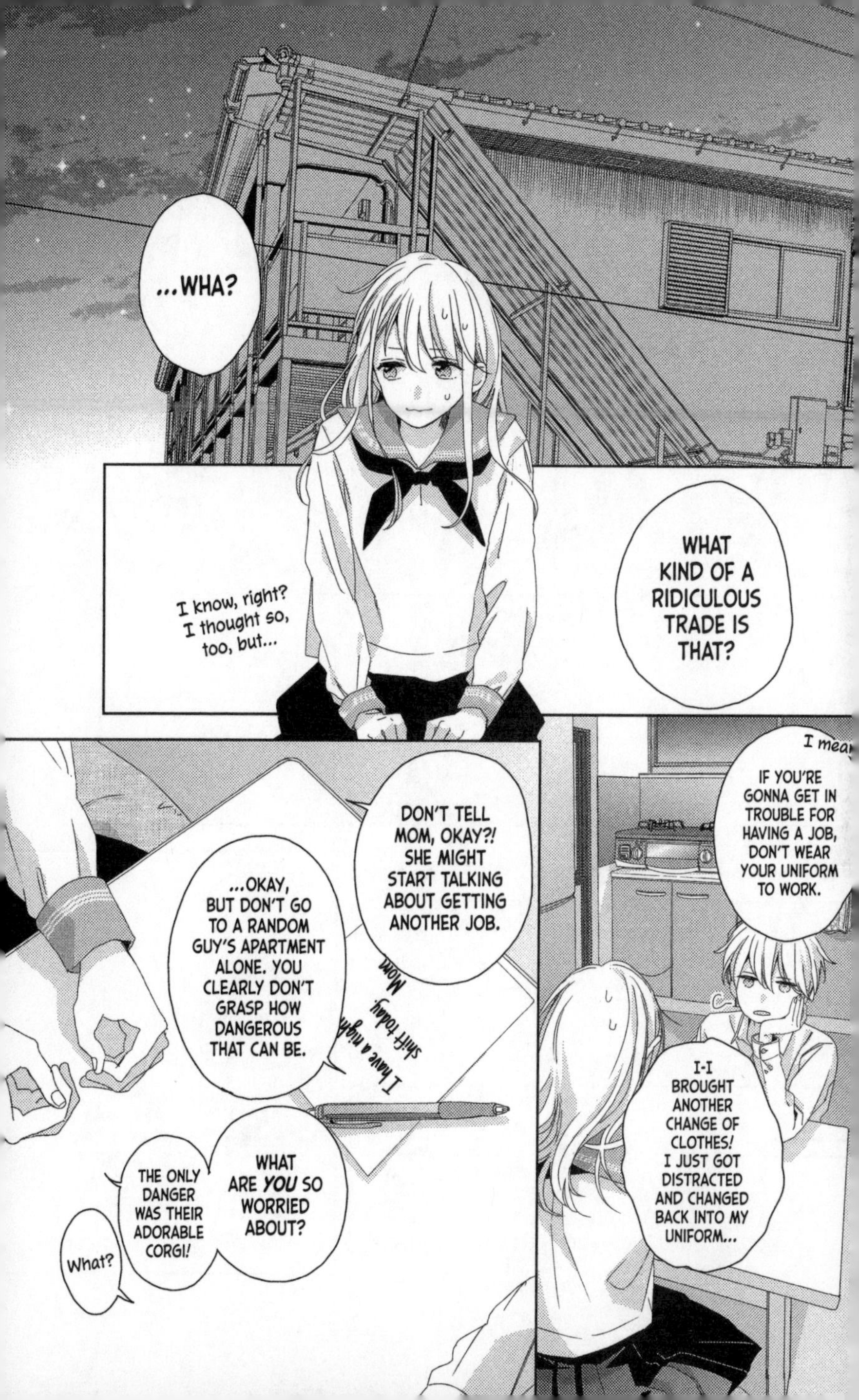
...WHA?
WHAT KIND OF A RIDICULOUS TRADE IS THAT?
I know, right? I thought so, too, but...
I mea
IF YOU'RE GONNA GET IN TROUBLE FOR HAVING A JOB, DON'T WEAR YOUR UNIFORM TO WORK.
I-I BROUGHT ANOTHER CHANGE OF CLOTHES! I JUST GOT DISTRACTED AND CHANGED BACK INTO MY UNIFORM...
DON'T TELL MOM, OKAY?! SHE MIGHT START TALKING ABOUT GETTING ANOTHER JOB.
...OKAY, BUT DON'T GO TO A RANDOM GUY'S APARTMENT ALONE. YOU CLEARLY DON'T GRASP HOW DANGEROUS THAT CAN BE.
I have a night shift today. Mom
WHAT ARE *YOU* SO WORRIED ABOUT?
THE ONLY DANGER WAS THEIR ADORABLE CORGI!
What?

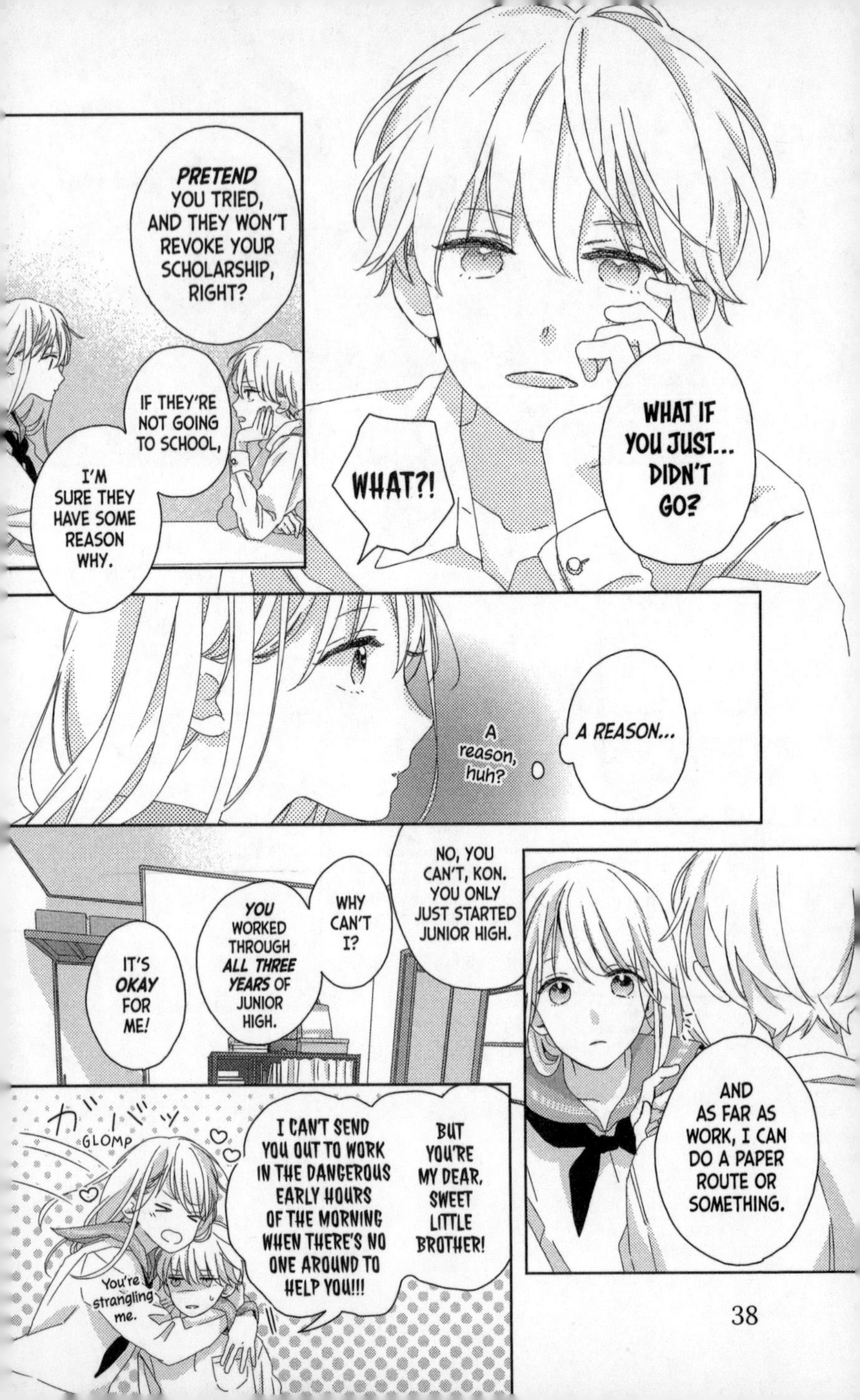
WHAT IF YOU JUST... DIDN'T GO?
WHAT?!
PRETEND YOU TRIED, AND THEY WON'T REVOKE YOUR SCHOLARSHIP, RIGHT?
IF THEY'RE NOT GOING TO SCHOOL,
I'M SURE THEY HAVE SOME REASON WHY.
A REASON...
A reason, huh?
AND AS FAR AS WORK, I CAN DO A PAPER ROUTE OR SOMETHING.
NO, YOU CAN'T, KON. YOU ONLY JUST STARTED JUNIOR HIGH.
WHY CAN'T I?
YOU WORKED THROUGH *ALL THREE YEARS* OF JUNIOR HIGH.
IT'S *OKAY* FOR ME!
GLOMP
BUT YOU'RE MY DEAR, SWEET LITTLE BROTHER!
I CAN'T SEND YOU OUT TO WORK IN THE DANGEROUS EARLY HOURS OF THE MORNING WHEN THERE'S NO ONE AROUND TO HELP YOU!!!
You're strangling me.

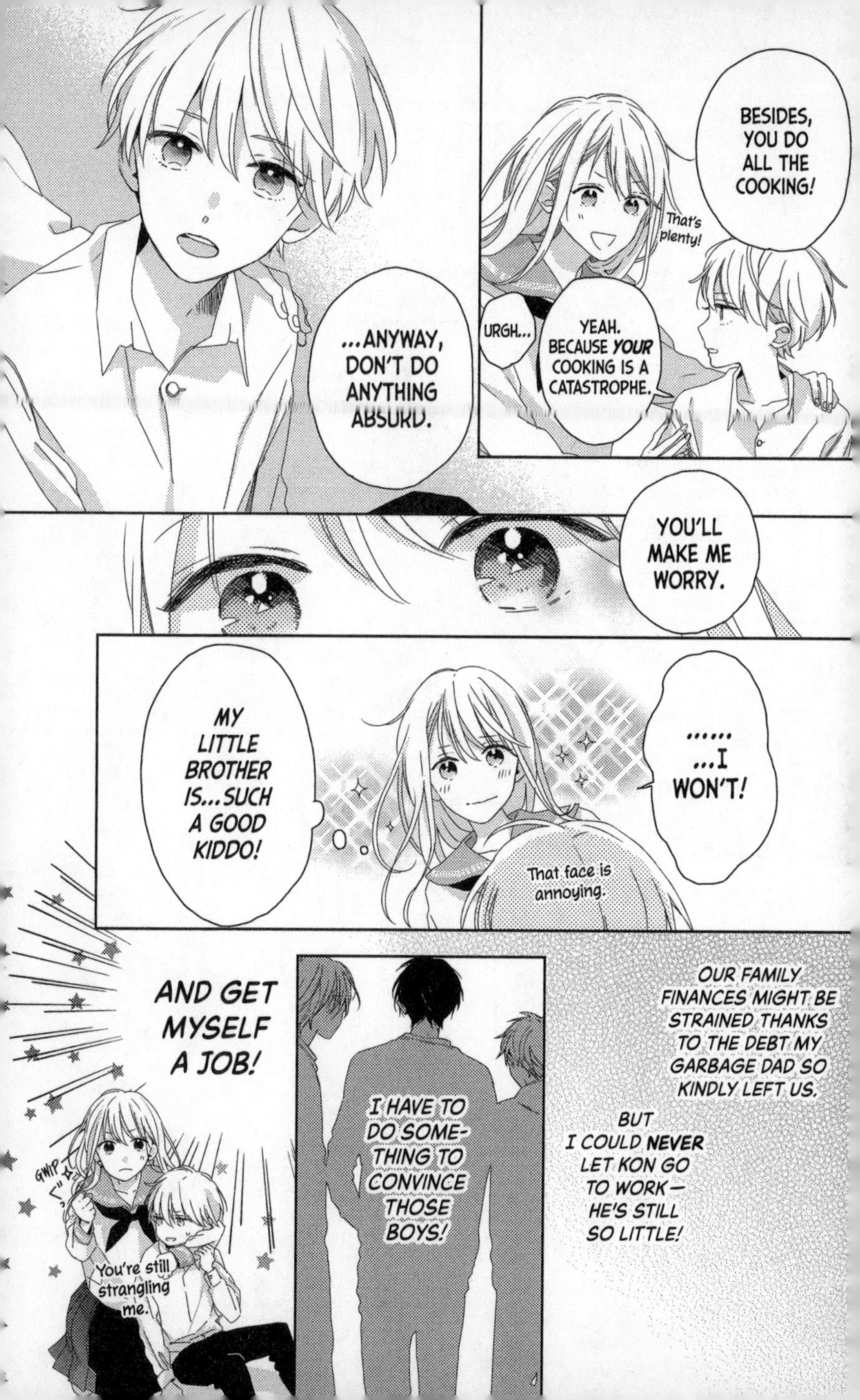
BESIDES, YOU DO ALL THE COOKING!
That's plenty!
YEAH. BECAUSE YOUR COOKING IS A CATASTROPHE.
URGH...
...ANYWAY, DON'T DO ANYTHING ABSURD.
YOU'LL MAKE ME WORRY.
....I WON'T!
That face is annoying.
MY LITTLE BROTHER IS...SUCH A GOOD KIDDO!
OUR FAMILY FINANCES MIGHT BE STRAINED THANKS TO THE DEBT MY GARBAGE DAD SO KINDLY LEFT US.
BUT I COULD NEVER LET KON GO TO WORK—HE'S STILL SO LITTLE!
I HAVE TO DO SOME-THING TO CONVINCE THOSE BOYS!
AND GET MYSELF A JOB!
GWIP
You're still strangling me.

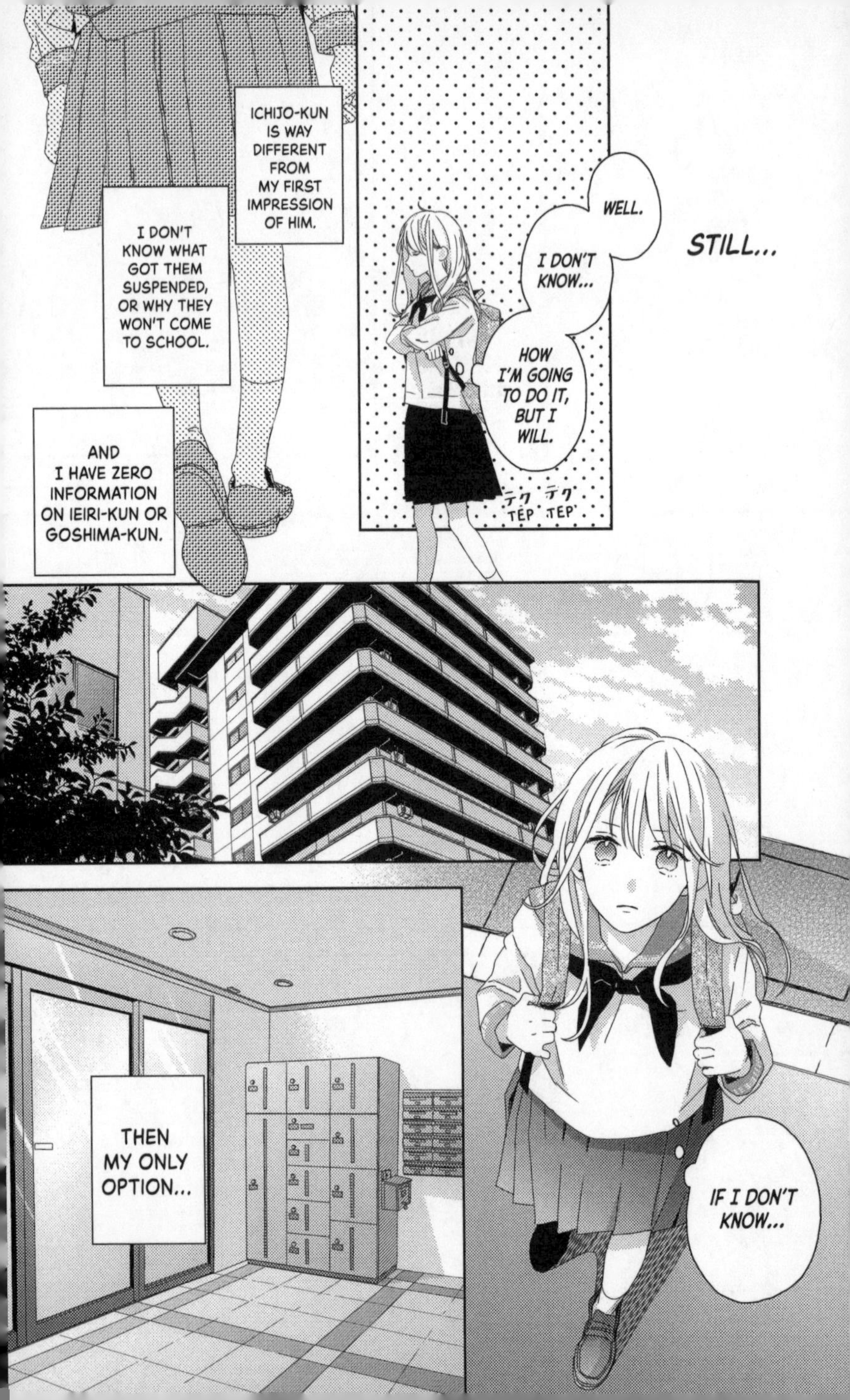
STILL...
WELL.
I DON'T KNOW...
HOW I'M GOING TO DO IT, BUT I WILL.
テク テク
TEP TEP
ICHIJO-KUN IS WAY DIFFERENT FROM MY FIRST IMPRESSION OF HIM.
I DON'T KNOW WHAT GOT THEM SUSPENDED, OR WHY THEY WON'T COME TO SCHOOL.
AND I HAVE ZERO INFORMATION ON IEIRI-KUN OR GOSHIMA-KUN.
IF I DON'T KNOW...
THEN MY ONLY OPTION...

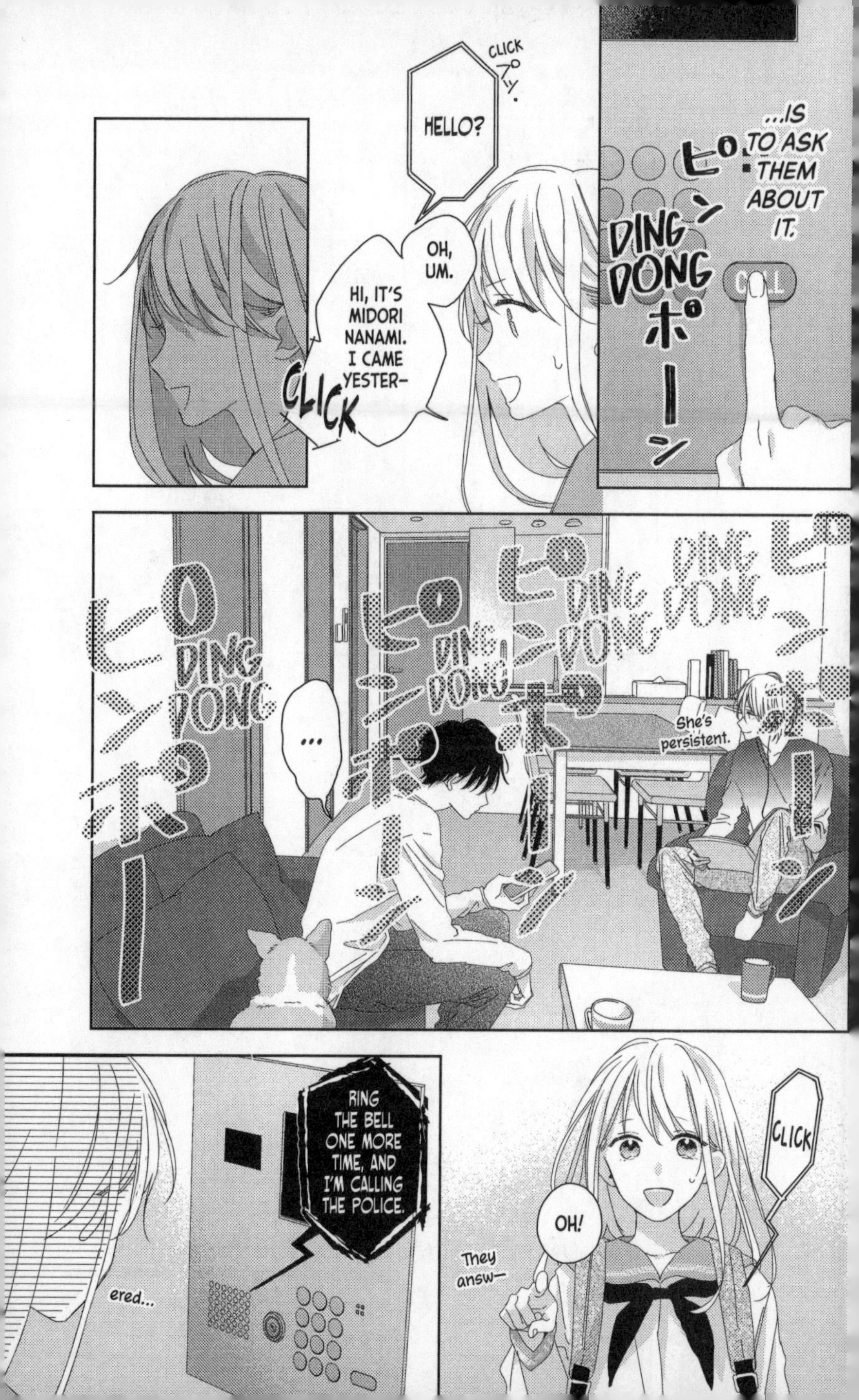
...IS TO ASK THEM ABOUT IT.
DING DONG
ピンポーン
CLICK
HELLO?
OH, UM.
HI, IT'S MIDORI NANAMI. I CAME YESTER—
CLICK
DING DONG
DING DONG
DING DONG
DING DONG
...
She's persistent.
CLICK
OH!
They answ—
RING THE BELL ONE MORE TIME, AND I'M CALLING THE POLICE.
ered...

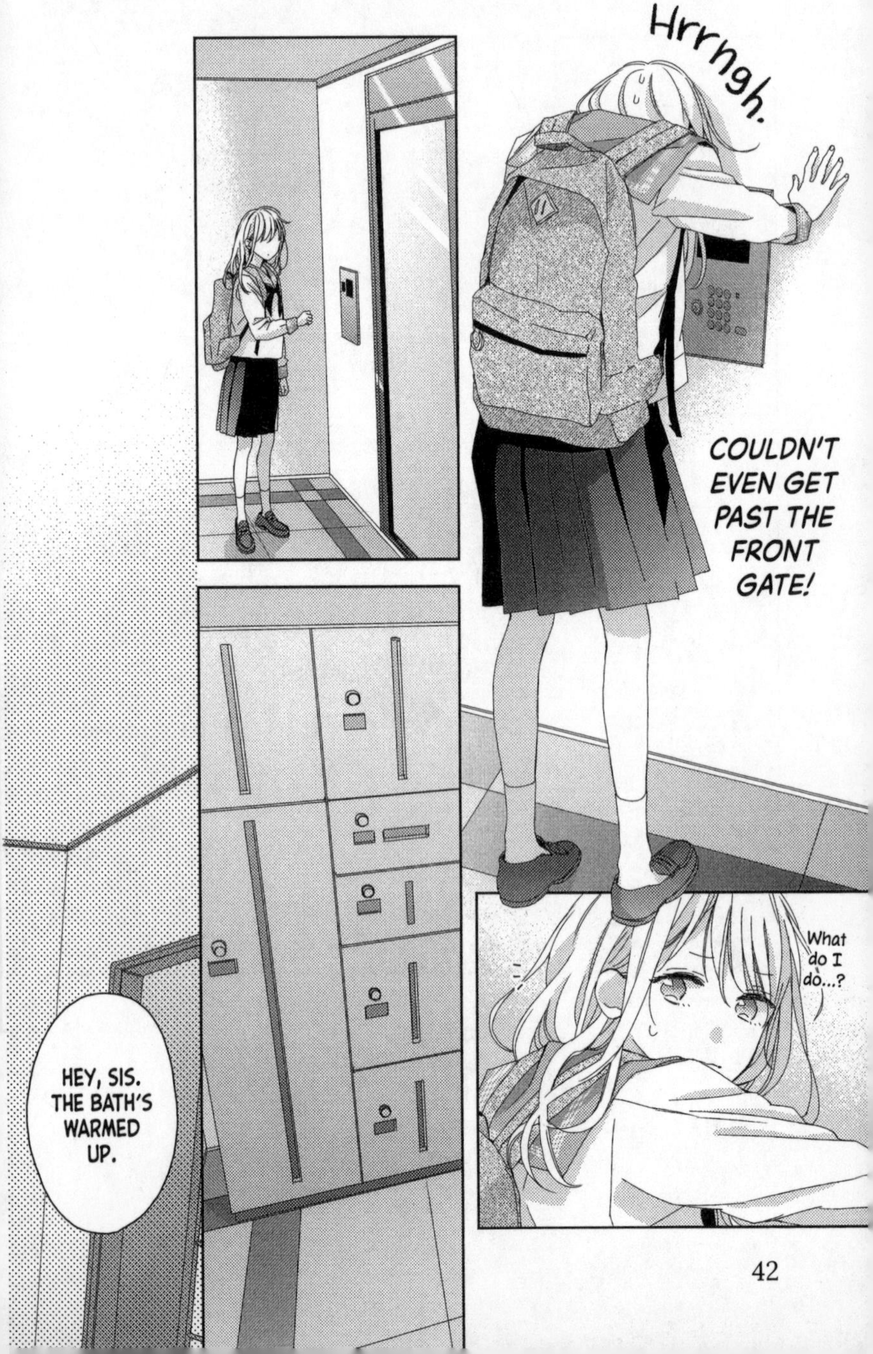
Hrrngh.
COULDN'T EVEN GET PAST THE FRONT GATE!
What do I do...?
HEY, SIS. THE BATH'S WARMED UP.

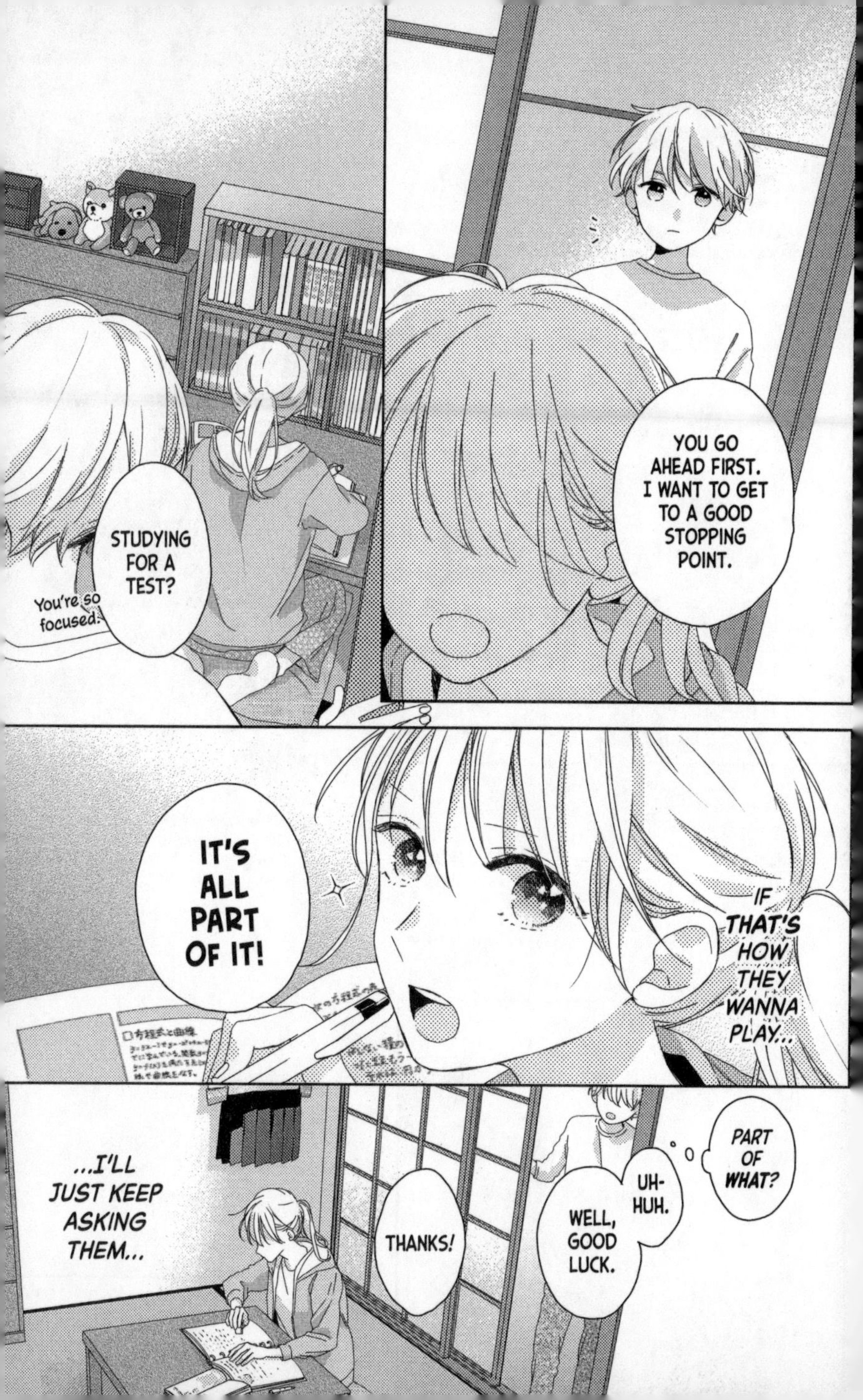
YOU GO AHEAD FIRST. I WANT TO GET TO A GOOD STOPPING POINT.
STUDYING FOR A TEST?
You're so focused.
IT'S ALL PART OF IT!
IF THAT'S HOW THEY WANNA PLAY...
PART OF WHAT?
UH-HUH.
WELL, GOOD LUCK.
THANKS!
...I'LL JUST KEEP ASKING THEM...

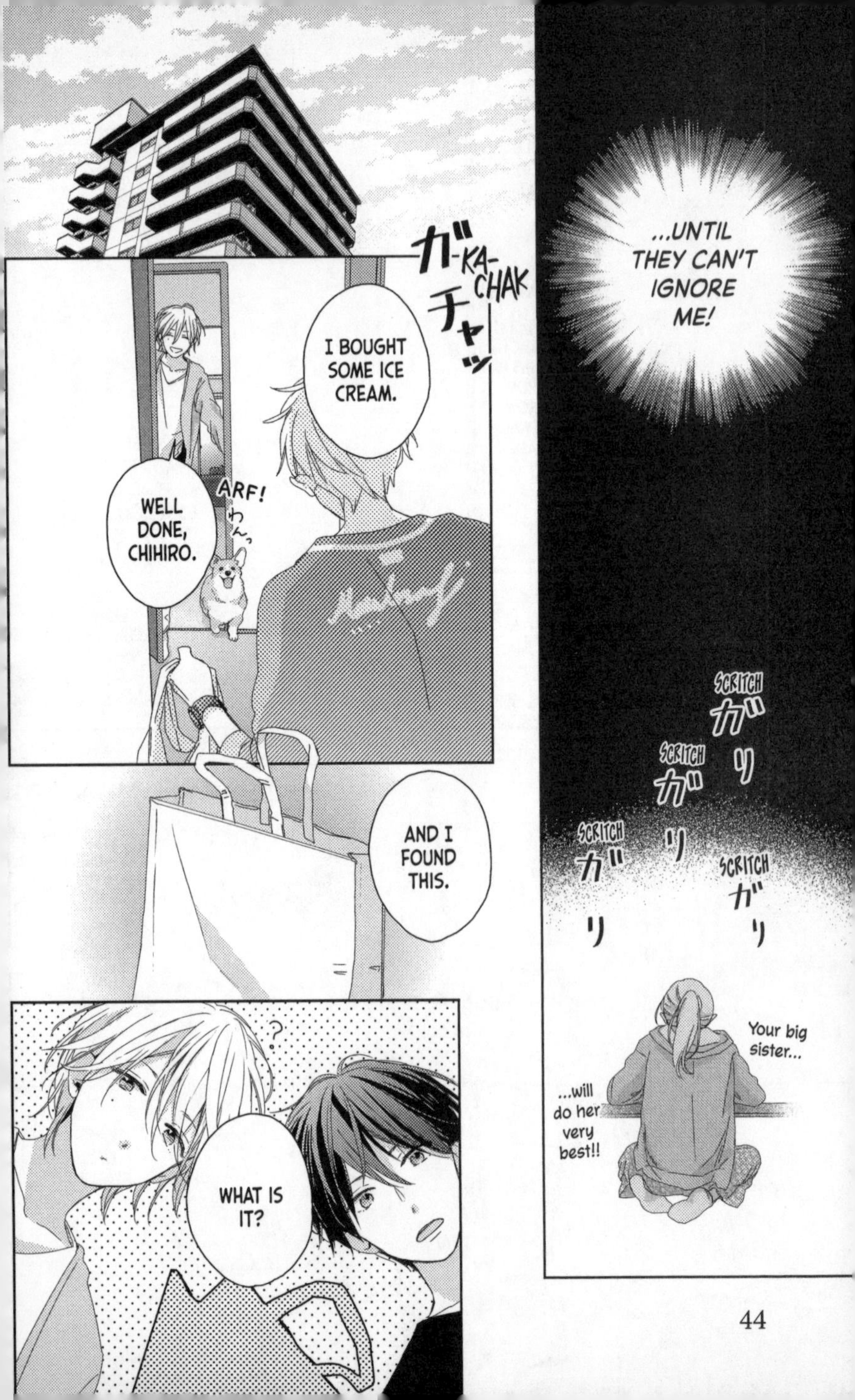

...UNTIL THEY CAN'T IGNORE ME!
SCRITCH
ガリ
SCRITCH
ガリ
SCRITCH
ガリ
SCRITCH
ガリ
Your big sister...
...will do her very best!!
ガチャッ
KA-CHAK
I BOUGHT SOME ICE CREAM.
WELL DONE, CHIHIRO.
ARF!
わんっ
AND I FOUND THIS.
?
WHAT IS IT?

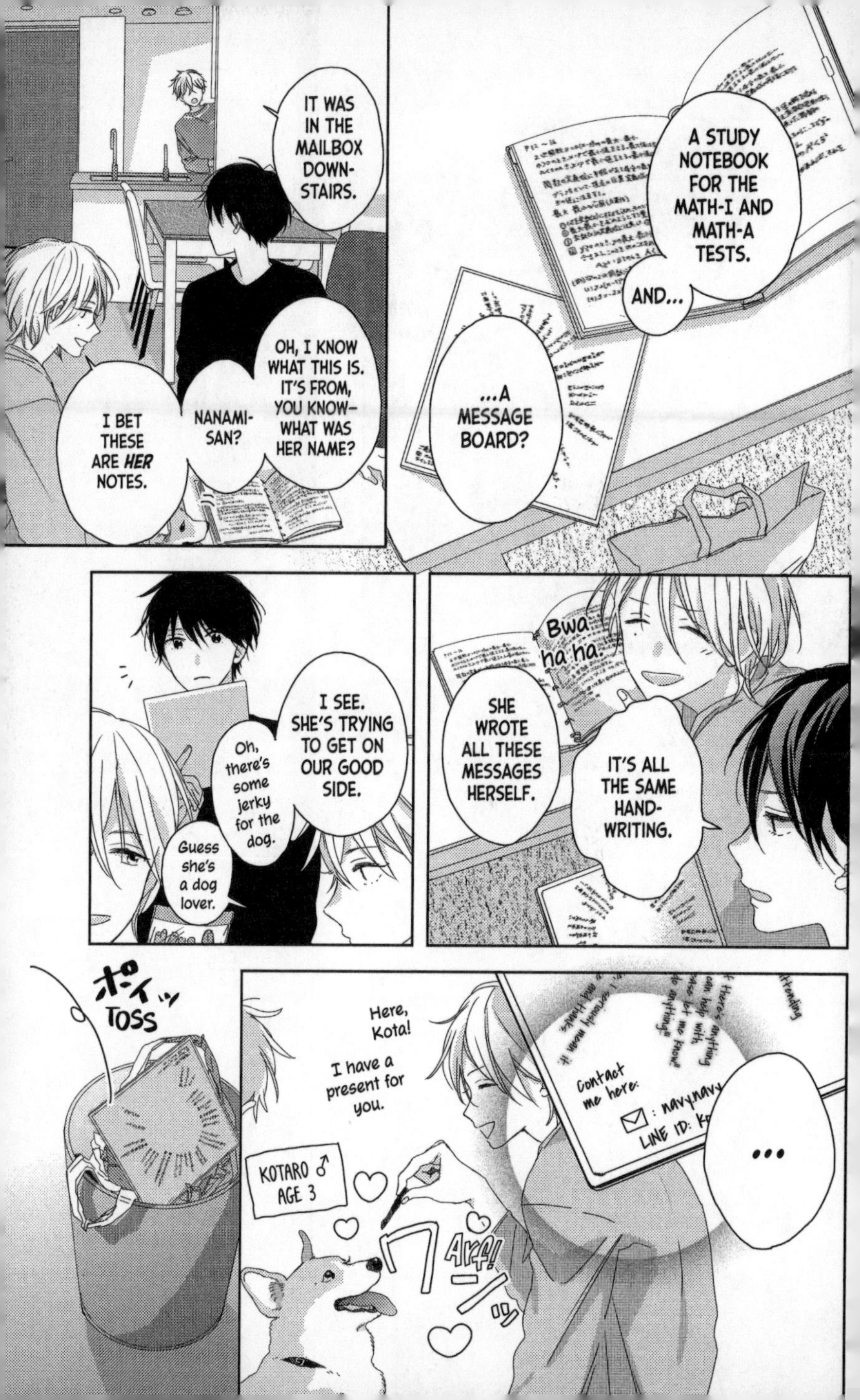
A STUDY NOTEBOOK FOR THE MATH-I AND MATH-A TESTS.
AND...
...A MESSAGE BOARD?
IT WAS IN THE MAILBOX DOWN-STAIRS.
OH, I KNOW WHAT THIS IS. IT'S FROM, YOU KNOW—WHAT WAS HER NAME?
NANAMI-SAN?
I BET THESE ARE HER NOTES.
Bwa ha ha.
SHE WROTE ALL THESE MESSAGES HERSELF.
IT'S ALL THE SAME HAND-WRITING.
I SEE. SHE'S TRYING TO GET ON OUR GOOD SIDE.
Oh, there's some jerky for the dog.
Guess she's a dog lover.
Contact me here:
LINE ID:
...
Here, Kota!
I have a present for you.
KOTARO ♂ AGE 3
Arf!
TOSS

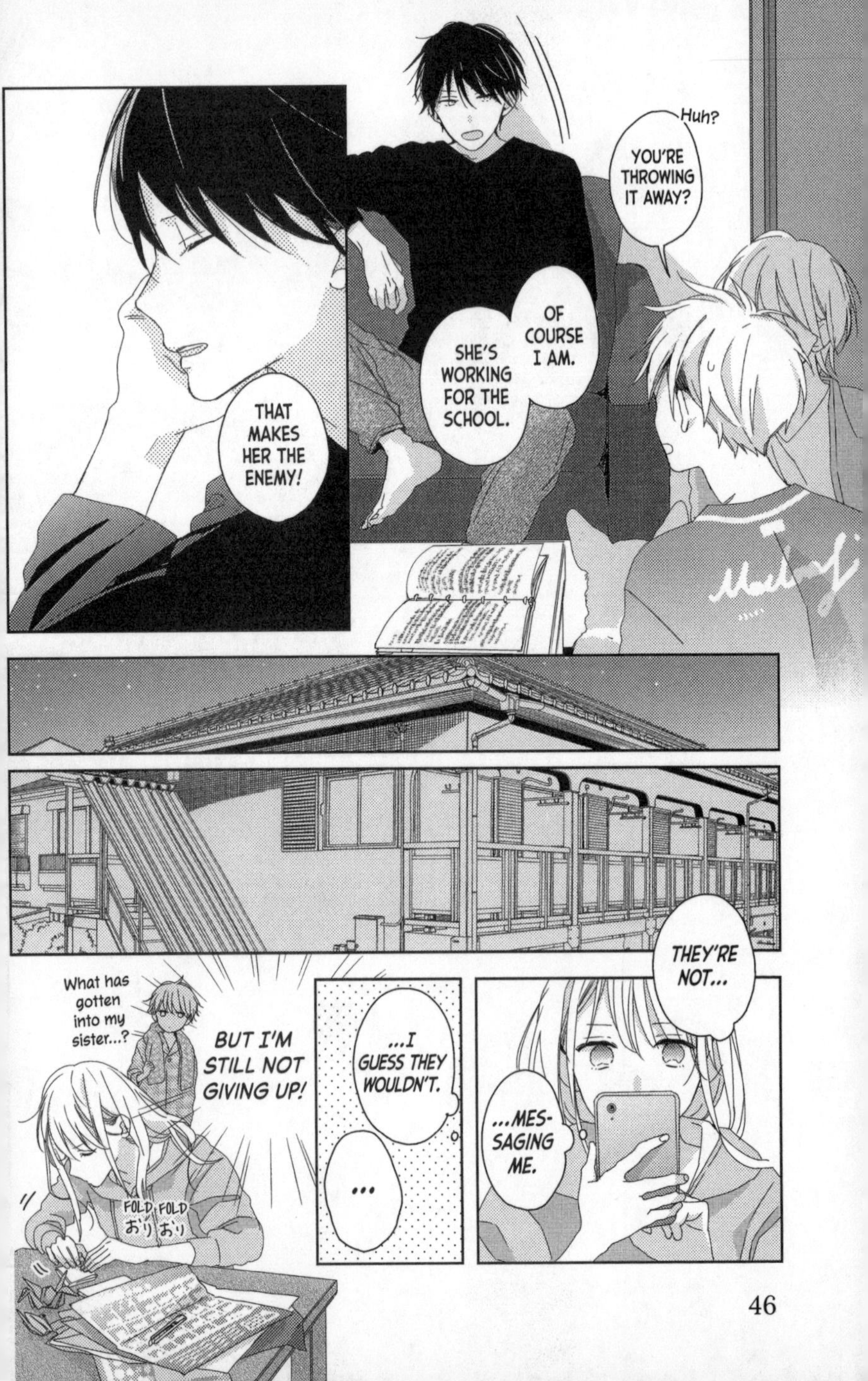
Huh?
YOU'RE THROWING IT AWAY?
OF COURSE I AM.
SHE'S WORKING FOR THE SCHOOL.
THAT MAKES HER THE ENEMY!
THEY'RE NOT...
...MES-SAGING ME.
...I GUESS THEY WOULDN'T.
...
BUT I'M STILL NOT GIVING UP!
What has gotten into my sister...?
FOLD FOLD
おりおり

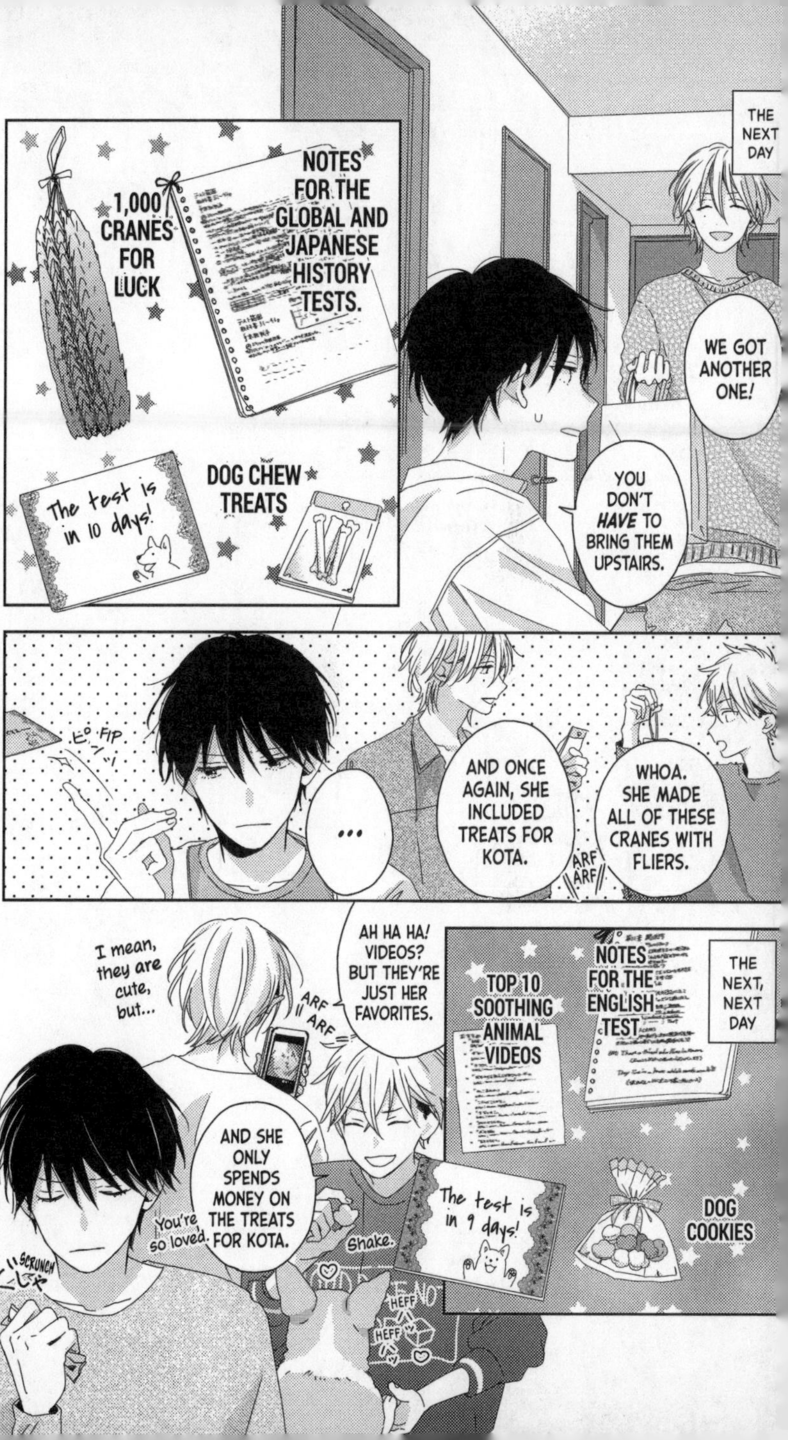
THE NEXT DAY
WE GOT ANOTHER ONE!
YOU DON'T *HAVE* TO BRING THEM UPSTAIRS.
NOTES FOR THE GLOBAL AND JAPANESE HISTORY TESTS.
1,000 CRANES FOR LUCK
The test is in 10 days!
DOG CHEW TREATS
WHOA. SHE MADE ALL OF THESE CRANES WITH FLIERS.
ARF ARF
AND ONCE AGAIN, SHE INCLUDED TREATS FOR KOTA.
...
FIP
THE NEXT, NEXT DAY
NOTES FOR THE ENGLISH TEST
TOP 10 SOOTHING ANIMAL VIDEOS
The test is in 9 days!
DOG COOKIES
AH HA HA! VIDEOS? BUT THEY'RE JUST HER FAVORITES.
ARF ARF
I mean, they are cute, but...
AND SHE ONLY SPENDS MONEY ON THE TREATS FOR KOTA.
Shake.
You're so loved.
HEFF HEFF
SCRUNCH

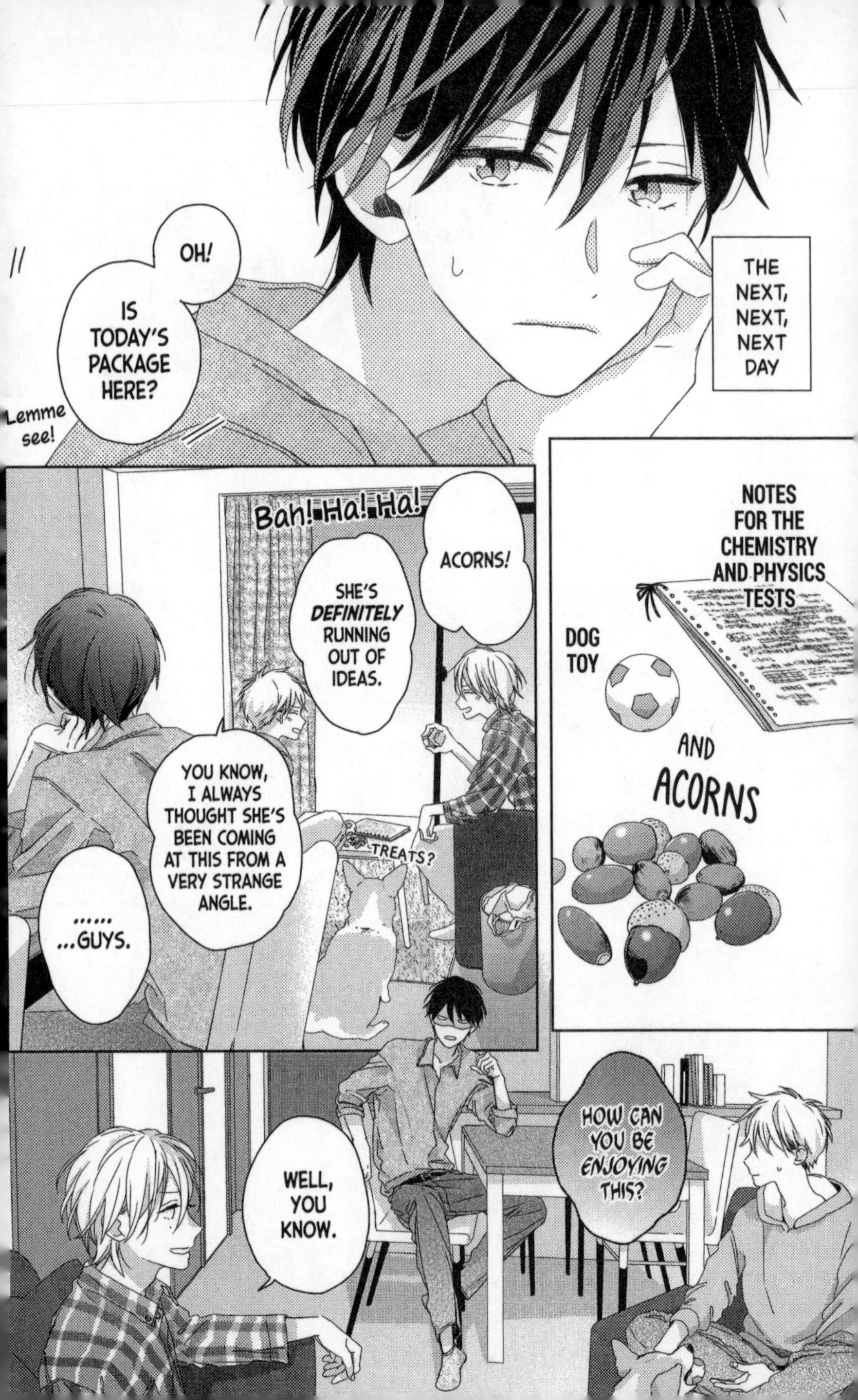
THE NEXT, NEXT, NEXT DAY
OH!
IS TODAY'S PACKAGE HERE?
Lemme see!
NOTES FOR THE CHEMISTRY AND PHYSICS TESTS
DOG TOY
AND ACORNS
Bah! Ha! Ha!
ACORNS!
SHE'S DEFINITELY RUNNING OUT OF IDEAS.
YOU KNOW, I ALWAYS THOUGHT SHE'S BEEN COMING AT THIS FROM A VERY STRANGE ANGLE.
TREATS?
....GUYS.
HOW CAN YOU BE ENJOYING THIS?
WELL, YOU KNOW.

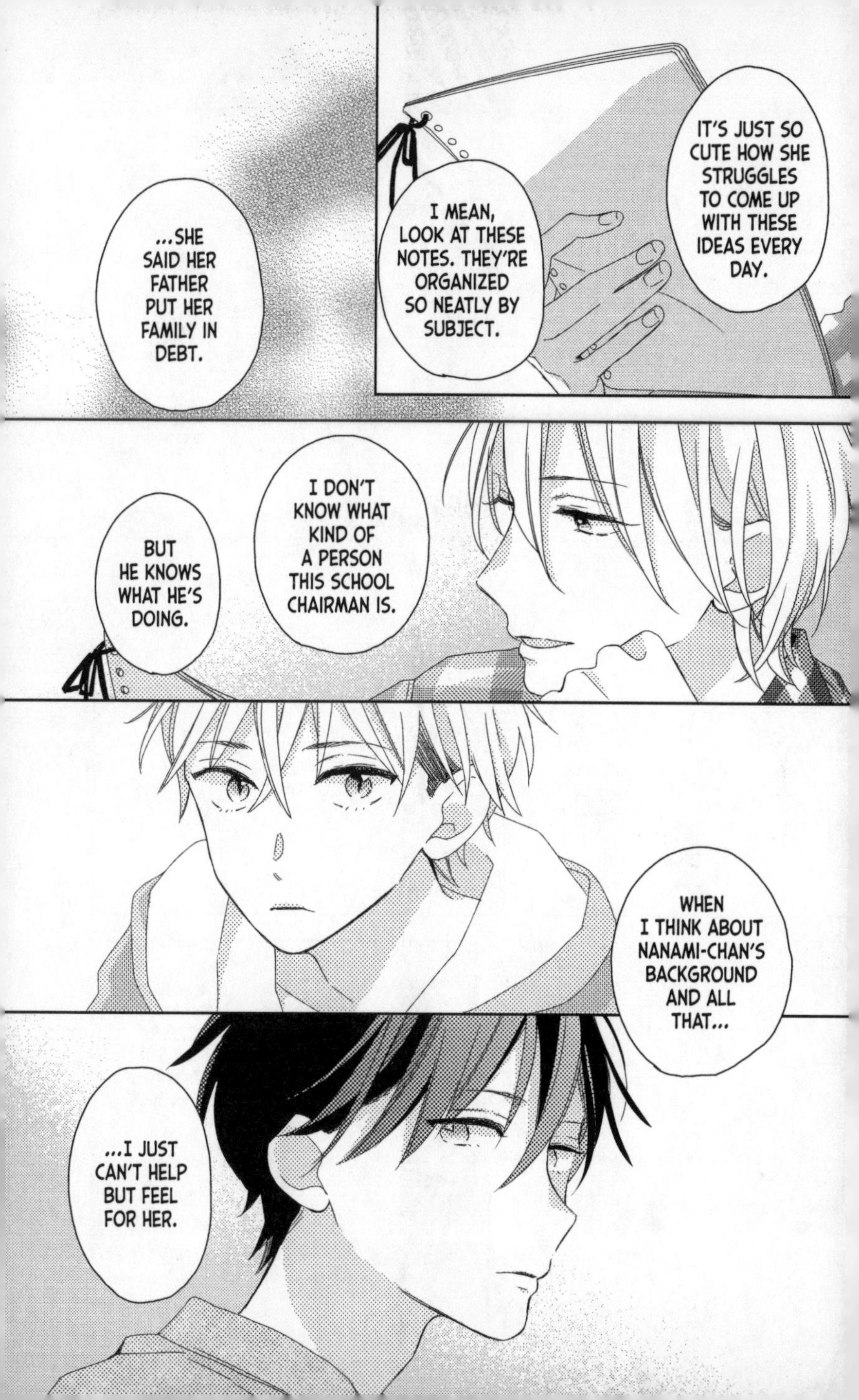
IT'S JUST SO CUTE HOW SHE STRUGGLES TO COME UP WITH THESE IDEAS EVERY DAY.
I MEAN, LOOK AT THESE NOTES. THEY'RE ORGANIZED SO NEATLY BY SUBJECT.
...SHE SAID HER FATHER PUT HER FAMILY IN DEBT.
I DON'T KNOW WHAT KIND OF A PERSON THIS SCHOOL CHAIRMAN IS.
BUT HE KNOWS WHAT HE'S DOING.
WHEN I THINK ABOUT NANAMI-CHAN'S BACKGROUND AND ALL THAT...
...I JUST CAN'T HELP BUT FEEL FOR HER.

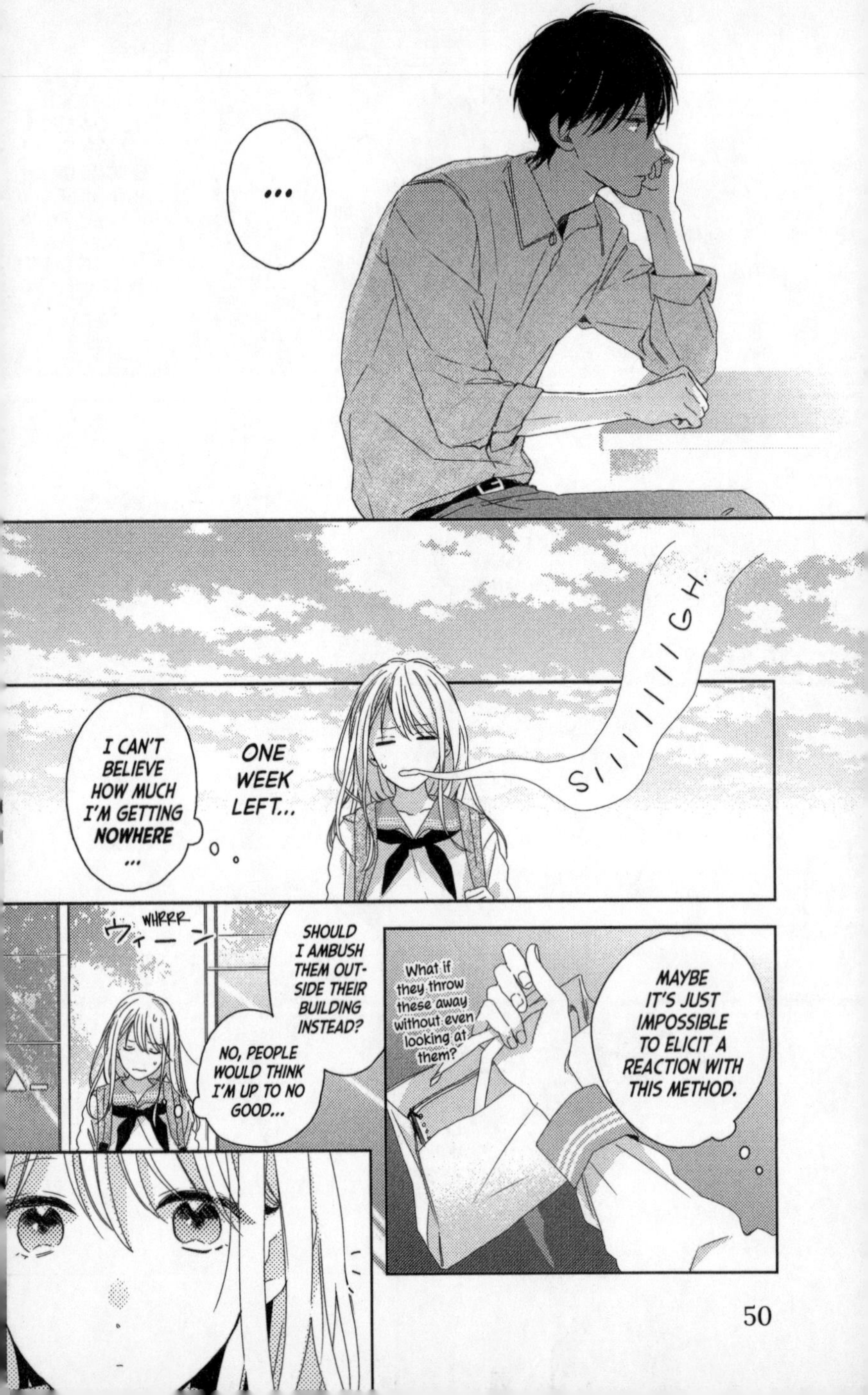
...
SIIIIIIIGH.
ONE WEEK LEFT...
I CAN'T BELIEVE HOW MUCH I'M GETTING NOWHERE...
MAYBE IT'S JUST IMPOSSIBLE TO ELICIT A REACTION WITH THIS METHOD.
What if they throw these away without even looking at them?
SHOULD I AMBUSH THEM OUT-SIDE THEIR BUILDING INSTEAD?
NO, PEOPLE WOULD THINK I'M UP TO NO GOOD...
WHRRR
ヴィーン

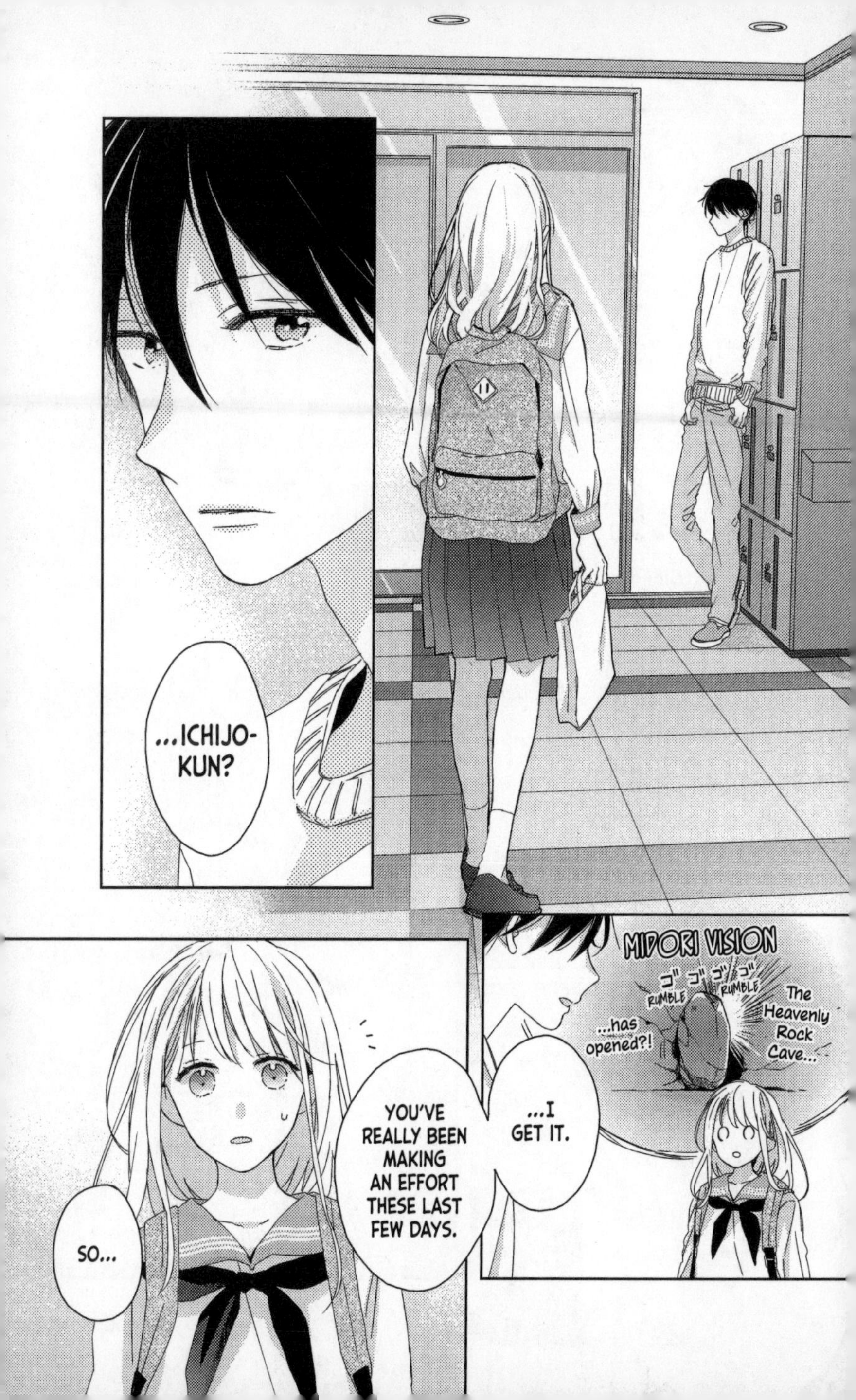
...ICHIJO-KUN?
MIDORI VISION
ゴゴ RUMBLE
ゴゴ RUMBLE
The Heavenly Rock Cave...
...has opened?!
...I GET IT.
YOU'VE REALLY BEEN MAKING AN EFFORT THESE LAST FEW DAYS.
SO...

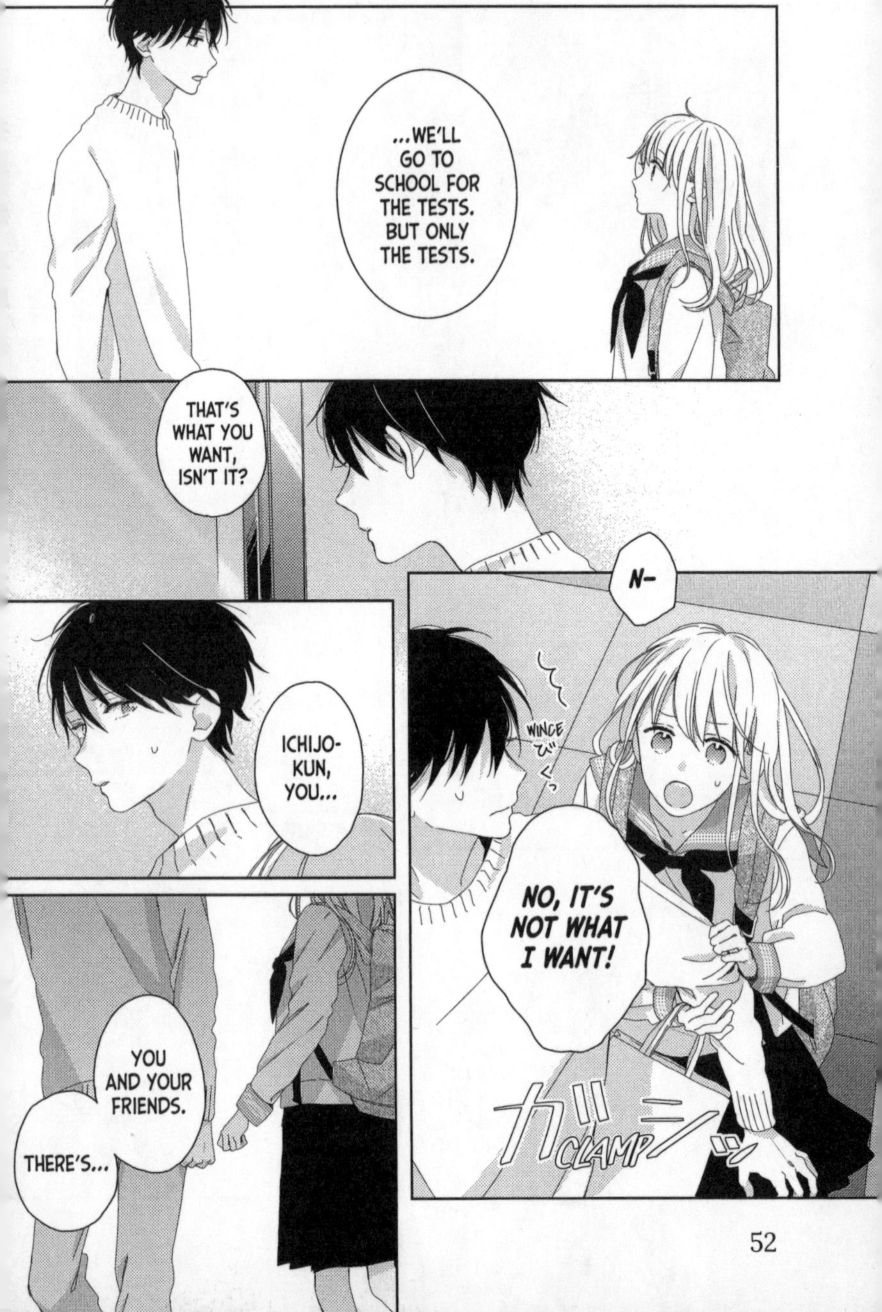
...WE'LL GO TO SCHOOL FOR THE TESTS. BUT ONLY THE TESTS.
THAT'S WHAT YOU WANT, ISN'T IT?
N-
WINCE
NO, IT'S NOT WHAT I WANT!
CLAMP
ICHIJO-KUN, YOU...
YOU AND YOUR FRIENDS.
THERE'S...

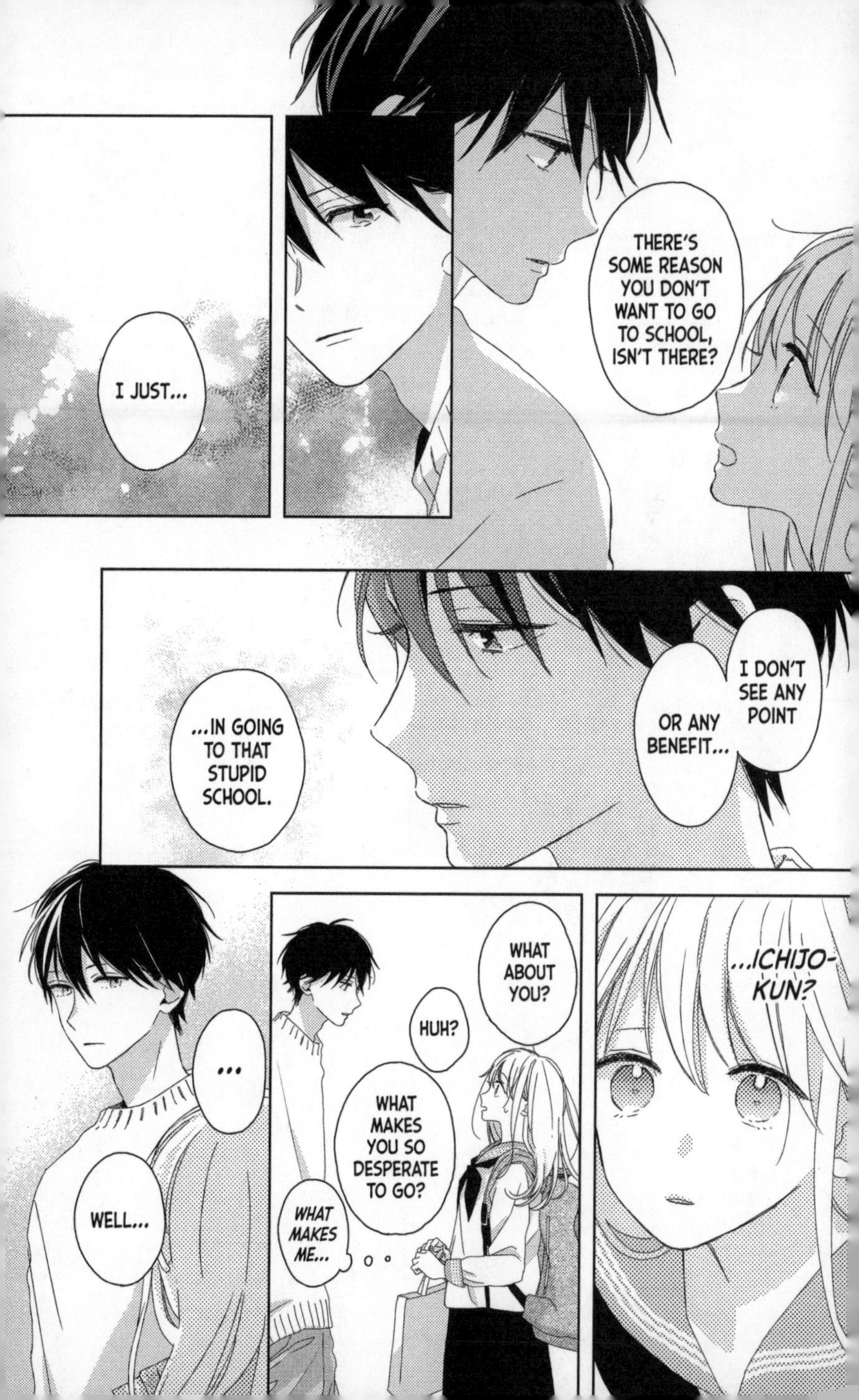
THERE'S SOME REASON YOU DON'T WANT TO GO TO SCHOOL, ISN'T THERE?
I JUST...
I DON'T SEE ANY POINT
OR ANY BENEFIT...
...IN GOING TO THAT STUPID SCHOOL.
...ICHIJO-KUN?
WHAT ABOUT YOU?
HUH?
WHAT MAKES YOU SO DESPERATE TO GO?
WHAT MAKES ME...
...
WELL...

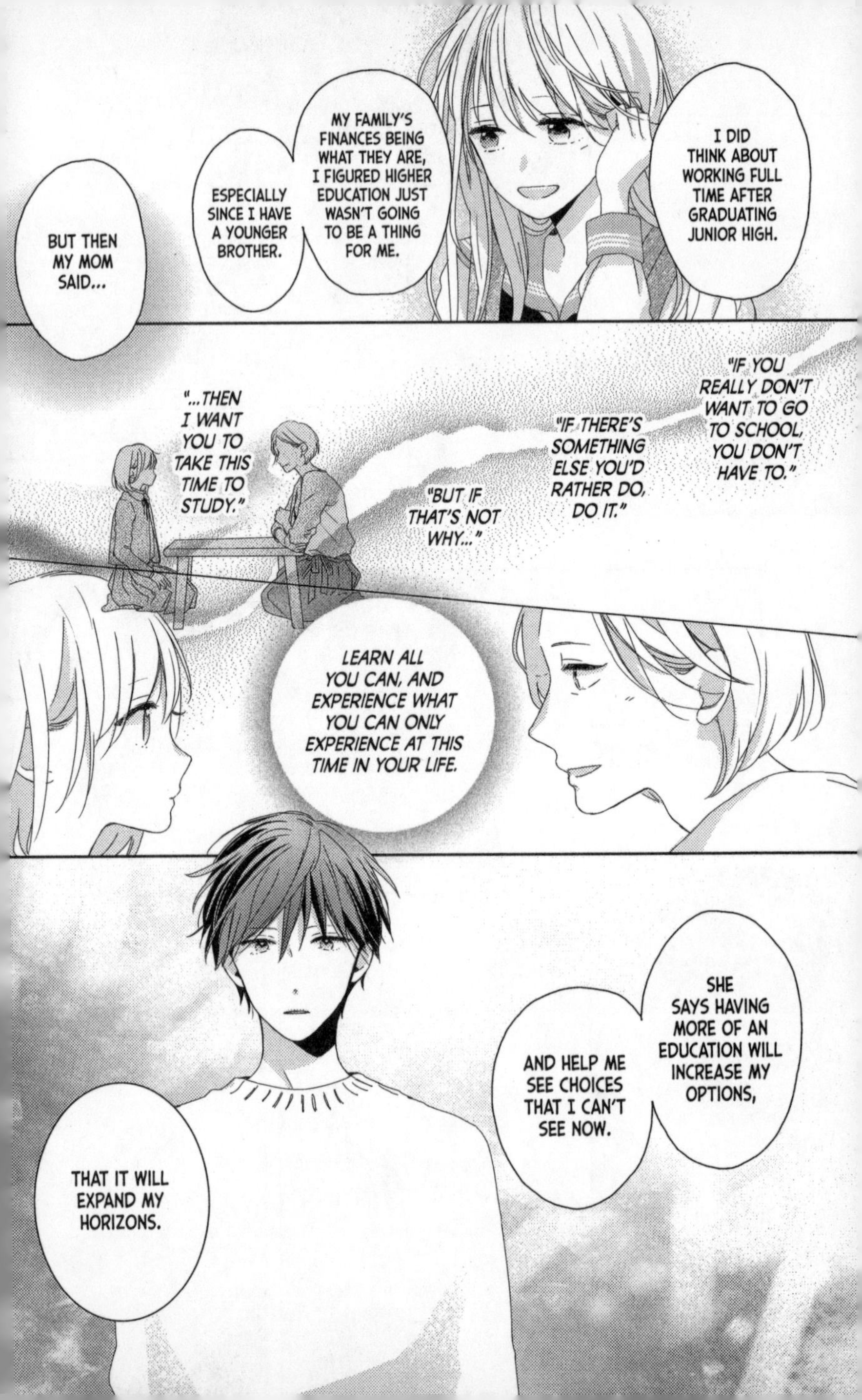
I DID THINK ABOUT WORKING FULL TIME AFTER GRADUATING JUNIOR HIGH.
MY FAMILY'S FINANCES BEING WHAT THEY ARE, I FIGURED HIGHER EDUCATION JUST WASN'T GOING TO BE A THING FOR ME.
ESPECIALLY SINCE I HAVE A YOUNGER BROTHER.
BUT THEN MY MOM SAID...
"IF YOU REALLY DON'T WANT TO GO TO SCHOOL, YOU DON'T HAVE TO."
"IF THERE'S SOMETHING ELSE YOU'D RATHER DO, DO IT."
"BUT IF THAT'S NOT WHY..."
"...THEN I WANT YOU TO TAKE THIS TIME TO STUDY."
LEARN ALL YOU CAN, AND EXPERIENCE WHAT YOU CAN ONLY EXPERIENCE AT THIS TIME IN YOUR LIFE.
SHE SAYS HAVING MORE OF AN EDUCATION WILL INCREASE MY OPTIONS,
AND HELP ME SEE CHOICES THAT I CAN'T SEE NOW.
THAT IT WILL EXPAND MY HORIZONS.

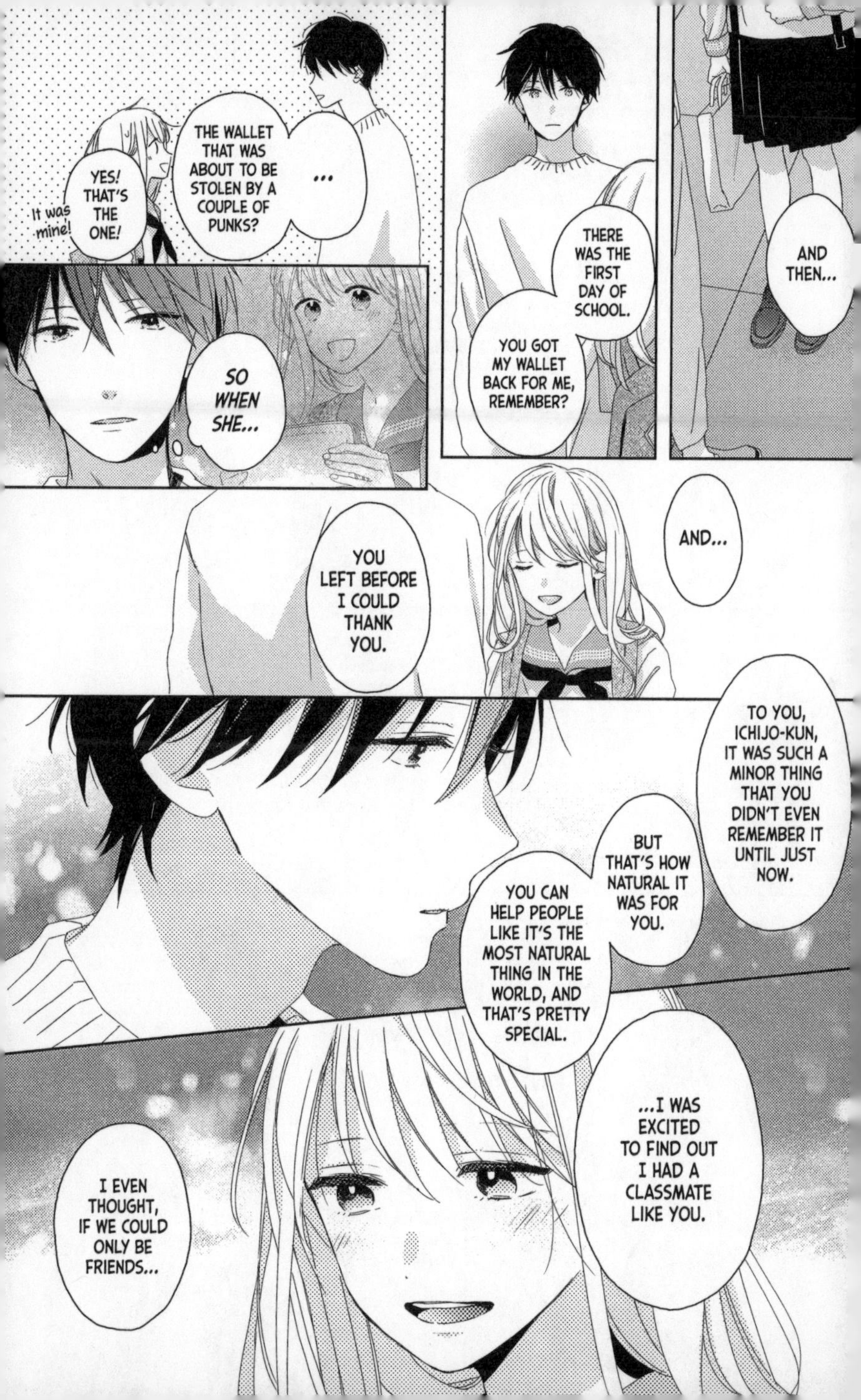
AND THEN...
THERE WAS THE FIRST DAY OF SCHOOL.
YOU GOT MY WALLET BACK FOR ME, REMEMBER?
...
THE WALLET THAT WAS ABOUT TO BE STOLEN BY A COUPLE OF PUNKS?
YES! THAT'S THE ONE!
It was mine!
SO WHEN SHE...
AND...
YOU LEFT BEFORE I COULD THANK YOU.
TO YOU, ICHIJO-KUN, IT WAS SUCH A MINOR THING THAT YOU DIDN'T EVEN REMEMBER IT UNTIL JUST NOW.
BUT THAT'S HOW NATURAL IT WAS FOR YOU.
YOU CAN HELP PEOPLE LIKE IT'S THE MOST NATURAL THING IN THE WORLD, AND THAT'S PRETTY SPECIAL.
...I WAS EXCITED TO FIND OUT I HAD A CLASSMATE LIKE YOU.
I EVEN THOUGHT, IF WE COULD ONLY BE FRIENDS...

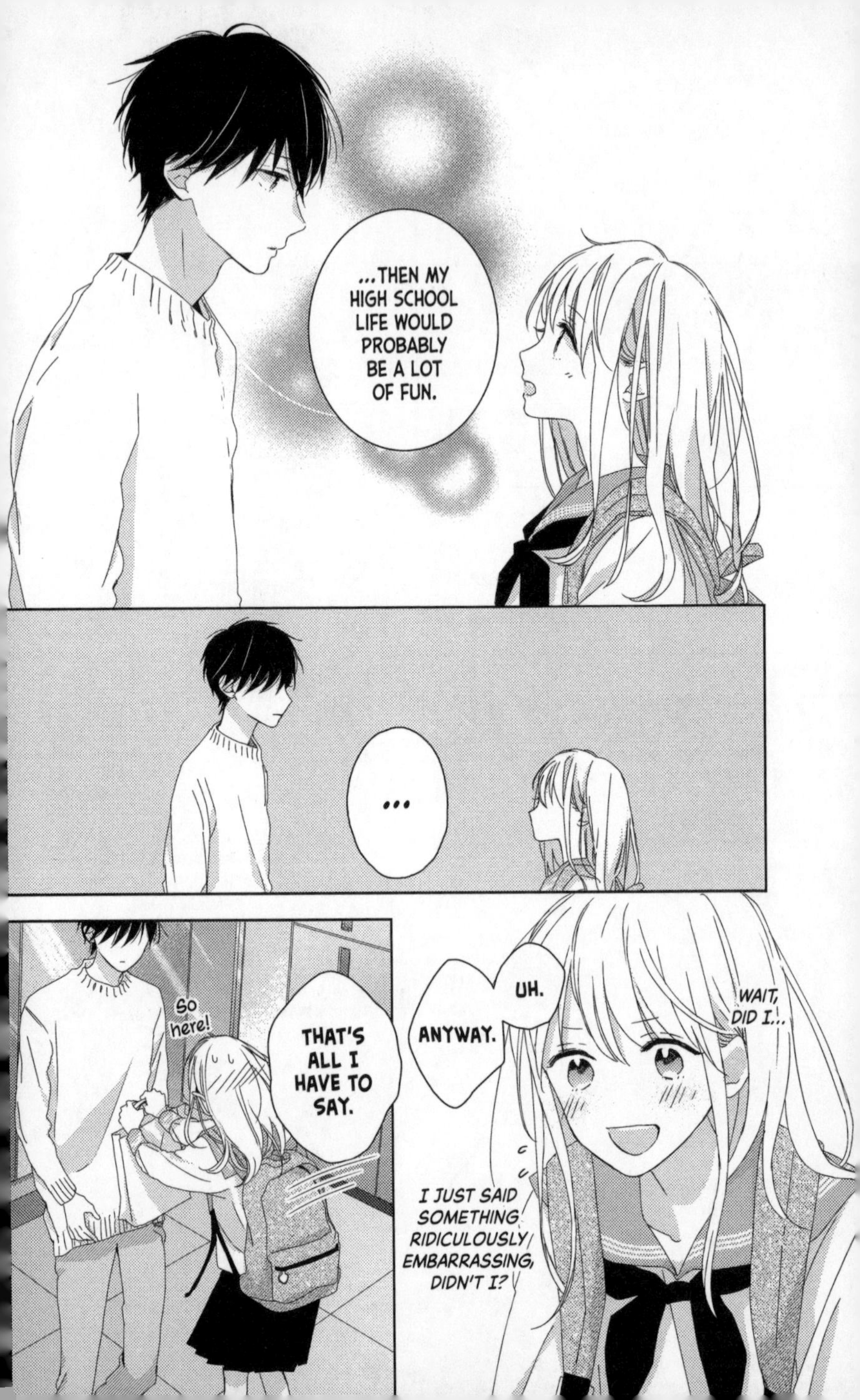
...THEN MY HIGH SCHOOL LIFE WOULD PROBABLY BE A LOT OF FUN.
...
WAIT, DID I...
UH.
ANYWAY.
I JUST SAID SOMETHING RIDICULOUSLY EMBARRASSING, DIDN'T I?
THAT'S ALL I HAVE TO SAY.
So here!

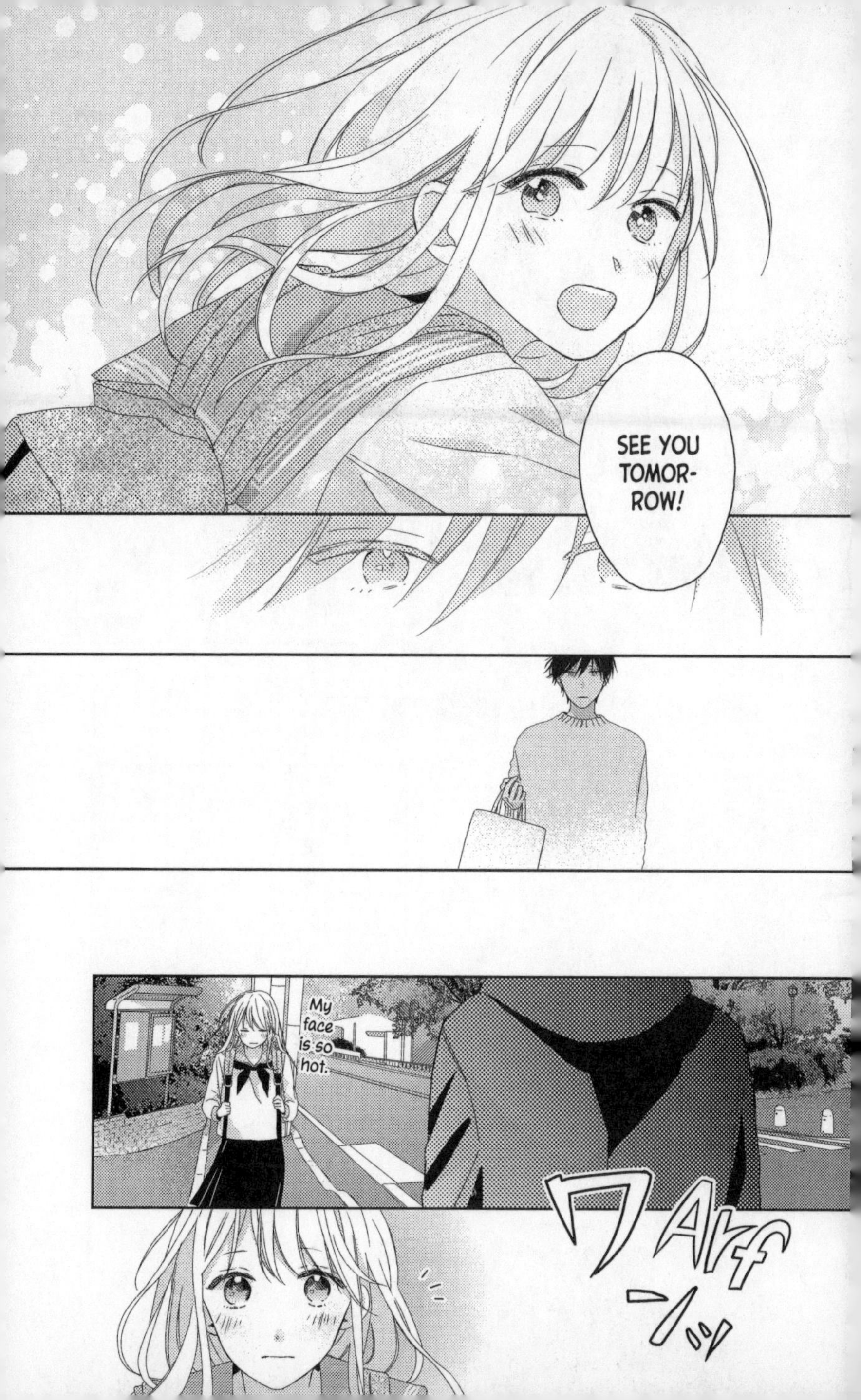

SEE YOU TOMORROW!
My face is so hot.
Arf

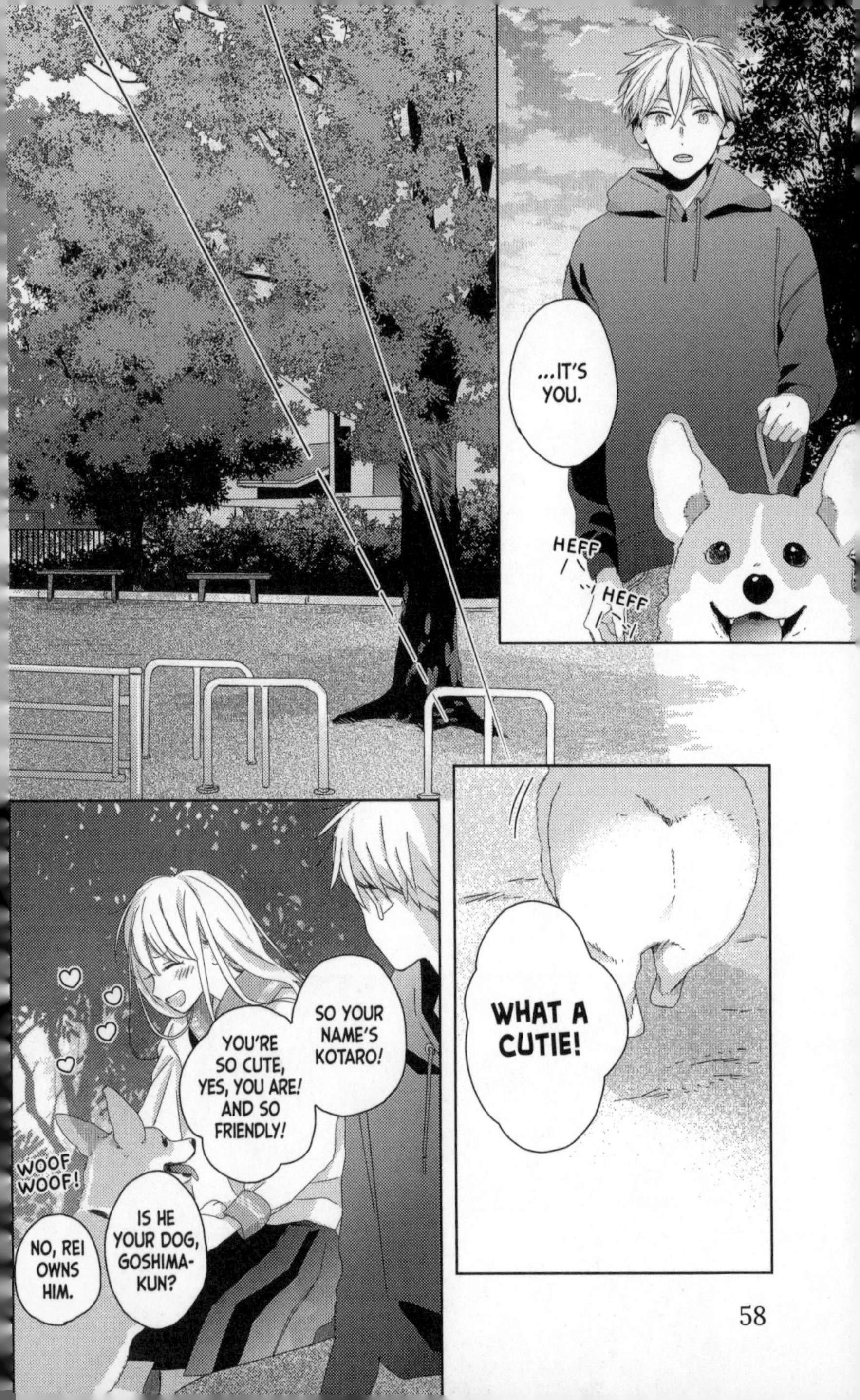
...IT'S YOU.
HEFF
HEFF
WHAT A CUTIE!
SO YOUR NAME'S KOTARO!
YOU'RE SO CUTE, YES, YOU ARE! AND SO FRIENDLY!
WOOF WOOF!
IS HE YOUR DOG, GOSHIMA-KUN?
NO, REI OWNS HIM.

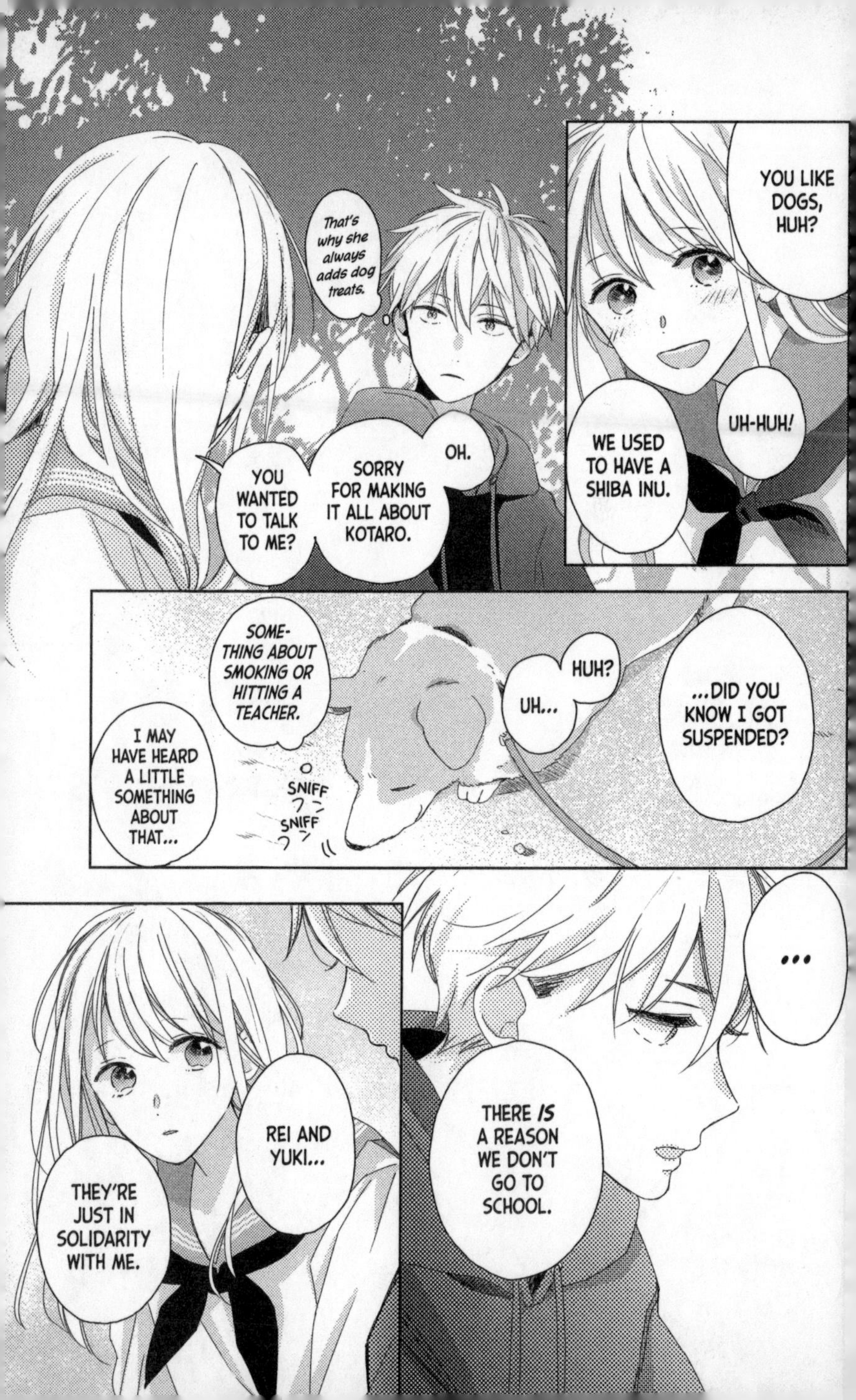
YOU LIKE DOGS, HUH?
UH-HUH!
WE USED TO HAVE A SHIBA INU.
That's why she always adds dog treats.
OH.
SORRY FOR MAKING IT ALL ABOUT KOTARO.
YOU WANTED TO TALK TO ME?
...DID YOU KNOW I GOT SUSPENDED?
HUH?
UH...
SOME-THING ABOUT SMOKING OR HITTING A TEACHER.
SNIFF
SNIFF
I MAY HAVE HEARD A LITTLE SOMETHING ABOUT THAT...
...
THERE *IS* A REASON WE DON'T GO TO SCHOOL.
REI AND YUKI...
THEY'RE JUST IN SOLIDARITY WITH ME.

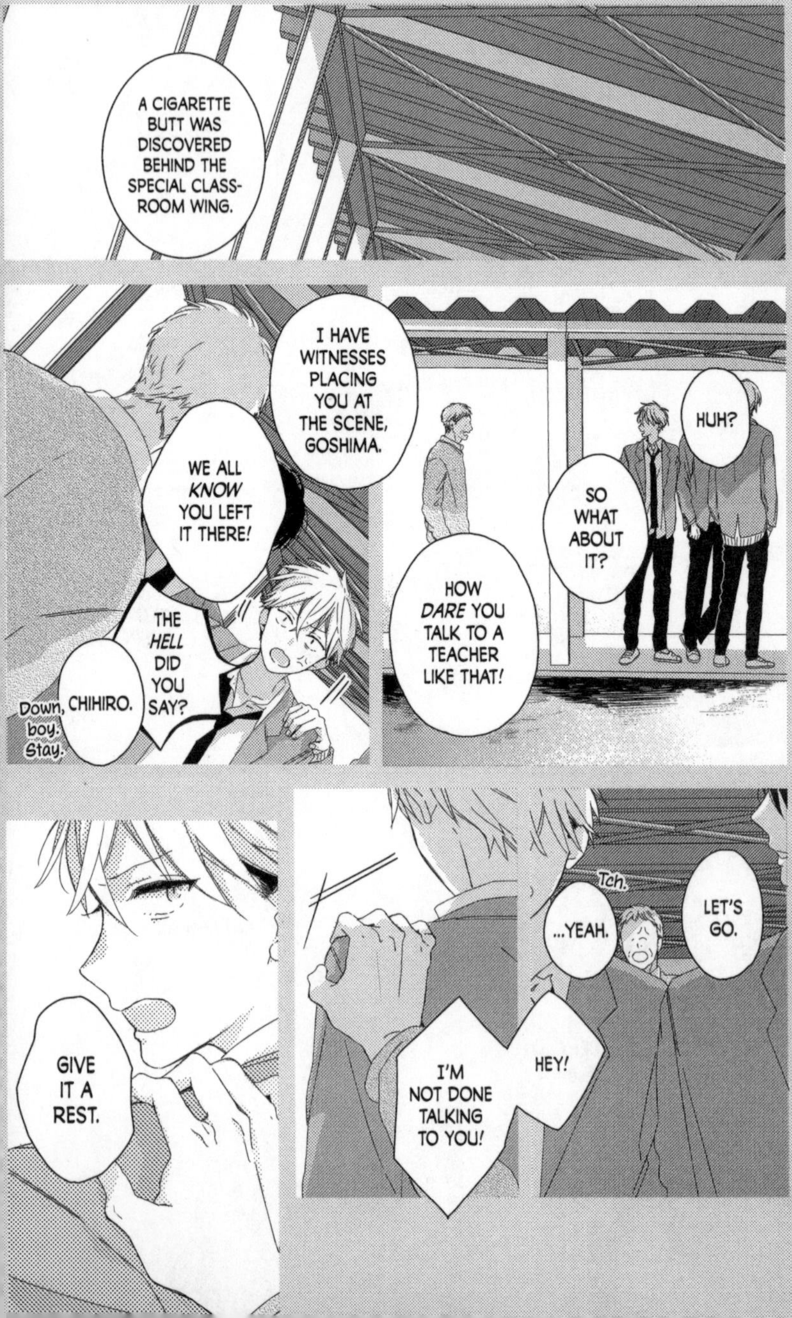
A CIGARETTE BUTT WAS DISCOVERED BEHIND THE SPECIAL CLASS-ROOM WING.
HUH?
SO WHAT ABOUT IT?
HOW *DARE* YOU TALK TO A TEACHER LIKE THAT!
I HAVE WITNESSES PLACING YOU AT THE SCENE, GOSHIMA.
WE ALL *KNOW* YOU LEFT IT THERE!
THE *HELL* DID YOU SAY?
CHIHIRO.
Down, boy. Stay.
LET'S GO.
Tch.
...YEAH.
HEY!
I'M NOT DONE TALKING TO YOU!
GIVE IT A REST.

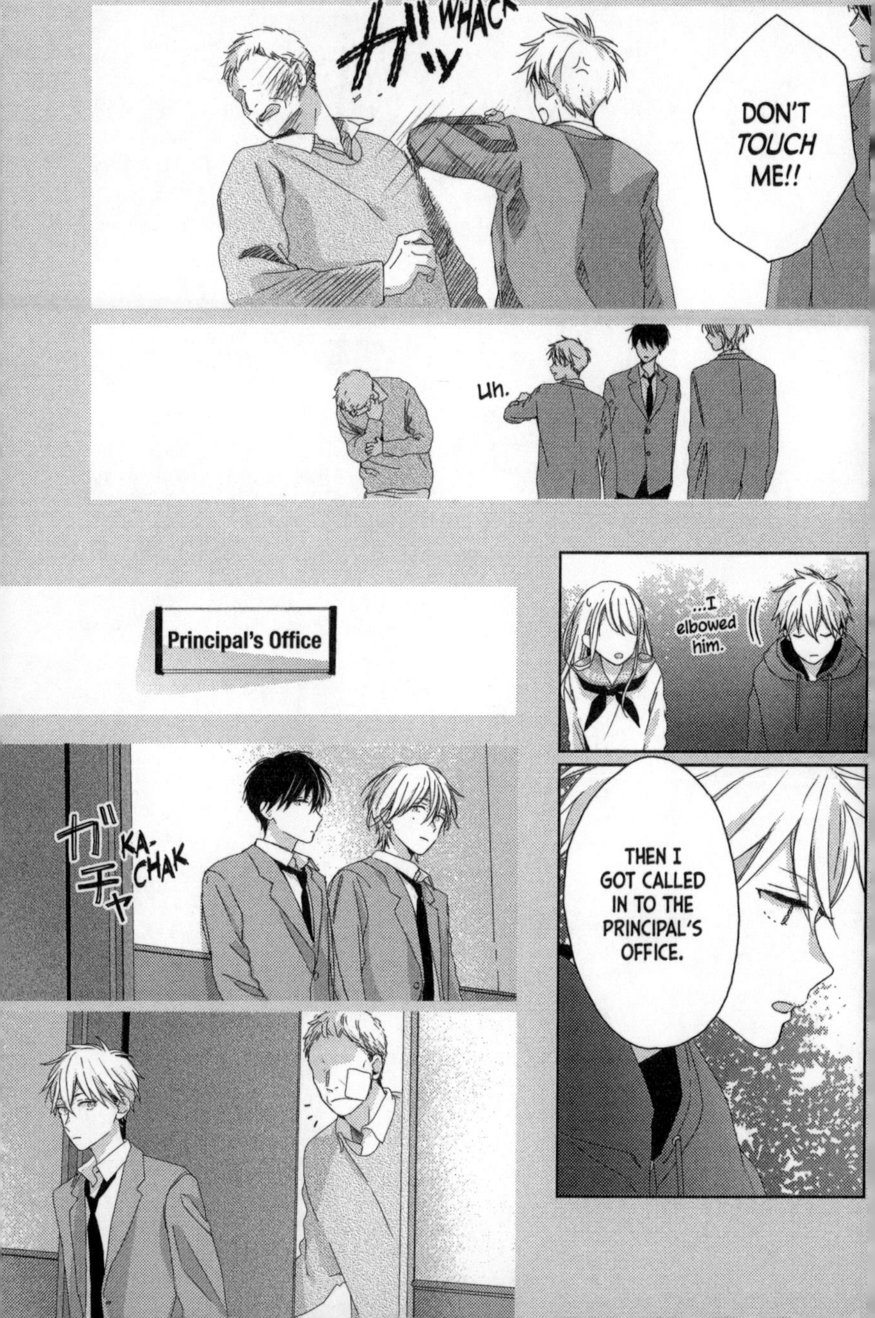
DON'T TOUCH ME!!
ガッ WHACK
Uh.
...I elbowed him.
THEN I GOT CALLED IN TO THE PRINCIPAL'S OFFICE.
Principal's Office
ガチャ KA-CHAK

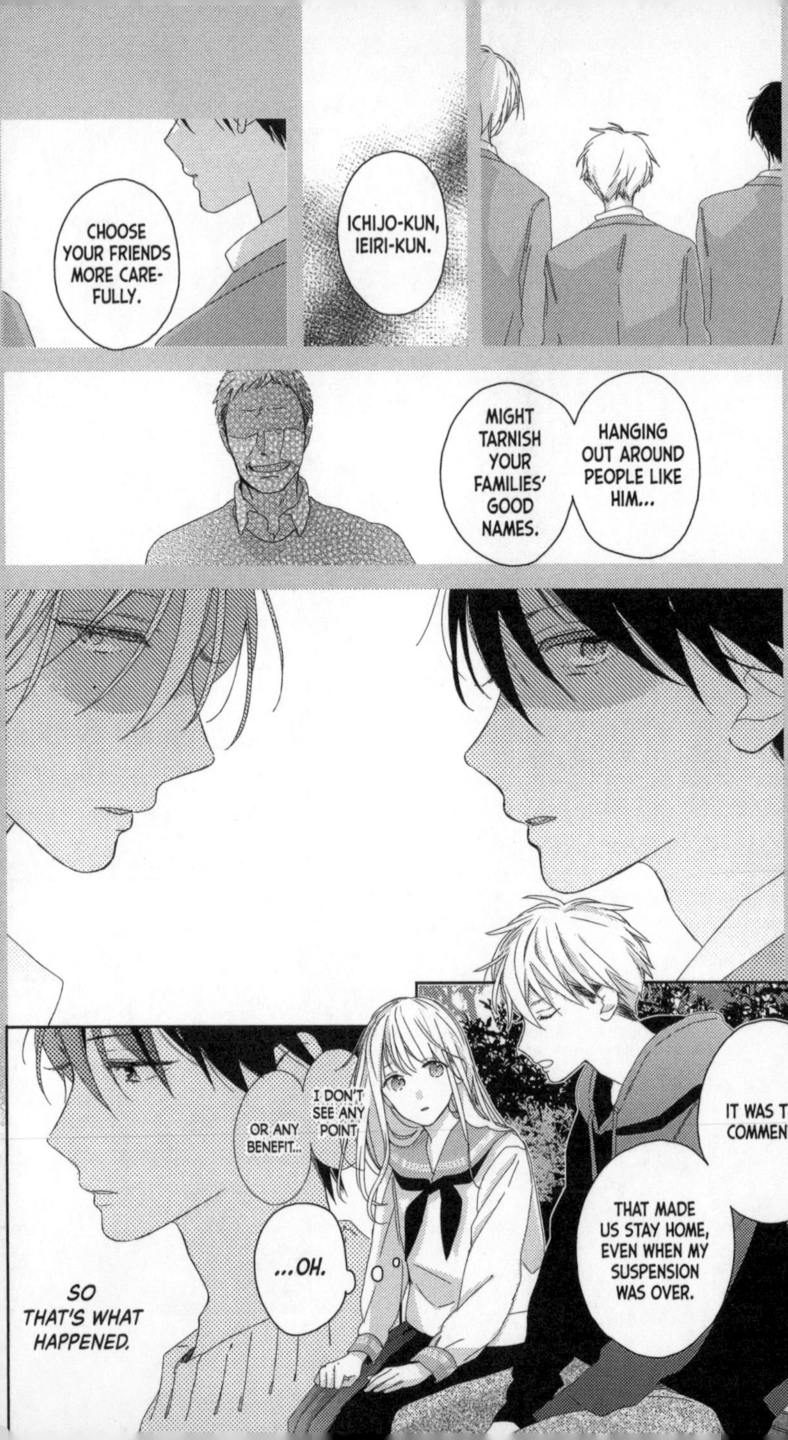
ICHIJO-KUN, IEIRI-KUN.
CHOOSE YOUR FRIENDS MORE CARE-FULLY.
HANGING OUT AROUND PEOPLE LIKE HIM...
MIGHT TARNISH YOUR FAMILIES' GOOD NAMES.
IT WAS THAT COMMENT...
THAT MADE US STAY HOME, EVEN WHEN MY SUSPENSION WAS OVER.
I DON'T SEE ANY POINT
OR ANY BENEFIT...
...OH.
SO THAT'S WHAT HAPPENED.

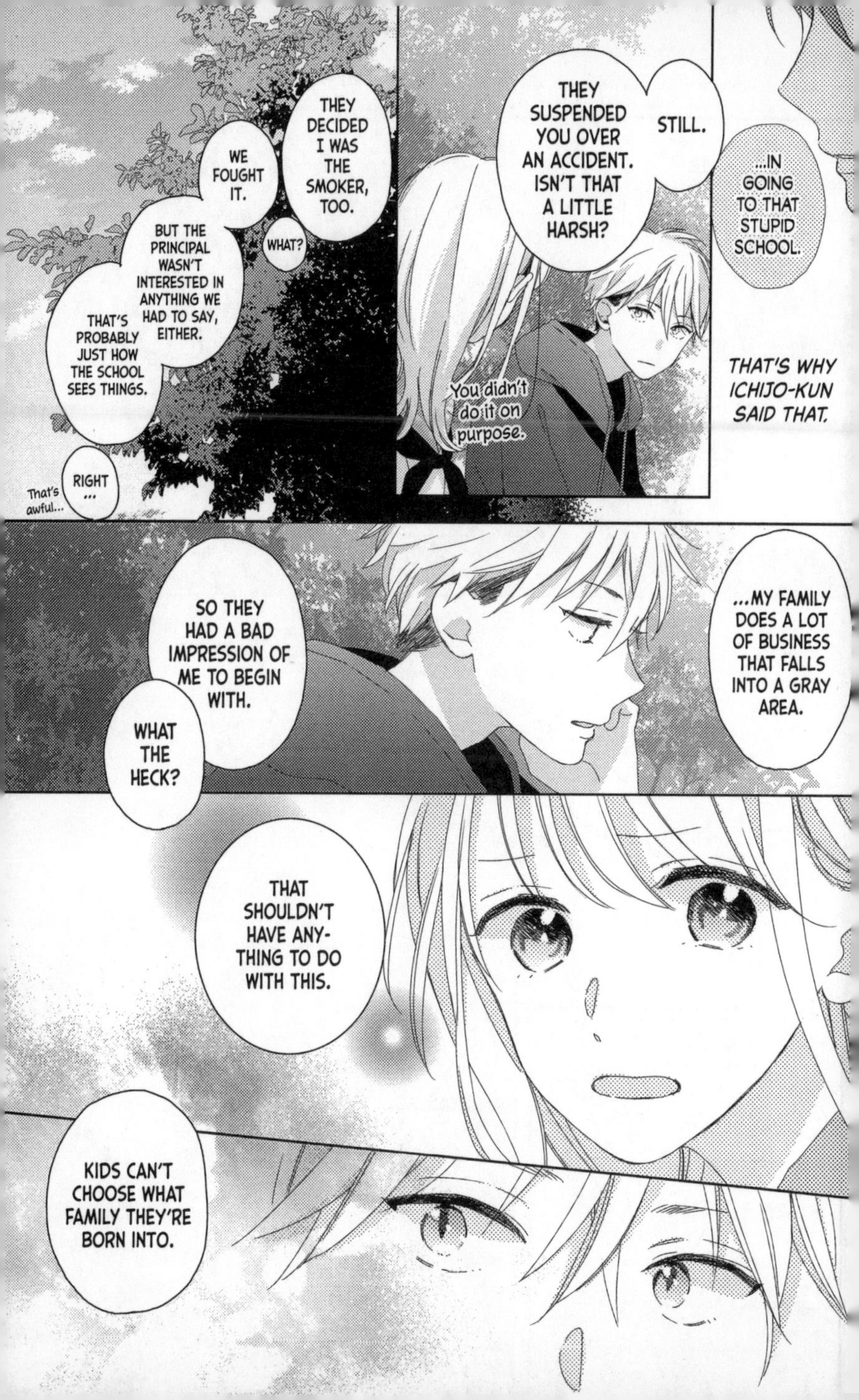
...IN GOING TO THAT STUPID SCHOOL.
STILL.
THEY SUSPENDED YOU OVER AN ACCIDENT. ISN'T THAT A LITTLE HARSH?
THAT'S WHY ICHIJO-KUN SAID THAT.
You didn't do it on purpose.
THEY DECIDED I WAS THE SMOKER, TOO.
WE FOUGHT IT.
WHAT?
BUT THE PRINCIPAL WASN'T INTERESTED IN ANYTHING WE HAD TO SAY, EITHER.
THAT'S PROBABLY JUST HOW THE SCHOOL SEES THINGS.
RIGHT...
That's awful...
...MY FAMILY DOES A LOT OF BUSINESS THAT FALLS INTO A GRAY AREA.
SO THEY HAD A BAD IMPRESSION OF ME TO BEGIN WITH.
WHAT THE HECK?
THAT SHOULDN'T HAVE ANYTHING TO DO WITH THIS.
KIDS CAN'T CHOOSE WHAT FAMILY THEY'RE BORN INTO.

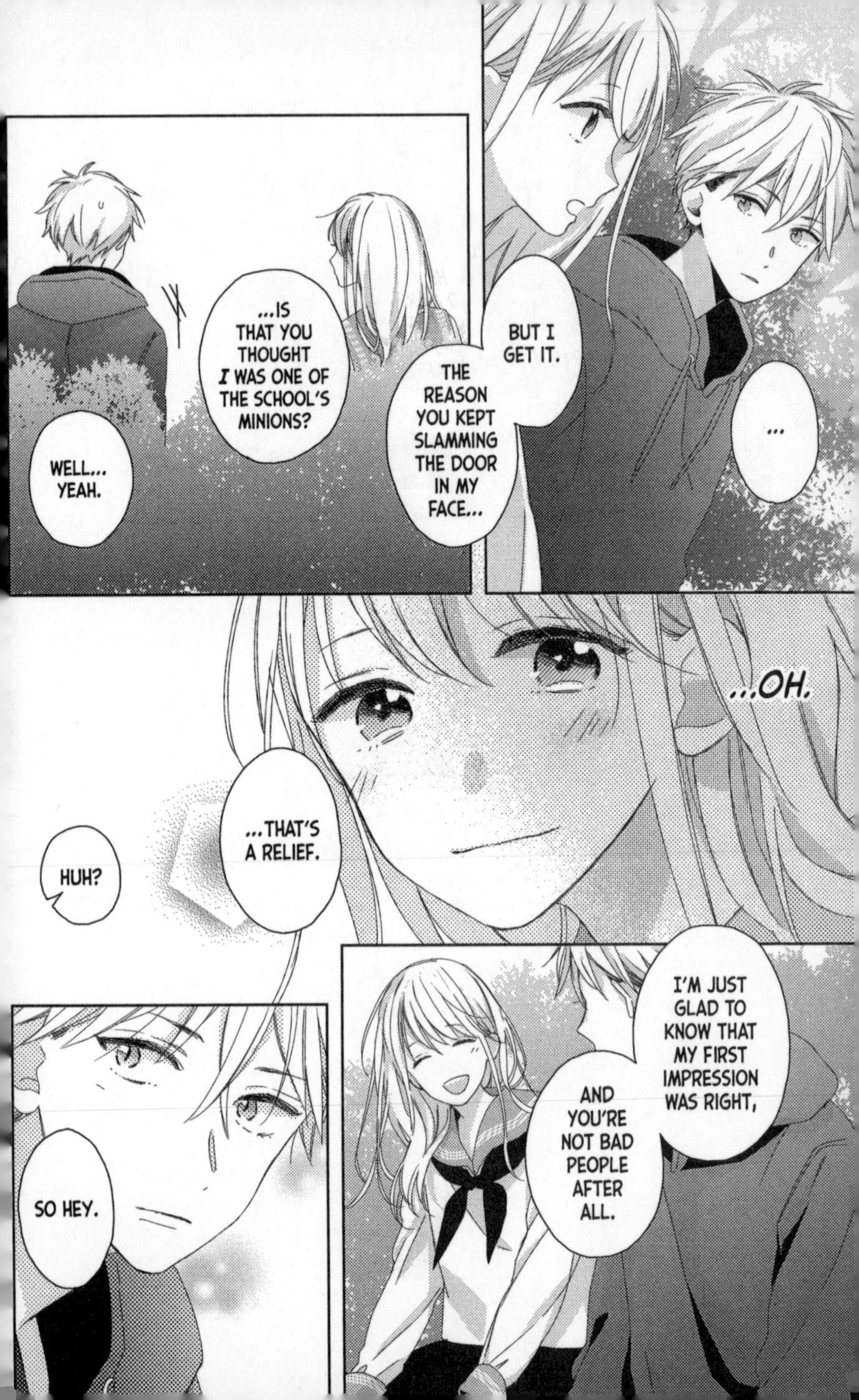

BUT I GET IT.
THE REASON YOU KEPT SLAMMING THE DOOR IN MY FACE...
...
...IS THAT YOU THOUGHT *I* WAS ONE OF THE SCHOOL'S MINIONS?
WELL... YEAH.
...OH.
...THAT'S A RELIEF.
HUH?
I'M JUST GLAD TO KNOW THAT MY FIRST IMPRESSION WAS RIGHT,
AND YOU'RE NOT BAD PEOPLE AFTER ALL.
SO HEY.

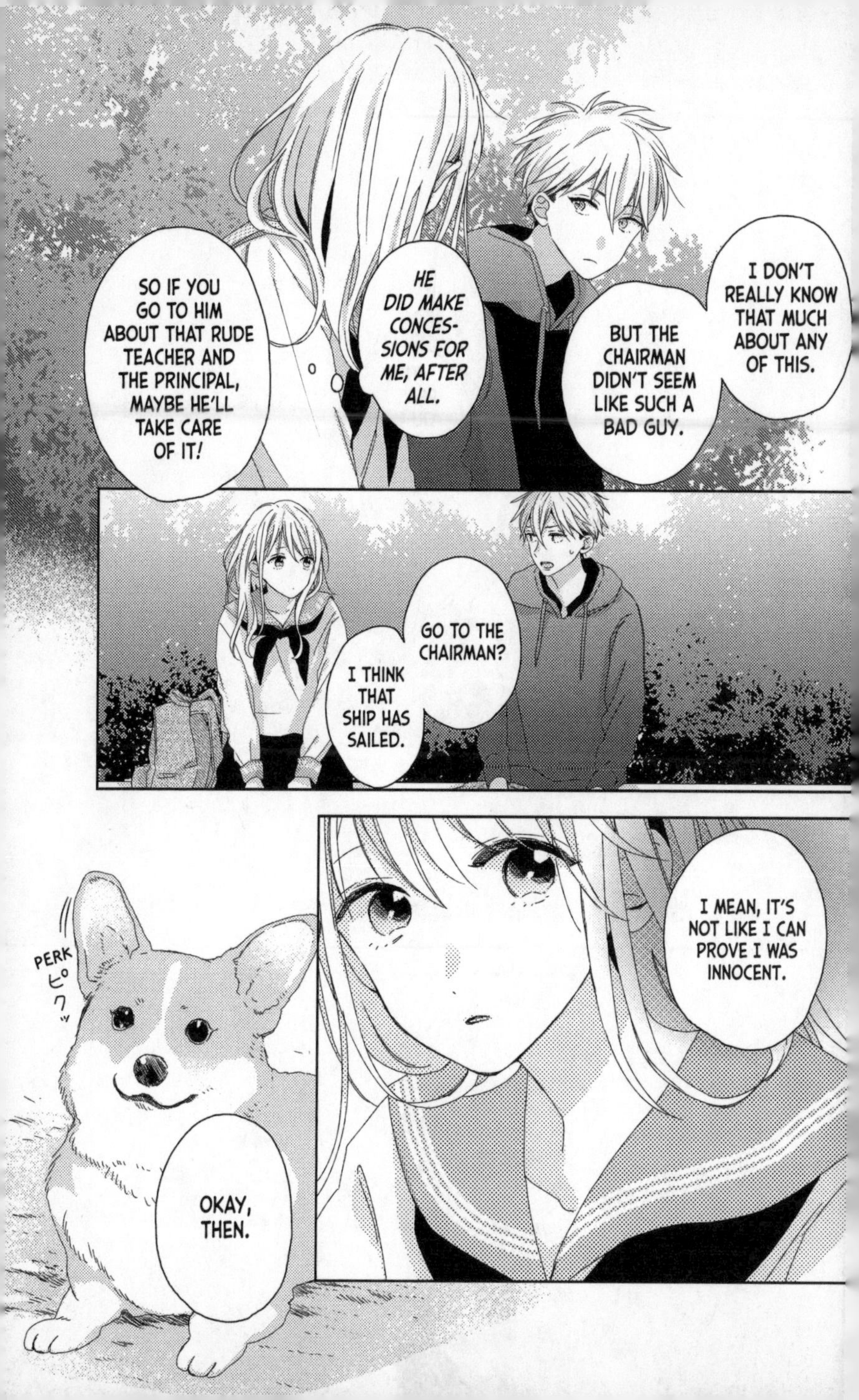
I DON'T REALLY KNOW THAT MUCH ABOUT ANY OF THIS.
BUT THE CHAIRMAN DIDN'T SEEM LIKE SUCH A BAD GUY.
HE DID MAKE CONCES-SIONS FOR ME, AFTER ALL.
SO IF YOU GO TO HIM ABOUT THAT RUDE TEACHER AND THE PRINCIPAL, MAYBE HE'LL TAKE CARE OF IT!
GO TO THE CHAIRMAN?
I THINK THAT SHIP HAS SAILED.
I MEAN, IT'S NOT LIKE I CAN PROVE I WAS INNOCENT.
PERK ピクッ
OKAY, THEN.

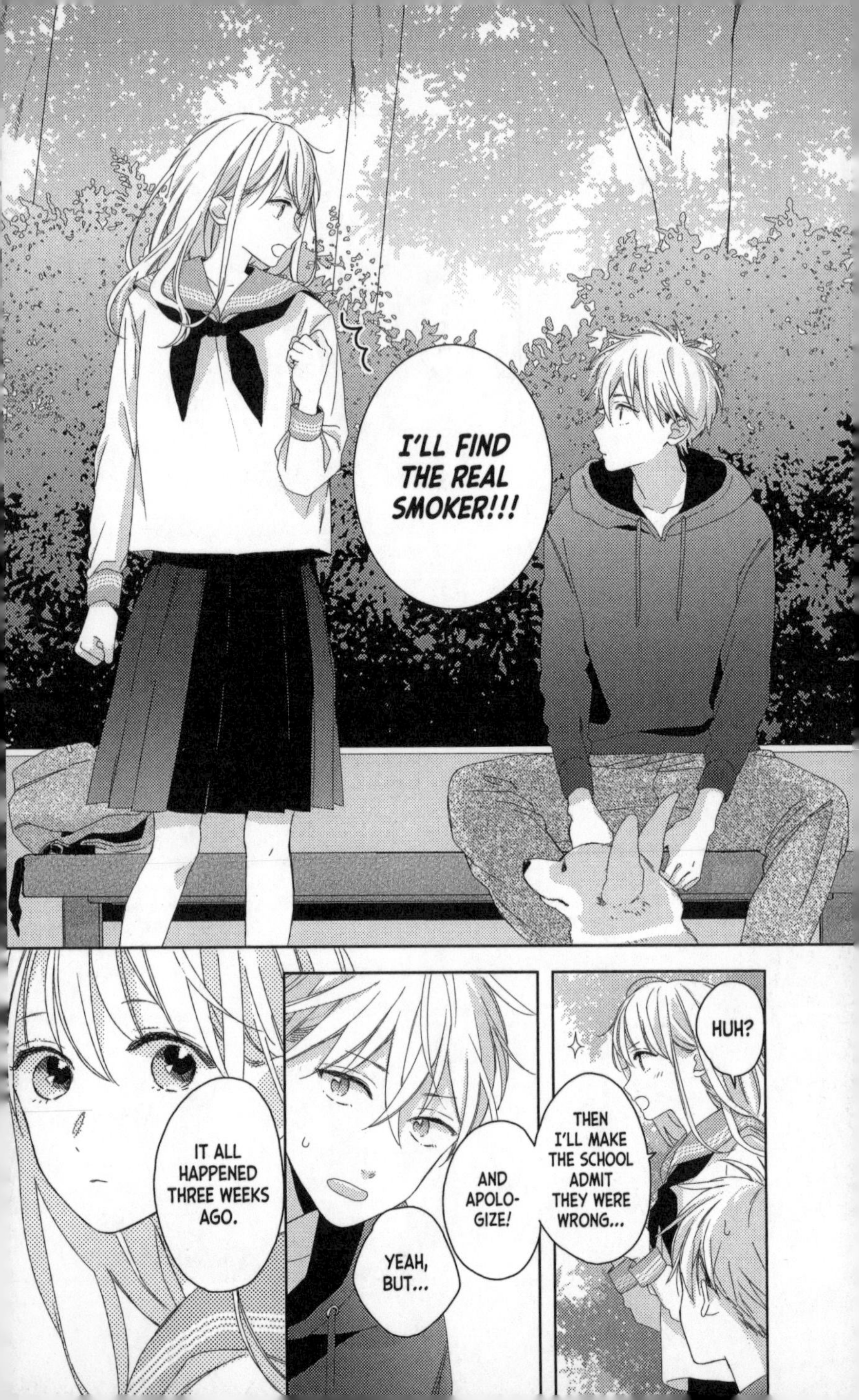
I'LL FIND THE REAL SMOKER!!!
HUH?
THEN I'LL MAKE THE SCHOOL ADMIT THEY WERE WRONG...
AND APOLO-GIZE!
YEAH, BUT...
IT ALL HAPPENED THREE WEEKS AGO.

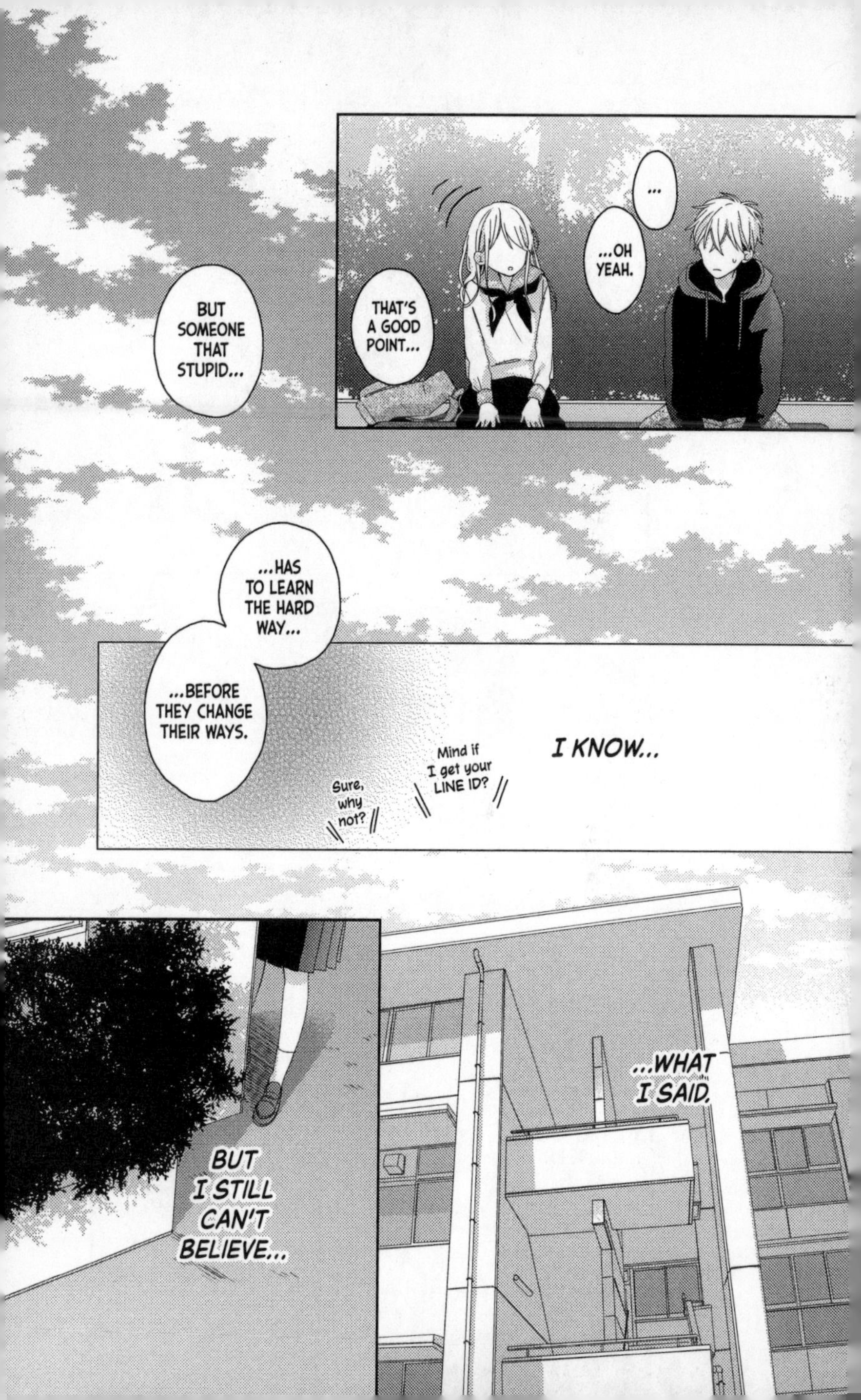
...
...OH YEAH.
THAT'S A GOOD POINT...
BUT SOMEONE THAT STUPID...
...HAS TO LEARN THE HARD WAY...
...BEFORE THEY CHANGE THEIR WAYS.
I KNOW...
Mind if I get your LINE ID?
Sure, why not?
...WHAT I SAID.
BUT I STILL CAN'T BELIEVE...

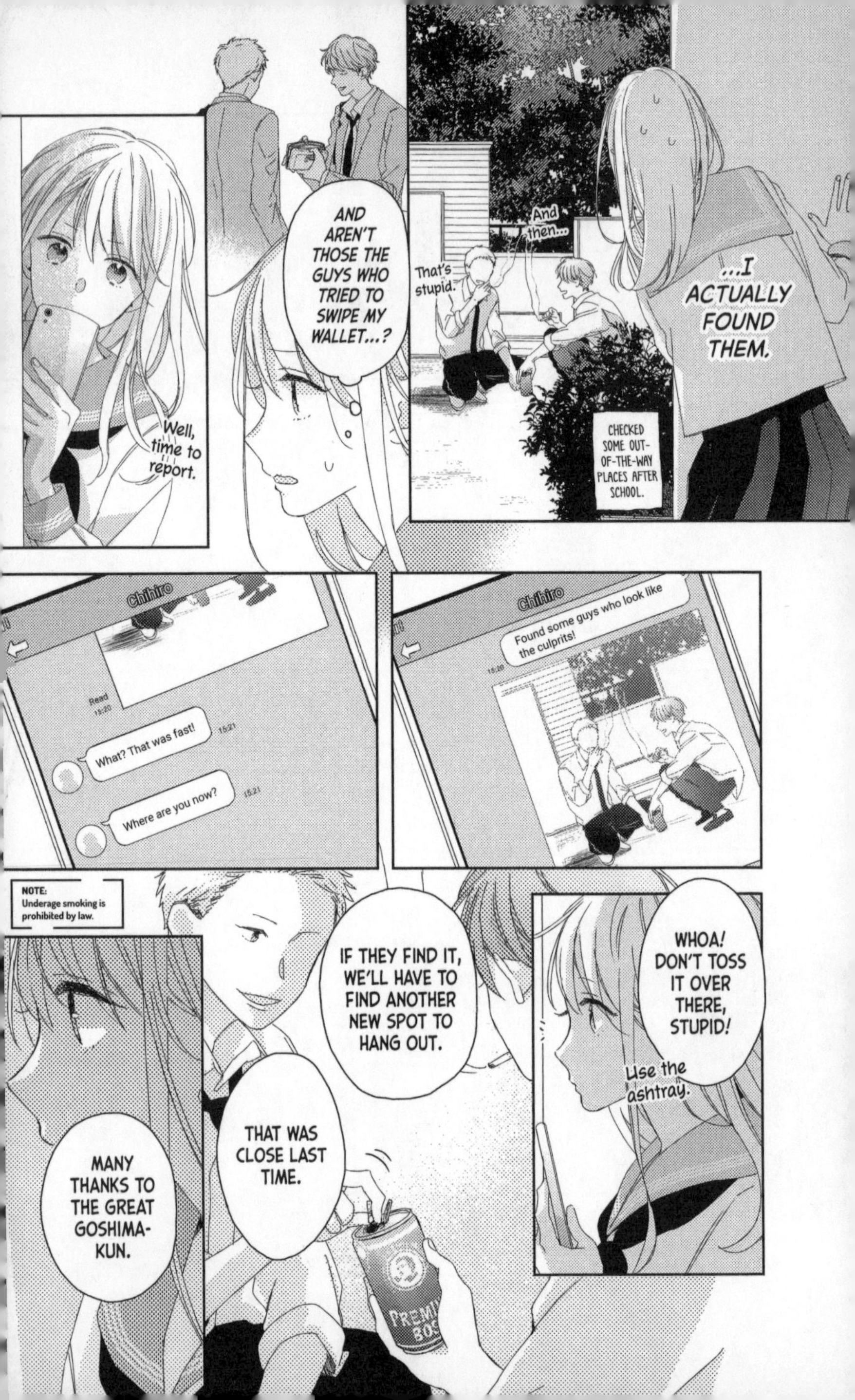
CHECKED SOME OUT-OF-THE-WAY PLACES AFTER SCHOOL.
...I ACTUALLY FOUND THEM.
And then...
That's stupid.
AND AREN'T THOSE THE GUYS WHO TRIED TO SWIPE MY WALLET...?
Well, time to report.
Chihiro
Found some guys who look like the culprits!
15:20
Chihiro
Read 15:20
What? That was fast!
15:21
Where are you now?
15:21
WHOA! DON'T TOSS IT OVER THERE, STUPID!
Use the ashtray.
IF THEY FIND IT, WE'LL HAVE TO FIND ANOTHER NEW SPOT TO HANG OUT.
THAT WAS CLOSE LAST TIME.
MANY THANKS TO THE GREAT GOSHIMA-KUN.
NOTE: Underage smoking is prohibited by law.

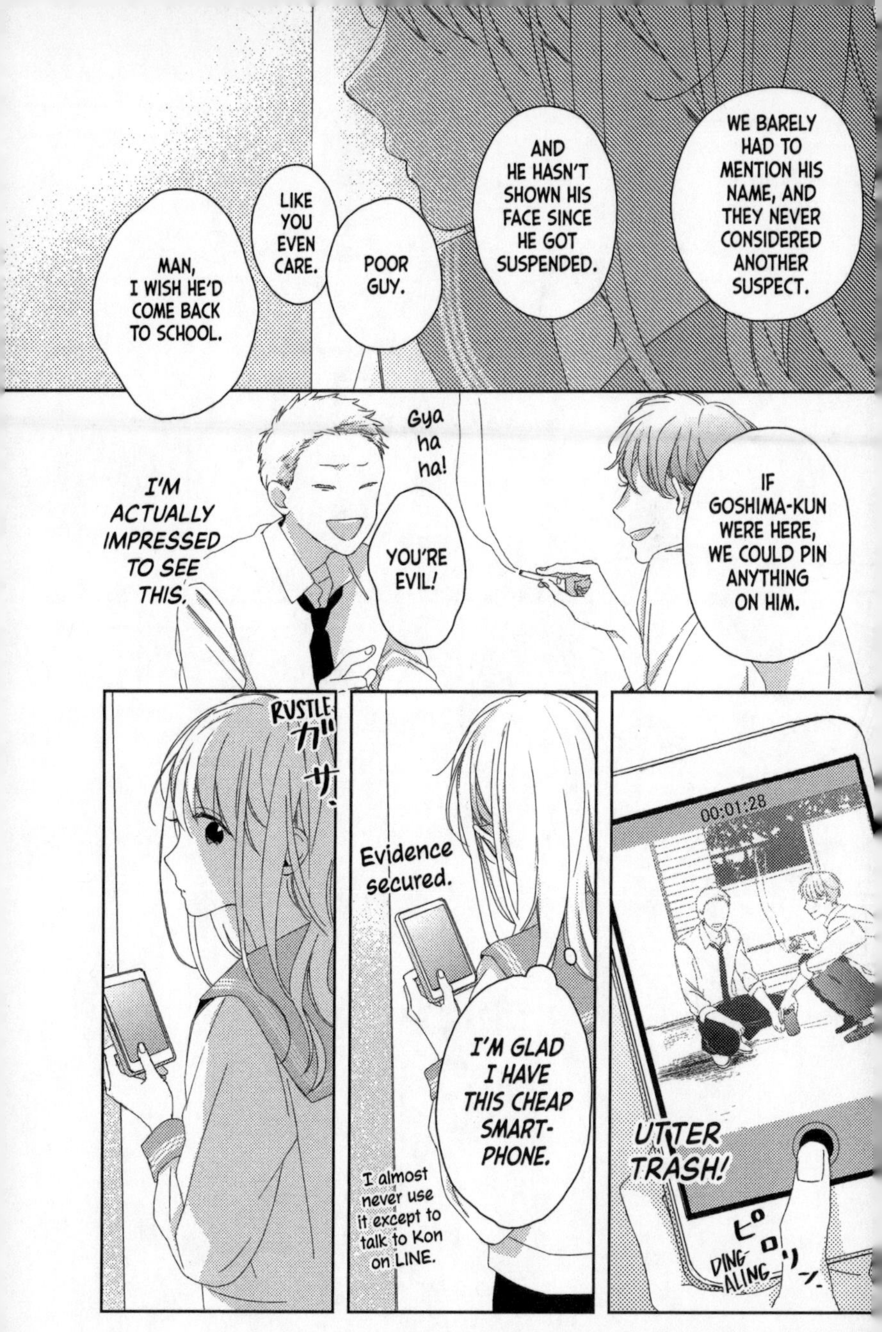
WE BARELY HAD TO MENTION HIS NAME, AND THEY NEVER CONSIDERED ANOTHER SUSPECT.
AND HE HASN'T SHOWN HIS FACE SINCE HE GOT SUSPENDED.
POOR GUY.
LIKE YOU EVEN CARE.
MAN, I WISH HE'D COME BACK TO SCHOOL.
IF GOSHIMA-KUN WERE HERE, WE COULD PIN ANYTHING ON HIM.
Gya ha ha!
YOU'RE EVIL!
I'M ACTUALLY IMPRESSED TO SEE THIS.
00:01:28
UTTER TRASH!
ピロリーン
DING-ALING
Evidence secured.
I'M GLAD I HAVE THIS CHEAP SMART-PHONE.
I almost never use it except to talk to Kon on LINE.
RUSTLE
ガサ

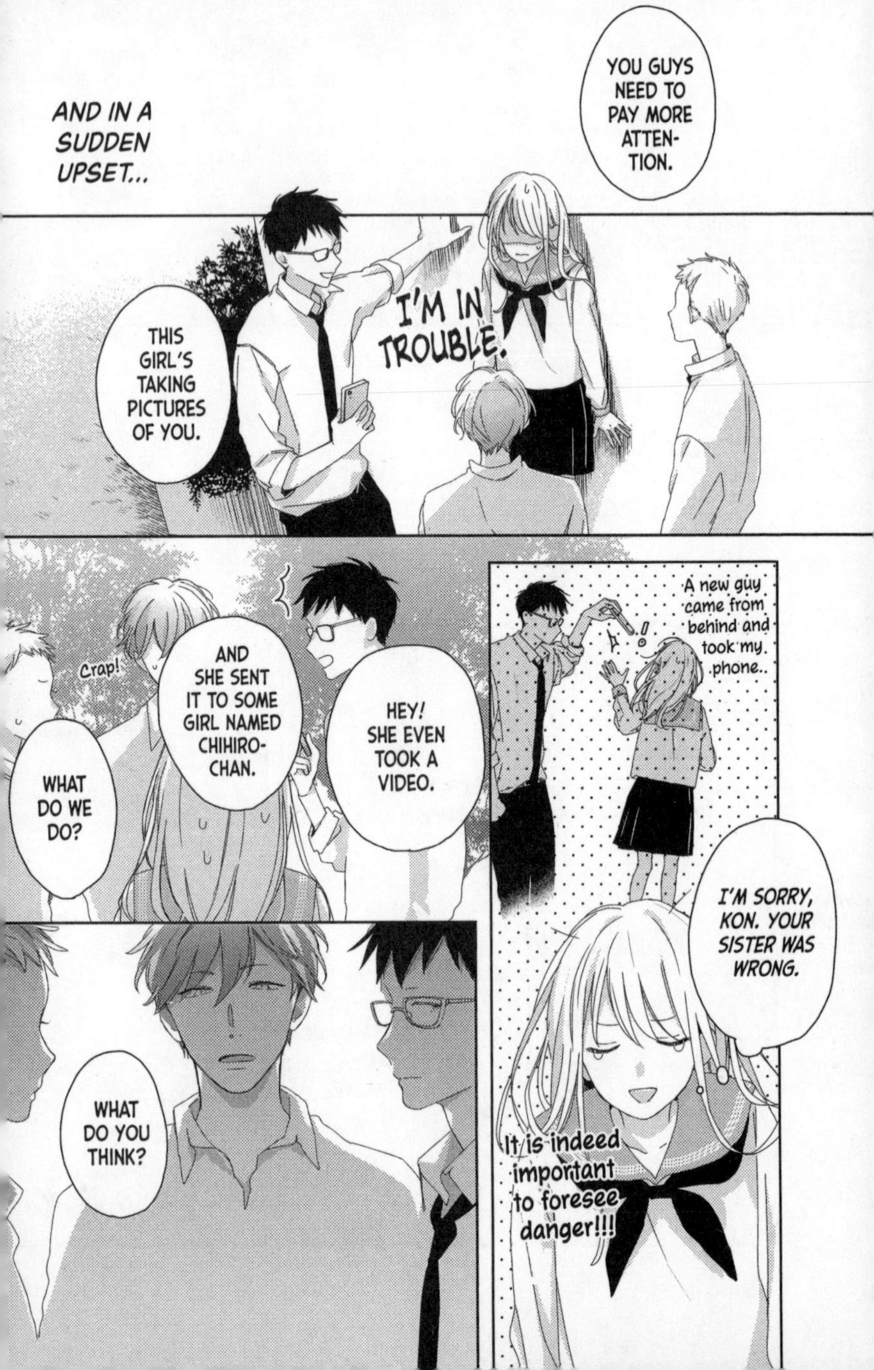
YOU GUYS NEED TO PAY MORE ATTEN-TION.
AND IN A SUDDEN UPSET...
I'M IN TROUBLE.
THIS GIRL'S TAKING PICTURES OF YOU.
A new guy came from behind and took my phone..
I'M SORRY, KON. YOUR SISTER WAS WRONG.
It is indeed important to foresee danger!!!
HEY! SHE EVEN TOOK A VIDEO.
AND SHE SENT IT TO SOME GIRL NAMED CHIHIRO-CHAN.
Crap!
WHAT DO WE DO?
WHAT DO YOU THINK?

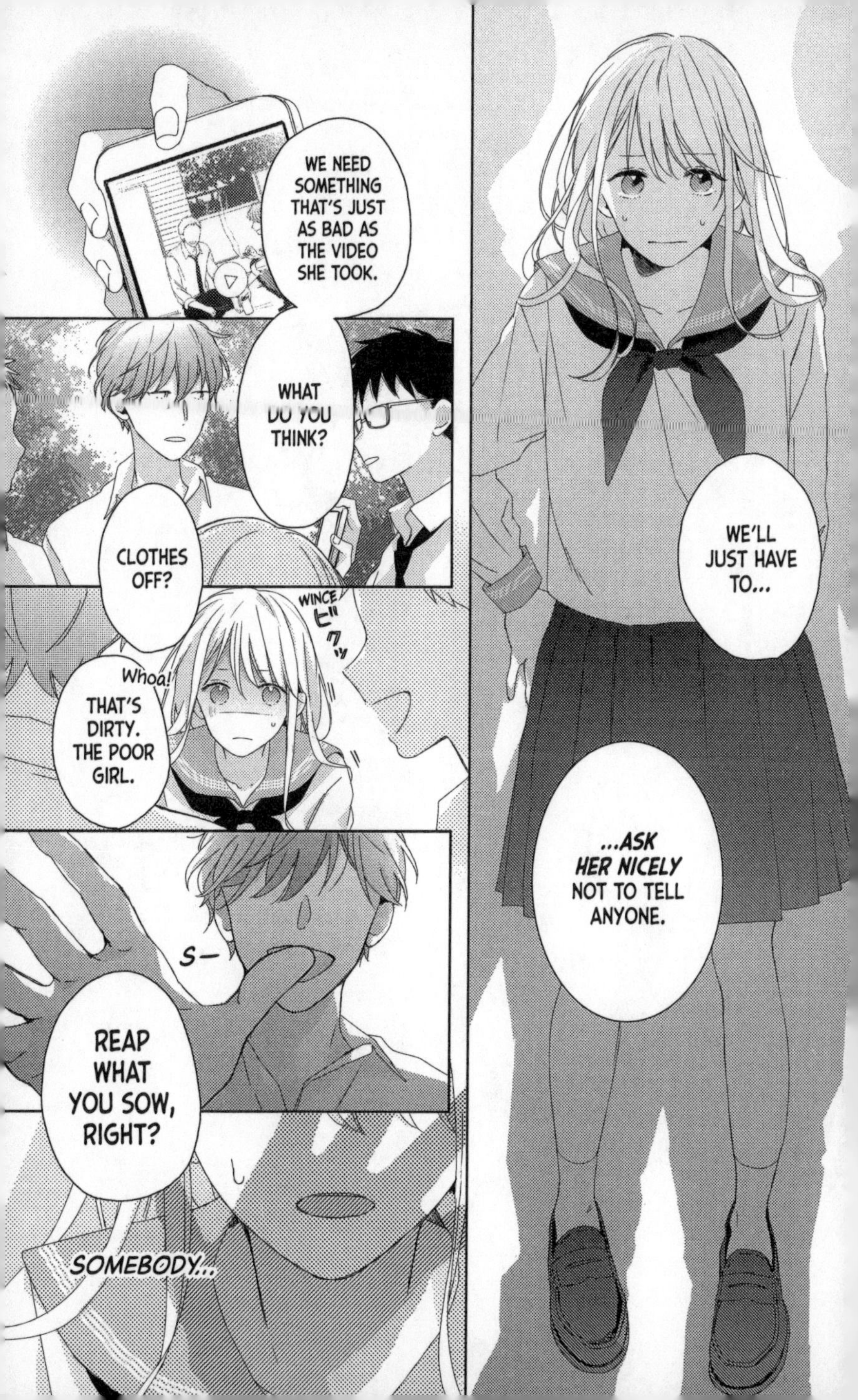
WE'LL JUST HAVE TO...
...ASK HER NICELY NOT TO TELL ANYONE.
WE NEED SOMETHING THAT'S JUST AS BAD AS THE VIDEO SHE TOOK.
WHAT DO YOU THINK?
CLOTHES OFF?
WINCE ビクッ
Whoa!
THAT'S DIRTY. THE POOR GIRL.
S—
REAP WHAT YOU SOW, RIGHT?
SOMEBODY...

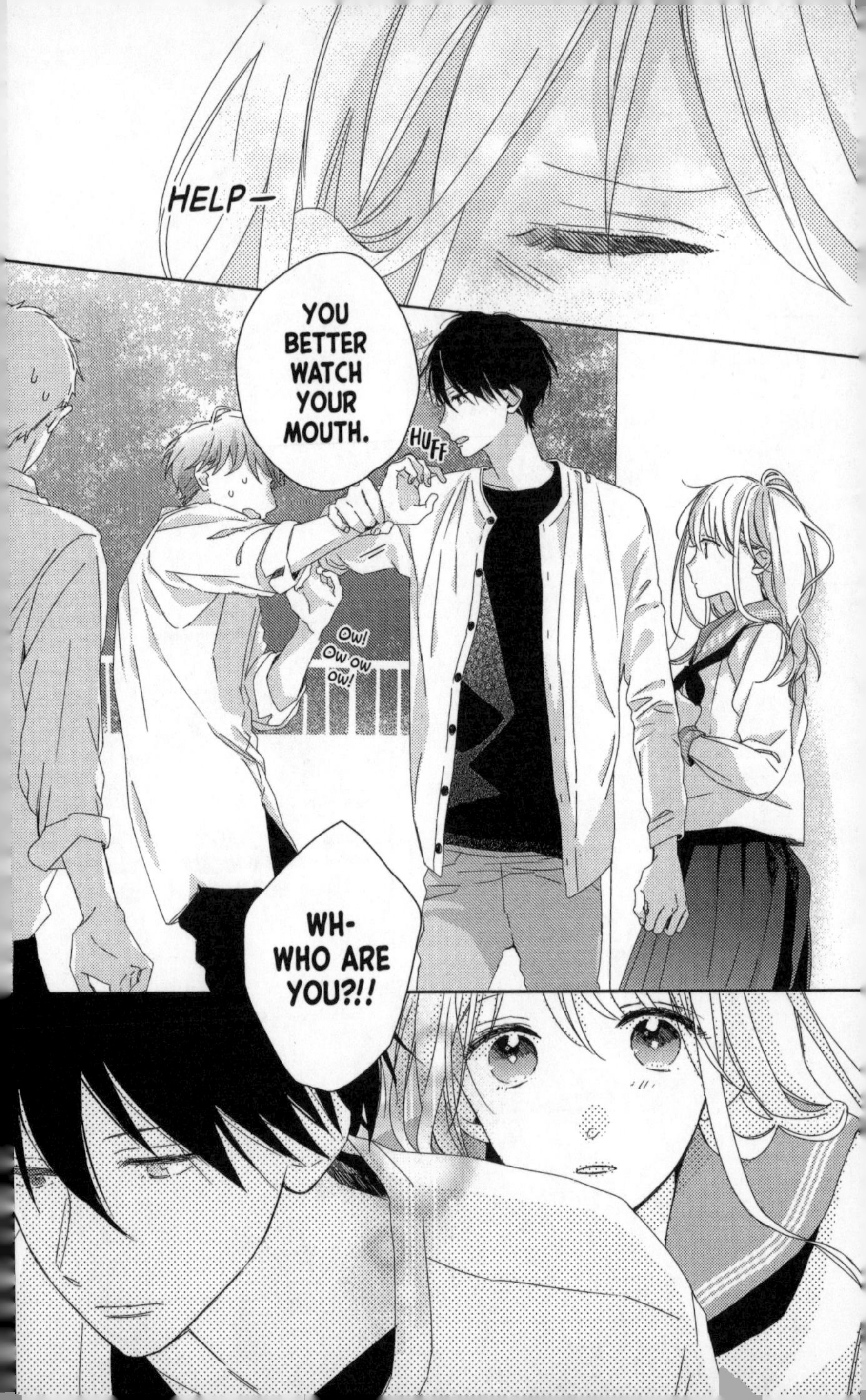
HELP—
YOU BETTER WATCH YOUR MOUTH.
HUFF
OW! OW OW OW!
WH- WHO ARE YOU?!!

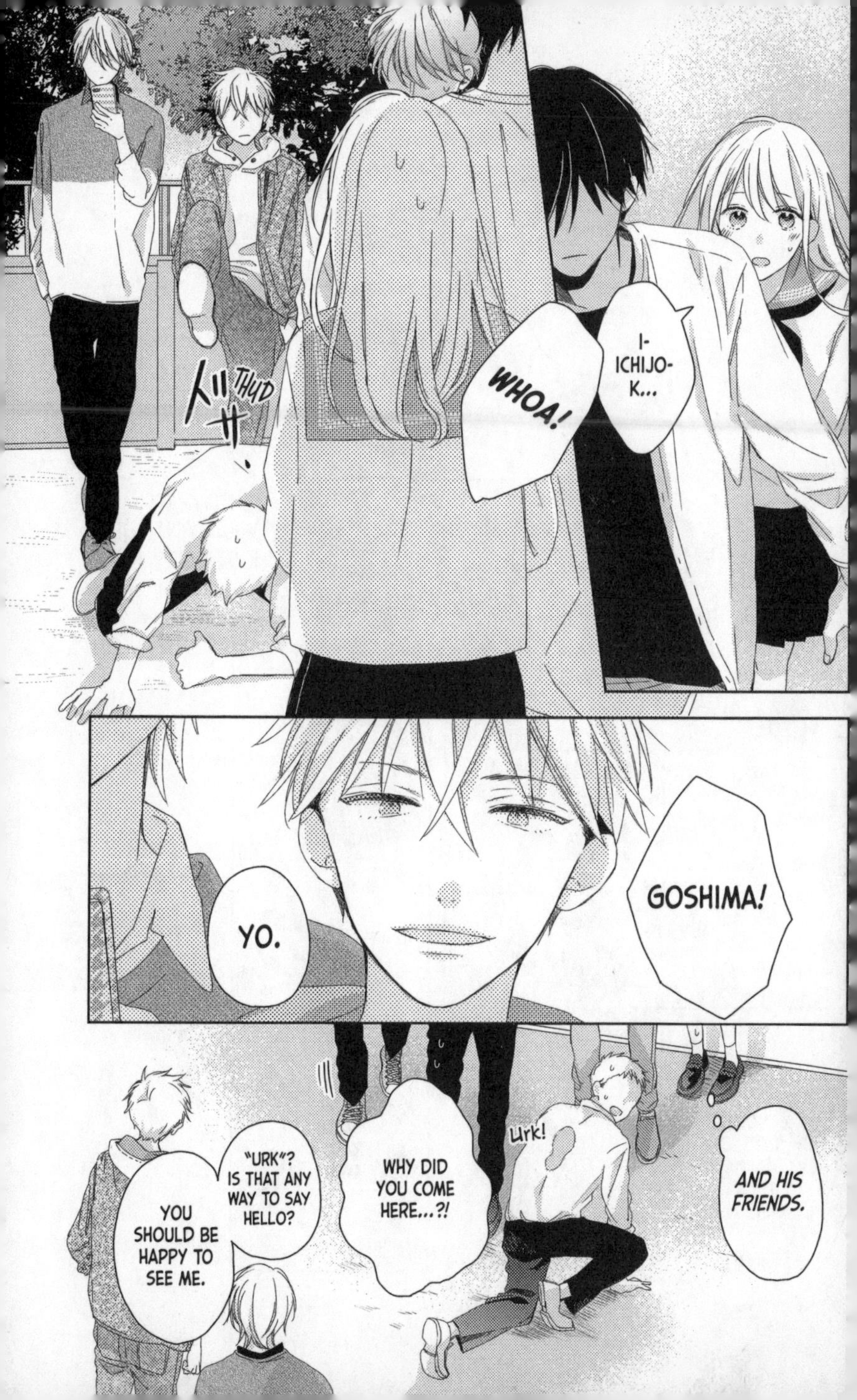
I-ICHIJO-K...
WHOA!
THUD
GOSHIMA!
YO.
AND HIS FRIENDS.
Urk!
WHY DID YOU COME HERE...?!
"URK"? IS THAT ANY WAY TO SAY HELLO?
YOU SHOULD BE HAPPY TO SEE ME.

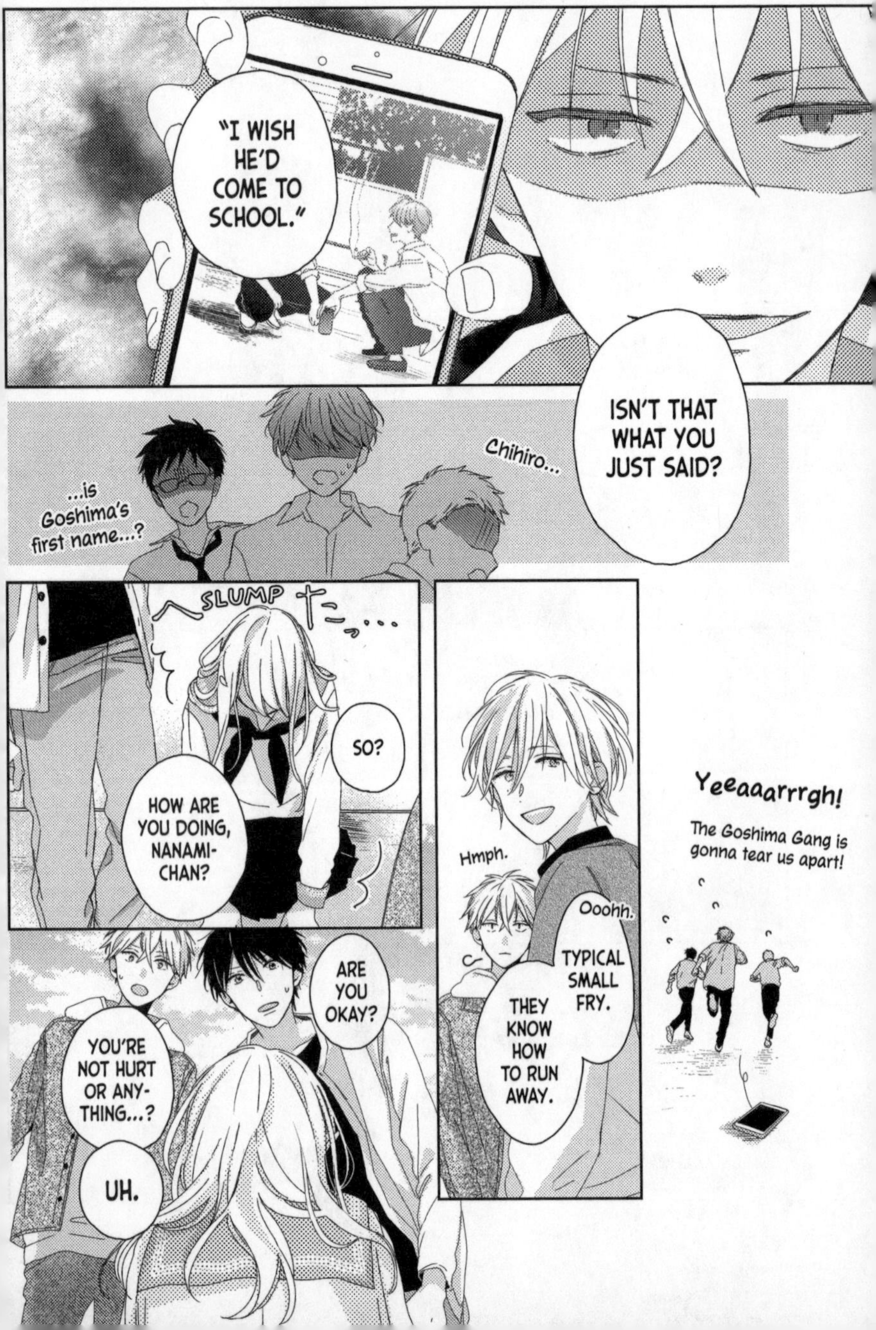
"I WISH HE'D COME TO SCHOOL."
ISN'T THAT WHAT YOU JUST SAID?
Chihiro...
...is Goshima's first name...?
Yeeaaarrrgh!
The Goshima Gang is gonna tear us apart!
Ooohh.
TYPICAL SMALL FRY.
THEY KNOW HOW TO RUN AWAY.
Hmph.
SLUMP
SO?
HOW ARE YOU DOING, NANAMI-CHAN?
ARE YOU OKAY?
YOU'RE NOT HURT OR ANYTHING...?
UH.

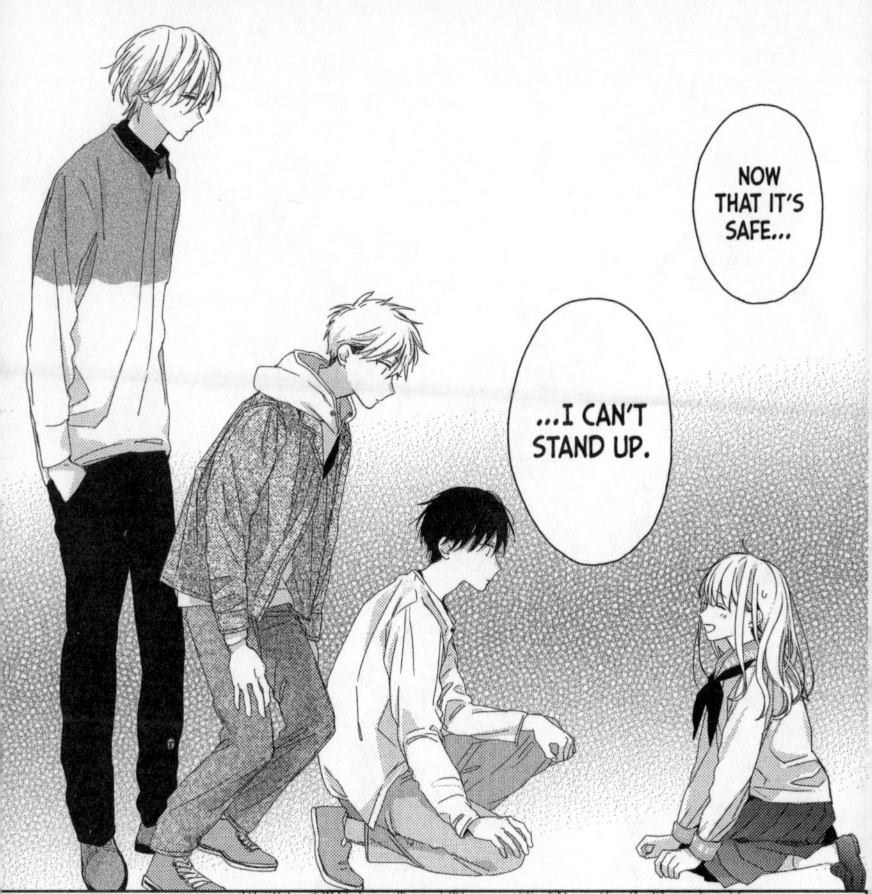
NOW THAT IT'S SAFE...
...I CAN'T STAND UP.
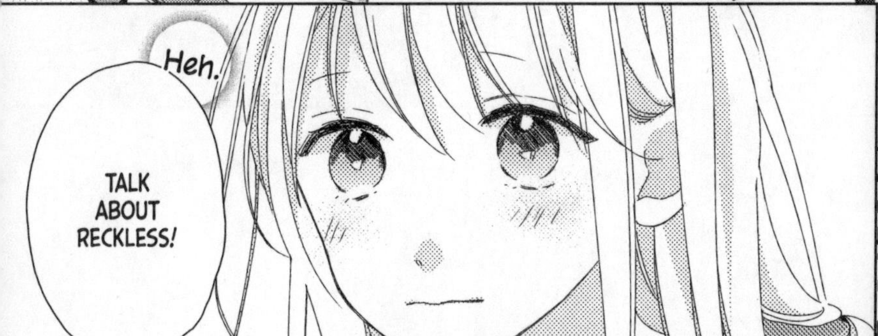
Heh.
TALK ABOUT RECKLESS!

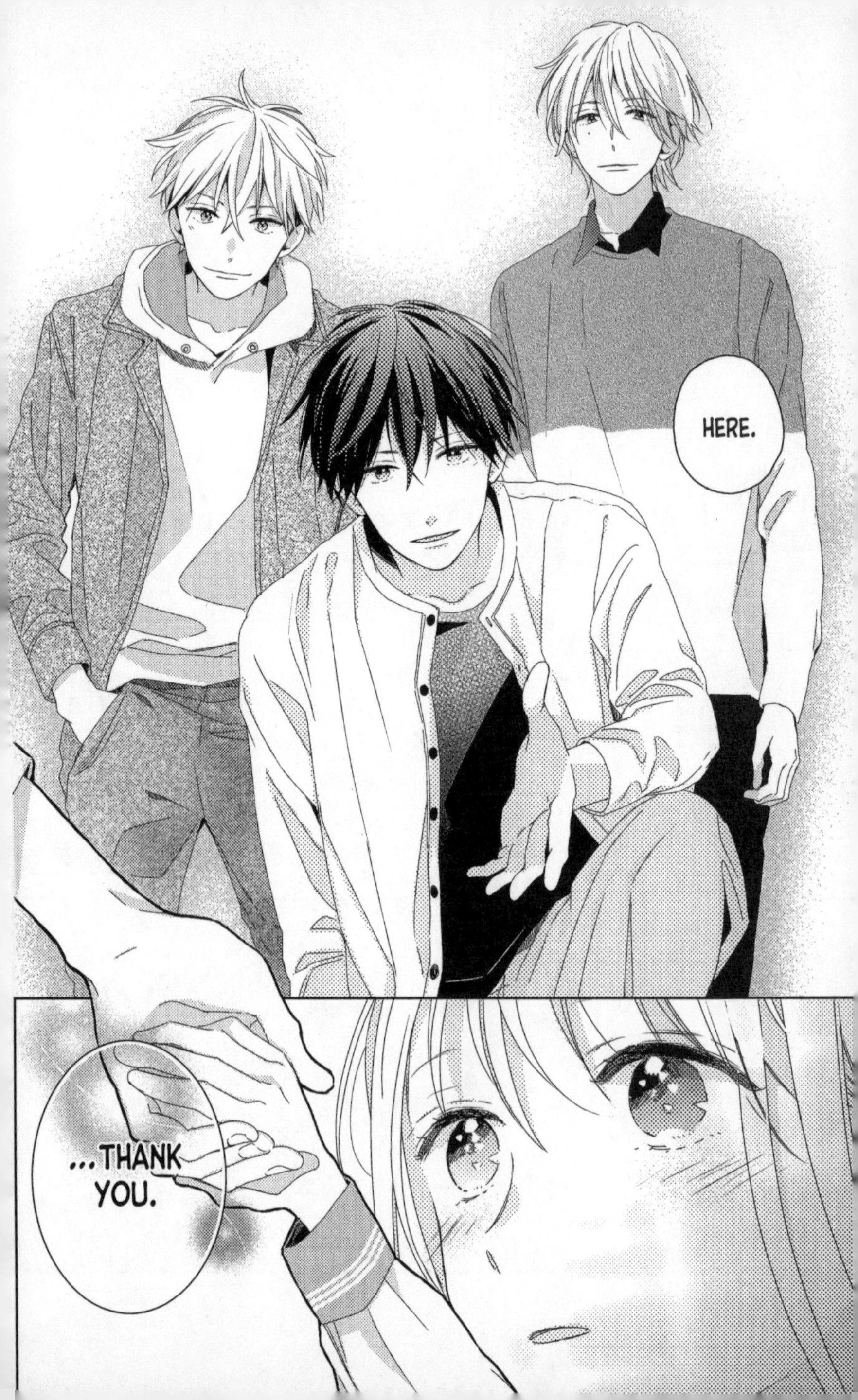
HERE.
...THANK YOU.

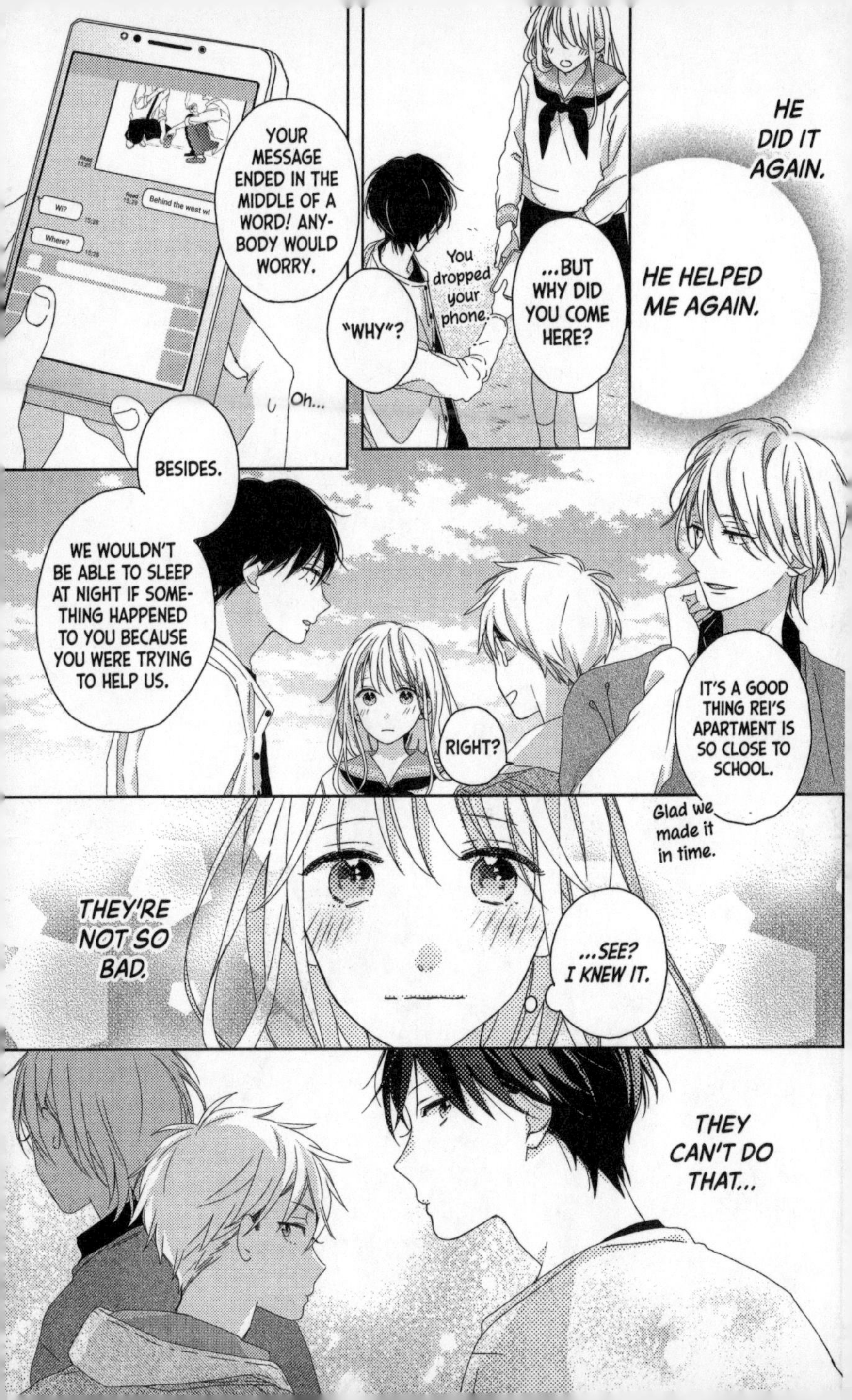
HE DID IT AGAIN.
HE HELPED ME AGAIN.
...BUT WHY DID YOU COME HERE?
You dropped your phone.
"WHY"?
Behind the west wi
Wi?
Where?
YOUR MESSAGE ENDED IN THE MIDDLE OF A WORD! ANYBODY WOULD WORRY.
Oh...
BESIDES.
WE WOULDN'T BE ABLE TO SLEEP AT NIGHT IF SOMETHING HAPPENED TO YOU BECAUSE YOU WERE TRYING TO HELP US.
IT'S A GOOD THING REI'S APARTMENT IS SO CLOSE TO SCHOOL.
RIGHT?
Glad we made it in time.
...SEE? I KNEW IT.
THEY'RE NOT SO BAD.
THEY CAN'T DO THAT...

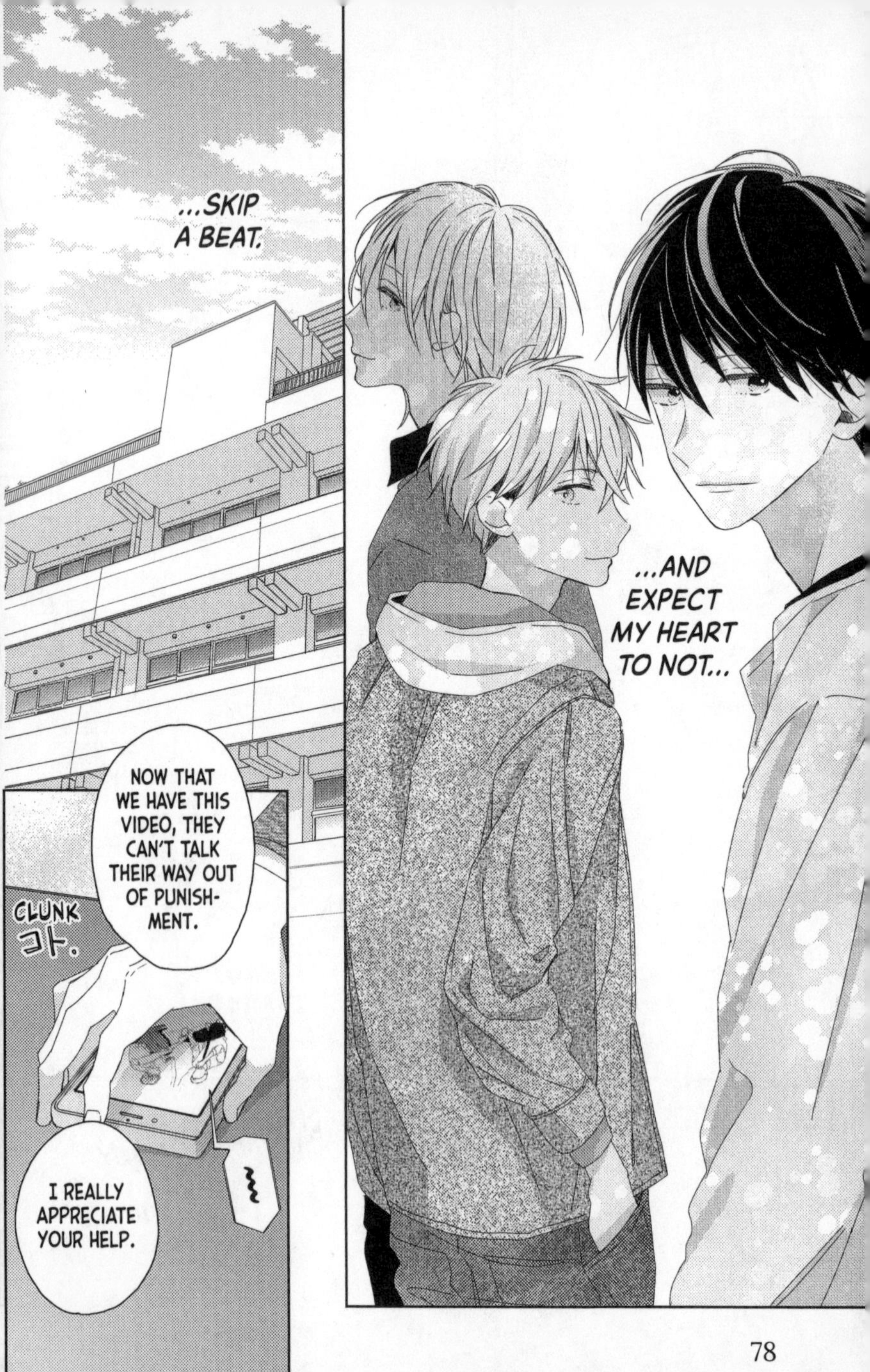
...AND EXPECT MY HEART TO NOT...
...SKIP A BEAT.
NOW THAT WE HAVE THIS VIDEO, THEY CAN'T TALK THEIR WAY OUT OF PUNISH-MENT.
CLUNK
コト.
I REALLY APPRECIATE YOUR HELP.

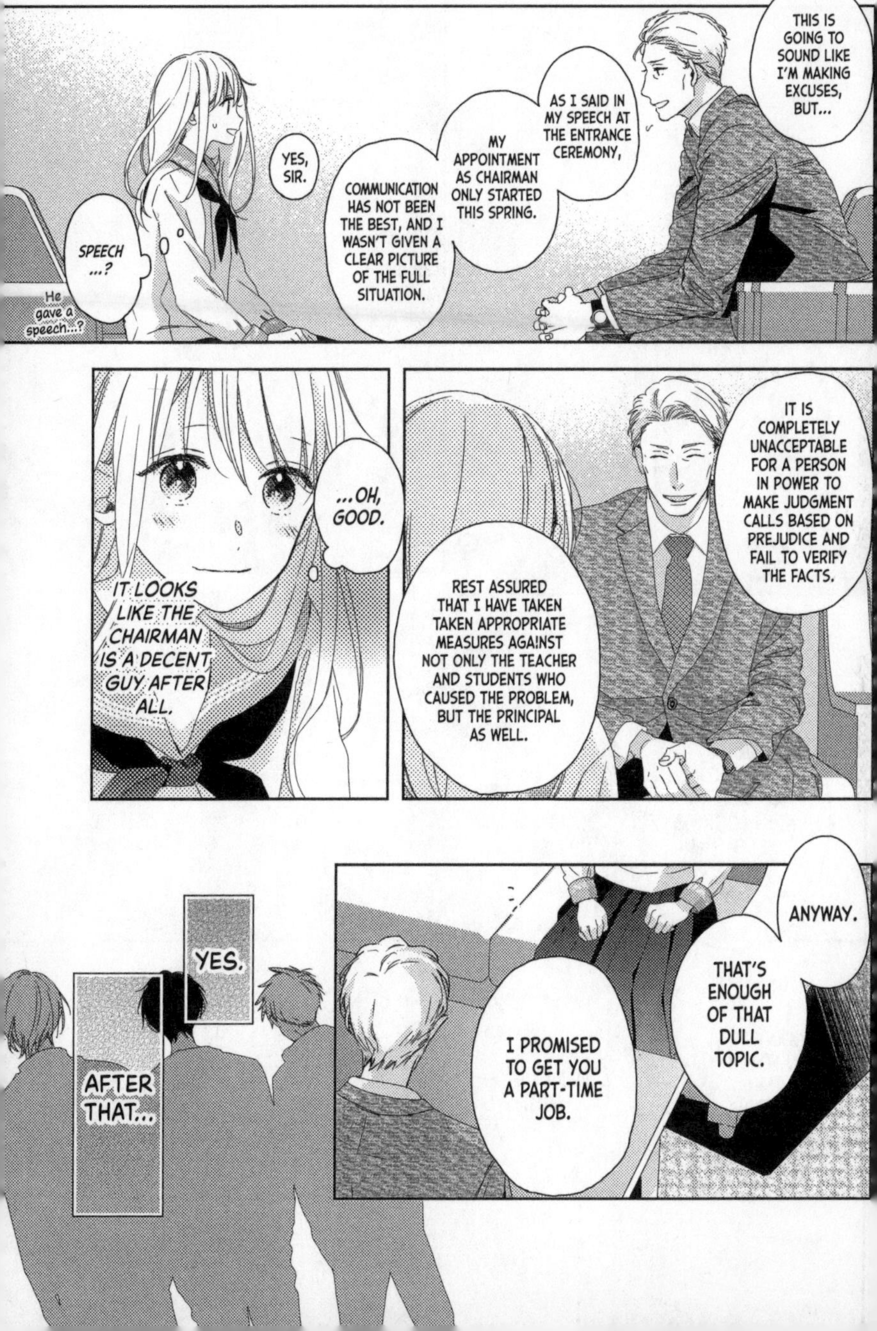
THIS IS GOING TO SOUND LIKE I'M MAKING EXCUSES, BUT...
AS I SAID IN MY SPEECH AT THE ENTRANCE CEREMONY,
MY APPOINTMENT AS CHAIRMAN ONLY STARTED THIS SPRING.
COMMUNICATION HAS NOT BEEN THE BEST, AND I WASN'T GIVEN A CLEAR PICTURE OF THE FULL SITUATION.
YES, SIR.
SPEECH ...?
He gave a speech...?
IT IS COMPLETELY UNACCEPTABLE FOR A PERSON IN POWER TO MAKE JUDGMENT CALLS BASED ON PREJUDICE AND FAIL TO VERIFY THE FACTS.
REST ASSURED THAT I HAVE TAKEN TAKEN APPROPRIATE MEASURES AGAINST NOT ONLY THE TEACHER AND STUDENTS WHO CAUSED THE PROBLEM, BUT THE PRINCIPAL AS WELL.
...OH, GOOD.
IT LOOKS LIKE THE CHAIRMAN IS A DECENT GUY AFTER ALL.
ANYWAY.
THAT'S ENOUGH OF THAT DULL TOPIC.
I PROMISED TO GET YOU A PART-TIME JOB.
YES.
AFTER THAT...

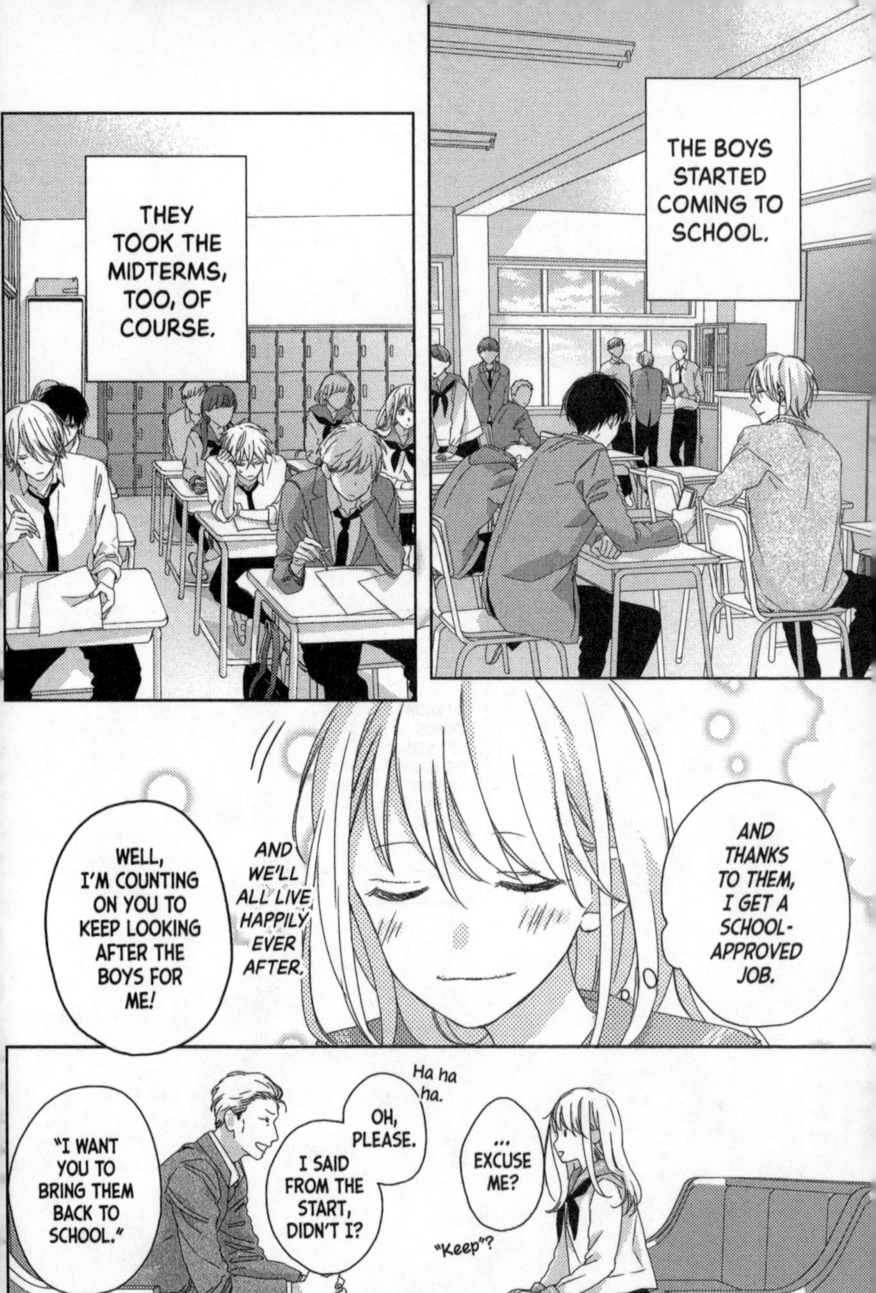
THE BOYS STARTED COMING TO SCHOOL.
THEY TOOK THE MIDTERMS, TOO, OF COURSE.
AND THANKS TO THEM, I GET A SCHOOL-APPROVED JOB.
AND WE'LL ALL LIVE HAPPILY EVER AFTER.
WELL, I'M COUNTING ON YOU TO KEEP LOOKING AFTER THE BOYS FOR ME!
Ha ha ha.
... EXCUSE ME?
"Keep"?
OH, PLEASE.
I SAID FROM THE START, DIDN'T I?
"I WANT YOU TO BRING THEM BACK TO SCHOOL."

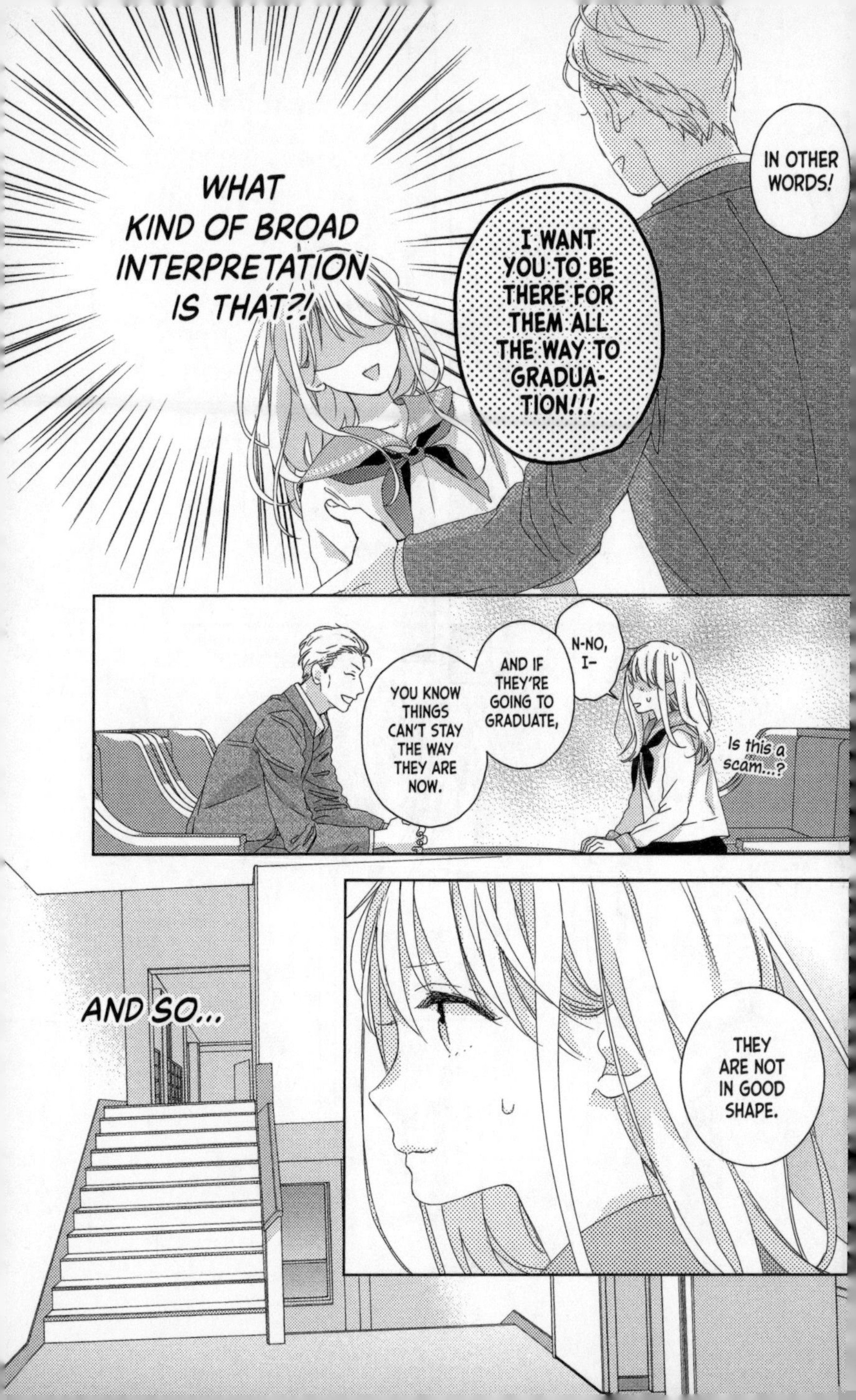
IN OTHER WORDS!
I WANT YOU TO BE THERE FOR THEM ALL THE WAY TO GRADUATION!!!
WHAT KIND OF BROAD INTERPRETATION IS THAT?!
Is this a scam...?
N-NO, I–
AND IF THEY'RE GOING TO GRADUATE,
YOU KNOW THINGS CAN'T STAY THE WAY THEY ARE NOW.
THEY ARE NOT IN GOOD SHAPE.
AND SO...

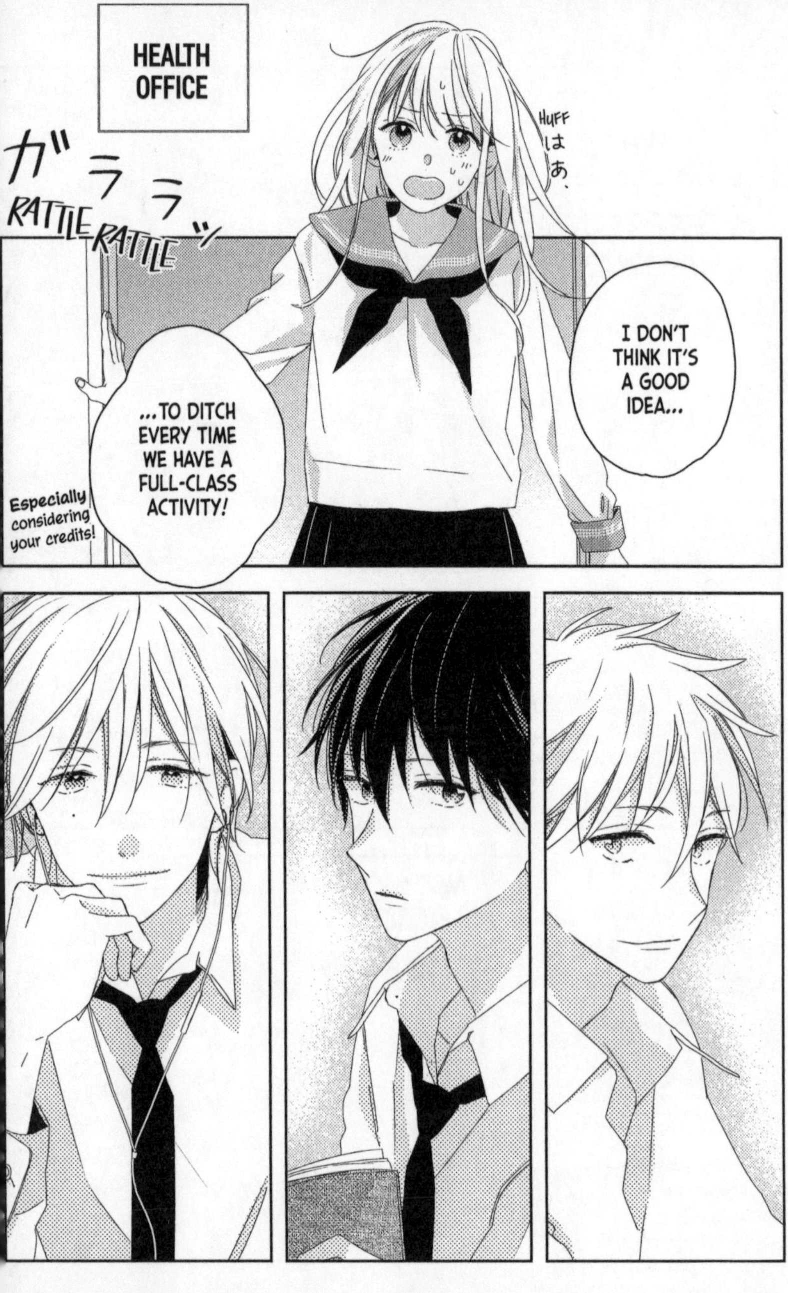
HEALTH OFFICE
ガラララッ
RATTLE RATTLE
HUFF はぁ、
I DON'T THINK IT'S A GOOD IDEA...
...TO DITCH EVERY TIME WE HAVE A FULL-CLASS ACTIVITY!
Especially considering your credits!

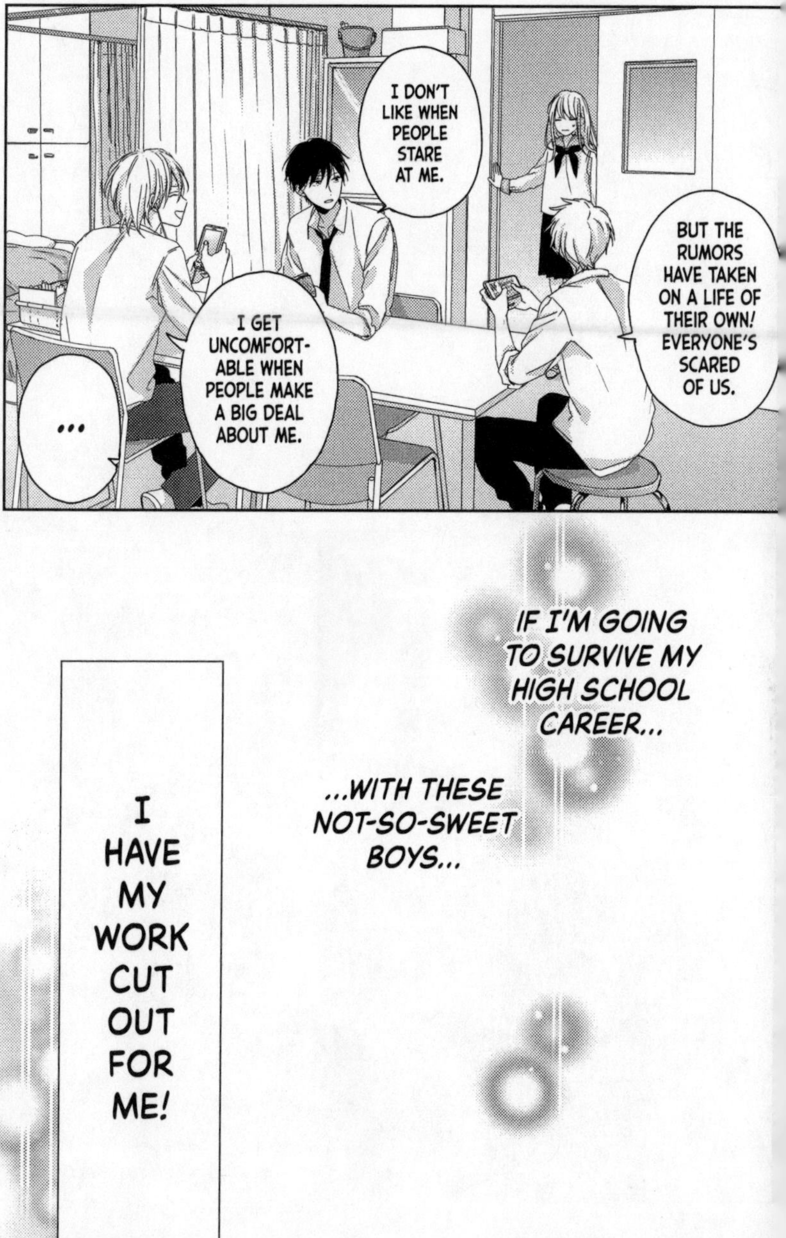
BUT THE RUMORS HAVE TAKEN ON A LIFE OF THEIR OWN! EVERYONE'S SCARED OF US.
I DON'T LIKE WHEN PEOPLE STARE AT ME.
I GET UNCOMFORT-ABLE WHEN PEOPLE MAKE A BIG DEAL ABOUT ME.
...
IF I'M GOING TO SURVIVE MY HIGH SCHOOL CAREER...
...WITH THESE NOT-SO-SWEET BOYS...
I HAVE MY WORK CUT OUT FOR ME!

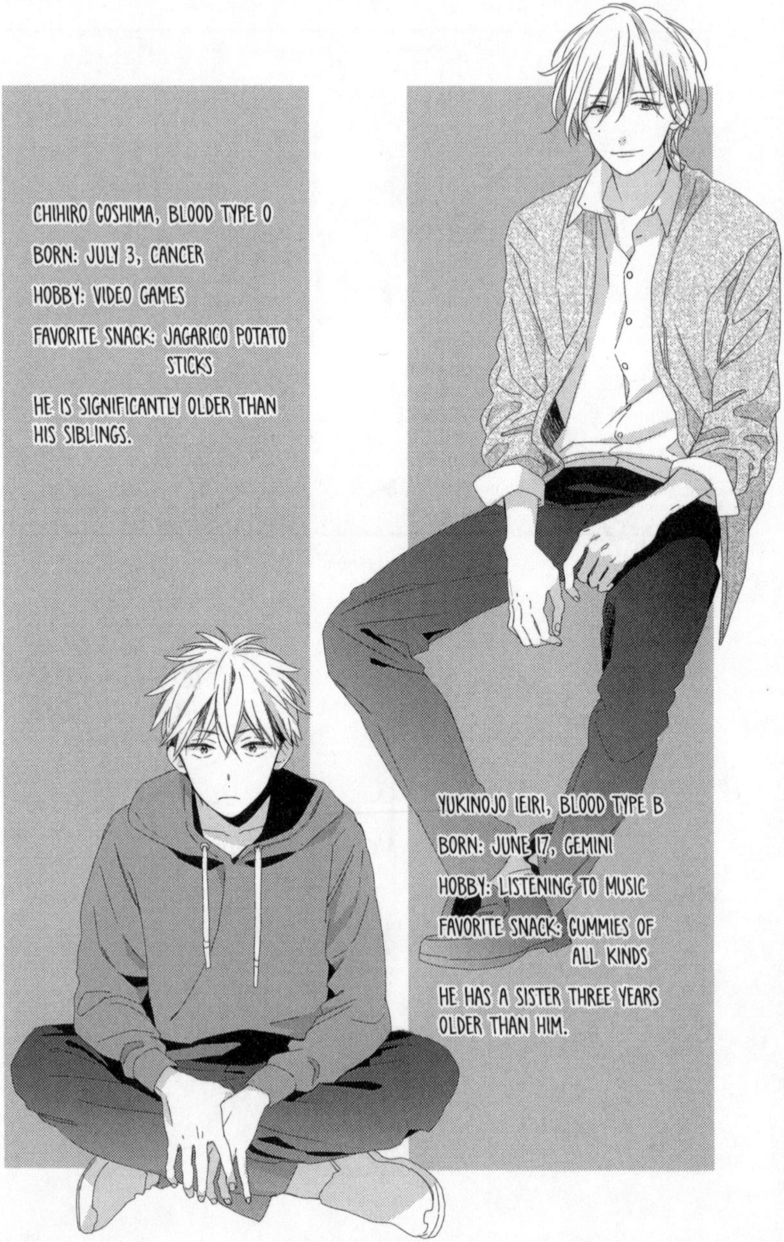
YUKINOJO IEIRI, BLOOD TYPE B
BORN: JUNE 17, GEMINI
HOBBY: LISTENING TO MUSIC
FAVORITE SNACK: GUMMIES OF ALL KINDS
HE HAS A SISTER THREE YEARS OLDER THAN HIM.
CHIHIRO GOSHIMA, BLOOD TYPE O
BORN: JULY 3, CANCER
HOBBY: VIDEO GAMES
FAVORITE SNACK: JAGARICO POTATO STICKS
HE IS SIGNIFICANTLY OLDER THAN HIS SIBLINGS.

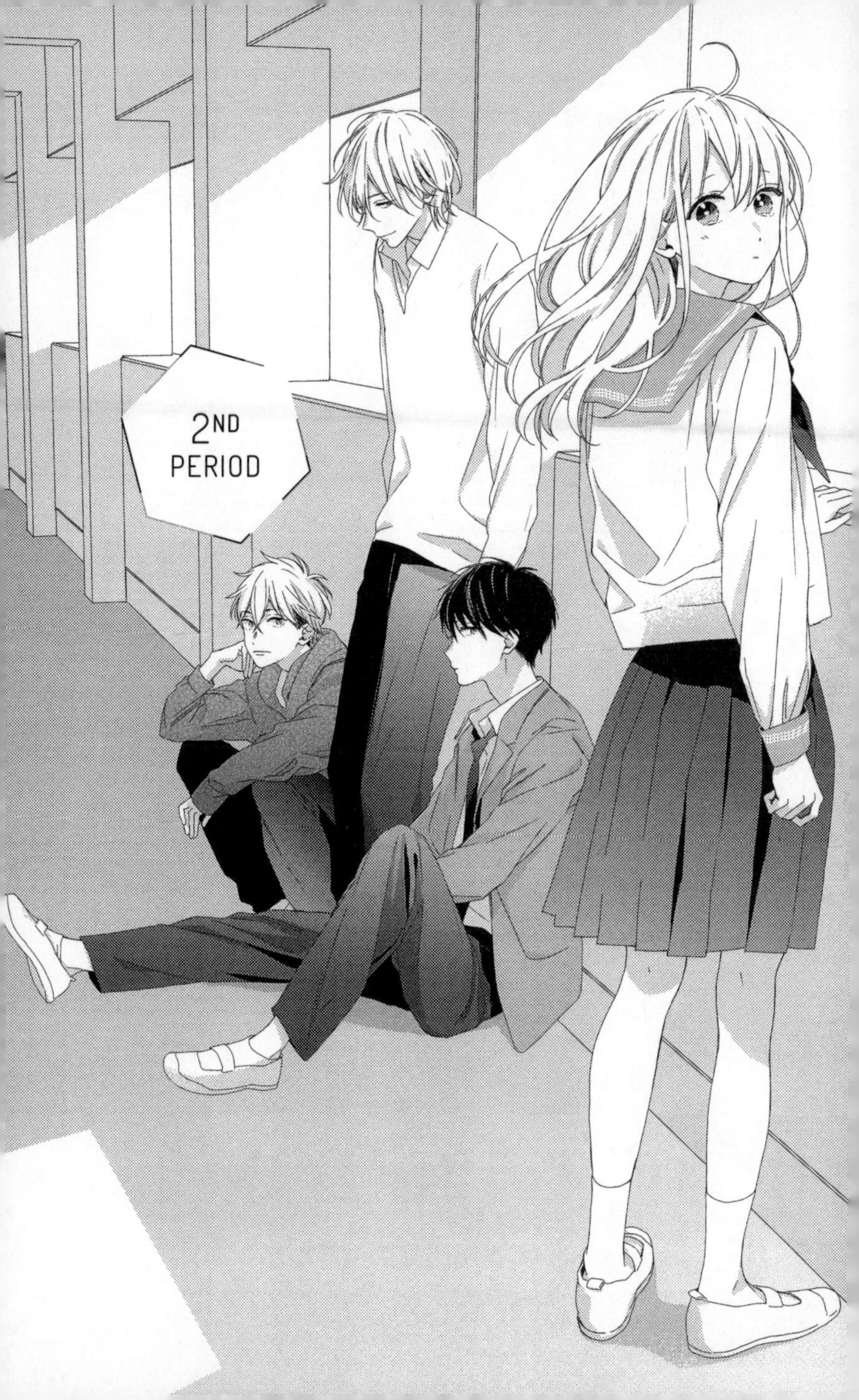
2ND PERIOD

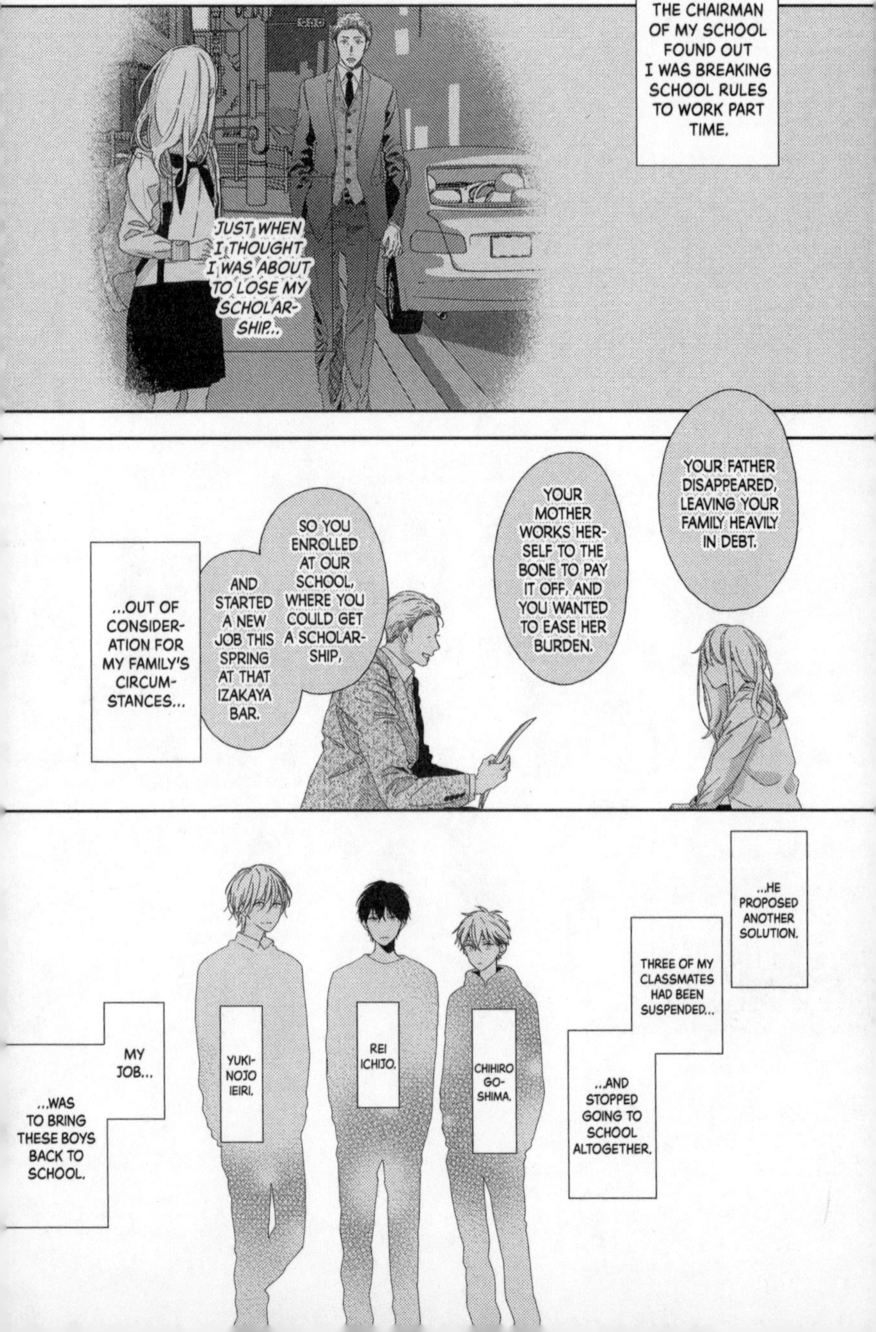
THE CHAIRMAN OF MY SCHOOL FOUND OUT I WAS BREAKING SCHOOL RULES TO WORK PART TIME.
JUST WHEN I THOUGHT I WAS ABOUT TO LOSE MY SCHOLAR-SHIP...
YOUR FATHER DISAPPEARED, LEAVING YOUR FAMILY HEAVILY IN DEBT.
YOUR MOTHER WORKS HER-SELF TO THE BONE TO PAY IT OFF, AND YOU WANTED TO EASE HER BURDEN.
SO YOU ENROLLED AT OUR SCHOOL, WHERE YOU COULD GET A SCHOLAR-SHIP,
AND STARTED A NEW JOB THIS SPRING AT THAT IZAKAYA BAR.
...OUT OF CONSIDER-ATION FOR MY FAMILY'S CIRCUM-STANCES...
...HE PROPOSED ANOTHER SOLUTION.
THREE OF MY CLASSMATES HAD BEEN SUSPENDED...
...AND STOPPED GOING TO SCHOOL ALTOGETHER.
CHIHIRO GO-SHIMA.
REI ICHIJO.
YUKI-NOJO IEIRI.
MY JOB...
...WAS TO BRING THESE BOYS BACK TO SCHOOL.

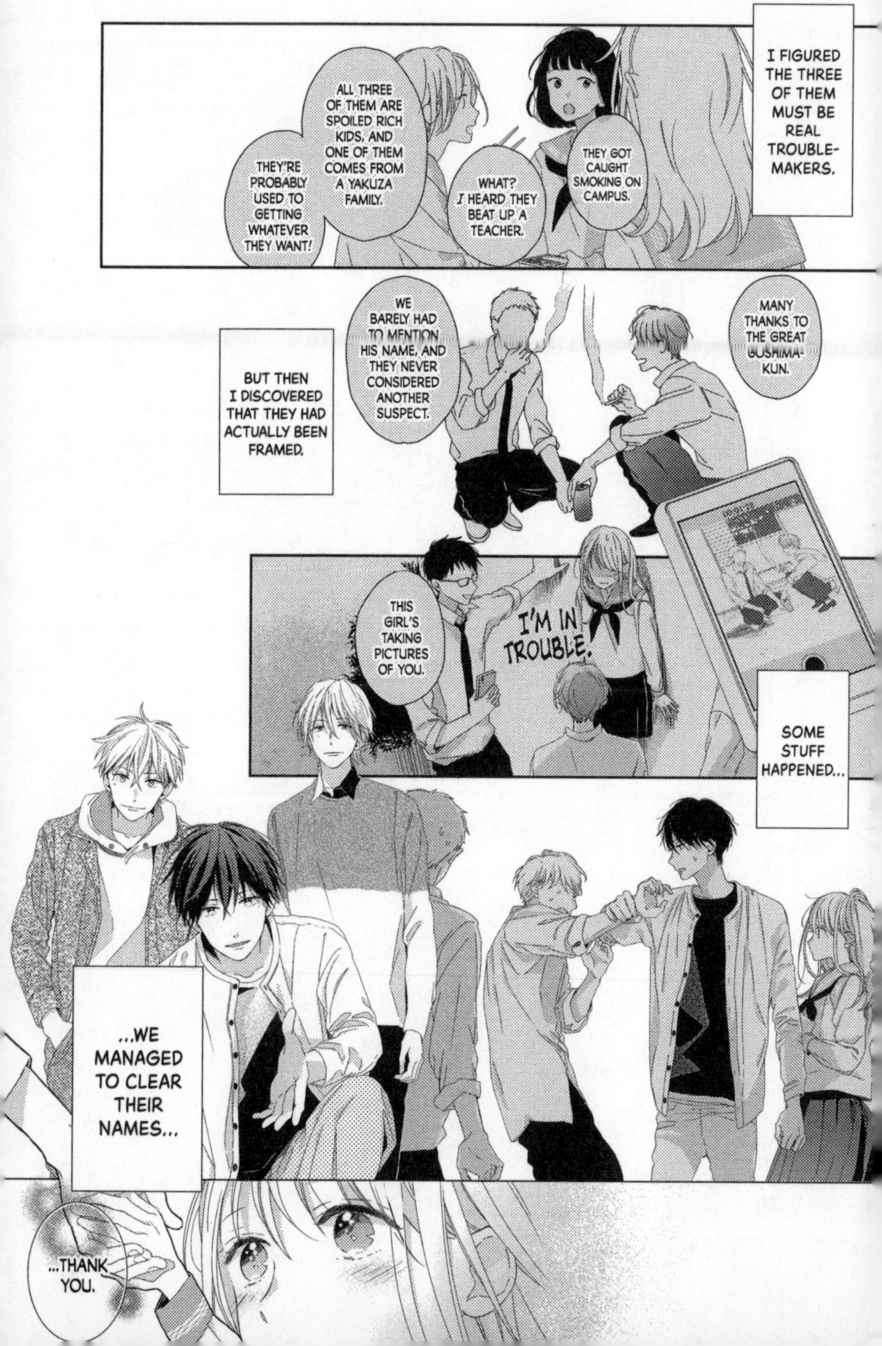
I FIGURED THE THREE OF THEM MUST BE REAL TROUBLE-MAKERS.
THEY GOT CAUGHT SMOKING ON CAMPUS.
WHAT? I HEARD THEY BEAT UP A TEACHER.
ALL THREE OF THEM ARE SPOILED RICH KIDS, AND ONE OF THEM COMES FROM A YAKUZA FAMILY.
THEY'RE PROBABLY USED TO GETTING WHATEVER THEY WANT!
MANY THANKS TO THE GREAT GUSHIMA-KUN.
WE BARELY HAD TO MENTION HIS NAME, AND THEY NEVER CONSIDERED ANOTHER SUSPECT.
BUT THEN I DISCOVERED THAT THEY HAD ACTUALLY BEEN FRAMED.
I'M IN TROUBLE.
THIS GIRL'S TAKING PICTURES OF YOU.
SOME STUFF HAPPENED...
...WE MANAGED TO CLEAR THEIR NAMES...
...THANK YOU.

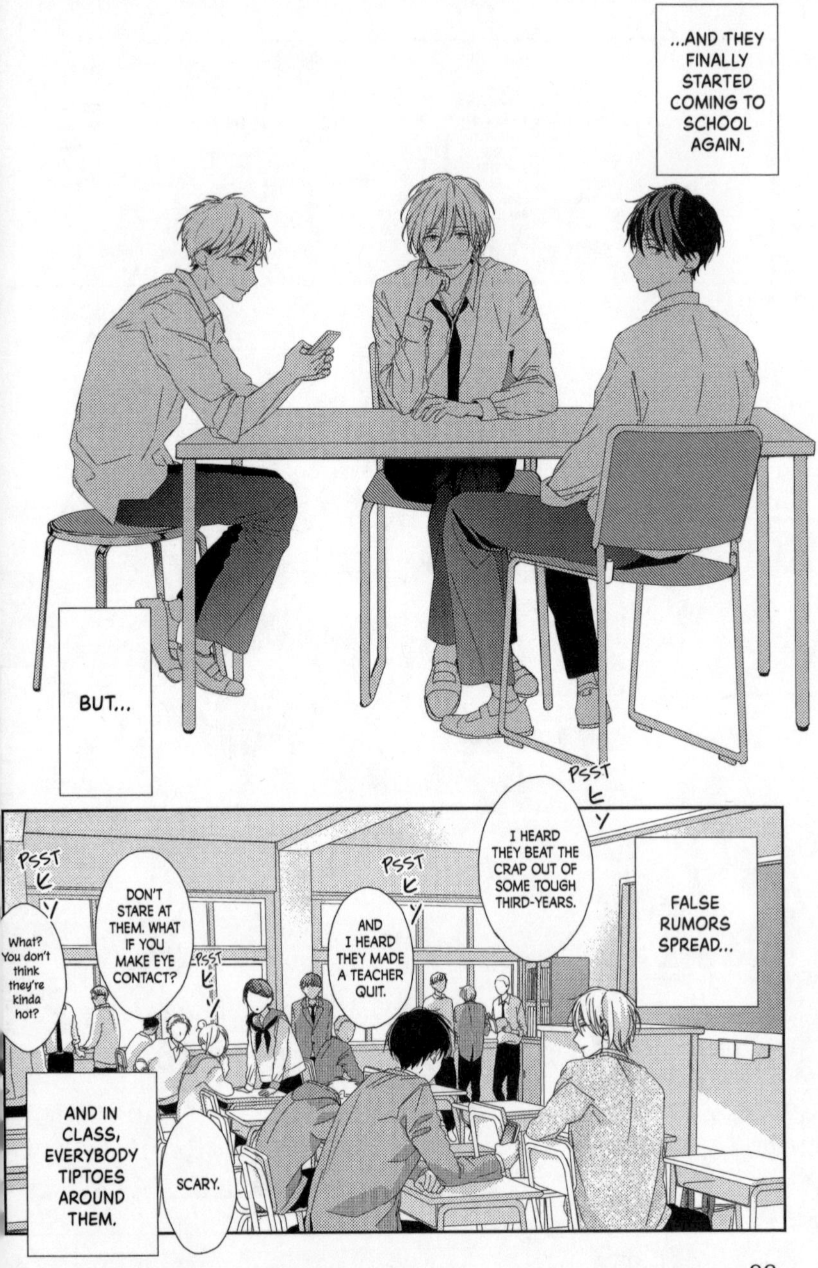
...AND THEY FINALLY STARTED COMING TO SCHOOL AGAIN.
BUT...
FALSE RUMORS SPREAD...
PSST
I HEARD THEY BEAT THE CRAP OUT OF SOME TOUGH THIRD-YEARS.
PSST
AND I HEARD THEY MADE A TEACHER QUIT.
PSST
DON'T STARE AT THEM. WHAT IF YOU MAKE EYE CONTACT?
PSST
What? You don't think they're kinda hot?
SCARY.
AND IN CLASS, EVERYBODY TIPTOES AROUND THEM.

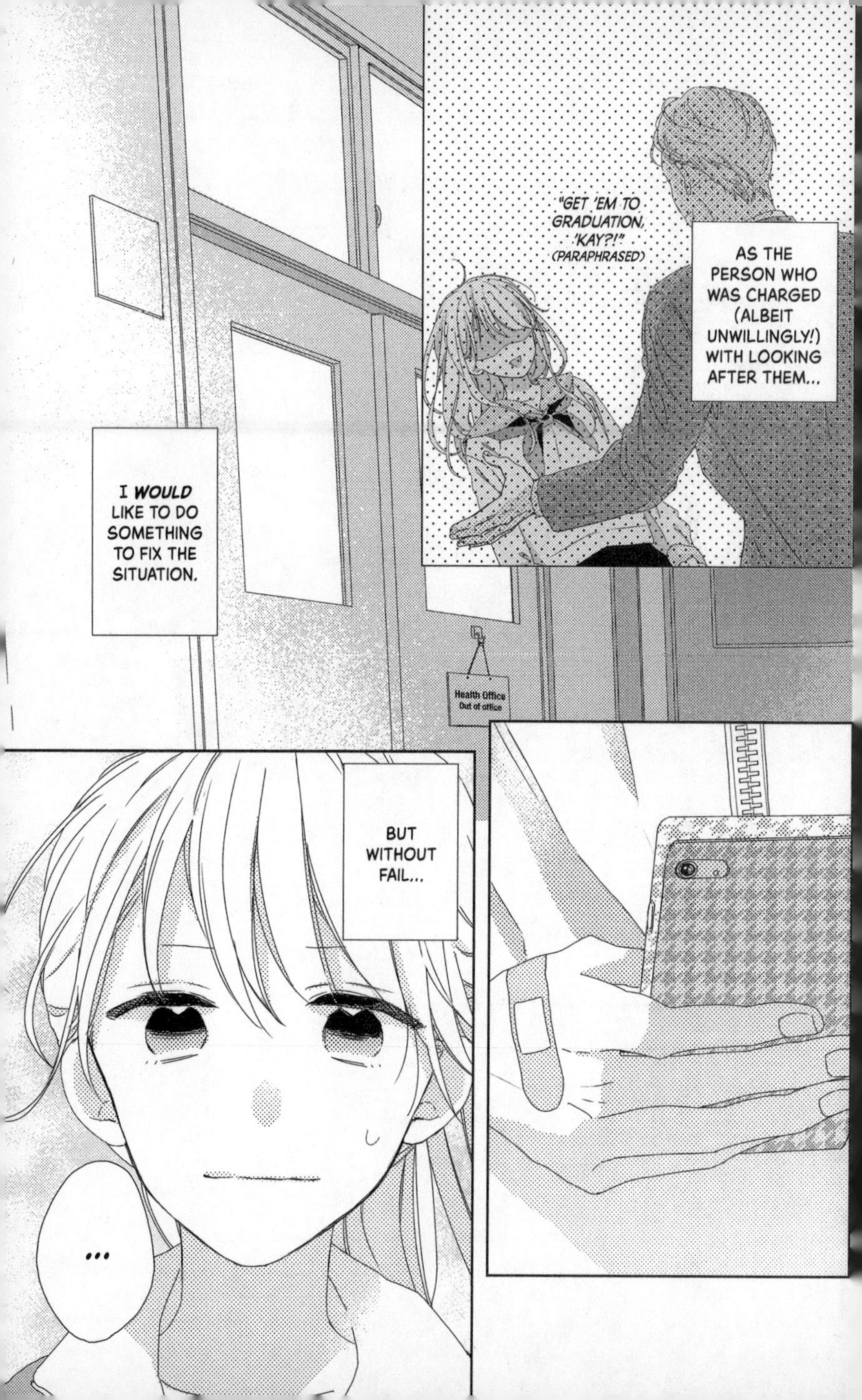
AS THE PERSON WHO WAS CHARGED (ALBEIT UNWILLINGLY!) WITH LOOKING AFTER THEM...
"GET 'EM TO GRADUATION, 'KAY?!"
(PARAPHRASED)
I *WOULD* LIKE TO DO SOMETHING TO FIX THE SITUATION.
Health Office
Out of office
BUT WITHOUT FAIL...
...

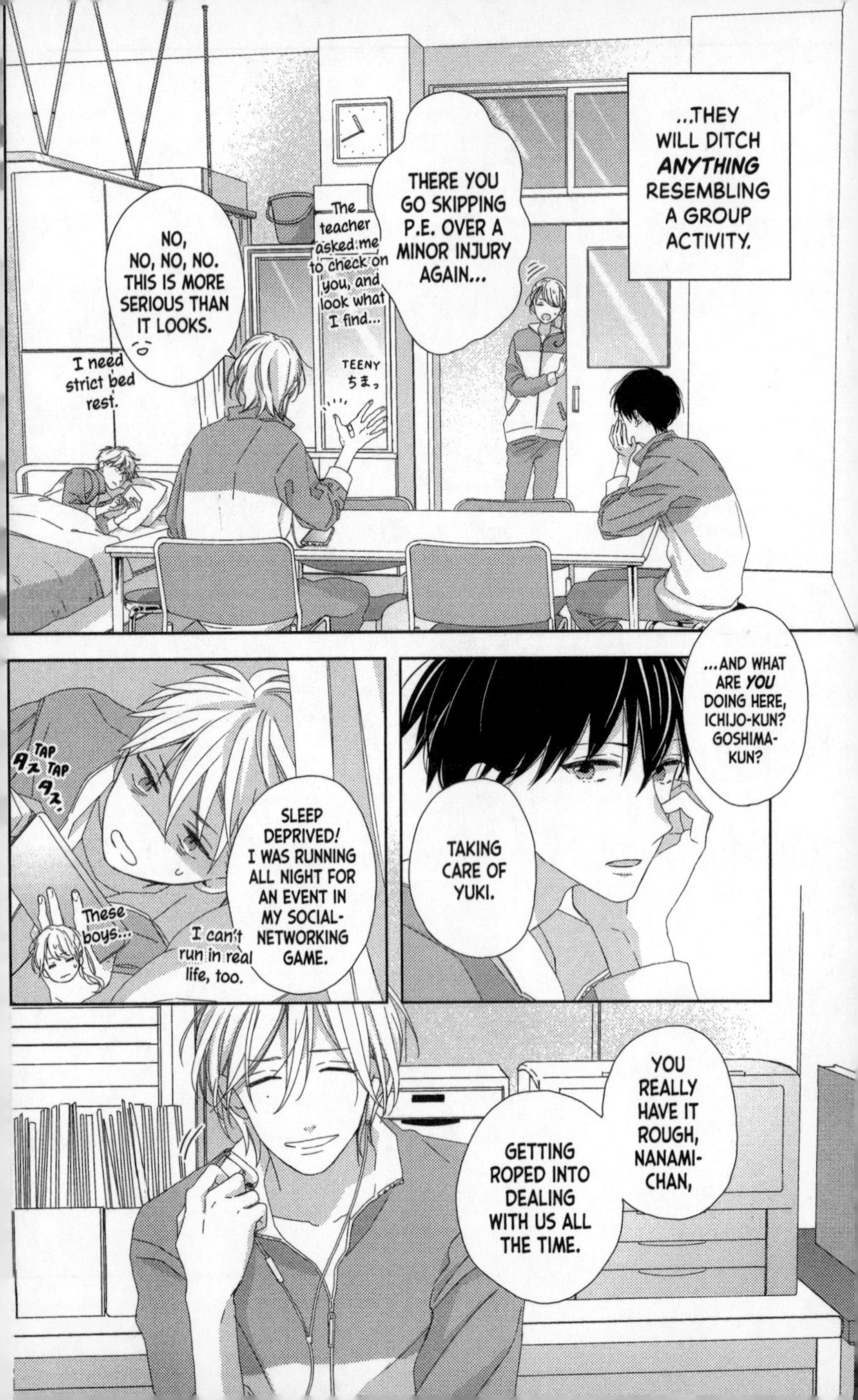

...THEY WILL DITCH ANYTHING RESEMBLING A GROUP ACTIVITY.
THERE YOU GO SKIPPING P.E. OVER A MINOR INJURY AGAIN...
The teacher asked me to check on you, and look what I find...
NO, NO, NO, NO. THIS IS MORE SERIOUS THAN IT LOOKS.
TEENY ちまっ
I need strict bed rest.
...AND WHAT ARE YOU DOING HERE, ICHIJO-KUN? GOSHIMA-KUN?
TAKING CARE OF YUKI.
SLEEP DEPRIVED! I WAS RUNNING ALL NIGHT FOR AN EVENT IN MY SOCIAL-NETWORKING GAME.
I can't run in real life, too.
TAP タス TAP タス
These boys...
YOU REALLY HAVE IT ROUGH, NANAMI-CHAN,
GETTING ROPED INTO DEALING WITH US ALL THE TIME.

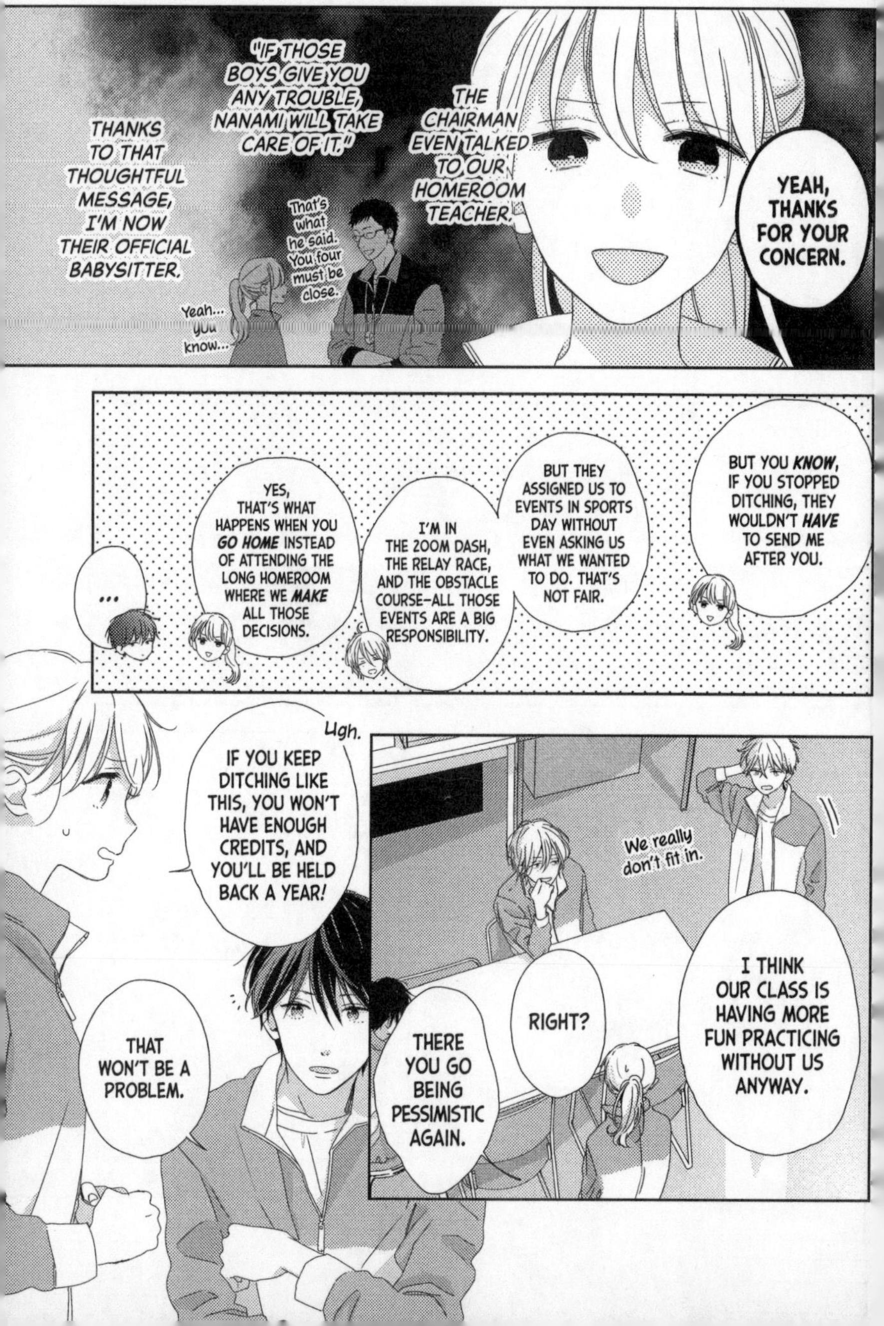
YEAH, THANKS FOR YOUR CONCERN.
THE CHAIRMAN EVEN TALKED TO OUR HOMEROOM TEACHER.
"IF THOSE BOYS GIVE YOU ANY TROUBLE, NANAMI WILL TAKE CARE OF IT."
That's what he said. You four must be close.
Yeah... you know...
THANKS TO THAT THOUGHTFUL MESSAGE, I'M NOW THEIR OFFICIAL BABYSITTER.
BUT YOU *KNOW*, IF YOU STOPPED DITCHING, THEY WOULDN'T *HAVE* TO SEND ME AFTER YOU.
BUT THEY ASSIGNED US TO EVENTS IN SPORTS DAY WITHOUT EVEN ASKING US WHAT WE WANTED TO DO. THAT'S NOT FAIR.
I'M IN THE ZOOM DASH, THE RELAY RACE, AND THE OBSTACLE COURSE–ALL THOSE EVENTS ARE A BIG RESPONSIBILITY.
YES, THAT'S WHAT HAPPENS WHEN YOU *GO HOME* INSTEAD OF ATTENDING THE LONG HOMEROOM WHERE WE *MAKE* ALL THOSE DECISIONS.
...
I THINK OUR CLASS IS HAVING MORE FUN PRACTICING WITHOUT US ANYWAY.
We really don't fit in.
RIGHT?
THERE YOU GO BEING PESSIMISTIC AGAIN.
Ugh.
IF YOU KEEP DITCHING LIKE THIS, YOU WON'T HAVE ENOUGH CREDITS, AND YOU'LL BE HELD BACK A YEAR!
THAT WON'T BE A PROBLEM.

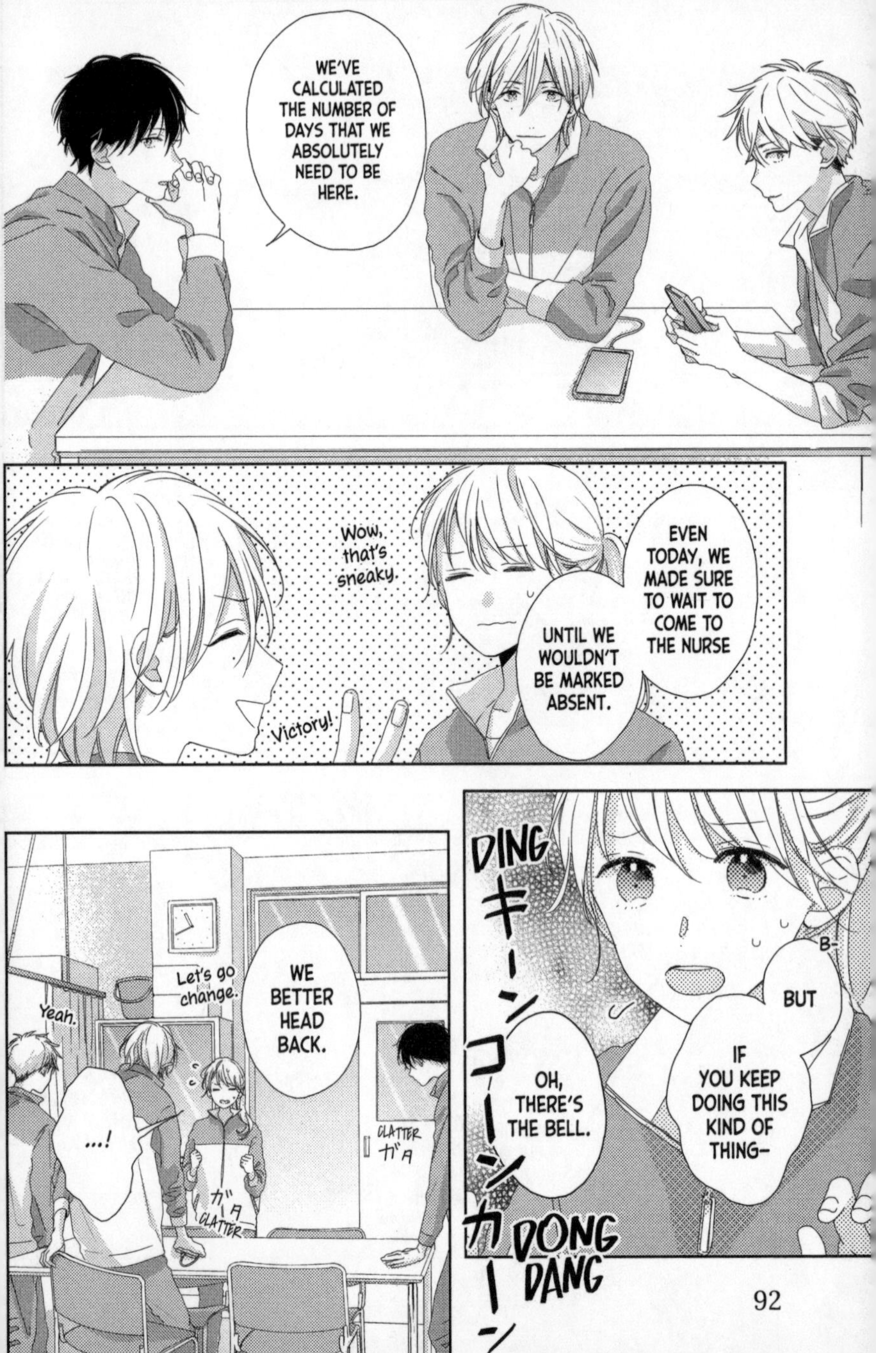
WE'VE CALCULATED THE NUMBER OF DAYS THAT WE ABSOLUTELY NEED TO BE HERE.
EVEN TODAY, WE MADE SURE TO WAIT TO COME TO THE NURSE
UNTIL WE WOULDN'T BE MARKED ABSENT.
Wow, that's sneaky.
Victory!
B-
BUT
IF YOU KEEP DOING THIS KIND OF THING–
DING キーンコーンカーン DONG DANG
OH, THERE'S THE BELL.
WE BETTER HEAD BACK.
Let's go change.
Yeah.
...!
CLATTER ガタ
ガタ CLATTER

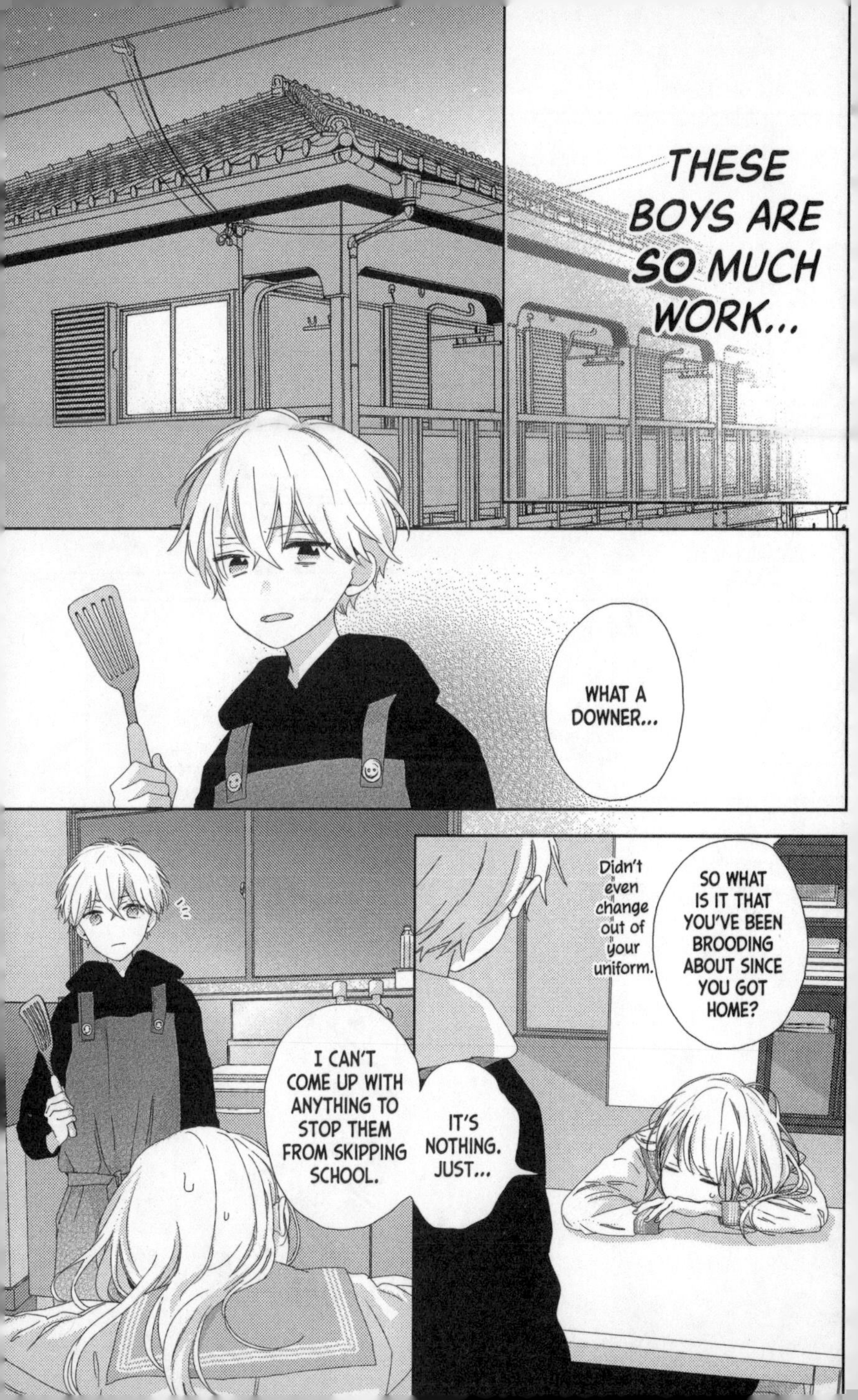
THESE BOYS ARE SO MUCH WORK...
WHAT A DOWNER...
SO WHAT IS IT THAT YOU'VE BEEN BROODING ABOUT SINCE YOU GOT HOME?
Didn't even change out of your uniform.
IT'S NOTHING. JUST...
I CAN'T COME UP WITH ANYTHING TO STOP THEM FROM SKIPPING SCHOOL.

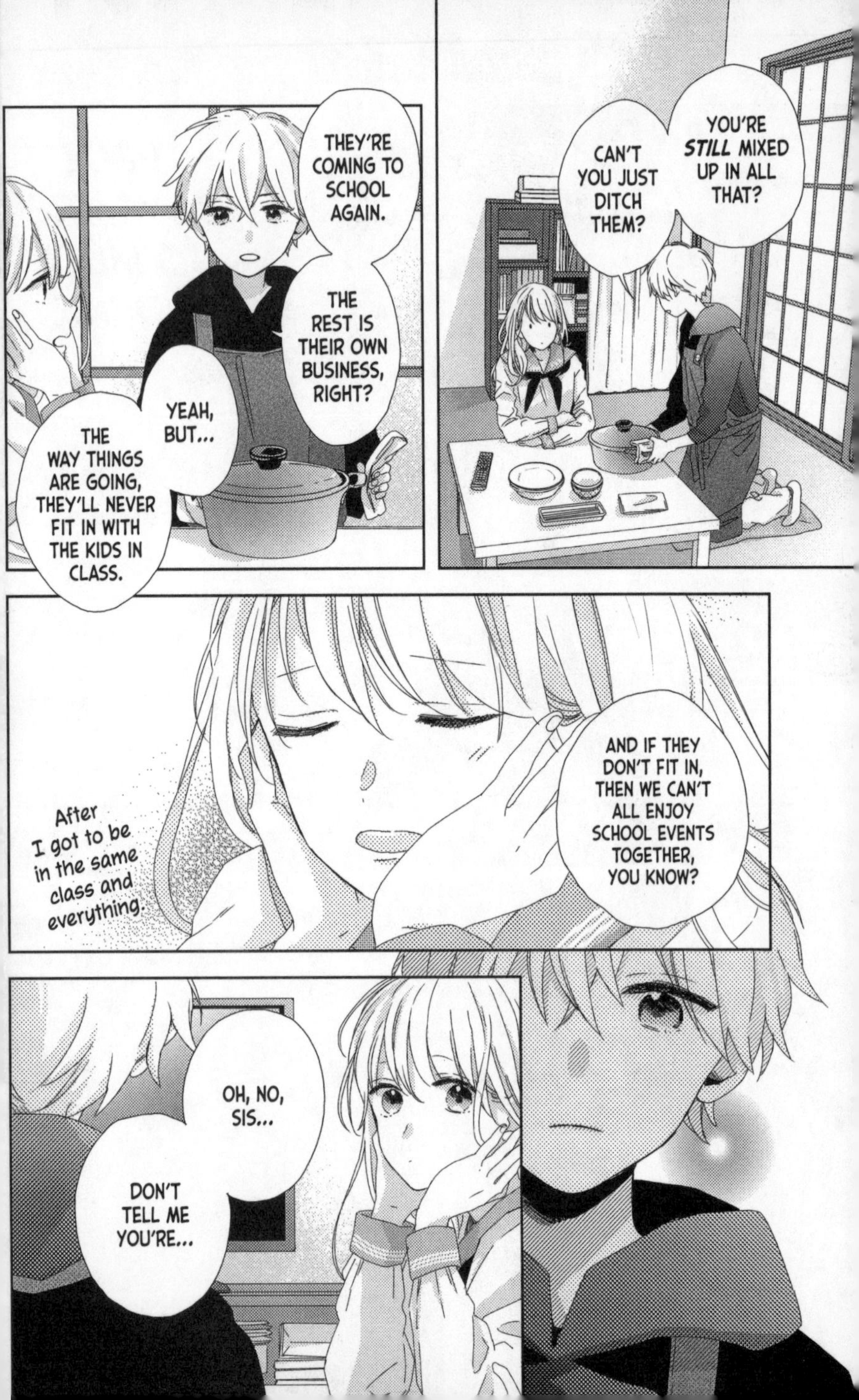
YOU'RE *STILL* MIXED UP IN ALL THAT?
CAN'T YOU JUST DITCH THEM?
THEY'RE COMING TO SCHOOL AGAIN.
THE REST IS THEIR OWN BUSINESS, RIGHT?
YEAH, BUT...
THE WAY THINGS ARE GOING, THEY'LL NEVER FIT IN WITH THE KIDS IN CLASS.
AND IF THEY DON'T FIT IN, THEN WE CAN'T ALL ENJOY SCHOOL EVENTS TOGETHER, YOU KNOW?
After I got to be in the same class and everything.
OH, NO, SIS...
DON'T TELL ME YOU'RE...

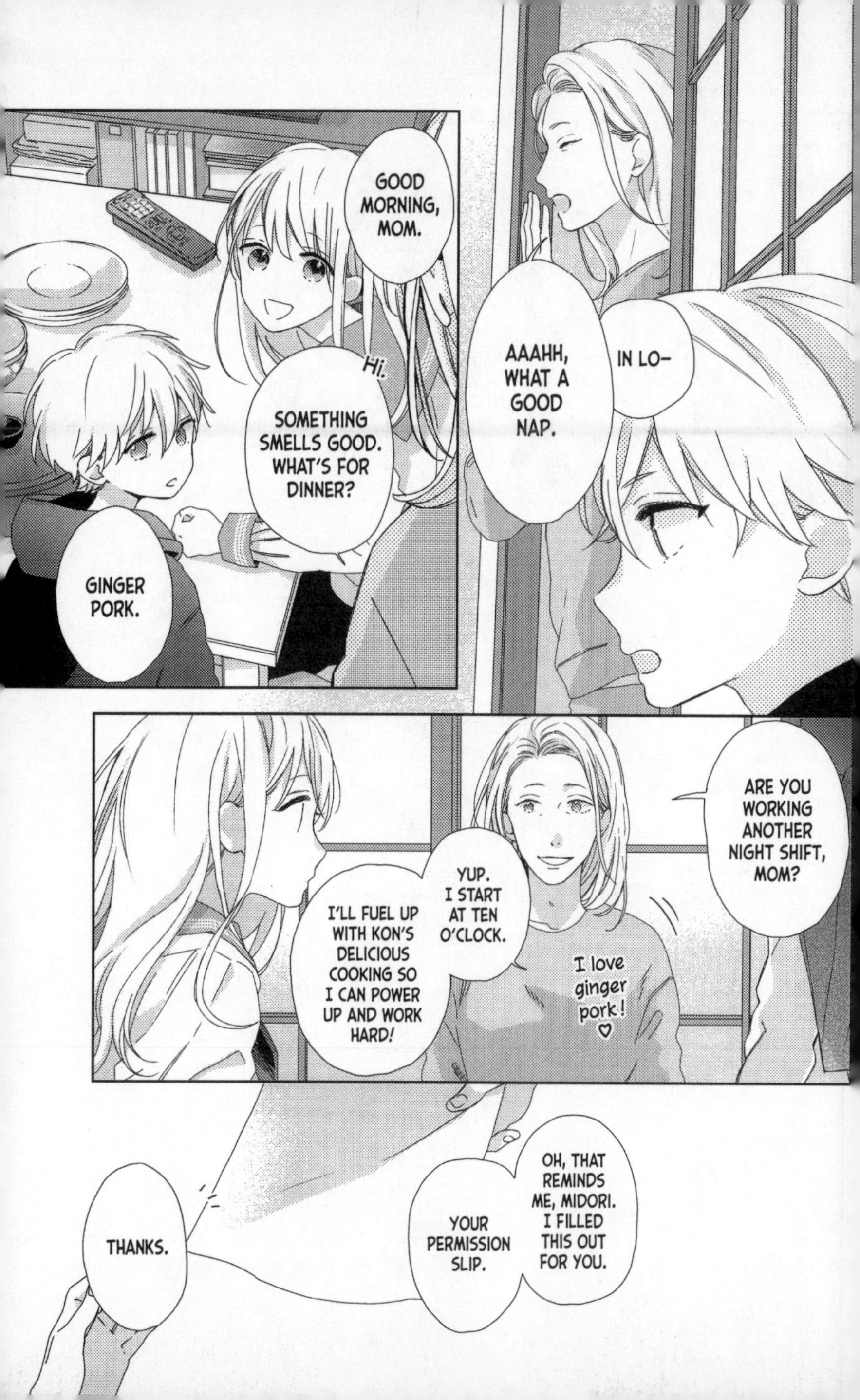
IN LO—
AAAHH, WHAT A GOOD NAP.
GOOD MORNING, MOM.
Hi.
SOMETHING SMELLS GOOD. WHAT'S FOR DINNER?
GINGER PORK.
ARE YOU WORKING ANOTHER NIGHT SHIFT, MOM?
YUP. I START AT TEN O'CLOCK.
I love ginger pork! ♡
I'LL FUEL UP WITH KON'S DELICIOUS COOKING SO I CAN POWER UP AND WORK HARD!
OH, THAT REMINDS ME, MIDORI. I FILLED THIS OUT FOR YOU.
YOUR PERMISSION SLIP.
THANKS.

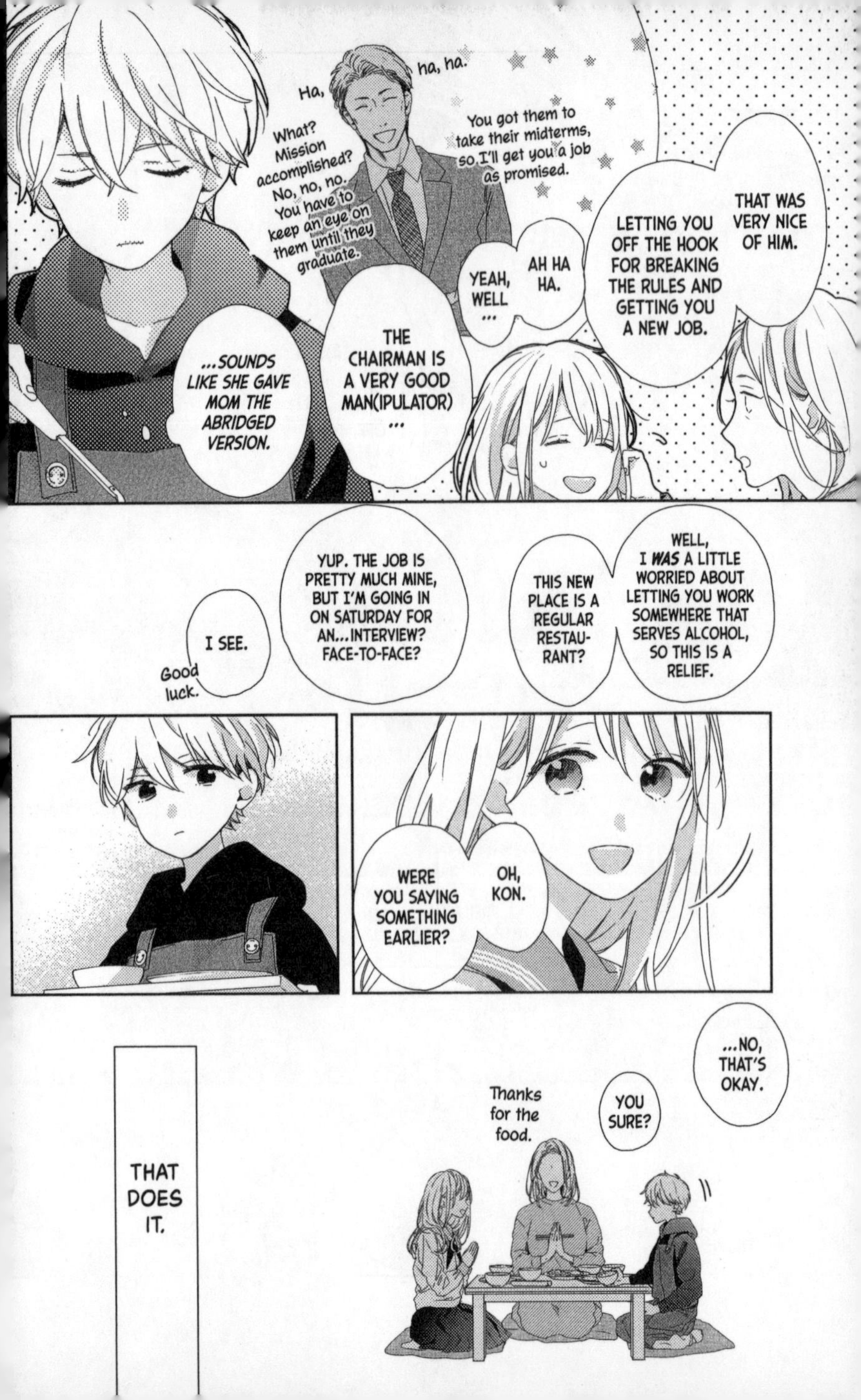
THAT WAS VERY NICE OF HIM.
LETTING YOU OFF THE HOOK FOR BREAKING THE RULES AND GETTING YOU A NEW JOB.
AH HA HA.
YEAH, WELL...
Ha, ha, ha.
You got them to take their midterms, so I'll get you a job as promised.
What? Mission accomplished? No, no, no. You have to keep an eye on them until they graduate.
THE CHAIRMAN IS A VERY GOOD MAN(IPULATOR)...
...SOUNDS LIKE SHE GAVE MOM THE ABRIDGED VERSION.
WELL, I *WAS* A LITTLE WORRIED ABOUT LETTING YOU WORK SOMEWHERE THAT SERVES ALCOHOL, SO THIS IS A RELIEF.
THIS NEW PLACE IS A REGULAR RESTAU-RANT?
YUP. THE JOB IS PRETTY MUCH MINE, BUT I'M GOING IN ON SATURDAY FOR AN...INTERVIEW? FACE-TO-FACE?
I SEE.
Good luck.
OH, KON.
WERE YOU SAYING SOMETHING EARLIER?
...NO, THAT'S OKAY.
YOU SURE?
Thanks for the food.
THAT DOES IT.

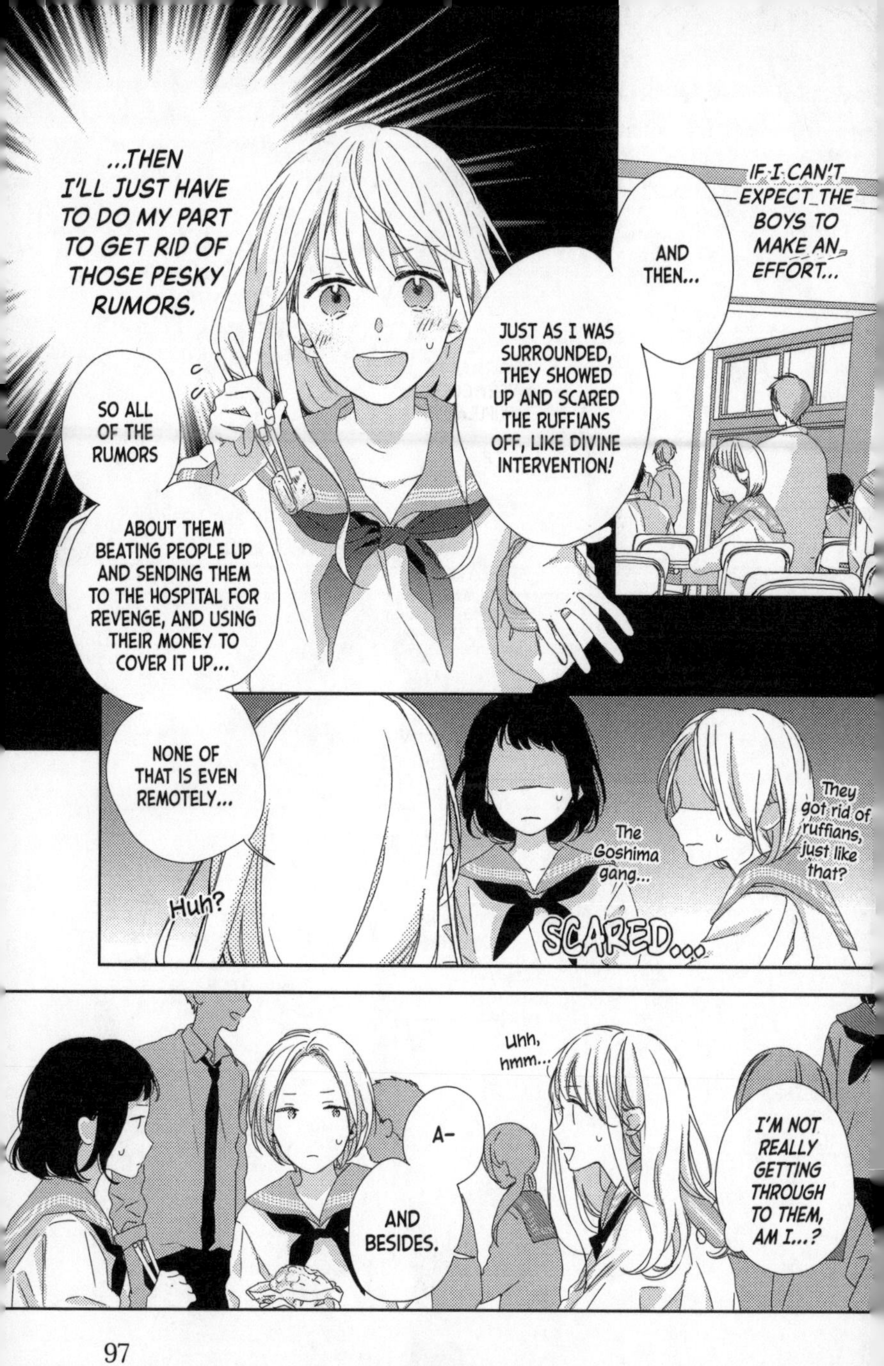
IF I CAN'T EXPECT THE BOYS TO MAKE AN EFFORT...
...THEN I'LL JUST HAVE TO DO MY PART TO GET RID OF THOSE PESKY RUMORS.
AND THEN...
JUST AS I WAS SURROUNDED, THEY SHOWED UP AND SCARED THE RUFFIANS OFF, LIKE DIVINE INTERVENTION!
SO ALL OF THE RUMORS
ABOUT THEM BEATING PEOPLE UP AND SENDING THEM TO THE HOSPITAL FOR REVENGE, AND USING THEIR MONEY TO COVER IT UP...
NONE OF THAT IS EVEN REMOTELY...
They got rid of ruffians, just like that?
The Goshima gang...
SCARED...
Huh?
I'M NOT REALLY GETTING THROUGH TO THEM, AM I...?
Uhh, hmm...
A-
AND BESIDES.

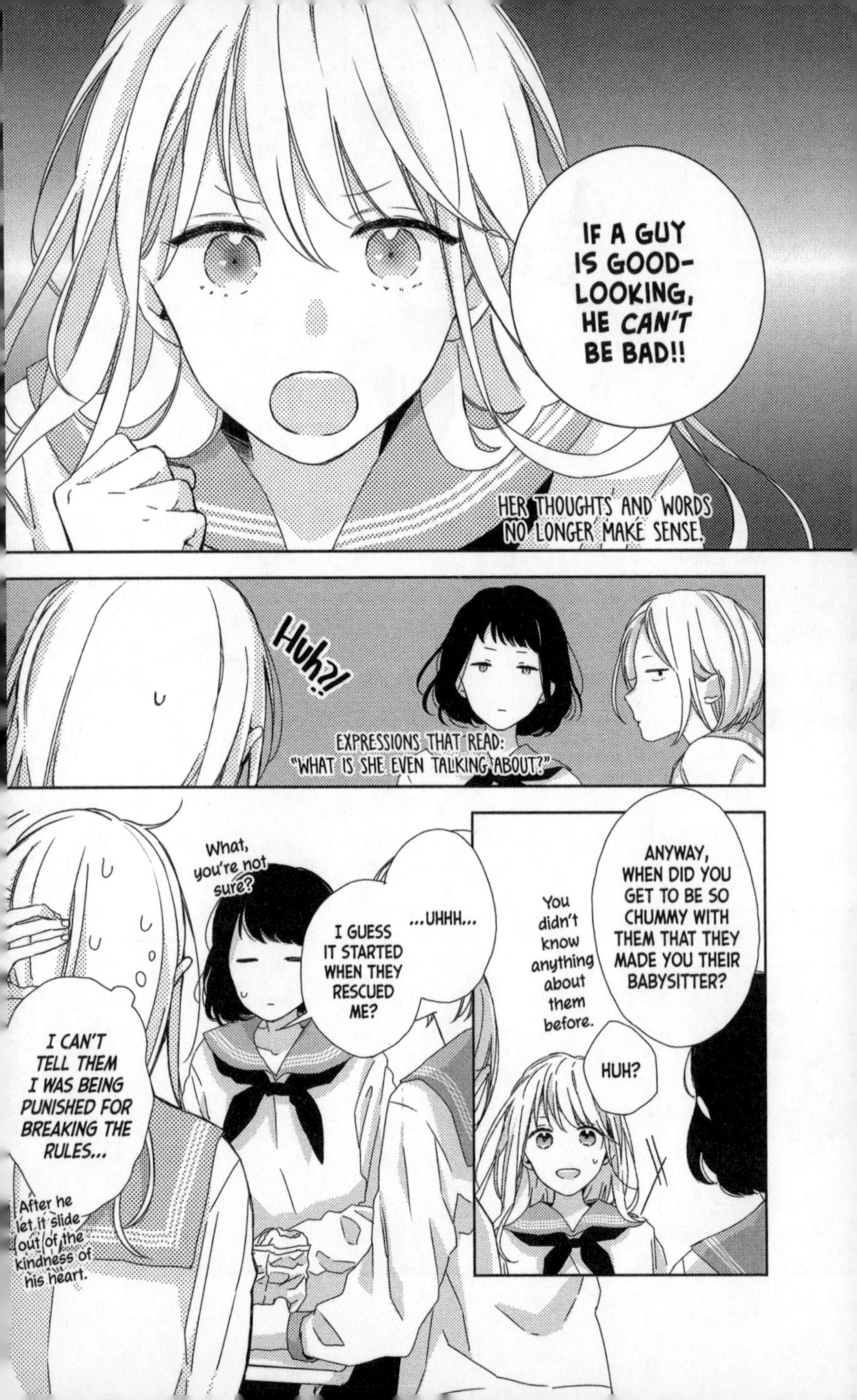
IF A GUY IS GOOD-LOOKING, HE *CAN'T* BE BAD!!
HER THOUGHTS AND WORDS NO LONGER MAKE SENSE.
Huh?!
EXPRESSIONS THAT READ: "WHAT IS SHE EVEN TALKING ABOUT?"
ANYWAY, WHEN DID YOU GET TO BE SO CHUMMY WITH THEM THAT THEY MADE YOU THEIR BABYSITTER?
You didn't know anything about them before.
HUH?
...UHHH...
I GUESS IT STARTED WHEN THEY RESCUED ME?
What, you're not sure?
I CAN'T TELL THEM I WAS BEING PUNISHED FOR BREAKING THE RULES...
After he let it slide out of the kindness of his heart.

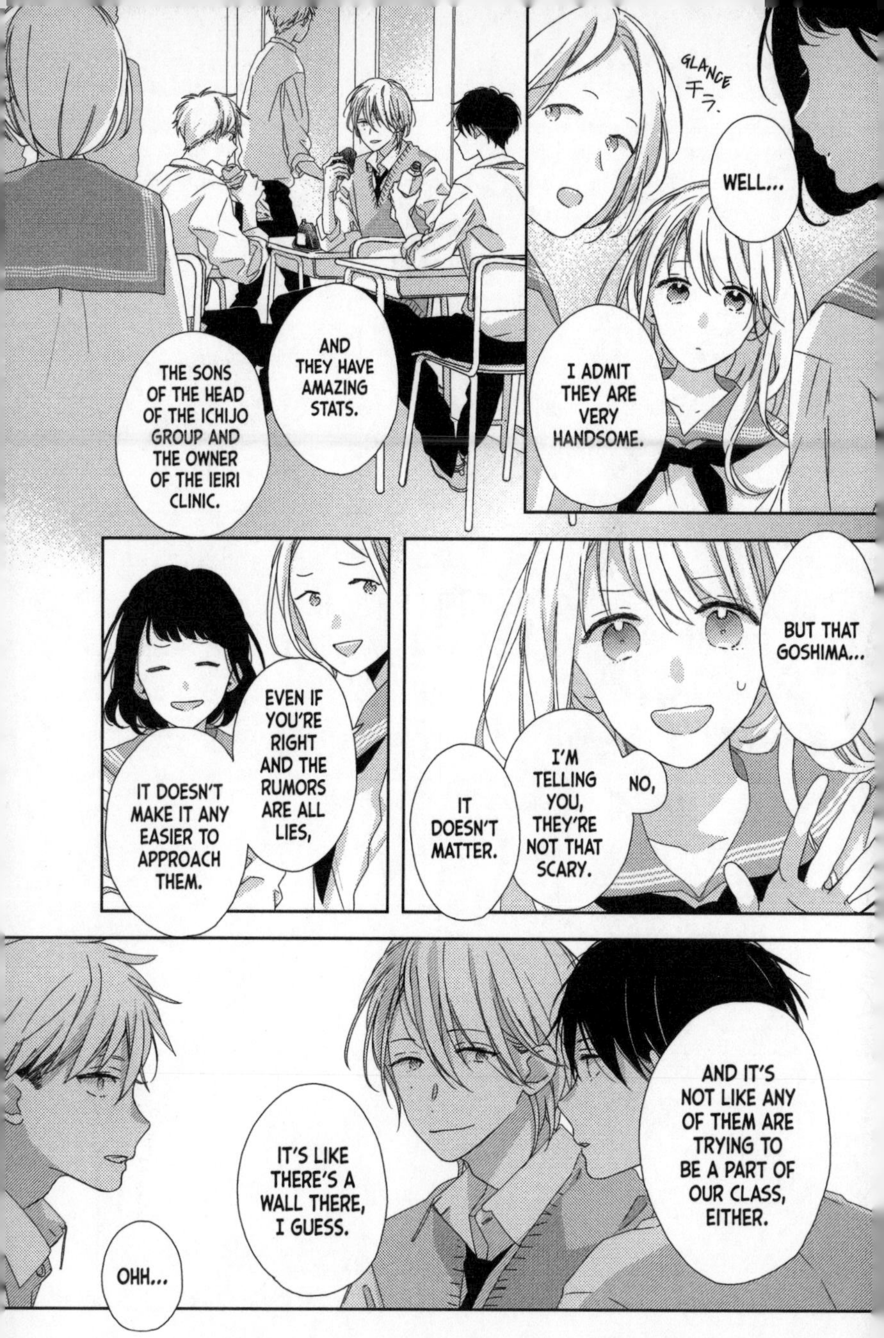
GLANCE チラ
WELL...
I ADMIT THEY ARE VERY HANDSOME.
AND THEY HAVE AMAZING STATS.
THE SONS OF THE HEAD OF THE ICHIJO GROUP AND THE OWNER OF THE IEIRI CLINIC.
BUT THAT GOSHIMA...
NO,
I'M TELLING YOU, THEY'RE NOT THAT SCARY.
IT DOESN'T MATTER.
EVEN IF YOU'RE RIGHT AND THE RUMORS ARE ALL LIES,
IT DOESN'T MAKE IT ANY EASIER TO APPROACH THEM.
AND IT'S NOT LIKE ANY OF THEM ARE TRYING TO BE A PART OF OUR CLASS, EITHER.
IT'S LIKE THERE'S A WALL THERE, I GUESS.
OHH...

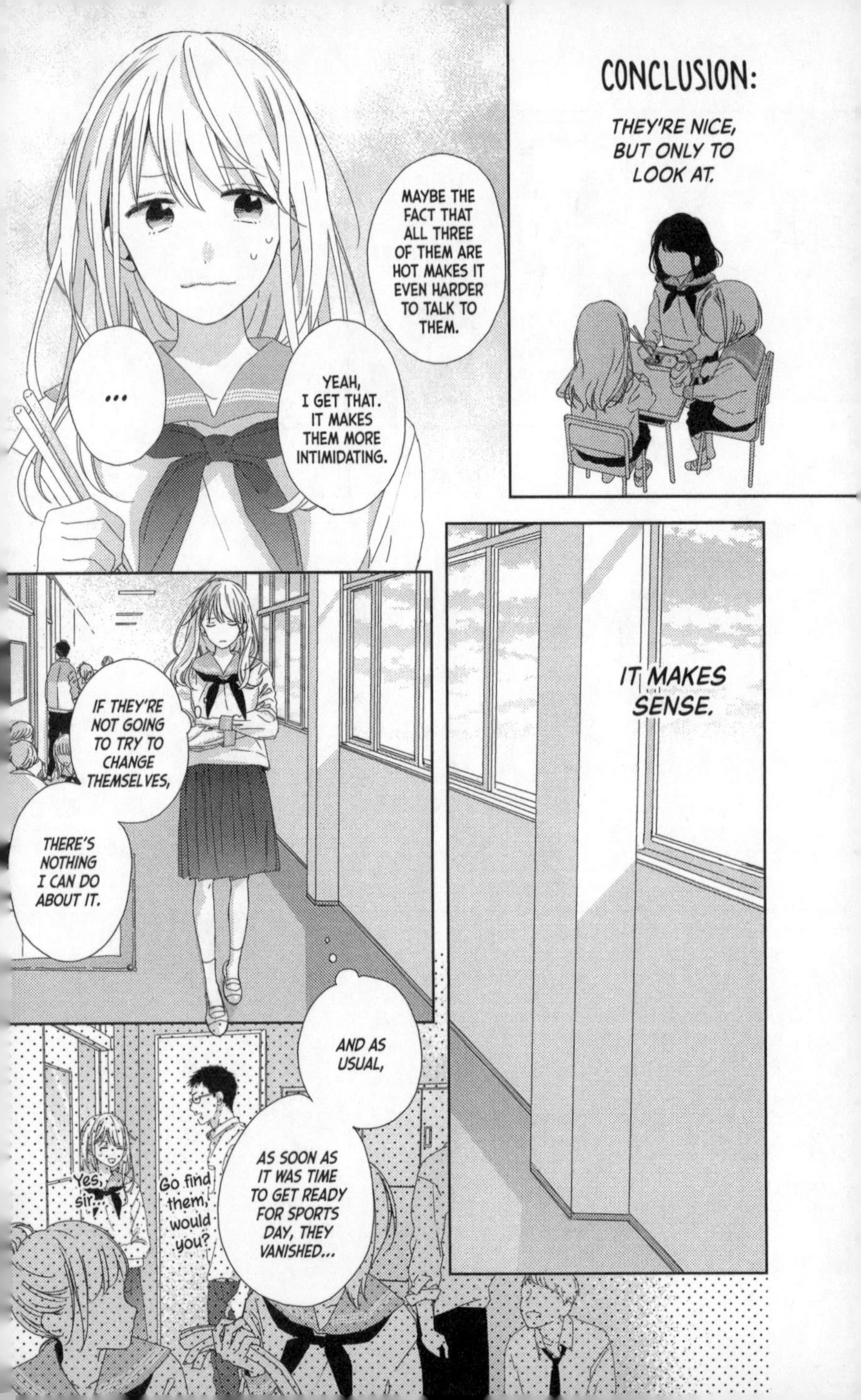

CONCLUSION:
THEY'RE NICE, BUT ONLY TO LOOK AT.
MAYBE THE FACT THAT ALL THREE OF THEM ARE HOT MAKES IT EVEN HARDER TO TALK TO THEM.
YEAH, I GET THAT. IT MAKES THEM MORE INTIMIDATING.
...
IT MAKES SENSE.
IF THEY'RE NOT GOING TO TRY TO CHANGE THEMSELVES,
THERE'S NOTHING I CAN DO ABOUT IT.
AND AS USUAL,
AS SOON AS IT WAS TIME TO GET READY FOR SPORTS DAY, THEY VANISHED...
Go find them, would you?
Yes, sir...

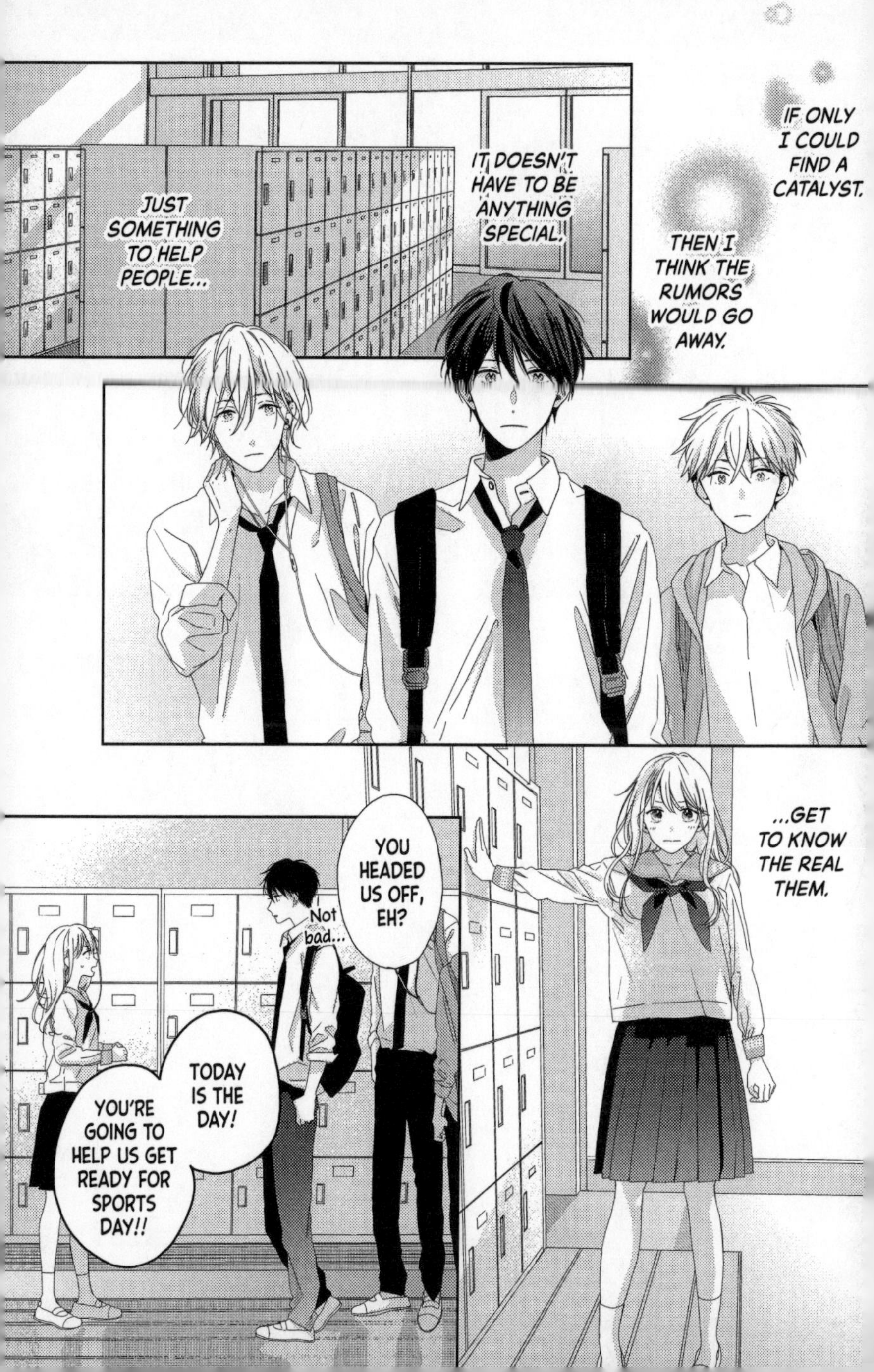
IF ONLY I COULD FIND A CATALYST.
THEN I THINK THE RUMORS WOULD GO AWAY.
IT DOESN'T HAVE TO BE ANYTHING SPECIAL.
JUST SOMETHING TO HELP PEOPLE...
...GET TO KNOW THE REAL THEM.
YOU HEADED US OFF, EH?
Not bad...
TODAY IS THE DAY!
YOU'RE GOING TO HELP US GET READY FOR SPORTS DAY!!

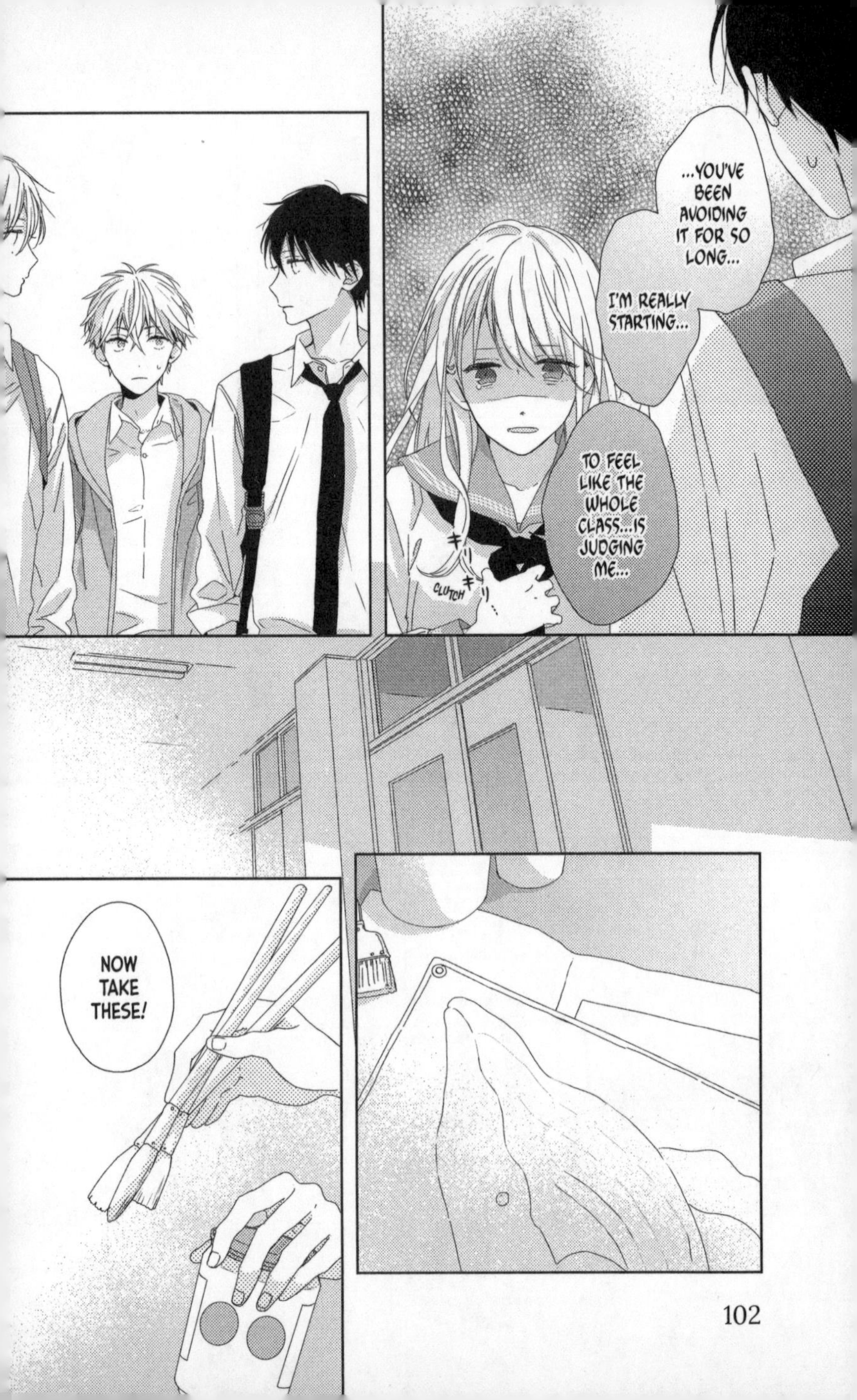
...YOU'VE BEEN AVOIDING IT FOR SO LONG...
I'M REALLY STARTING...
TO FEEL LIKE THE WHOLE CLASS...IS JUDGING ME...
キリキリ
CLUTCH
NOW TAKE THESE!

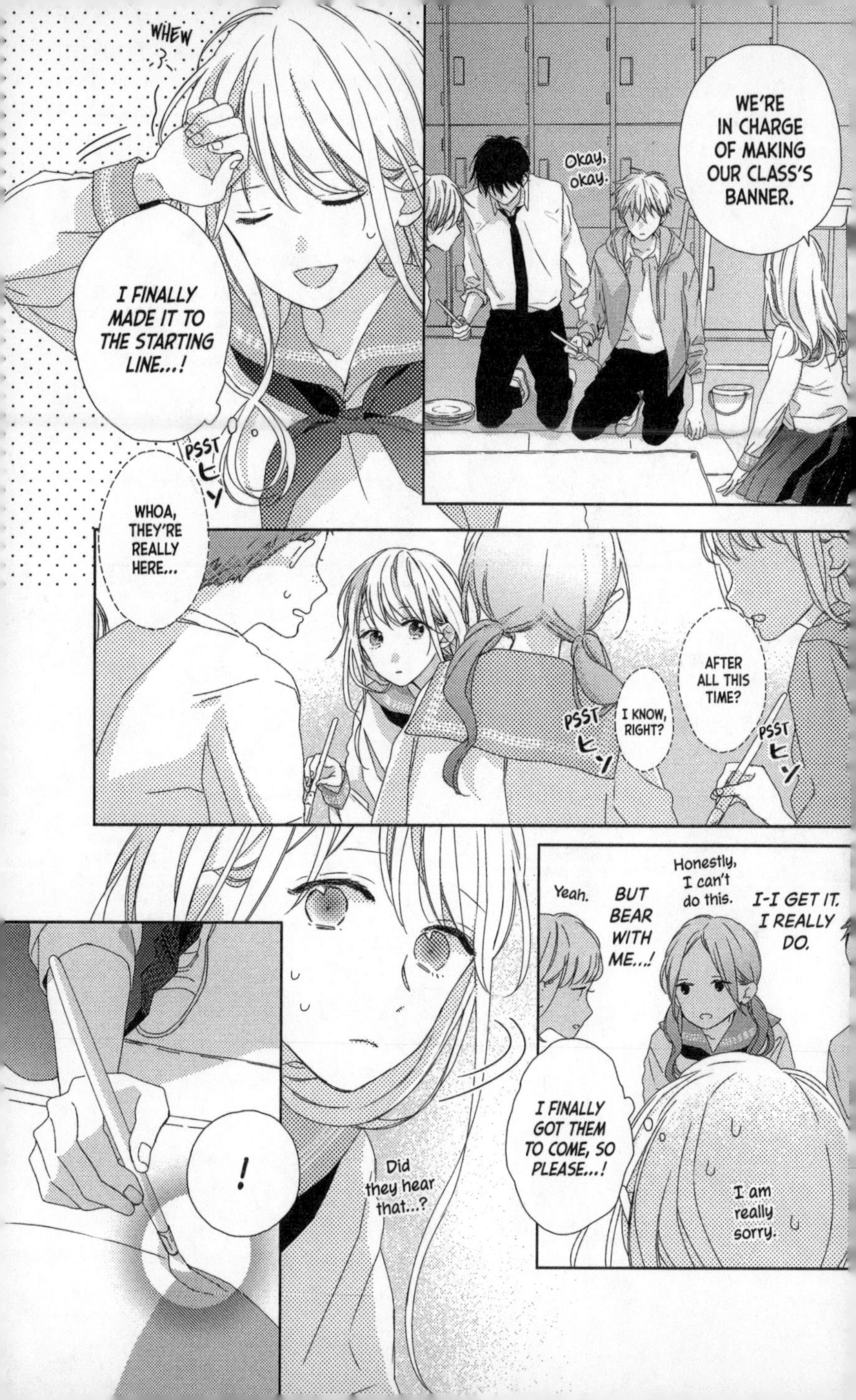
WE'RE IN CHARGE OF MAKING OUR CLASS'S BANNER.
Okay, okay.
WHEW
I FINALLY MADE IT TO THE STARTING LINE...!
PSST ヒソ
AFTER ALL THIS TIME?
I KNOW, RIGHT?
PSST ヒソ
WHOA, THEY'RE REALLY HERE...
PSST ヒソ
I-I GET IT. I REALLY DO.
Honestly, I can't do this.
BUT BEAR WITH ME...!
Yeah.
I FINALLY GOT THEM TO COME, SO PLEASE...!
I am really sorry.
Did they hear that...?
!

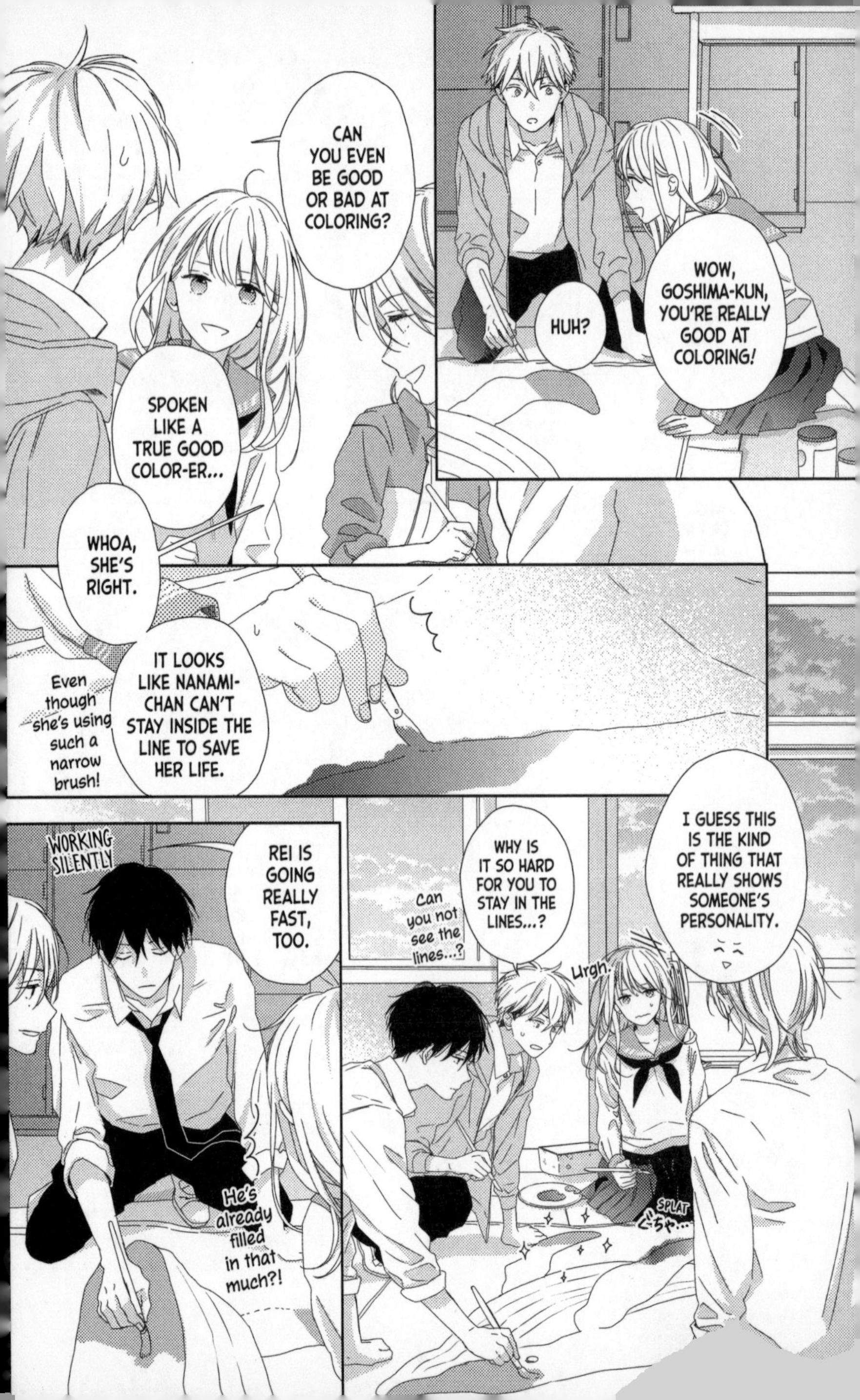
WOW, GOSHIMA-KUN, YOU'RE REALLY GOOD AT COLORING!
HUH?
CAN YOU EVEN BE GOOD OR BAD AT COLORING?
SPOKEN LIKE A TRUE GOOD COLOR-ER...
WHOA, SHE'S RIGHT.
IT LOOKS LIKE NANAMI-CHAN CAN'T STAY INSIDE THE LINE TO SAVE HER LIFE.
Even though she's using such a narrow brush!
I GUESS THIS IS THE KIND OF THING THAT REALLY SHOWS SOMEONE'S PERSONALITY.
WHY IS IT SO HARD FOR YOU TO STAY IN THE LINES...?
Can you not see the lines...?
Urgh.
SPLAT
ぐちゃ...
REI IS GOING REALLY FAST, TOO.
WORKING SILENTLY
He's already filled in that much?!

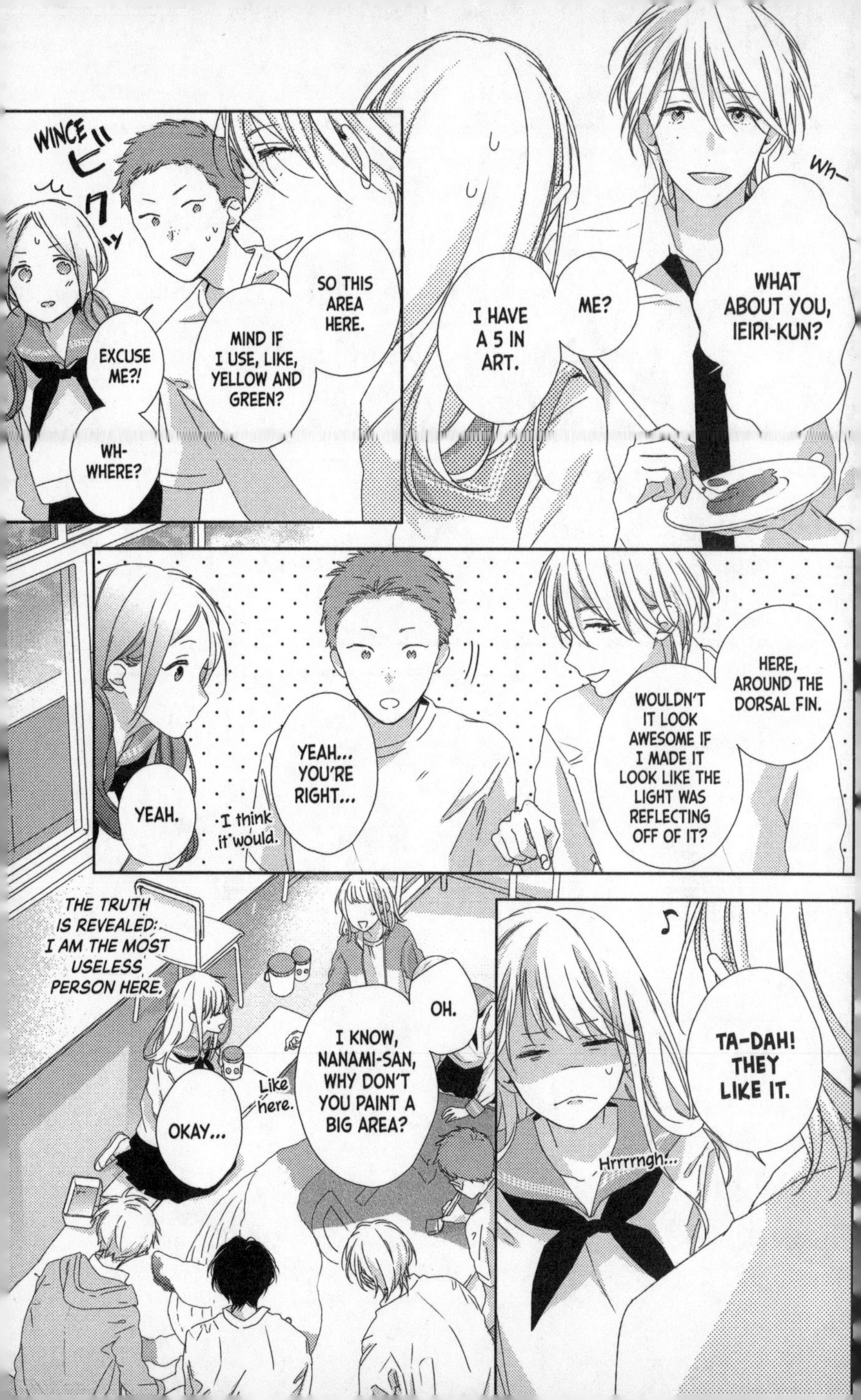
Wh—
WHAT ABOUT YOU, IEIRI-KUN?
ME?
I HAVE A 5 IN ART.
SO THIS AREA HERE.
MIND IF I USE, LIKE, YELLOW AND GREEN?
WINCE ビクッ
EXCUSE ME?!
WH- WHERE?
HERE, AROUND THE DORSAL FIN.
WOULDN'T IT LOOK AWESOME IF I MADE IT LOOK LIKE THE LIGHT WAS REFLECTING OFF OF IT?
YEAH... YOU'RE RIGHT...
I think it would.
YEAH.
TA-DAH! THEY LIKE IT.
Hrrrrngh...
OH.
I KNOW, NANAMI-SAN, WHY DON'T YOU PAINT A BIG AREA?
Like here.
OKAY...
THE TRUTH IS REVEALED: I AM THE MOST USELESS PERSON HERE.

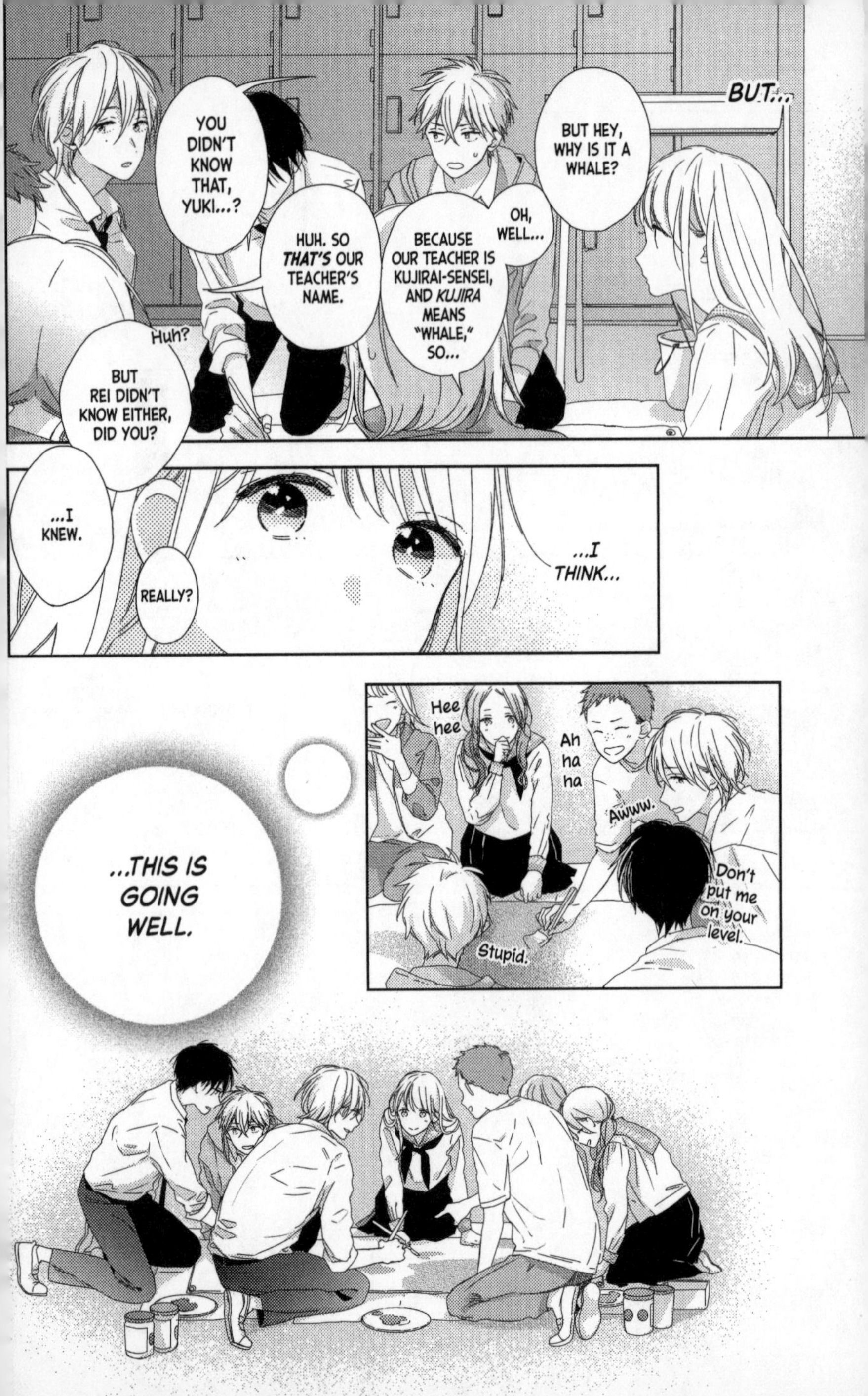
BUT...
BUT HEY, WHY IS IT A WHALE?
OH, WELL...
BECAUSE OUR TEACHER IS KUJIRAI-SENSEI, AND *KUJIRA* MEANS "WHALE," SO...
HUH. SO *THAT'S* OUR TEACHER'S NAME.
YOU DIDN'T KNOW THAT, YUKI...?
Huh?
BUT REI DIDN'T KNOW EITHER, DID YOU?
...I KNEW.
REALLY?
...I THINK...
Don't put me on your level.
Awww.
Ah ha ha
Hee hee
Stupid.
...THIS IS GOING WELL.

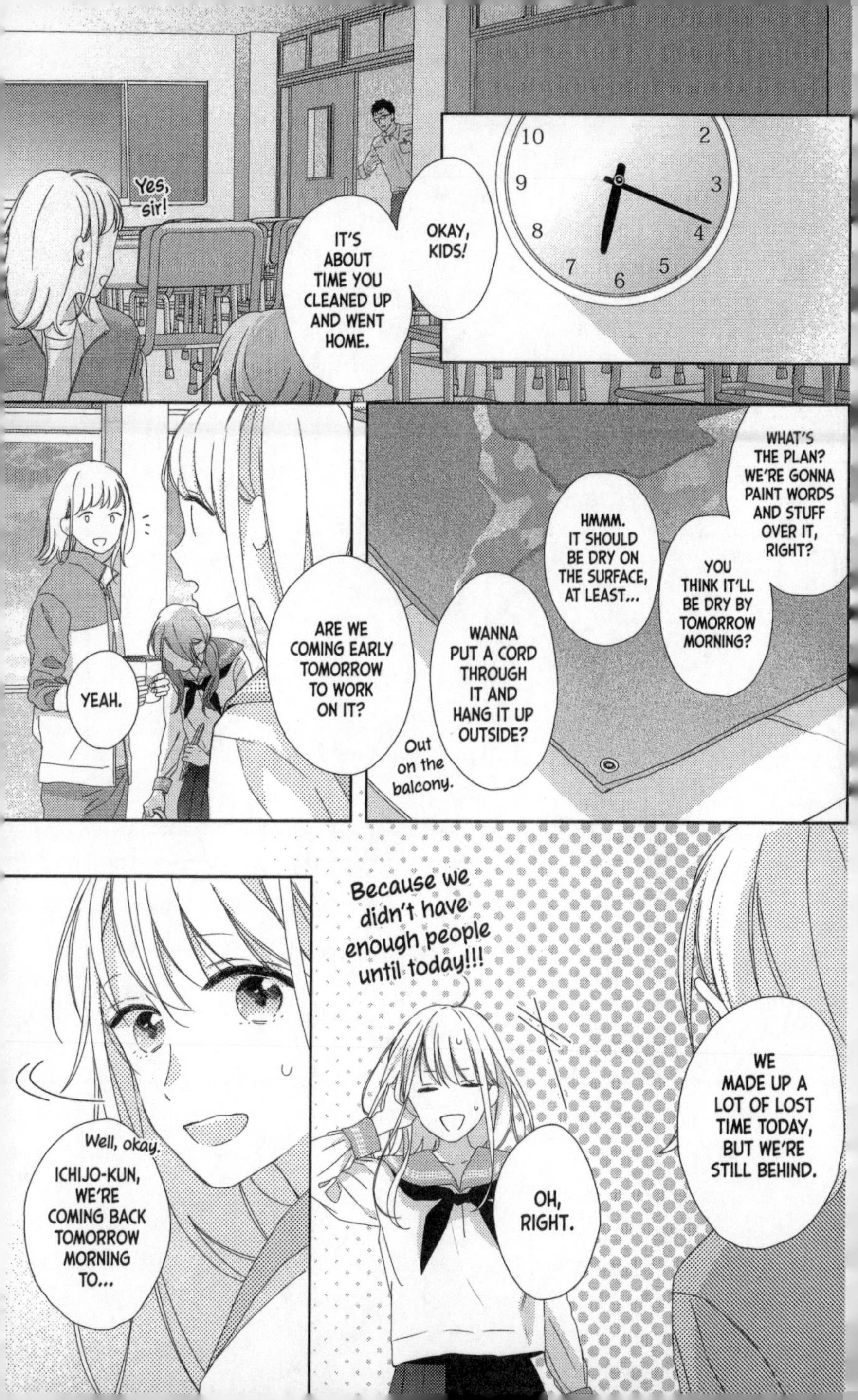
OKAY, KIDS!
IT'S ABOUT TIME YOU CLEANED UP AND WENT HOME.
Yes, sir!
WHAT'S THE PLAN? WE'RE GONNA PAINT WORDS AND STUFF OVER IT, RIGHT?
YOU THINK IT'LL BE DRY BY TOMORROW MORNING?
HMMM. IT SHOULD BE DRY ON THE SURFACE, AT LEAST...
WANNA PUT A CORD THROUGH IT AND HANG IT UP OUTSIDE?
Out on the balcony.
ARE WE COMING EARLY TOMORROW TO WORK ON IT?
YEAH.
WE MADE UP A LOT OF LOST TIME TODAY, BUT WE'RE STILL BEHIND.
Because we didn't have enough people until today!!!
OH, RIGHT.
Well, okay.
ICHIJO-KUN, WE'RE COMING BACK TOMORROW MORNING TO...

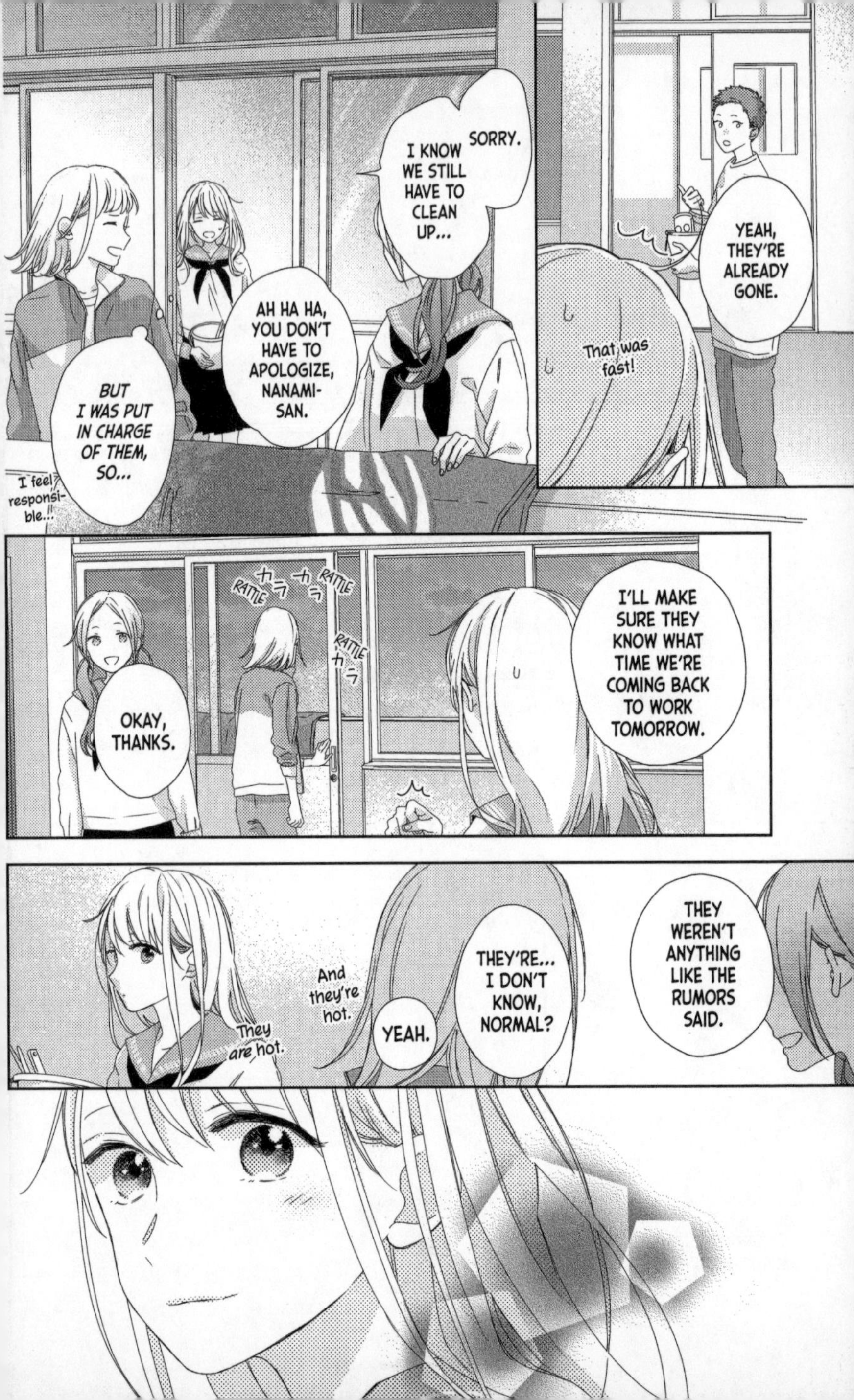
YEAH, THEY'RE ALREADY GONE.
That was fast!
SORRY.
I KNOW WE STILL HAVE TO CLEAN UP...
AH HA HA, YOU DON'T HAVE TO APOLOGIZE, NANAMI-SAN.
BUT I WAS PUT IN CHARGE OF THEM, SO...
I feel responsible..!!
I'LL MAKE SURE THEY KNOW WHAT TIME WE'RE COMING BACK TO WORK TOMORROW.
カラ RATTLE
カラ RATTLE
カラ RATTLE
OKAY, THANKS.
THEY WEREN'T ANYTHING LIKE THE RUMORS SAID.
THEY'RE... I DON'T KNOW, NORMAL?
YEAH.
And they're hot.
They are hot.

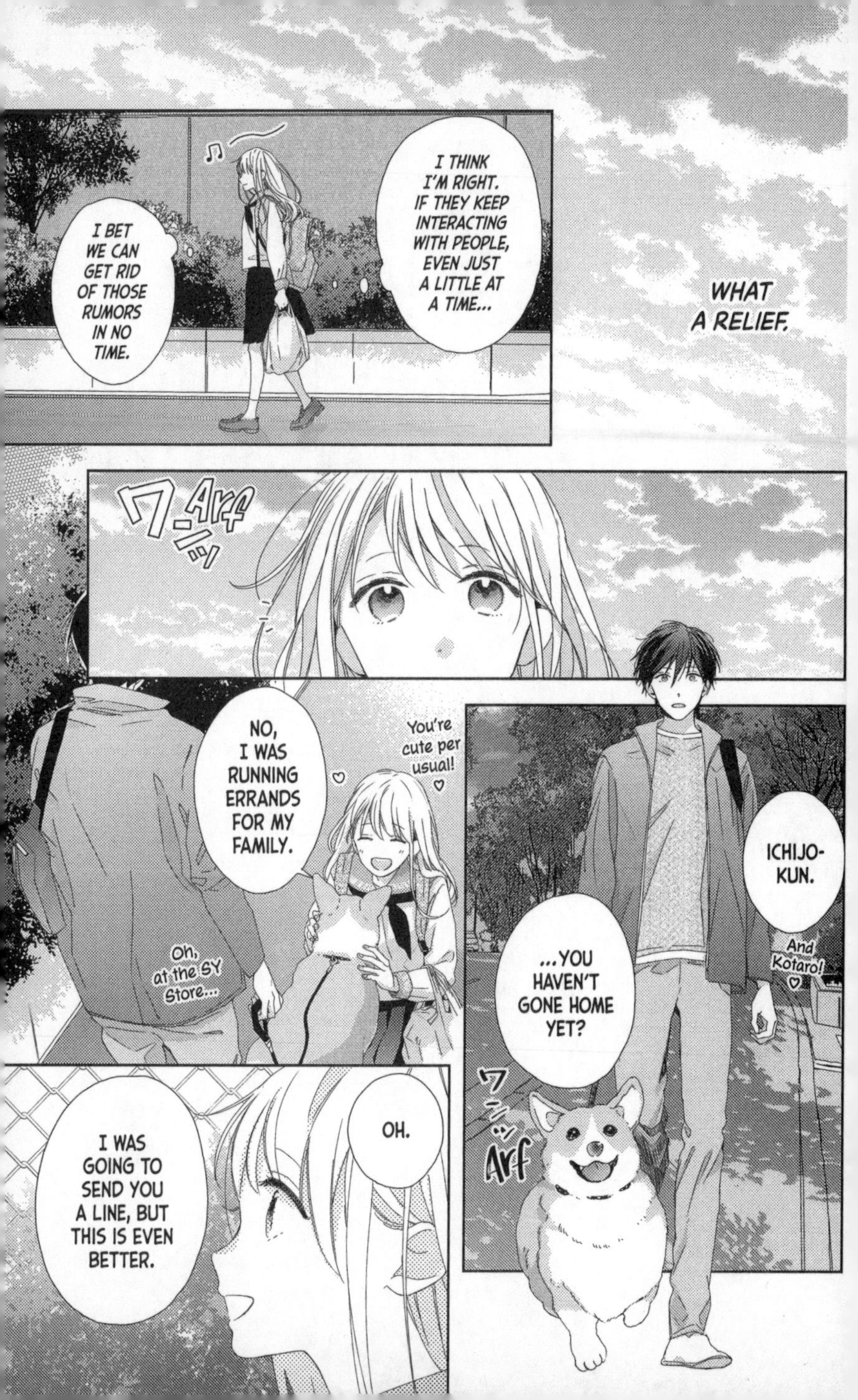
WHAT A RELIEF.
I THINK I'M RIGHT. IF THEY KEEP INTERACTING WITH PEOPLE, EVEN JUST A LITTLE AT A TIME...
I BET WE CAN GET RID OF THOSE RUMORS IN NO TIME.
Arf
ICHIJO-KUN.
And Kotaro! ♡
...YOU HAVEN'T GONE HOME YET?
Arf
NO, I WAS RUNNING ERRANDS FOR MY FAMILY.
You're cute per usual! ♡
Oh, at the SY Store...
OH.
I WAS GOING TO SEND YOU A LINE, BUT THIS IS EVEN BETTER.

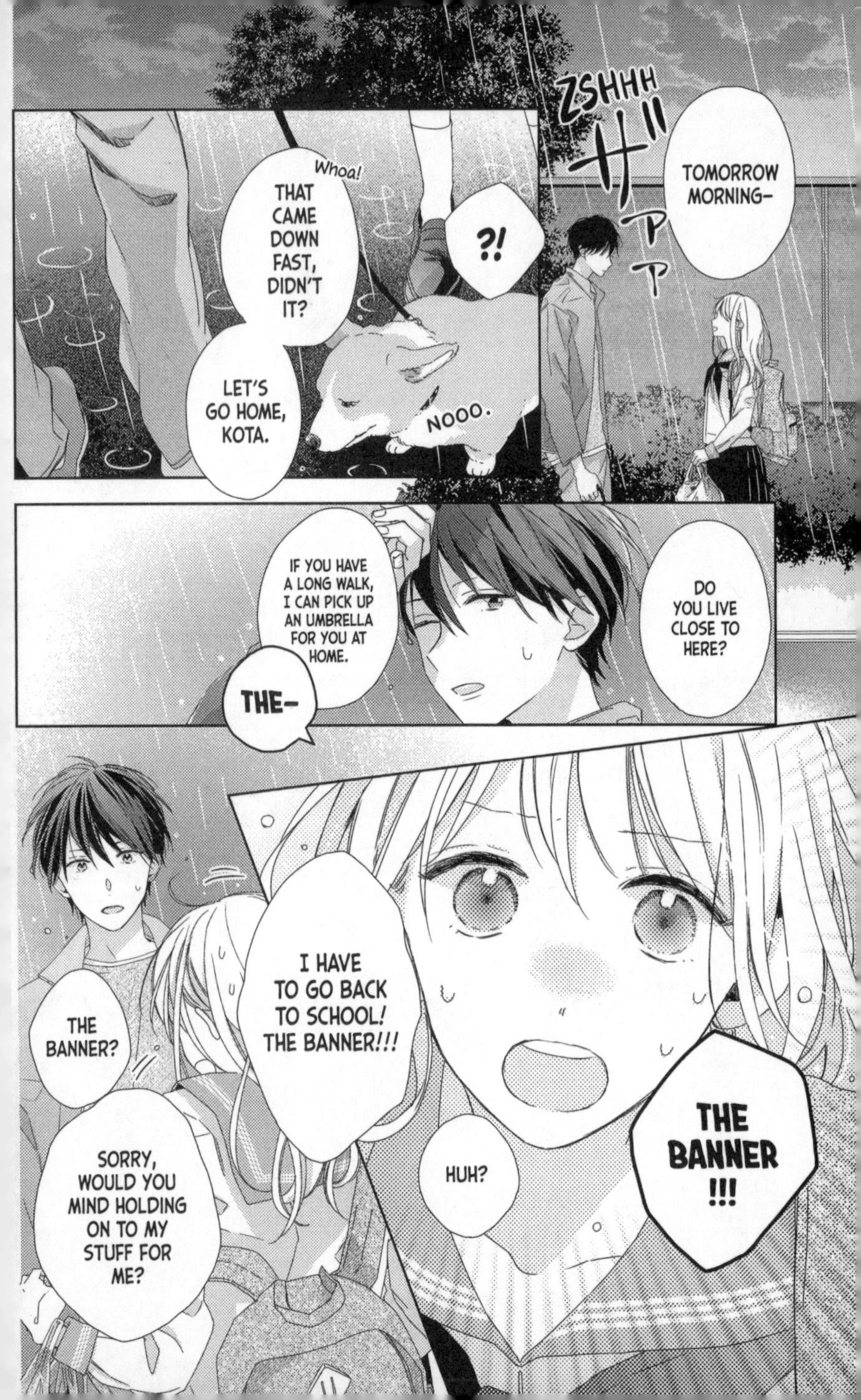
ZSHHH
TOMORROW MORNING–
Whoa!
THAT CAME DOWN FAST, DIDN'T IT?
?!
LET'S GO HOME, KOTA.
NOOO.
DO YOU LIVE CLOSE TO HERE?
IF YOU HAVE A LONG WALK, I CAN PICK UP AN UMBRELLA FOR YOU AT HOME.
THE–
THE BANNER!!!
HUH?
I HAVE TO GO BACK TO SCHOOL! THE BANNER!!!
THE BANNER?
SORRY, WOULD YOU MIND HOLDING ON TO MY STUFF FOR ME?

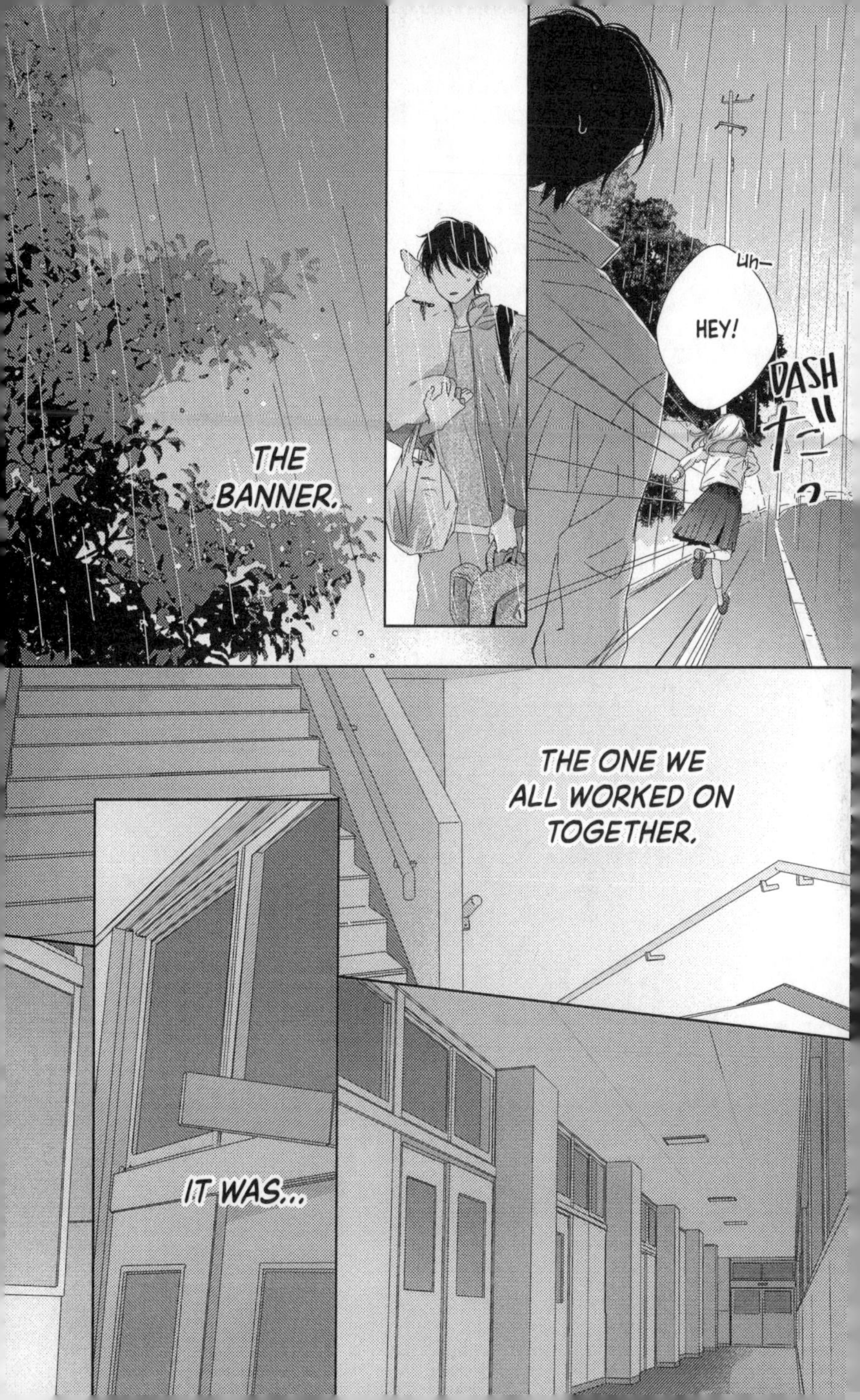
uh—
HEY!
DASH
THE BANNER.
THE ONE WE ALL WORKED ON TOGETHER.
IT WAS...

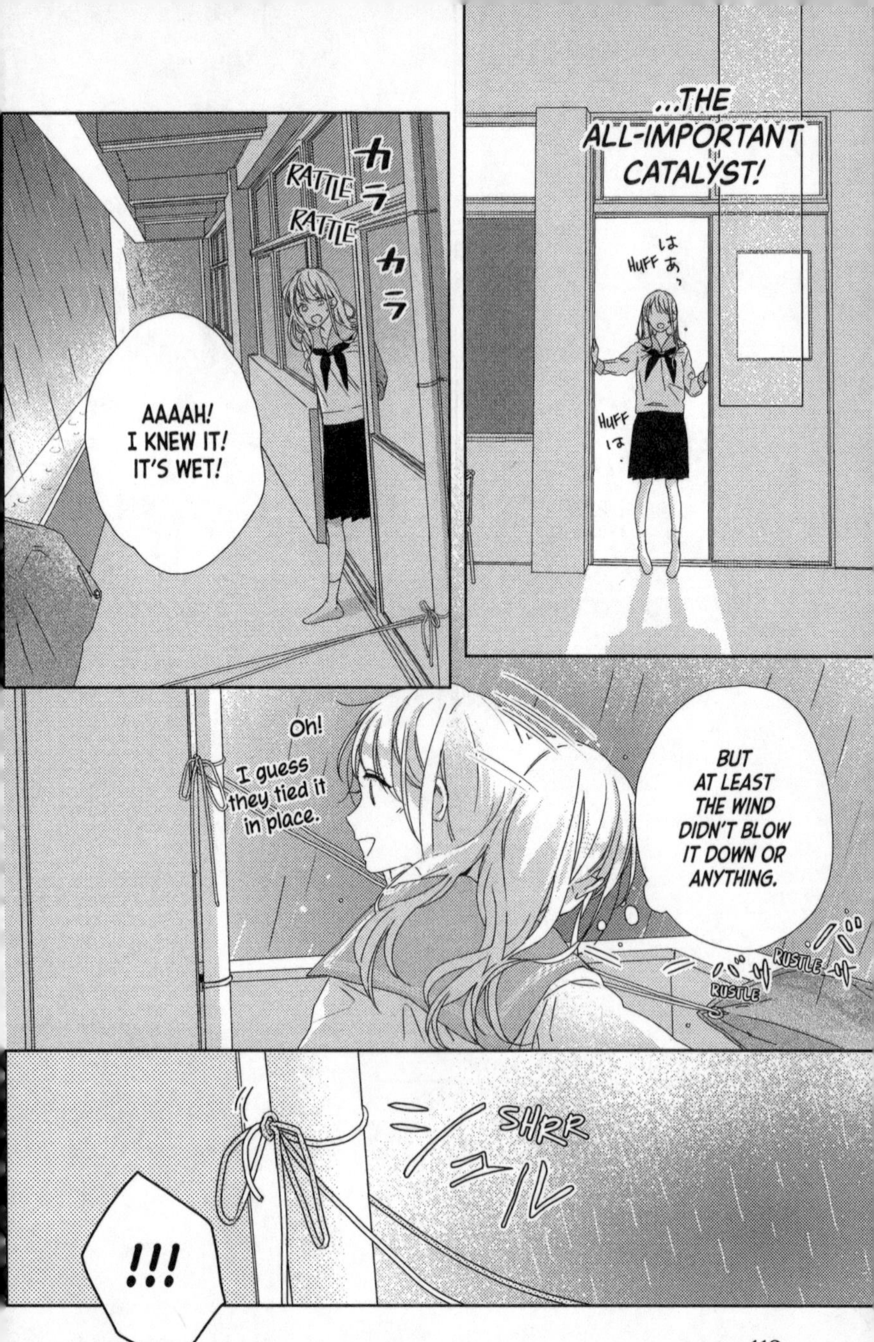
...THE ALL-IMPORTANT CATALYST!
HUFF はあ、
HUFF は.
カラ RATTLE
カラ RATTLE
AAAAH! I KNEW IT! IT'S WET!
BUT AT LEAST THE WIND DIDN'T BLOW IT DOWN OR ANYTHING.
バサ RUSTLE
バサ RUSTLE
Oh!
I guess they tied it in place.
シュル SHRR
!!!

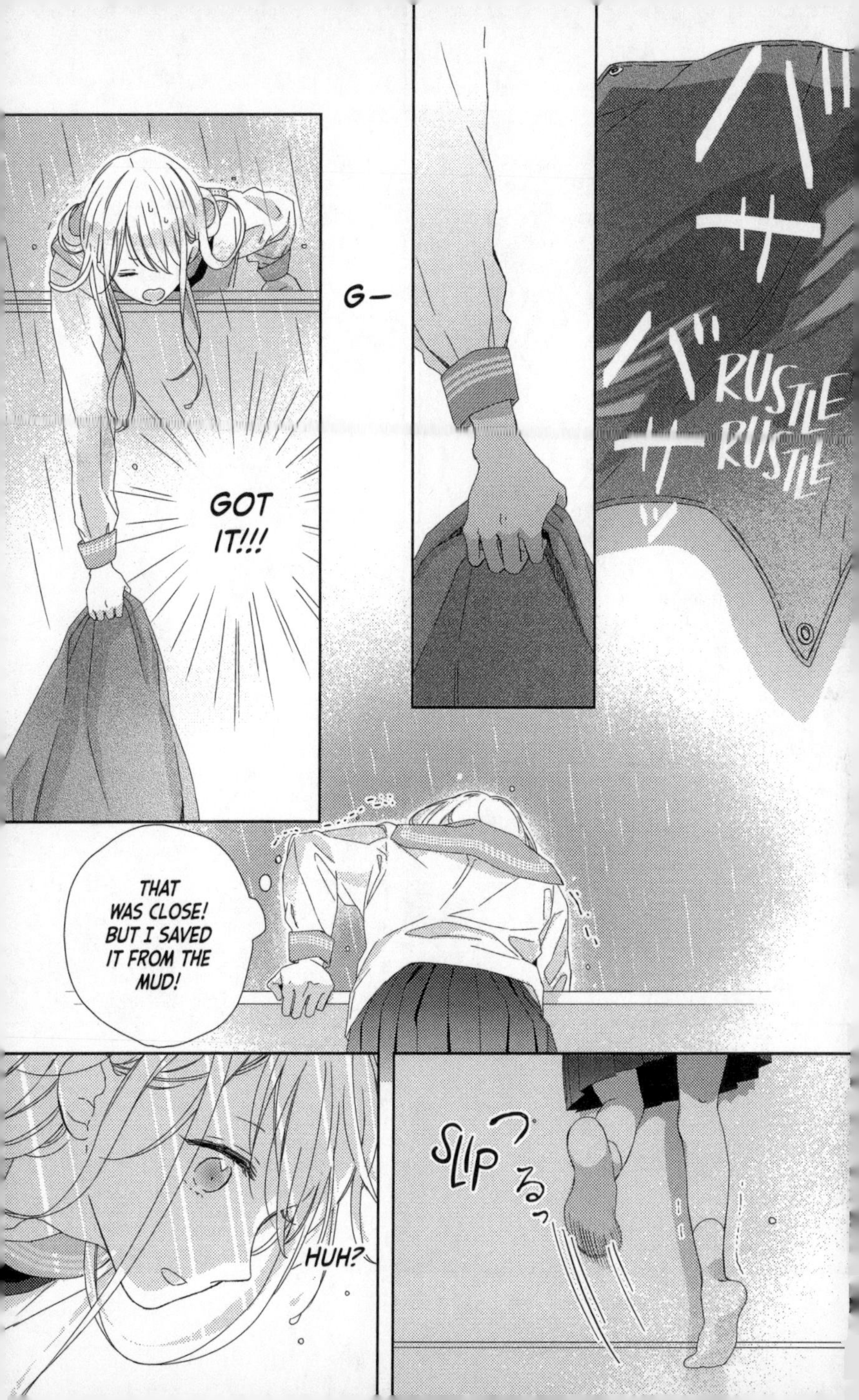
RUSTLE RUSTLE
G—
GOT IT!!!
THAT WAS CLOSE! BUT I SAVED IT FROM THE MUD!
SLIP
HUH?

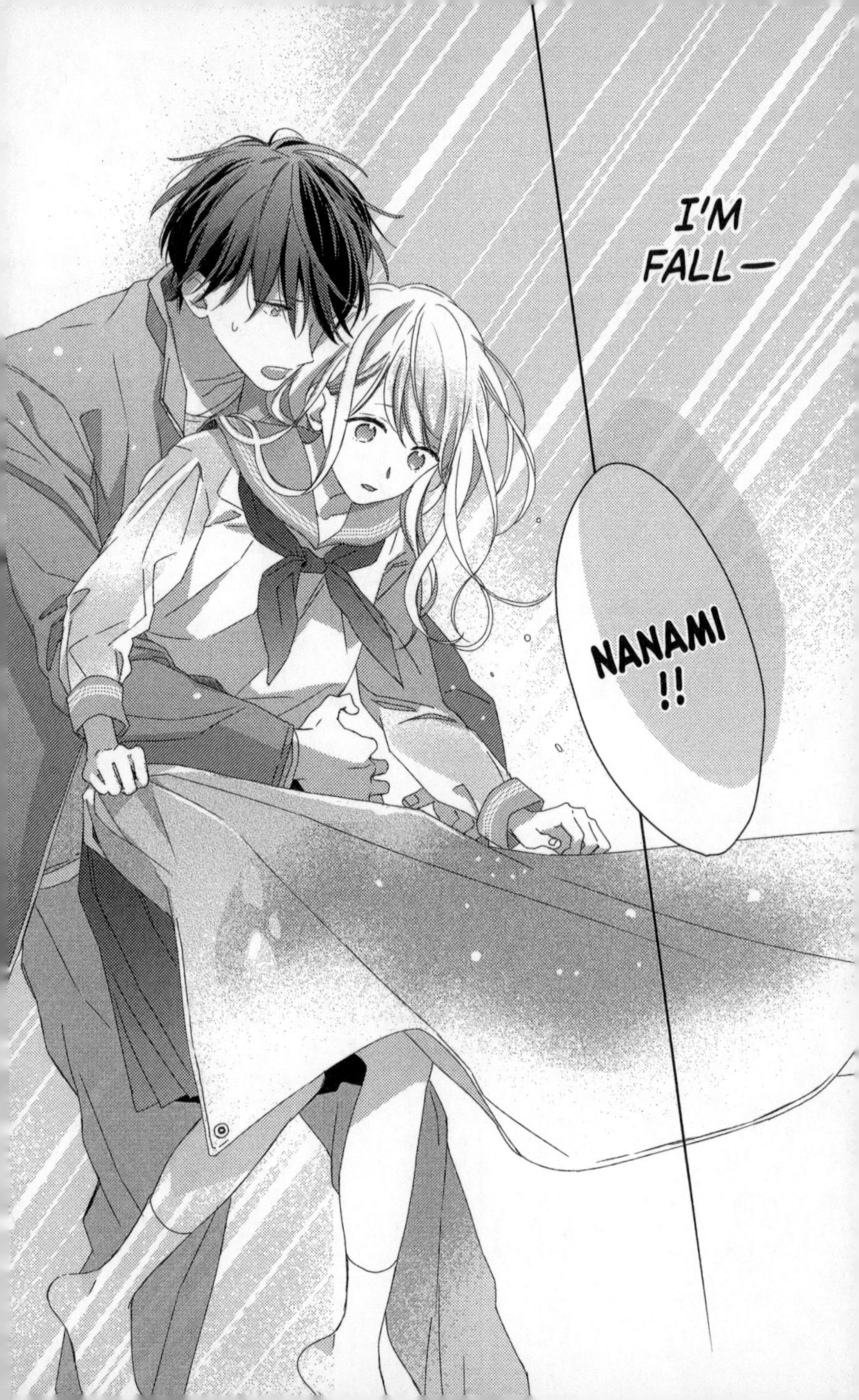
I'M FALL—
NANAMI !!

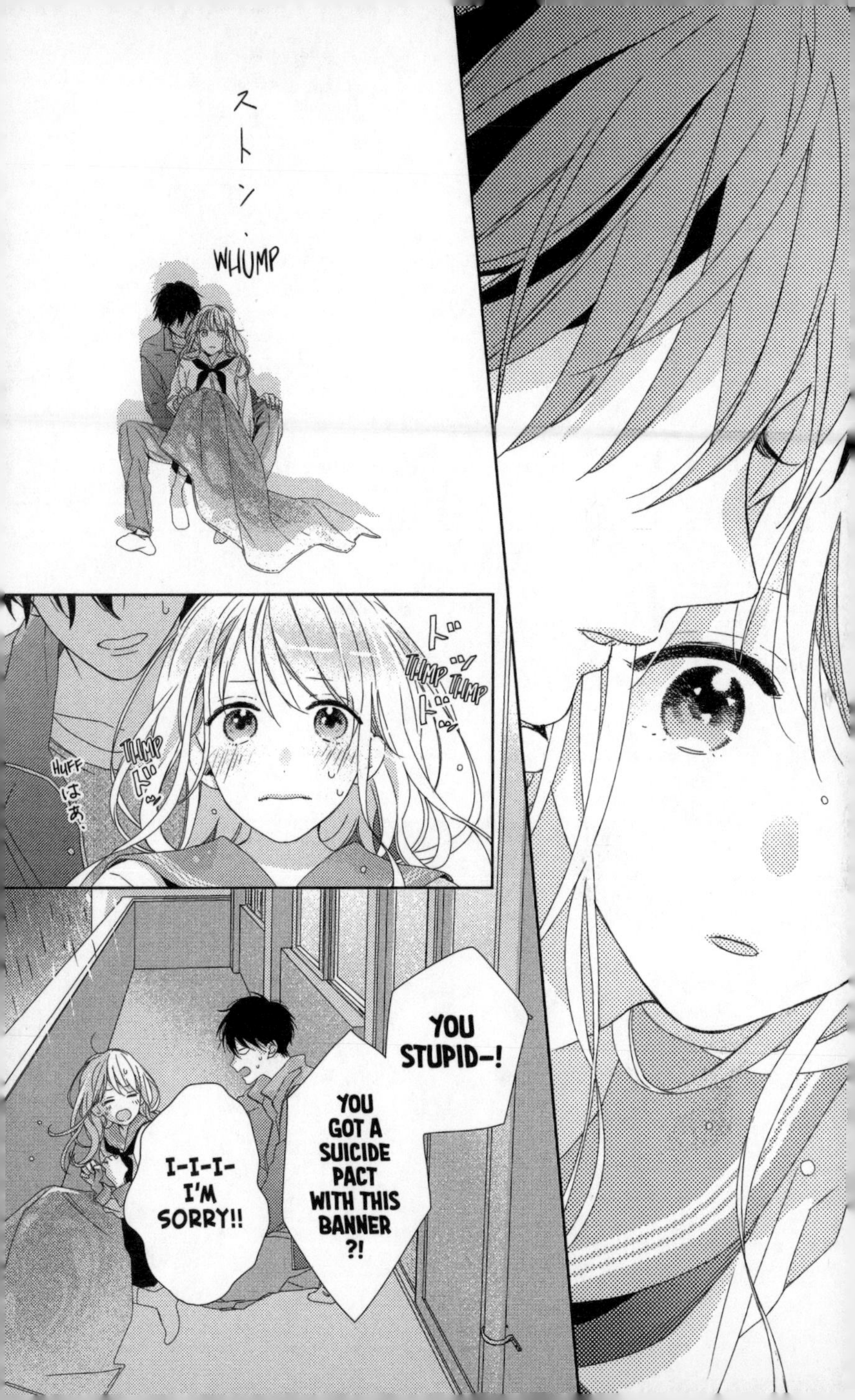
ストン
WHUMP
ドッ
THMP
ドッ
THMP
THMP
ドッ
HUFF
はぁ
YOU STUPID—!
YOU GOT A SUICIDE PACT WITH THIS BANNER?!
I-I-I- I'M SORRY!!

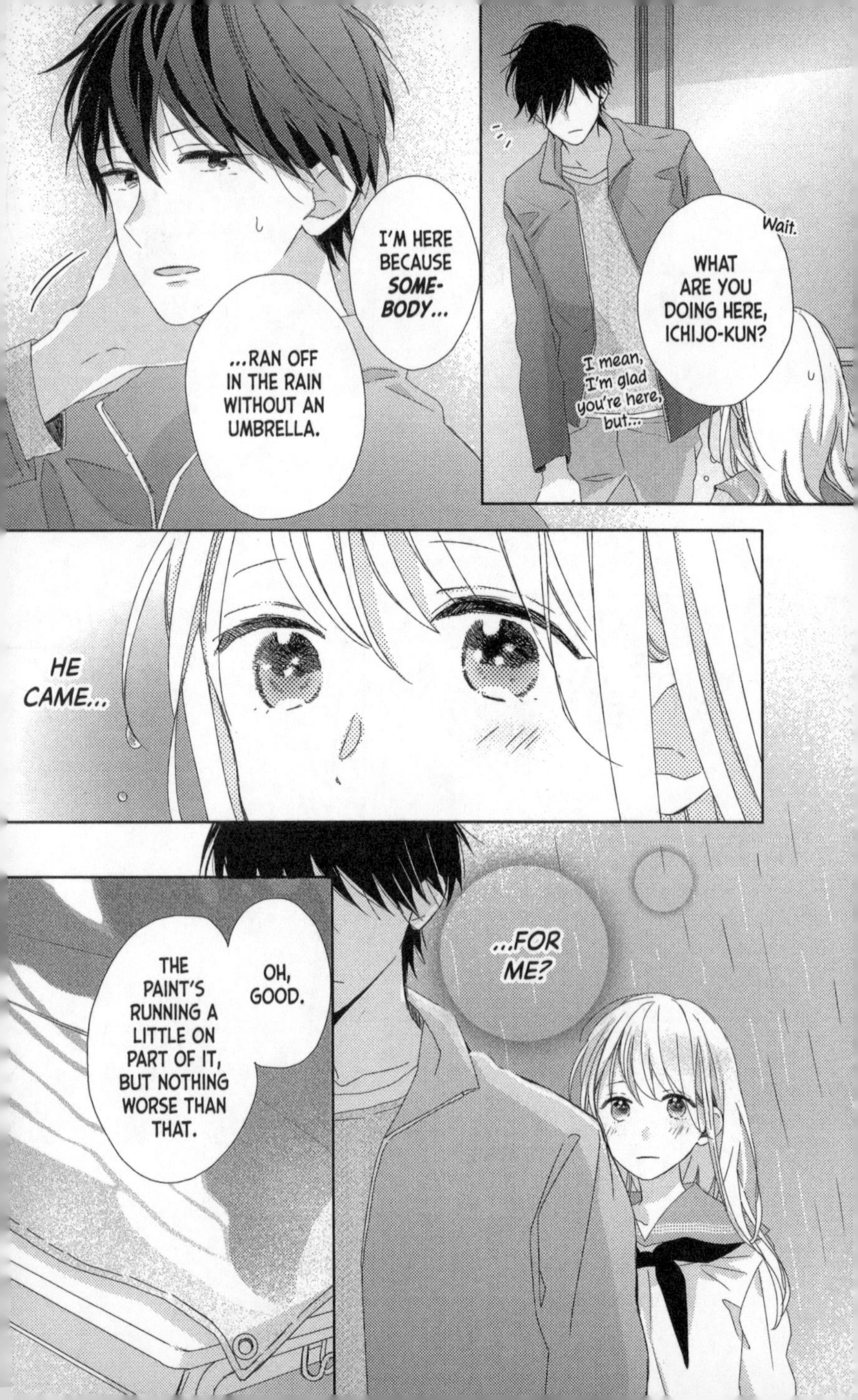
Wait.
WHAT ARE YOU DOING HERE, ICHIJO-KUN?
I mean, I'm glad you're here, but...
I'M HERE BECAUSE SOME-BODY...
...RAN OFF IN THE RAIN WITHOUT AN UMBRELLA.
HE CAME...
...FOR ME?
OH, GOOD.
THE PAINT'S RUNNING A LITTLE ON PART OF IT, BUT NOTHING WORSE THAN THAT.

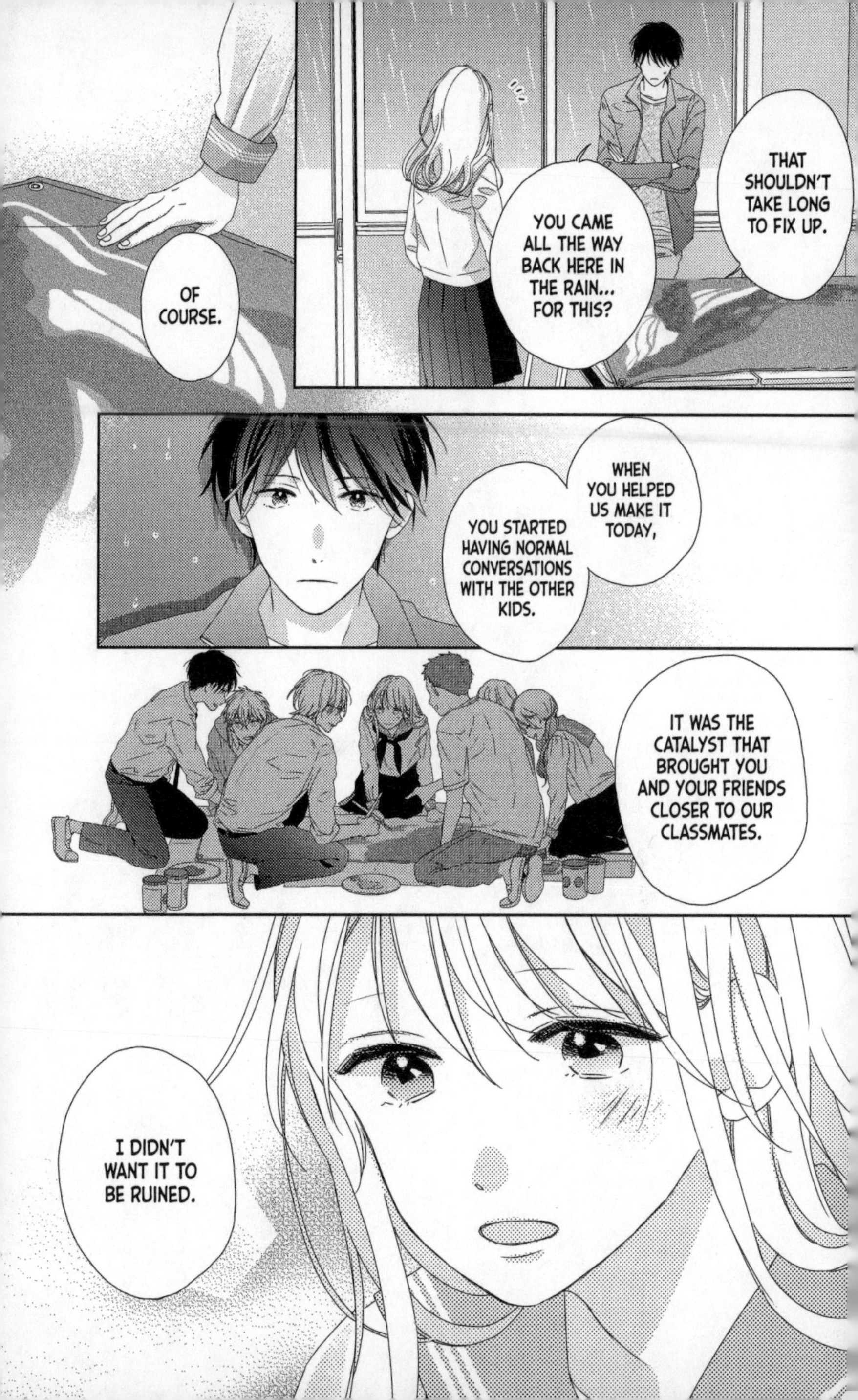
THAT SHOULDN'T TAKE LONG TO FIX UP.
YOU CAME ALL THE WAY BACK HERE IN THE RAIN... FOR THIS?
OF COURSE.
WHEN YOU HELPED US MAKE IT TODAY,
YOU STARTED HAVING NORMAL CONVERSATIONS WITH THE OTHER KIDS.
IT WAS THE CATALYST THAT BROUGHT YOU AND YOUR FRIENDS CLOSER TO OUR CLASSMATES.
I DIDN'T WANT IT TO BE RUINED.

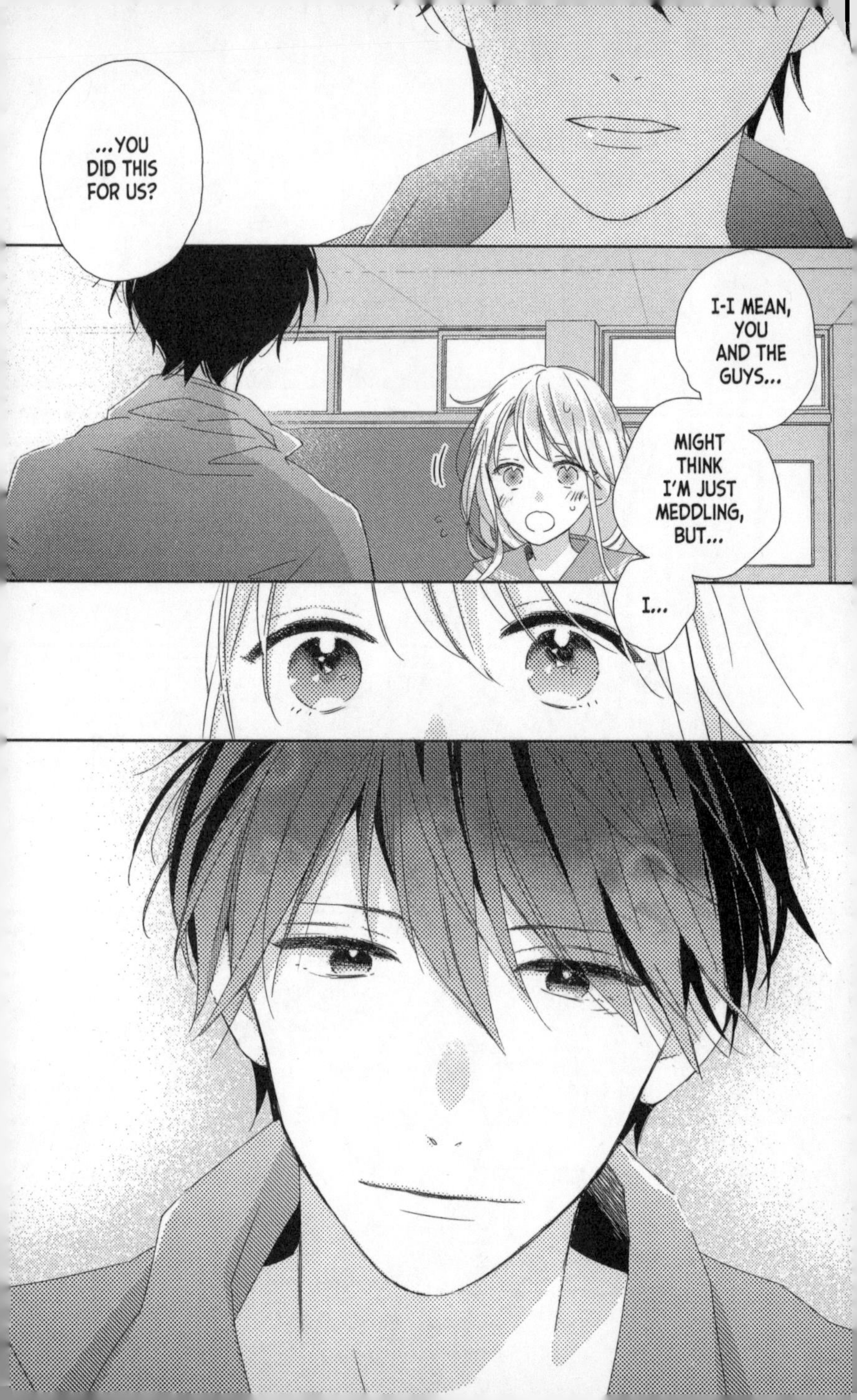
...YOU DID THIS FOR US?
I-I MEAN, YOU AND THE GUYS...
MIGHT THINK I'M JUST MEDDLING, BUT...
I...

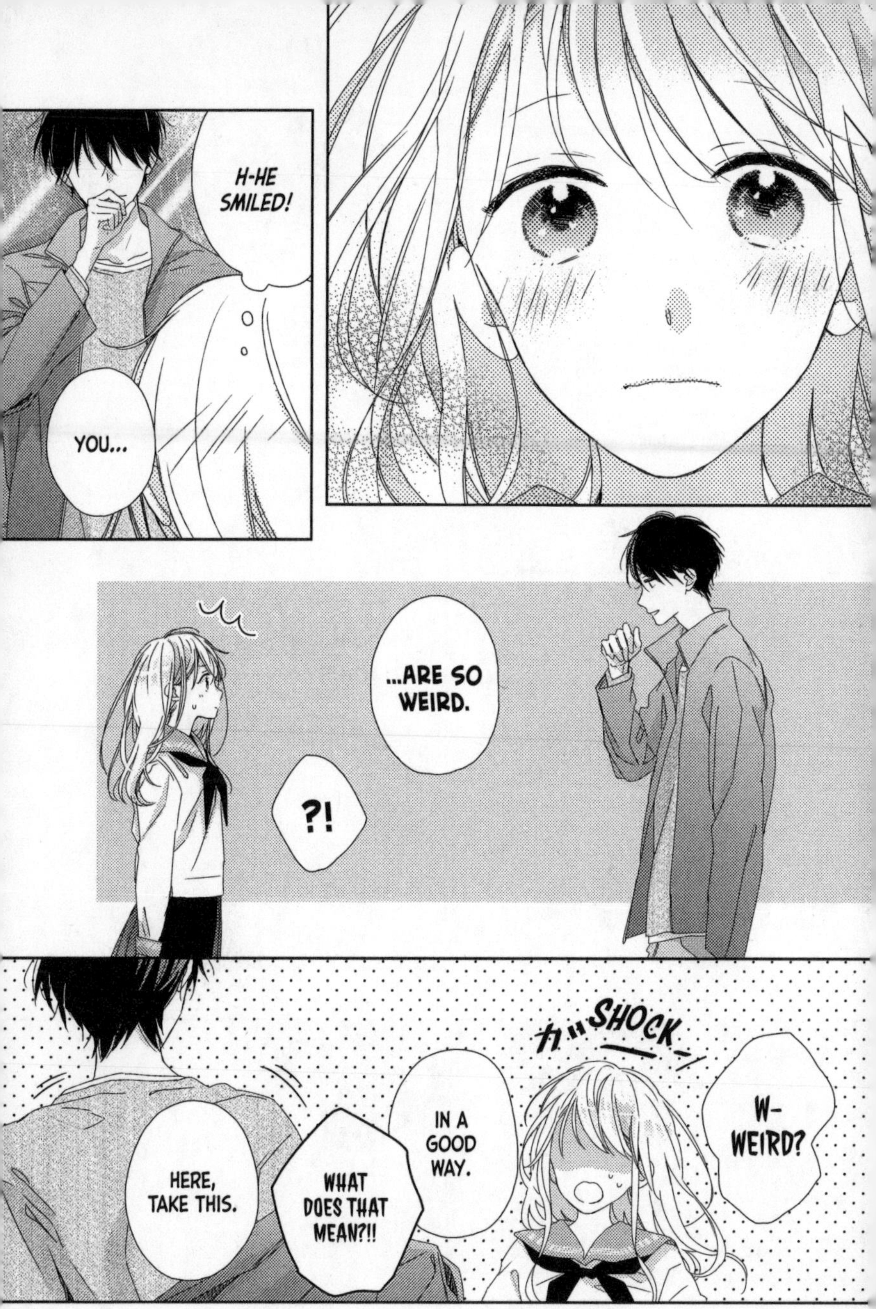
H-HE SMILED!
YOU...
...ARE SO WEIRD.
?!
SHOCK
W-WEIRD?
IN A GOOD WAY.
WHAT DOES THAT MEAN?!!
HERE, TAKE THIS.

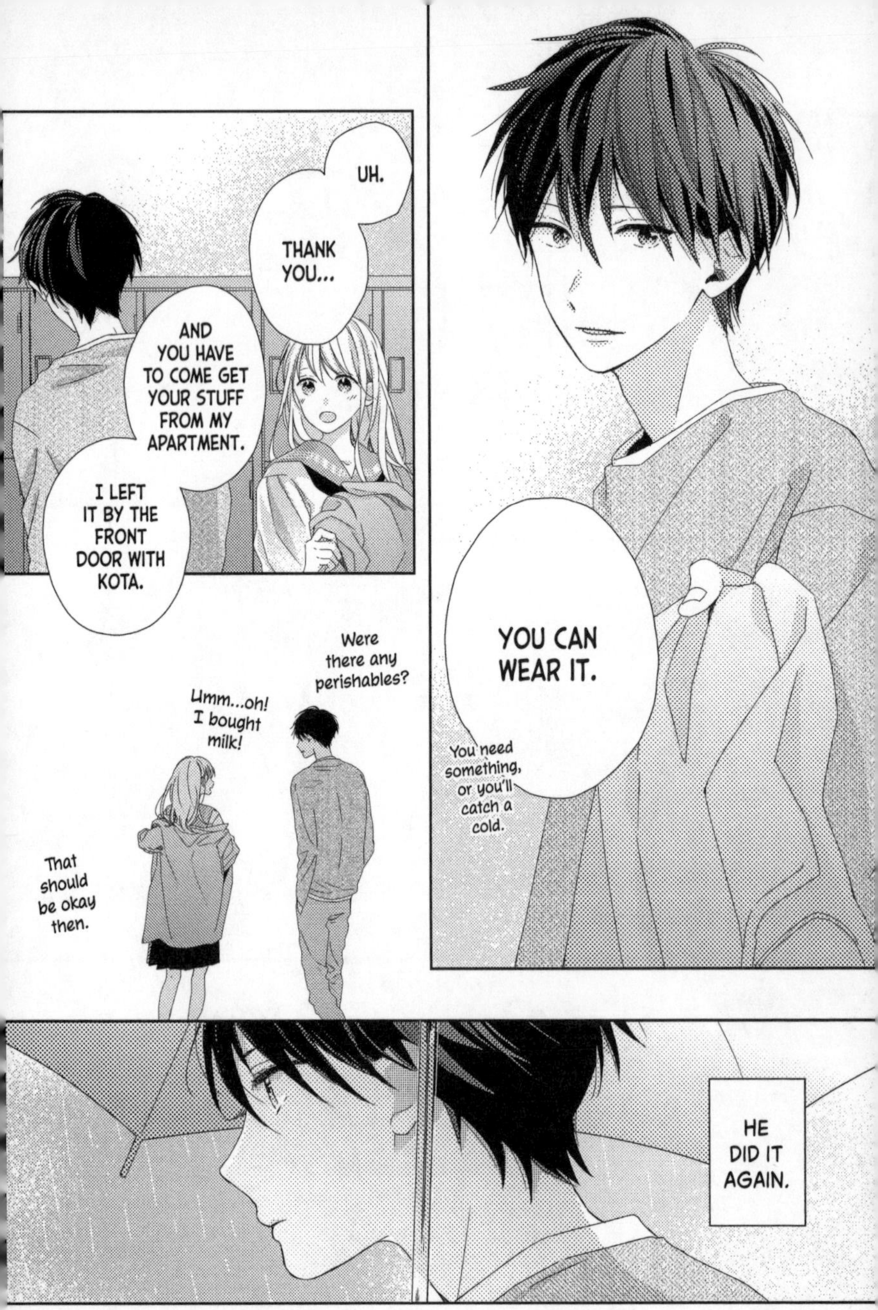
YOU CAN WEAR IT.
You need something, or you'll catch a cold.
UH.
THANK YOU...
AND YOU HAVE TO COME GET YOUR STUFF FROM MY APARTMENT.
I LEFT IT BY THE FRONT DOOR WITH KOTA.
Were there any perishables?
Umm...oh! I bought milk!
That should be okay then.
HE DID IT AGAIN.

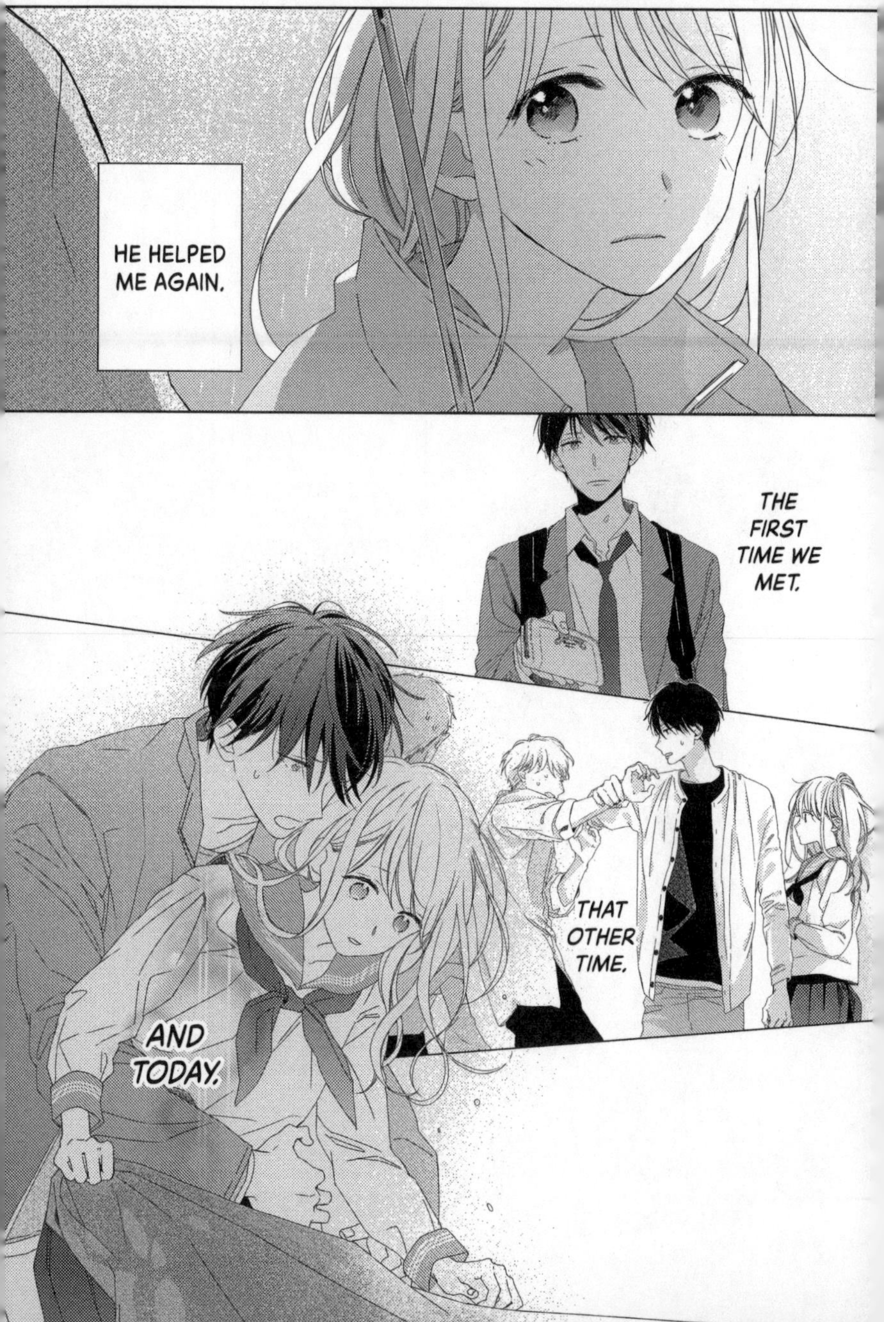
HE HELPED ME AGAIN.
THE FIRST TIME WE MET.
THAT OTHER TIME.
AND TODAY.

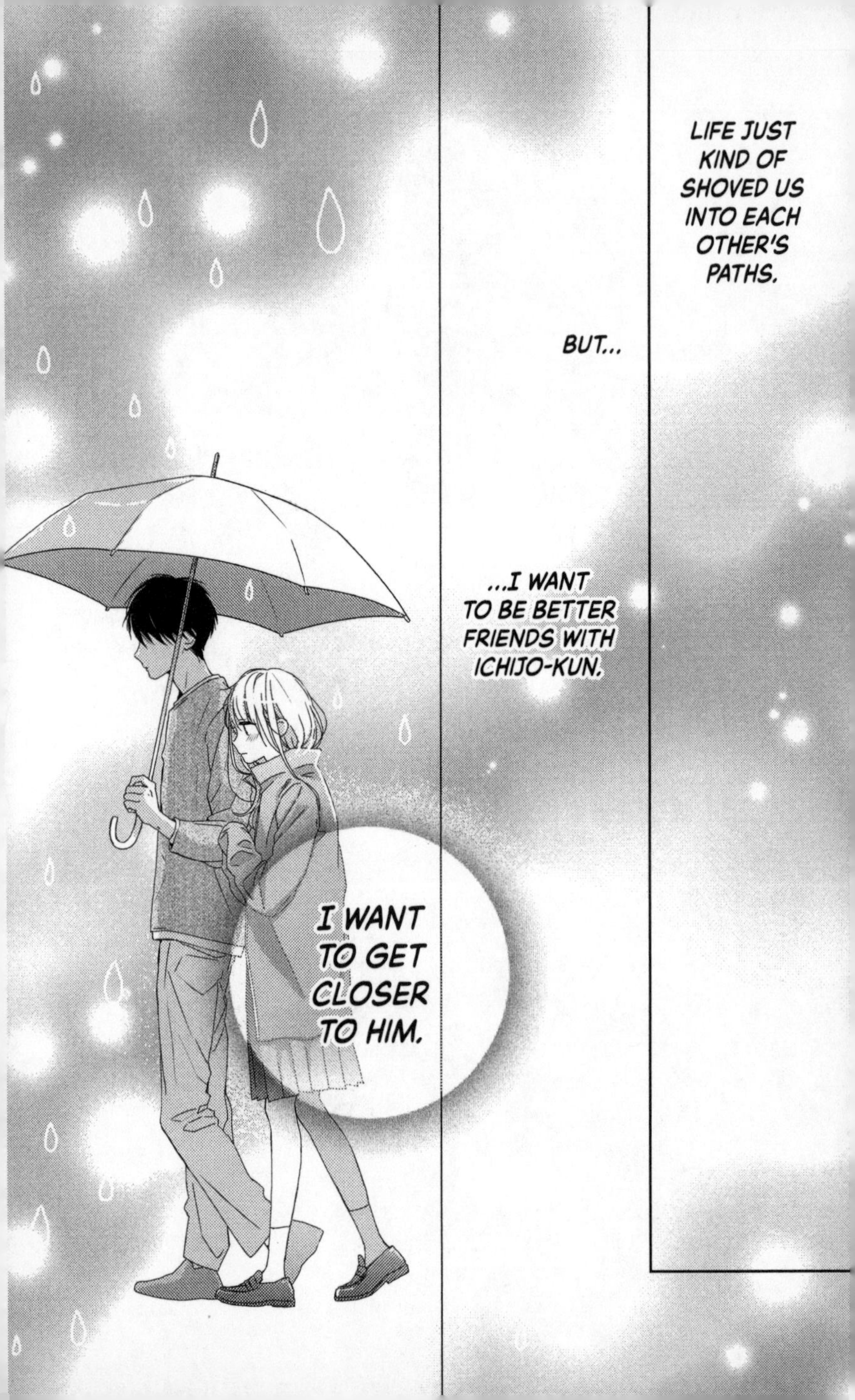
LIFE JUST KIND OF SHOVED US INTO EACH OTHER'S PATHS.
BUT...
...I WANT TO BE BETTER FRIENDS WITH ICHIJO-KUN.
I WANT TO GET CLOSER TO HIM.

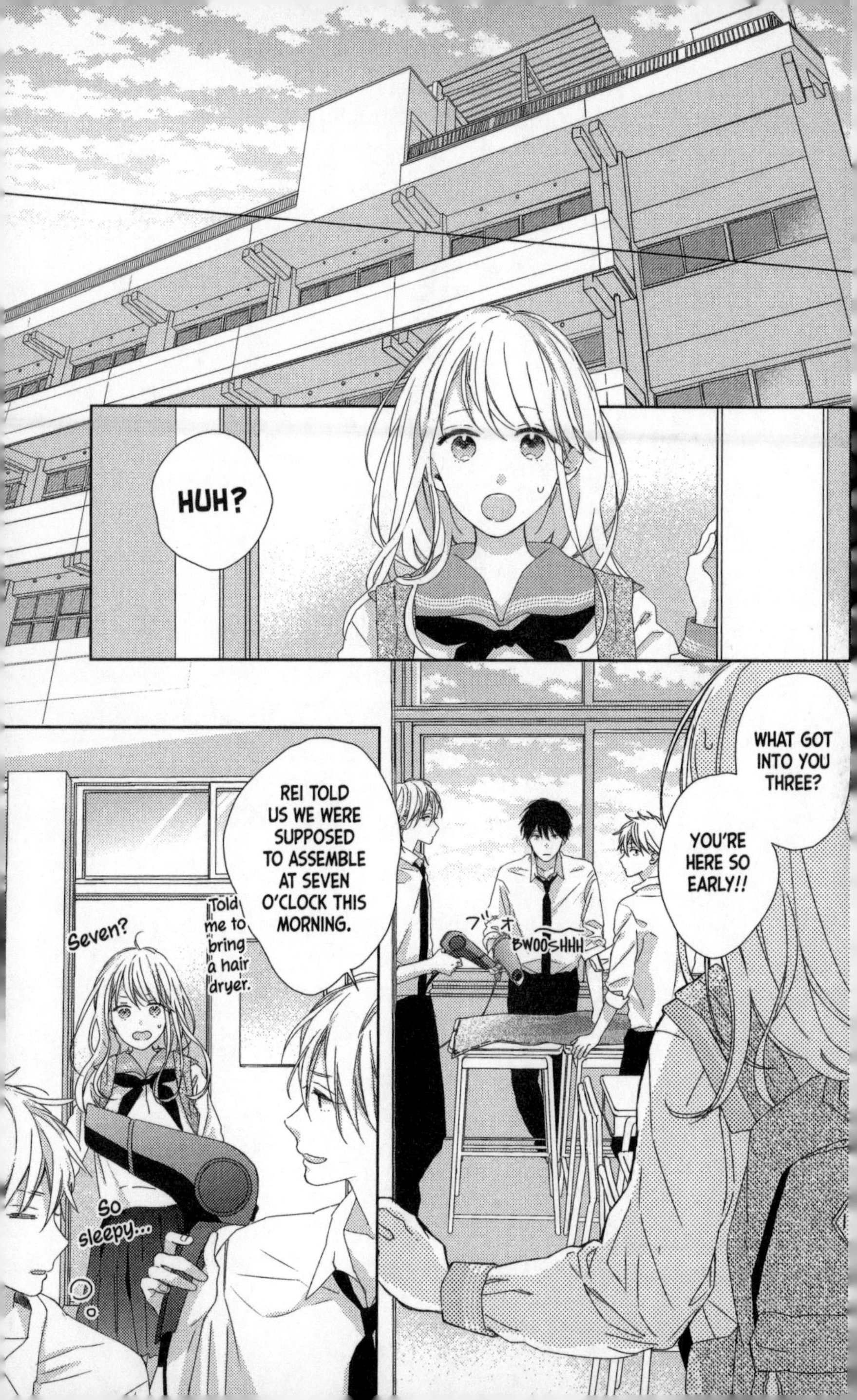
HUH?
WHAT GOT INTO YOU THREE?
YOU'RE HERE SO EARLY!!
ブォ
BWOOSHHH
REI TOLD US WE WERE SUPPOSED TO ASSEMBLE AT SEVEN O'CLOCK THIS MORNING.
Told me to bring a hair dryer.
Seven?
So sleepy...

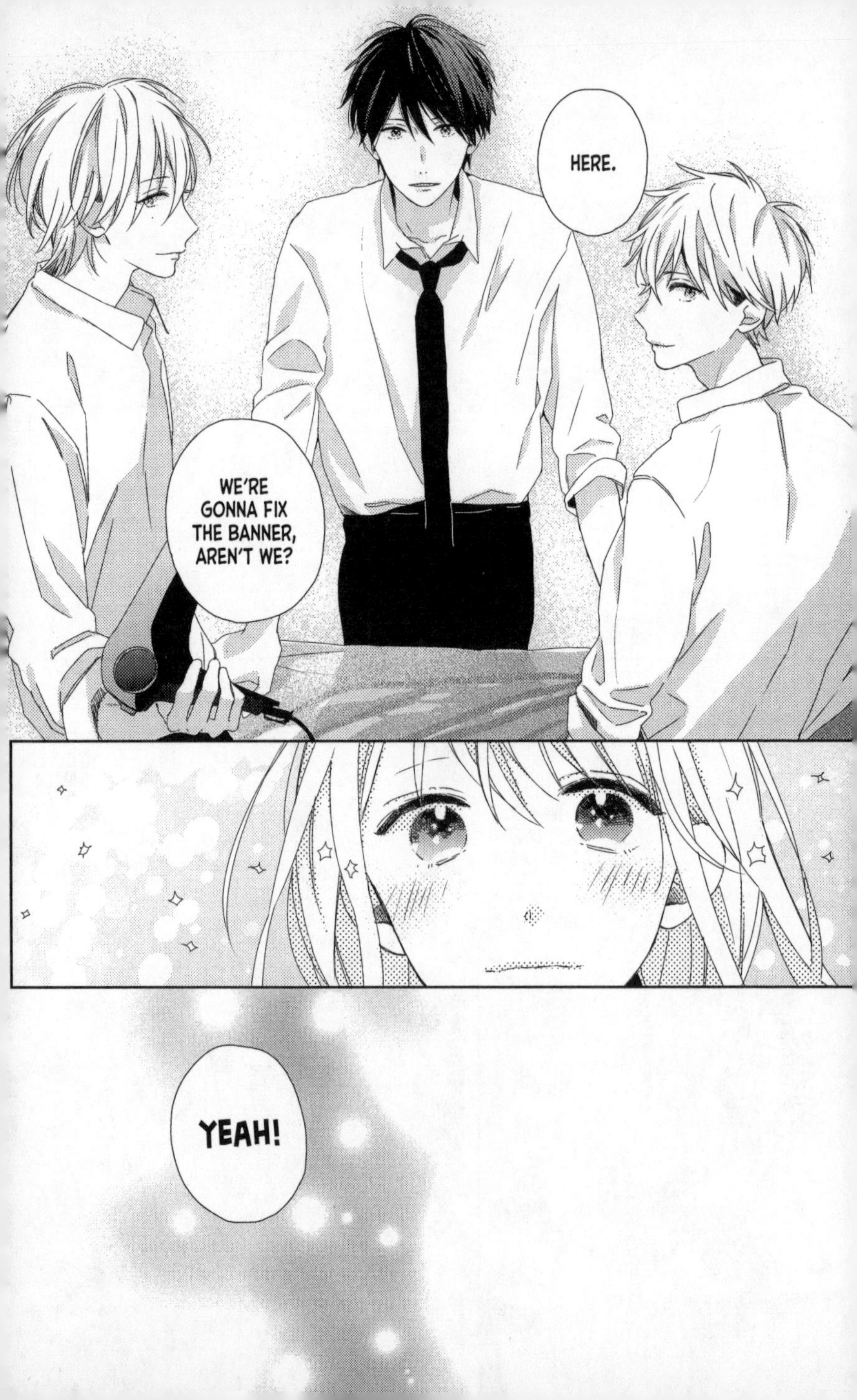
HERE.
WE'RE GONNA FIX THE BANNER, AREN'T WE?
YEAH!

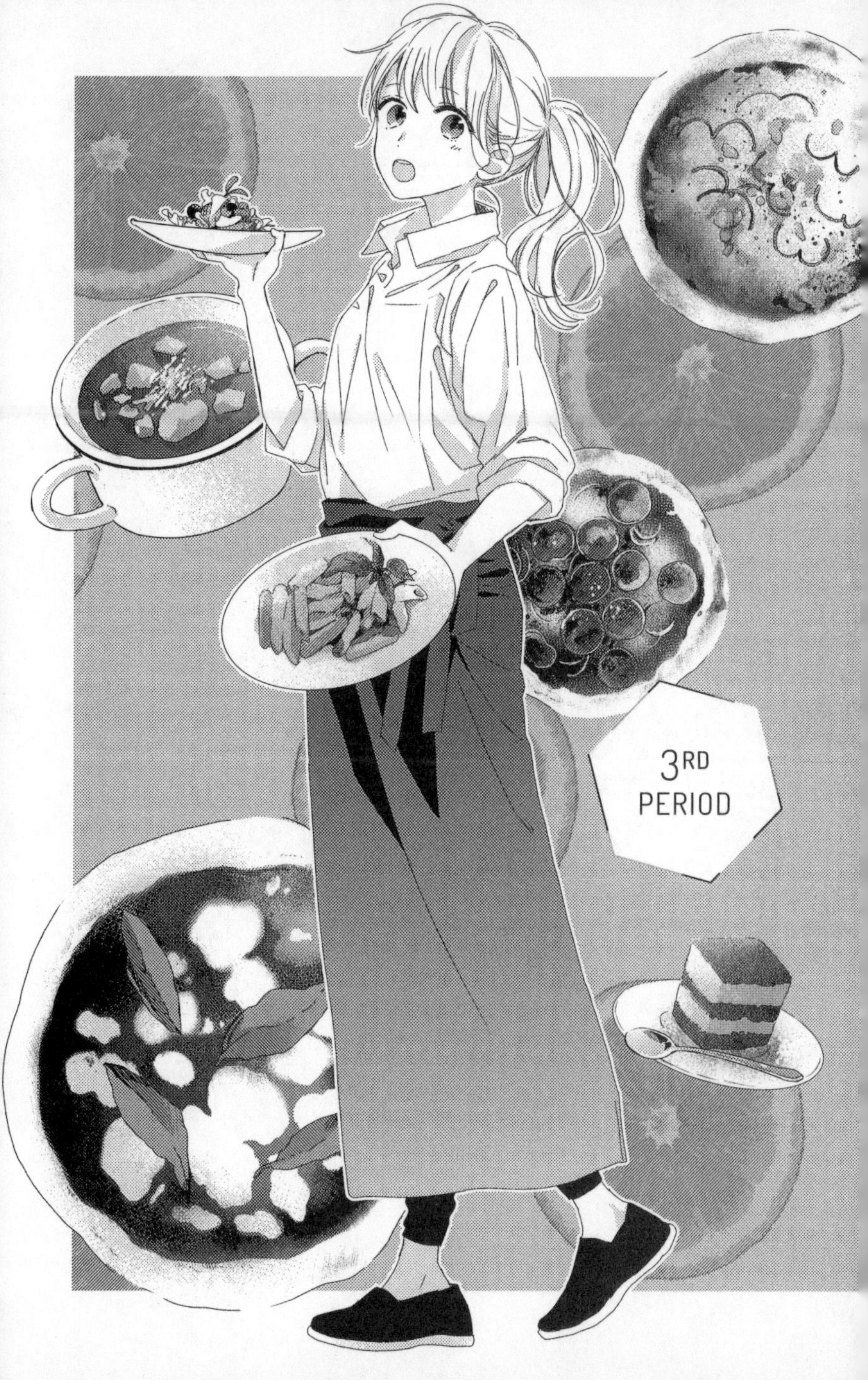
3RD
PERIOD

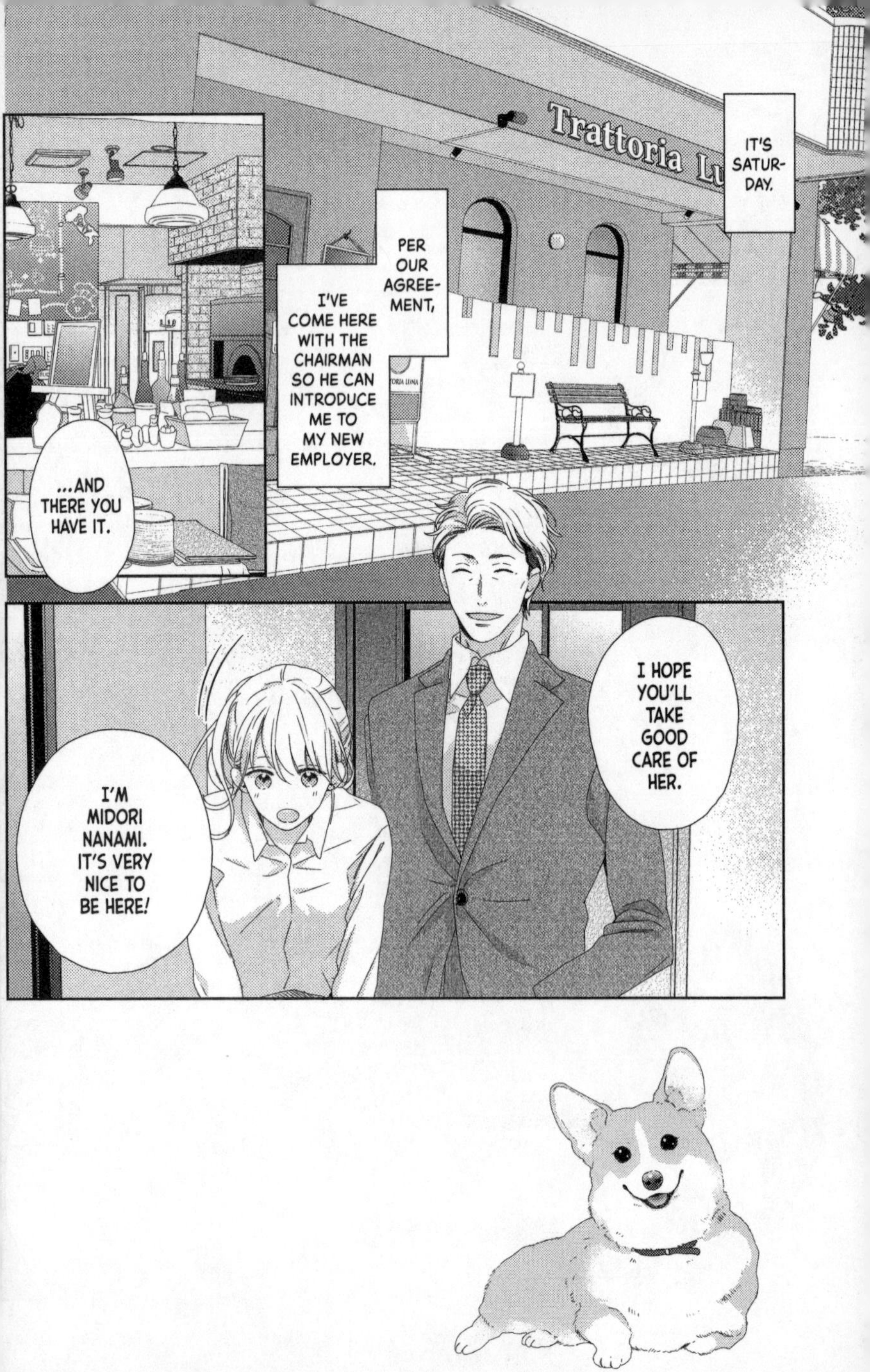
IT'S SATURDAY.
PER OUR AGREEMENT,
I'VE COME HERE WITH THE CHAIRMAN SO HE CAN INTRODUCE ME TO MY NEW EMPLOYER.
...AND THERE YOU HAVE IT.
I HOPE YOU'LL TAKE GOOD CARE OF HER.
I'M MIDORI NANAMI. IT'S VERY NICE TO BE HERE!

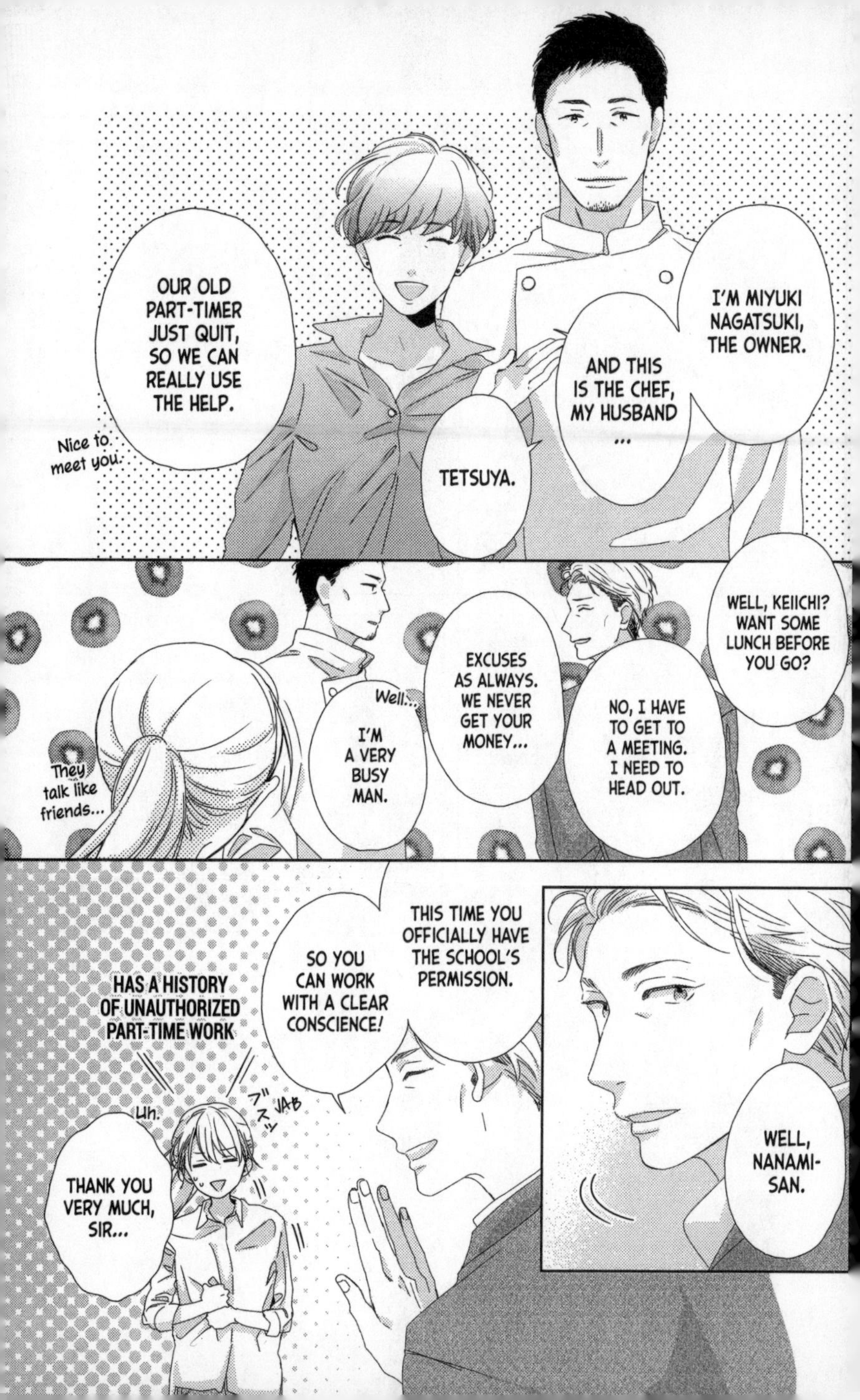
I'M MIYUKI NAGATSUKI, THE OWNER.
AND THIS IS THE CHEF, MY HUSBAND ...
TETSUYA.
OUR OLD PART-TIMER JUST QUIT, SO WE CAN REALLY USE THE HELP.
Nice to meet you.
WELL, KEIICHI? WANT SOME LUNCH BEFORE YOU GO?
NO, I HAVE TO GET TO A MEETING. I NEED TO HEAD OUT.
EXCUSES AS ALWAYS. WE NEVER GET YOUR MONEY...
Well...
I'M A VERY BUSY MAN.
They talk like friends...
WELL, NANAMI-SAN.
THIS TIME YOU OFFICIALLY HAVE THE SCHOOL'S PERMISSION.
SO YOU CAN WORK WITH A CLEAR CONSCIENCE!
HAS A HISTORY OF UNAUTHORIZED PART-TIME WORK
ブスッ JAB
Uh.
THANK YOU VERY MUCH, SIR...

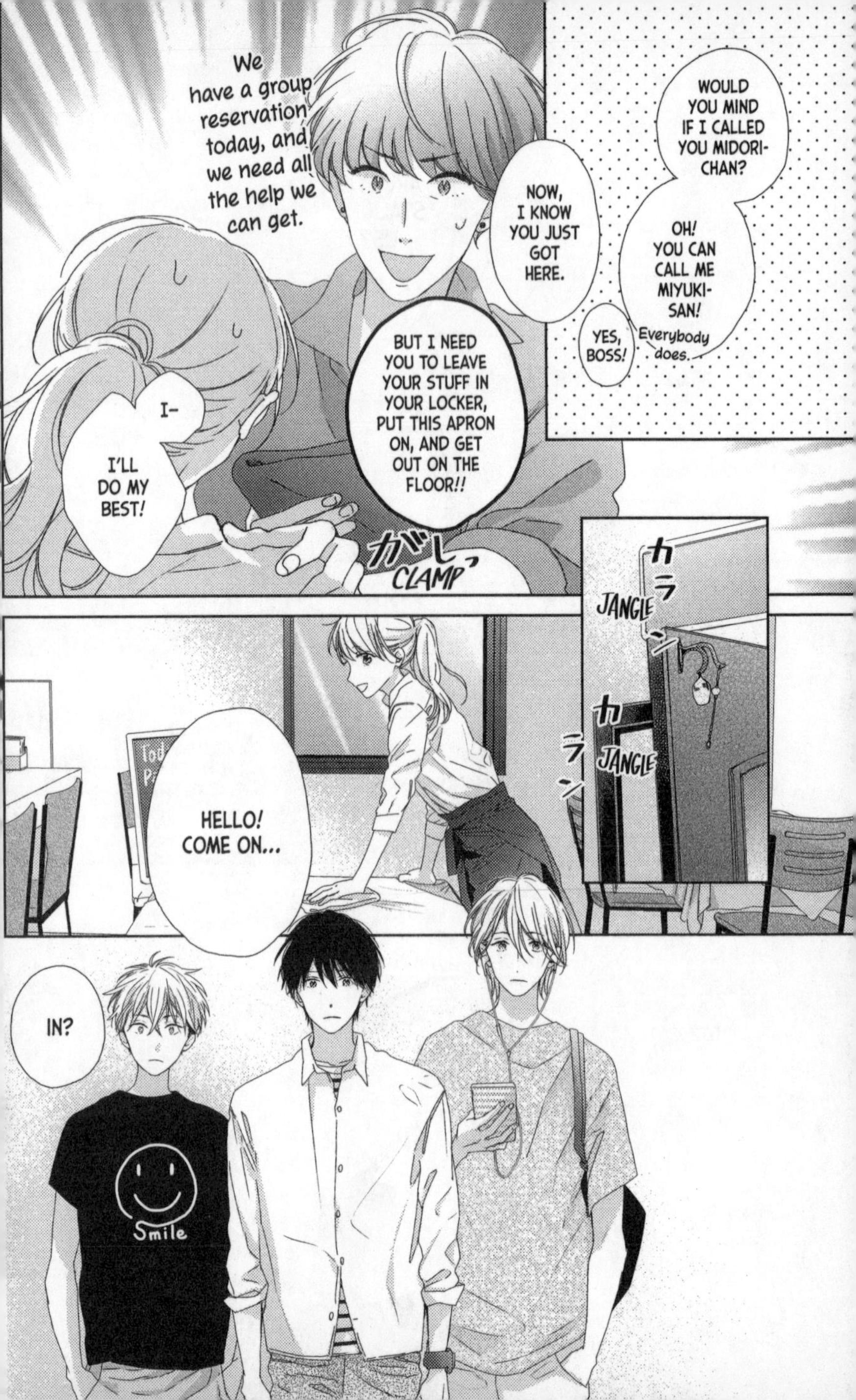
WOULD YOU MIND IF I CALLED YOU MIDORI-CHAN?
OH! YOU CAN CALL ME MIYUKI-SAN!
Everybody does.
YES, BOSS!
NOW, I KNOW YOU JUST GOT HERE.
We have a group reservation today, and we need all the help we can get.
BUT I NEED YOU TO LEAVE YOUR STUFF IN YOUR LOCKER, PUT THIS APRON ON, AND GET OUT ON THE FLOOR!!
I-
I'LL DO MY BEST!
がしっ
CLAMP
カラン
JANGLE
カラン
JANGLE
HELLO! COME ON...
IN?
Smile

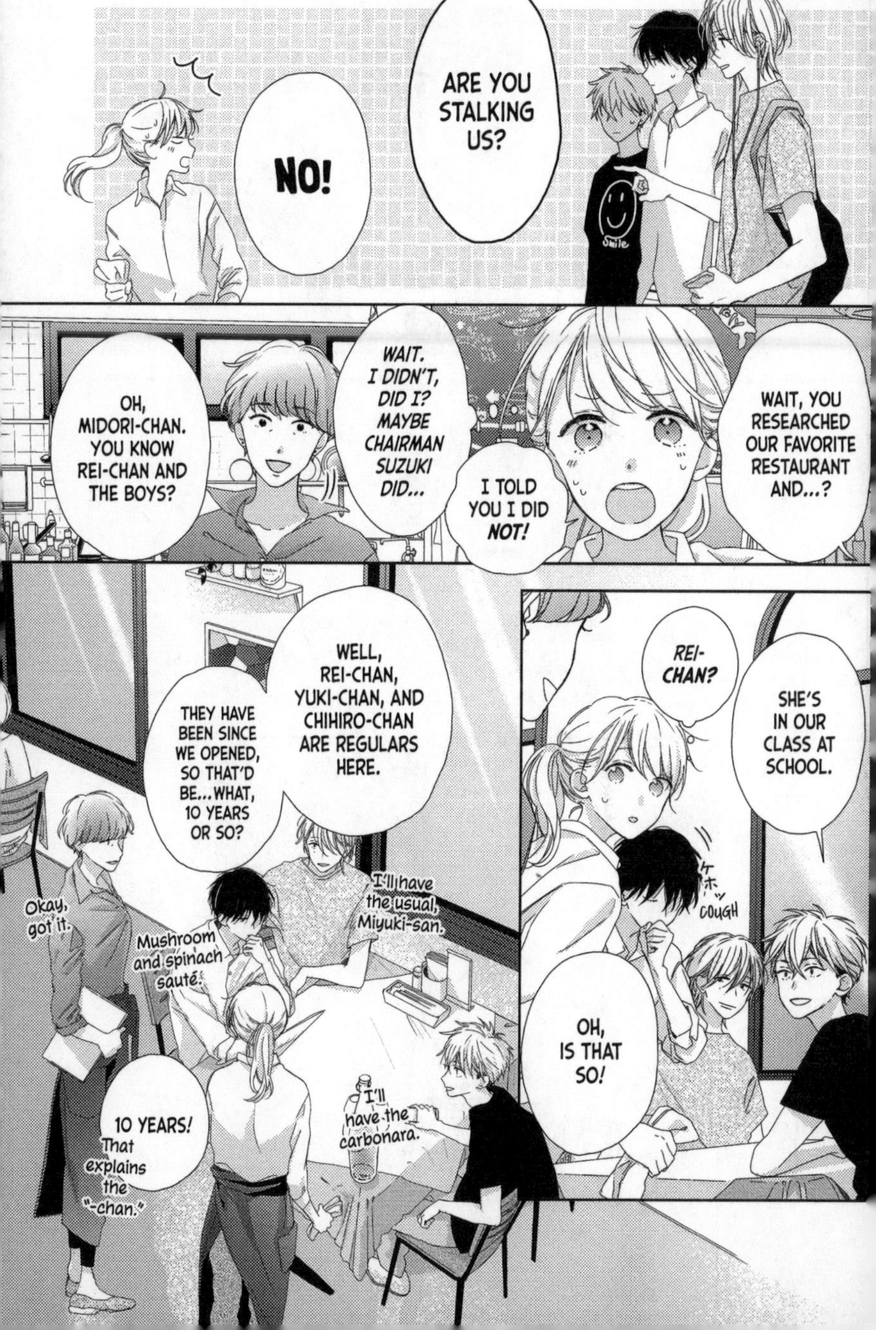
ARE YOU STALKING US?
NO!
WAIT, YOU RESEARCHED OUR FAVORITE RESTAURANT AND...?
I TOLD YOU I DID *NOT!*
WAIT. I DIDN'T, DID I? MAYBE CHAIRMAN SUZUKI DID...
OH, MIDORI-CHAN. YOU KNOW REI-CHAN AND THE BOYS?
REI-CHAN?
SHE'S IN OUR CLASS AT SCHOOL.
ケホッ COUGH
OH, IS THAT SO!
WELL, REI-CHAN, YUKI-CHAN, AND CHIHIRO-CHAN ARE REGULARS HERE.
THEY HAVE BEEN SINCE WE OPENED, SO THAT'D BE...WHAT, 10 YEARS OR SO?
I'll have the usual, Miyuki-san.
Mushroom and spinach sauté.
Okay, got it.
I'll have the carbonara.
10 YEARS! That explains the "-chan."

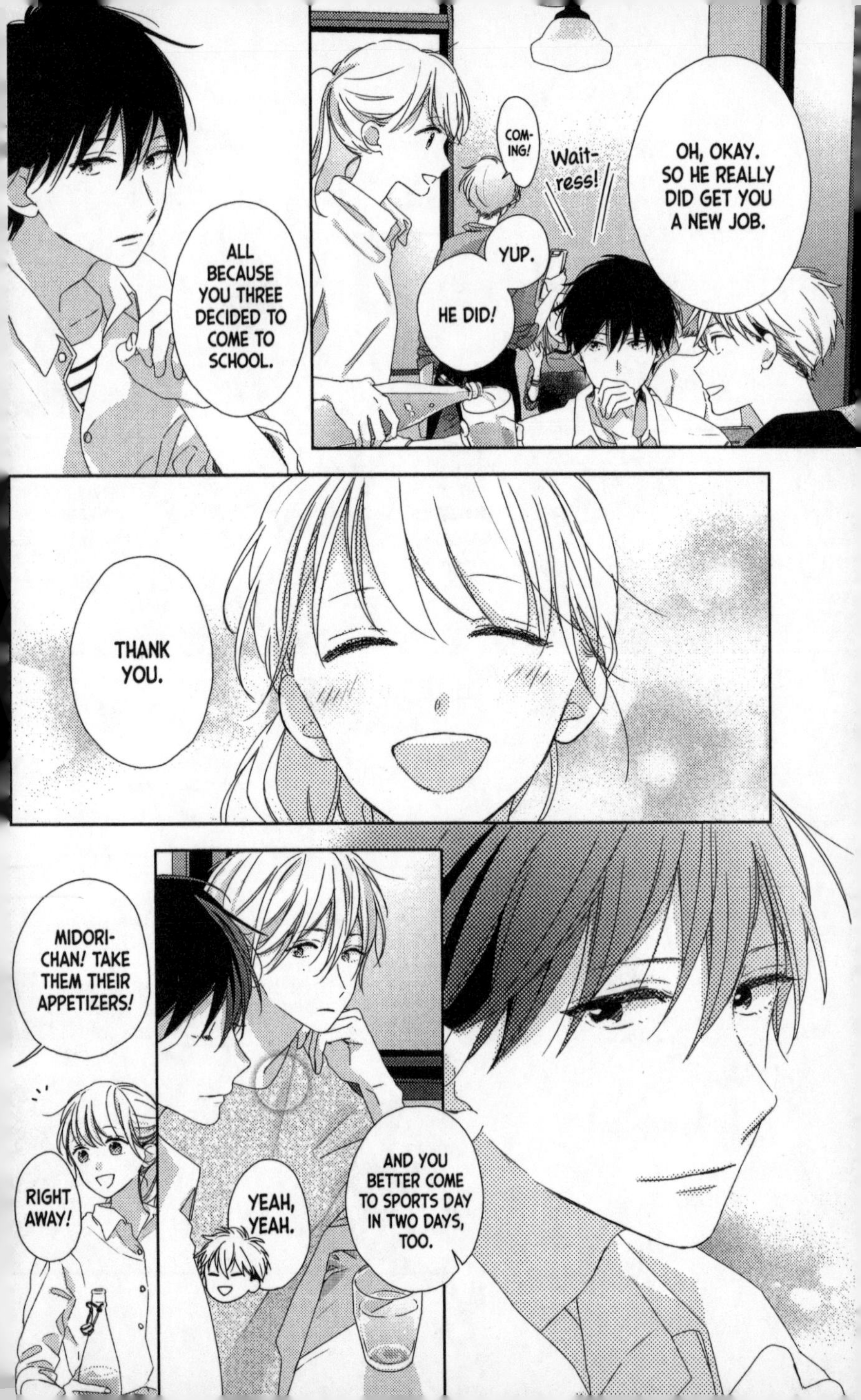
OH, OKAY. SO HE REALLY DID GET YOU A NEW JOB.
Wait-ress!
COM-ING!
YUP.
HE DID!
ALL BECAUSE YOU THREE DECIDED TO COME TO SCHOOL.
THANK YOU.
AND YOU BETTER COME TO SPORTS DAY IN TWO DAYS, TOO.
YEAH, YEAH.
MIDORI-CHAN! TAKE THEM THEIR APPETIZERS!
RIGHT AWAY!

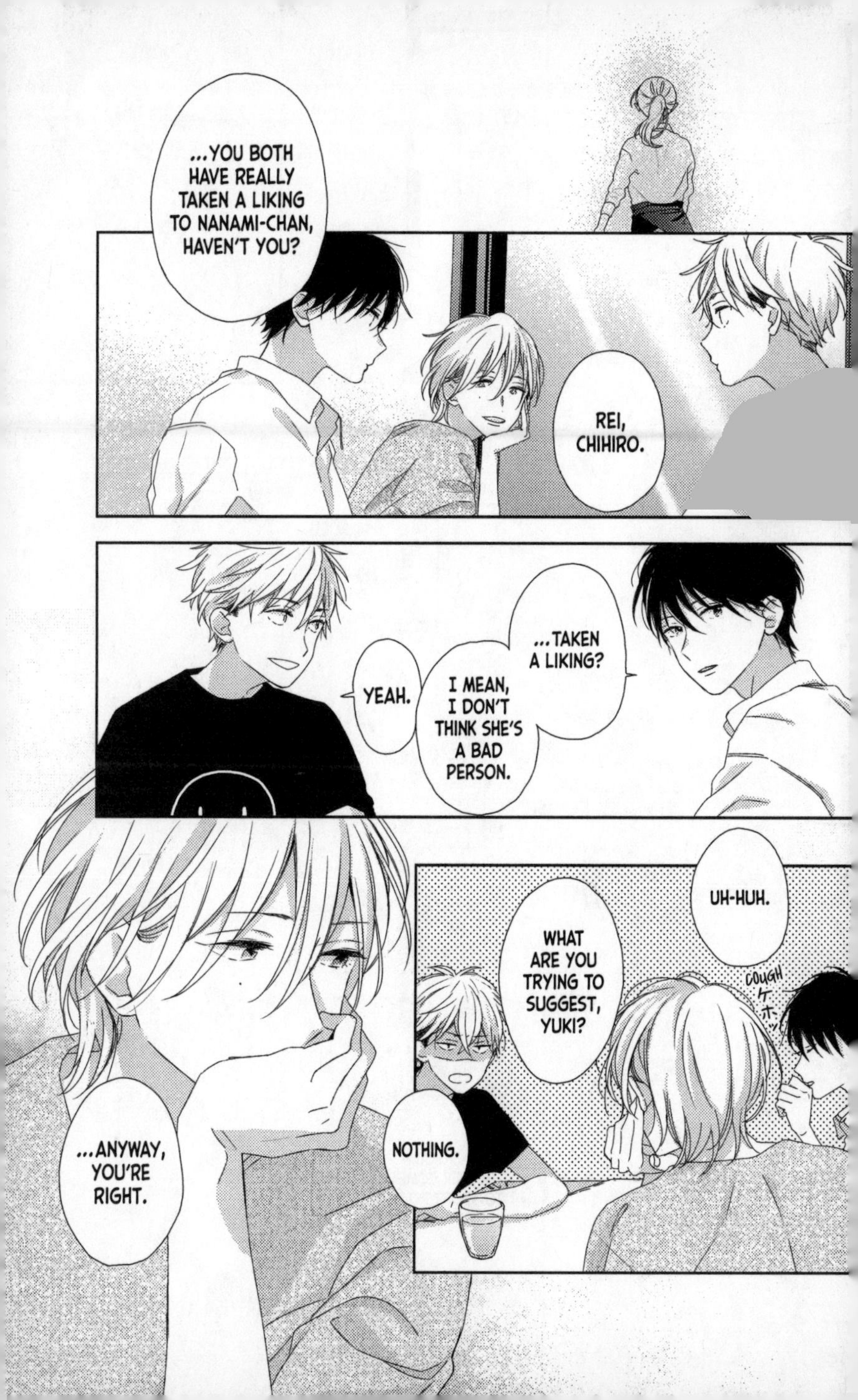
...YOU BOTH HAVE REALLY TAKEN A LIKING TO NANAMI-CHAN, HAVEN'T YOU?
REI, CHIHIRO.
...TAKEN A LIKING?
I MEAN, I DON'T THINK SHE'S A BAD PERSON.
YEAH.
UH-HUH.
WHAT ARE YOU TRYING TO SUGGEST, YUKI?
COUGH
ケホッ
NOTHING.
...ANYWAY, YOU'RE RIGHT.

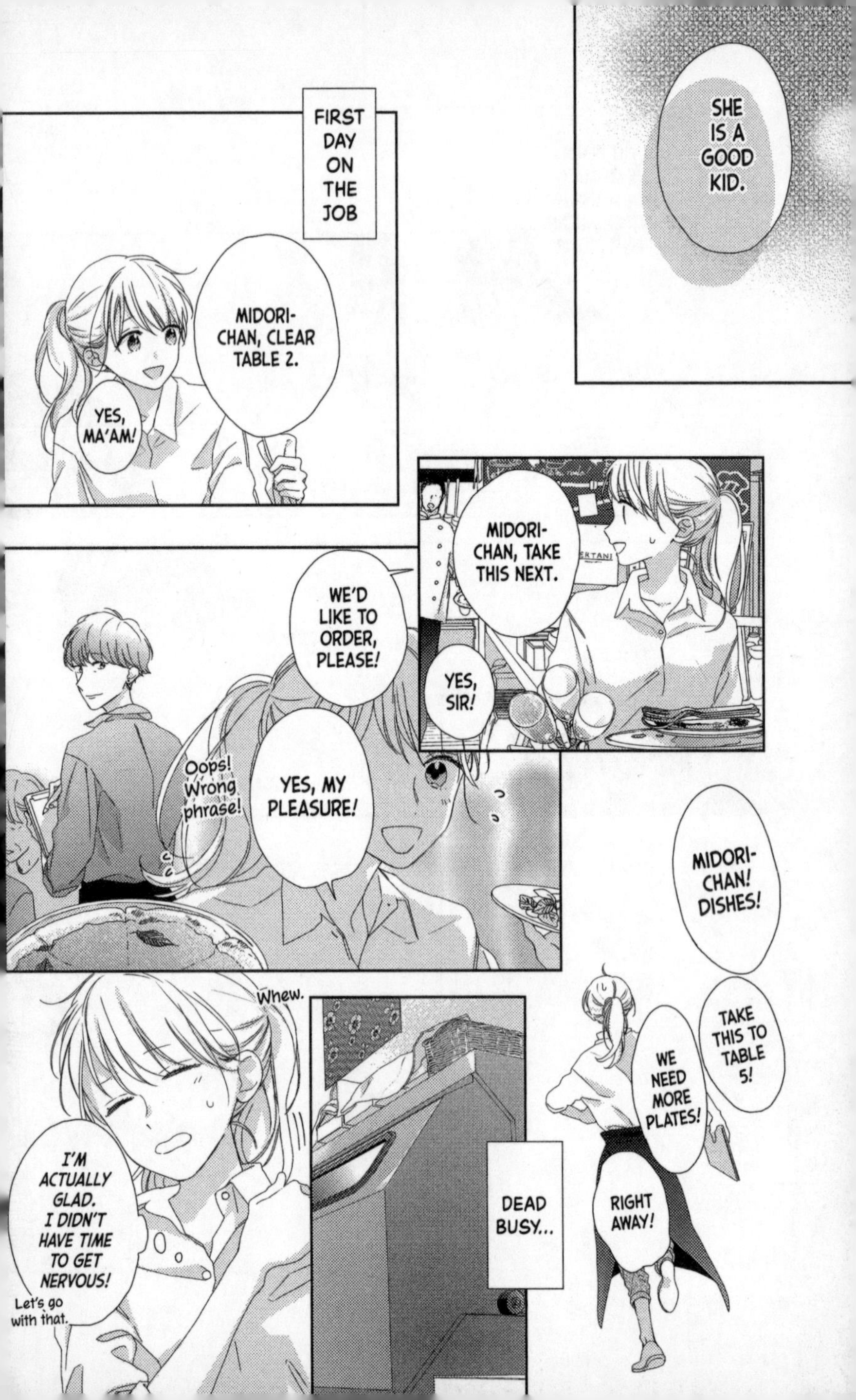
SHE IS A GOOD KID.
FIRST DAY ON THE JOB
MIDORI-CHAN, CLEAR TABLE 2.
YES, MA'AM!
MIDORI-CHAN, TAKE THIS NEXT.
YES, SIR!
WE'D LIKE TO ORDER, PLEASE!
YES, MY PLEASURE!
Oops! Wrong phrase!
MIDORI-CHAN! DISHES!
TAKE THIS TO TABLE 5!
WE NEED MORE PLATES!
RIGHT AWAY!
DEAD BUSY...
Whew.
I'M ACTUALLY GLAD. I DIDN'T HAVE TIME TO GET NERVOUS!
Let's go with that.

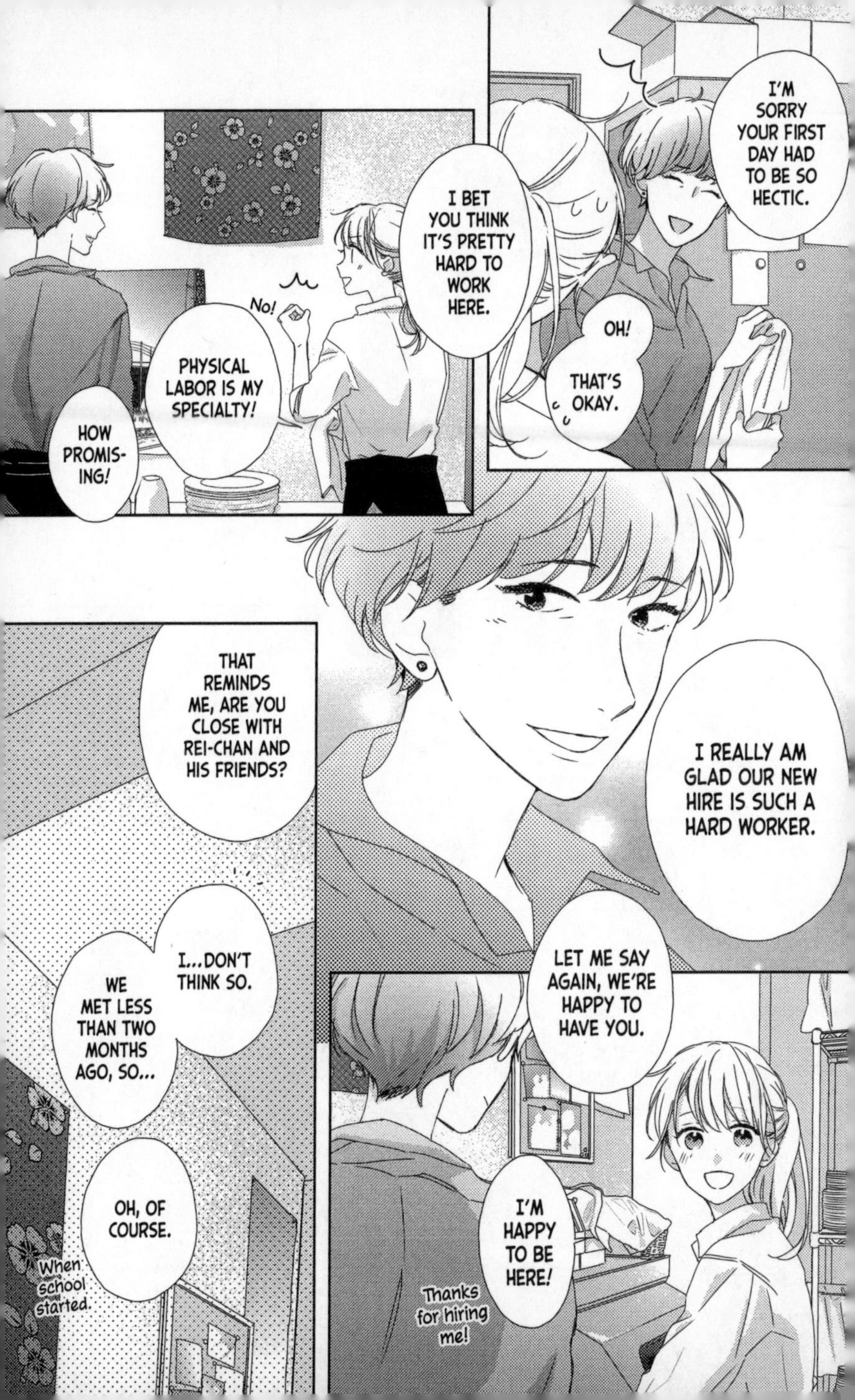
I'M SORRY YOUR FIRST DAY HAD TO BE SO HECTIC.
I BET YOU THINK IT'S PRETTY HARD TO WORK HERE.
OH!
THAT'S OKAY.
No!
PHYSICAL LABOR IS MY SPECIALTY!
HOW PROMISING!
I REALLY AM GLAD OUR NEW HIRE IS SUCH A HARD WORKER.
LET ME SAY AGAIN, WE'RE HAPPY TO HAVE YOU.
I'M HAPPY TO BE HERE!
Thanks for hiring me!
THAT REMINDS ME, ARE YOU CLOSE WITH REI-CHAN AND HIS FRIENDS?
I...DON'T THINK SO.
WE MET LESS THAN TWO MONTHS AGO, SO...
OH, OF COURSE.
When school started.

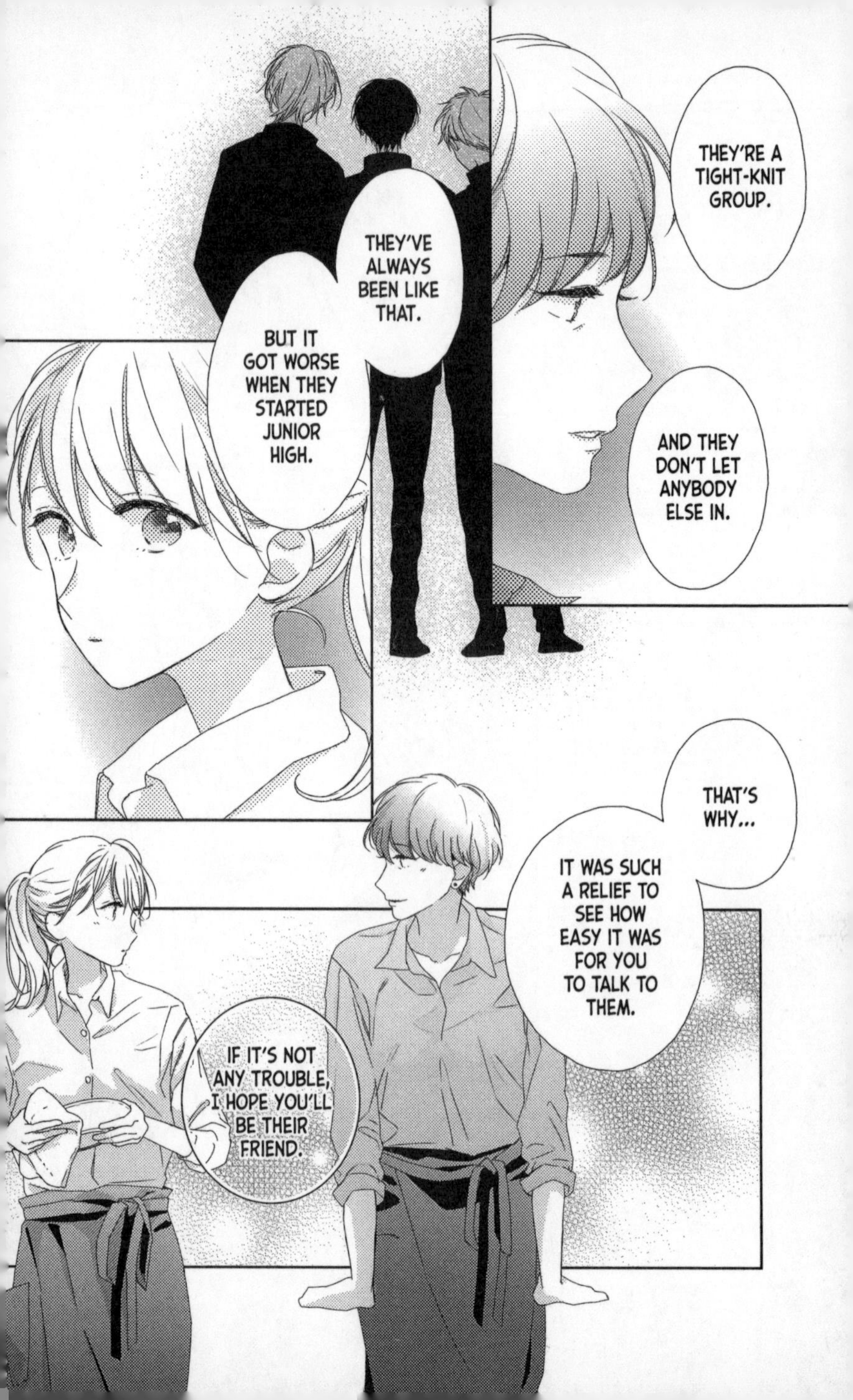
THEY'RE A TIGHT-KNIT GROUP.
AND THEY DON'T LET ANYBODY ELSE IN.
THEY'VE ALWAYS BEEN LIKE THAT.
BUT IT GOT WORSE WHEN THEY STARTED JUNIOR HIGH.
THAT'S WHY...
IT WAS SUCH A RELIEF TO SEE HOW EASY IT WAS FOR YOU TO TALK TO THEM.
IF IT'S NOT ANY TROUBLE, I HOPE YOU'LL BE THEIR FRIEND.

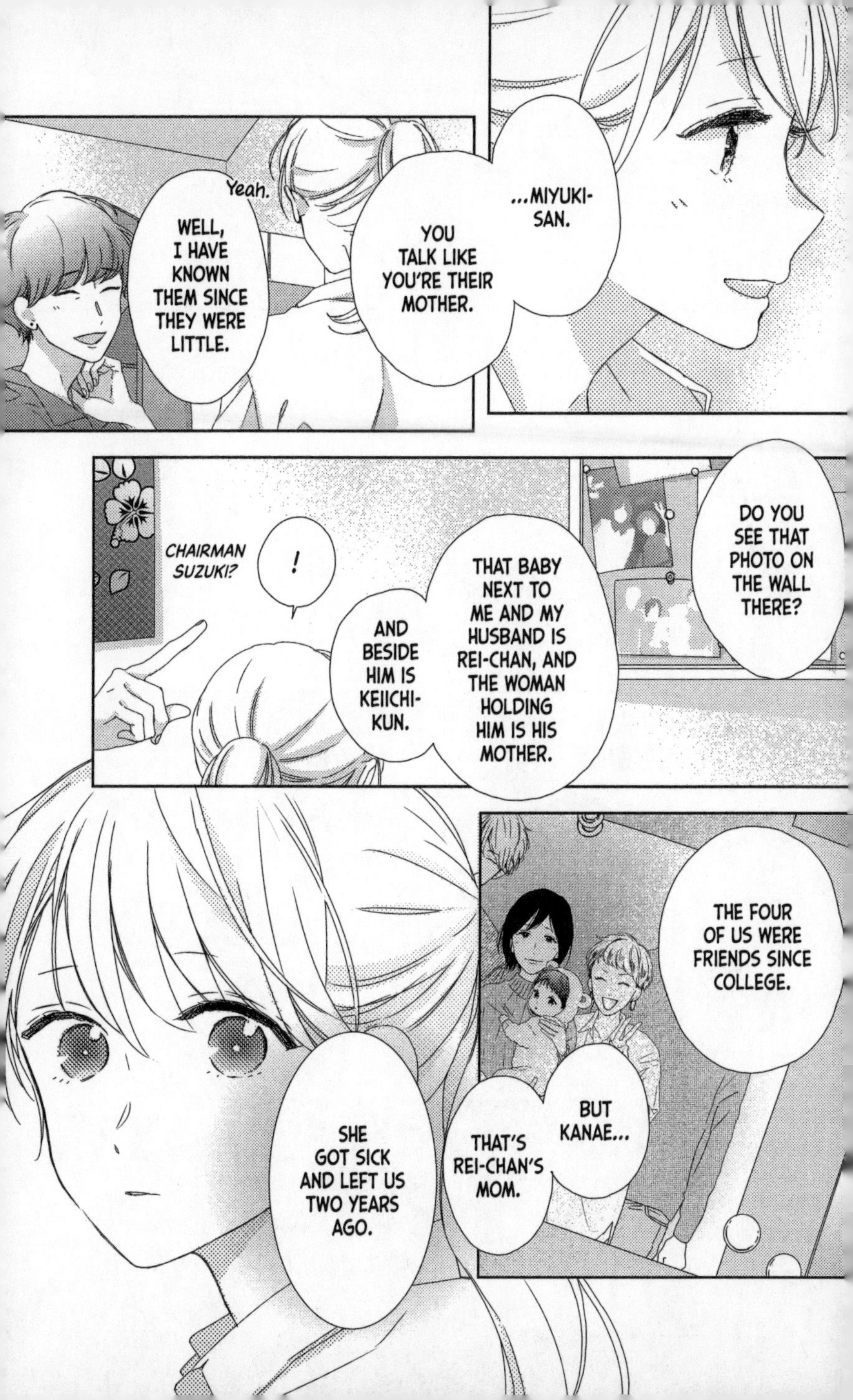
...MIYUKI-SAN.
YOU TALK LIKE YOU'RE THEIR MOTHER.
Yeah.
WELL, I HAVE KNOWN THEM SINCE THEY WERE LITTLE.
DO YOU SEE THAT PHOTO ON THE WALL THERE?
THAT BABY NEXT TO ME AND MY HUSBAND IS REI-CHAN, AND THE WOMAN HOLDING HIM IS HIS MOTHER.
AND BESIDE HIM IS KEIICHI-KUN.
!
CHAIRMAN SUZUKI?
THE FOUR OF US WERE FRIENDS SINCE COLLEGE.
BUT KANAE...
THAT'S REI-CHAN'S MOM.
SHE GOT SICK AND LEFT US TWO YEARS AGO.

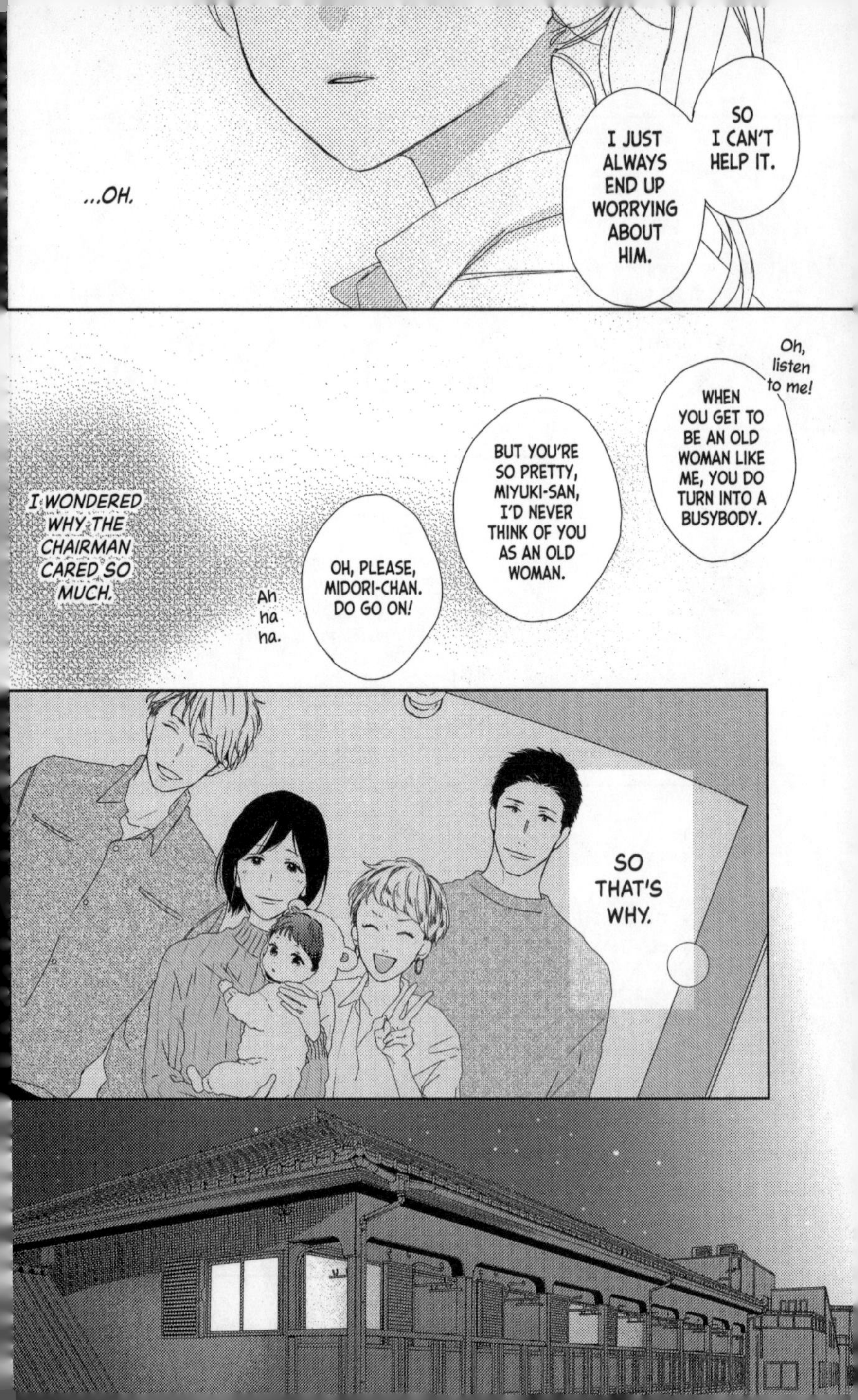
SO I CAN'T HELP IT.
I JUST ALWAYS END UP WORRYING ABOUT HIM.
...OH.
Oh, listen to me!
WHEN YOU GET TO BE AN OLD WOMAN LIKE ME, YOU DO TURN INTO A BUSYBODY.
BUT YOU'RE SO PRETTY, MIYUKI-SAN, I'D NEVER THINK OF YOU AS AN OLD WOMAN.
OH, PLEASE, MIDORI-CHAN. DO GO ON!
Ah ha ha.
I WONDERED WHY THE CHAIRMAN CARED SO MUCH.
SO THAT'S WHY.

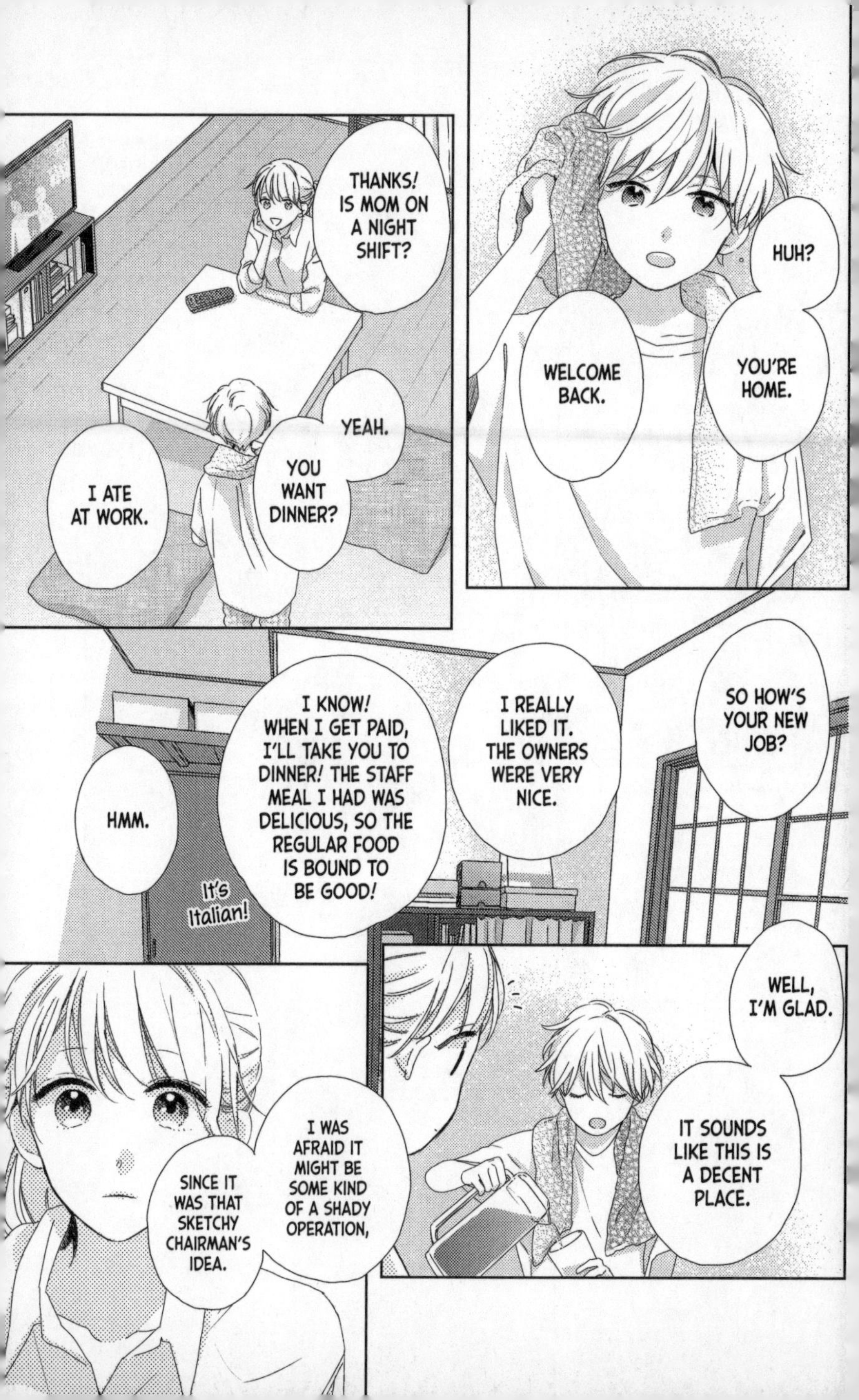
HUH?
YOU'RE HOME.
WELCOME BACK.
THANKS! IS MOM ON A NIGHT SHIFT?
YEAH.
YOU WANT DINNER?
I ATE AT WORK.
SO HOW'S YOUR NEW JOB?
I REALLY LIKED IT. THE OWNERS WERE VERY NICE.
I KNOW! WHEN I GET PAID, I'LL TAKE YOU TO DINNER! THE STAFF MEAL I HAD WAS DELICIOUS, SO THE REGULAR FOOD IS BOUND TO BE GOOD!
It's Italian!
HMM.
WELL, I'M GLAD.
IT SOUNDS LIKE THIS IS A DECENT PLACE.
I WAS AFRAID IT MIGHT BE SOME KIND OF A SHADY OPERATION,
SINCE IT WAS THAT SKETCHY CHAIRMAN'S IDEA.

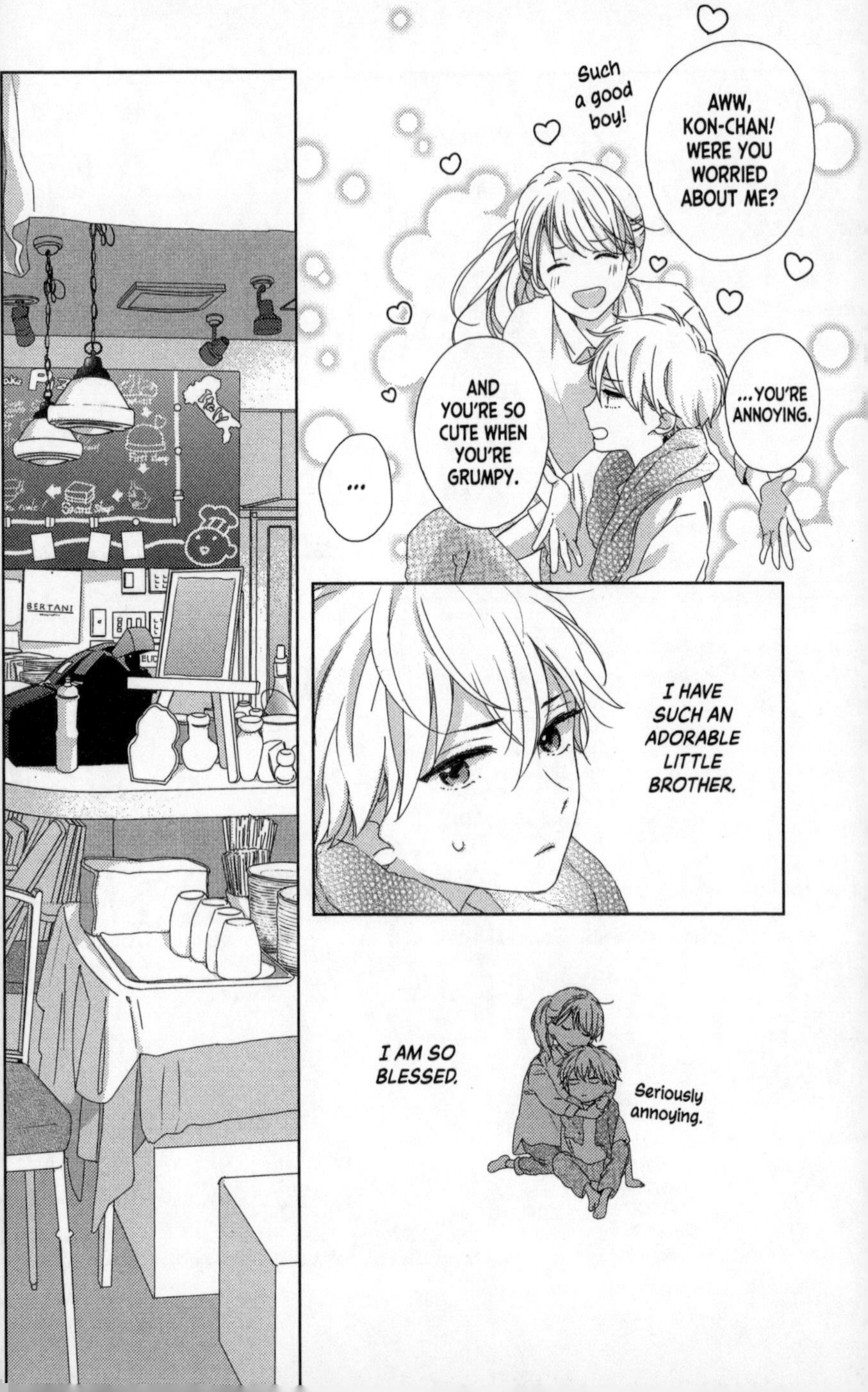
AWW, KON-CHAN! WERE YOU WORRIED ABOUT ME?
Such a good boy!
...YOU'RE ANNOYING.
AND YOU'RE SO CUTE WHEN YOU'RE GRUMPY.
...
I HAVE SUCH AN ADORABLE LITTLE BROTHER.
Seriously annoying.
I AM SO BLESSED.
BERTANI

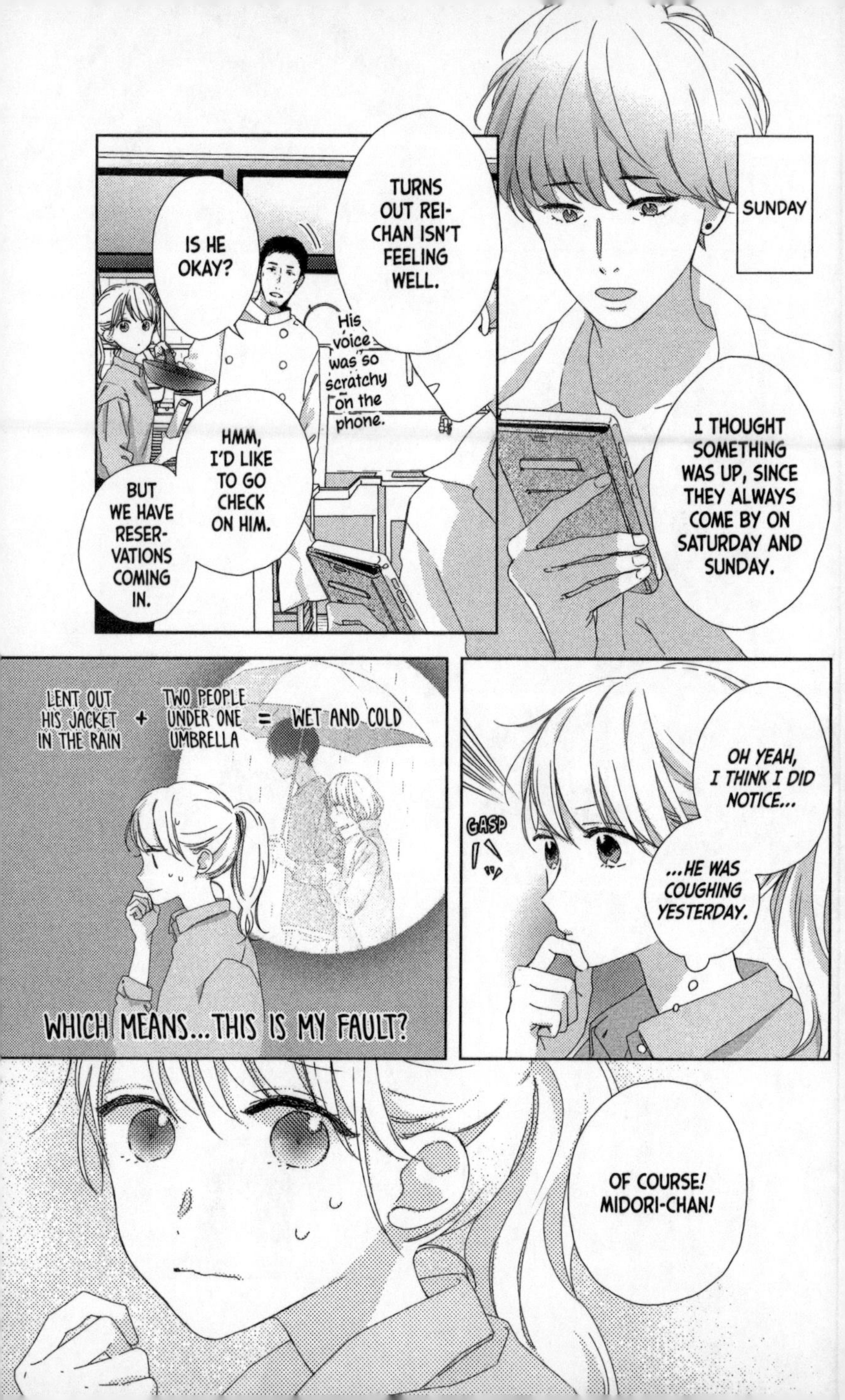
SUNDAY
TURNS OUT REI-CHAN ISN'T FEELING WELL.
I THOUGHT SOMETHING WAS UP, SINCE THEY ALWAYS COME BY ON SATURDAY AND SUNDAY.
IS HE OKAY?
His voice was so scratchy on the phone.
HMM, I'D LIKE TO GO CHECK ON HIM.
BUT WE HAVE RESERVATIONS COMING IN.
GASP
OH YEAH, I THINK I DID NOTICE...
...HE WAS COUGHING YESTERDAY.
LENT OUT HIS JACKET IN THE RAIN + TWO PEOPLE UNDER ONE UMBRELLA = WET AND COLD
WHICH MEANS... THIS IS MY FAULT?
OF COURSE! MIDORI-CHAN!

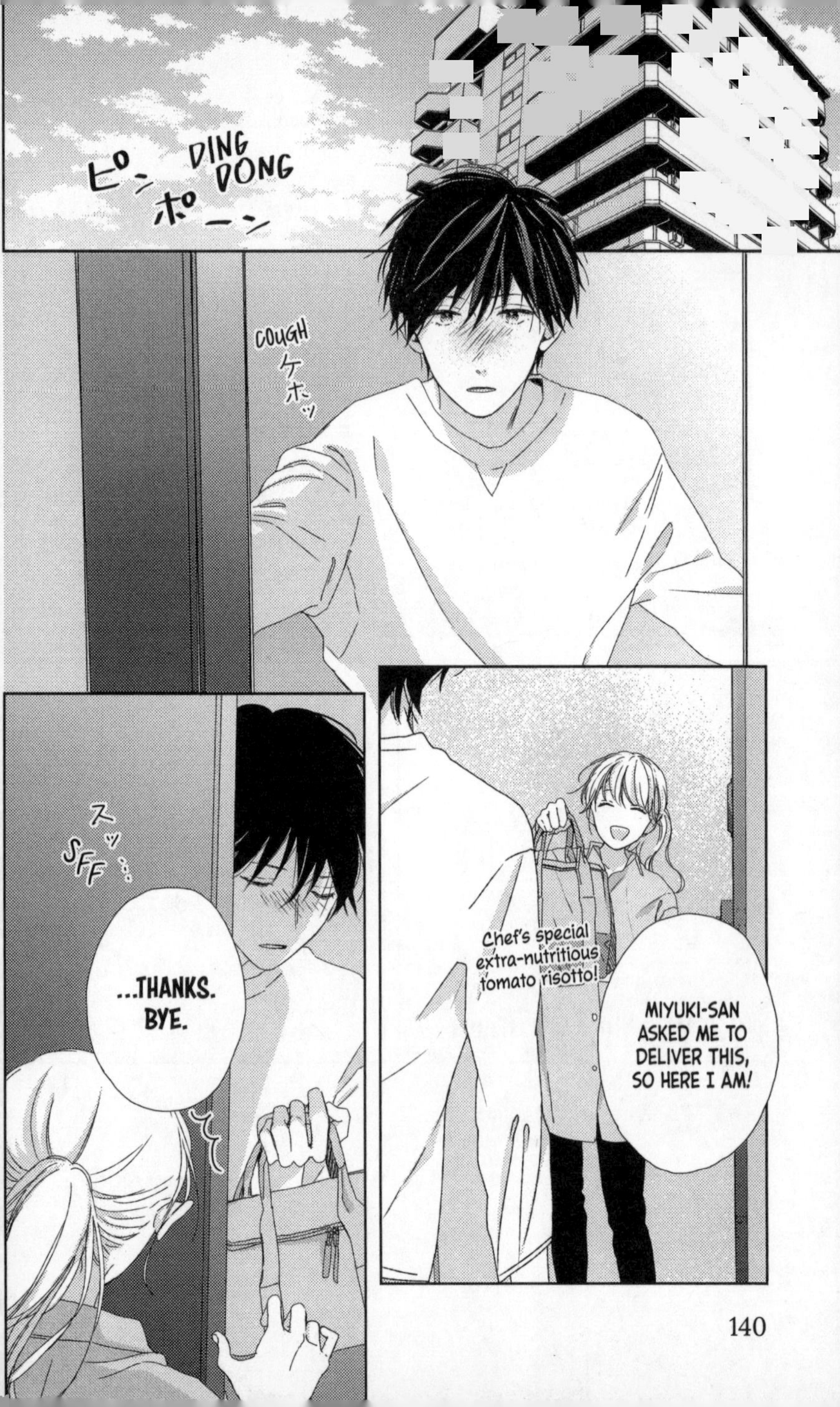
ピンポーン
DING DONG
ケホッ
COUGH
MIYUKI-SAN ASKED ME TO DELIVER THIS, SO HERE I AM!
Chef's special extra-nutritious tomato risotto!
スッ…
SFF
...THANKS. BYE.

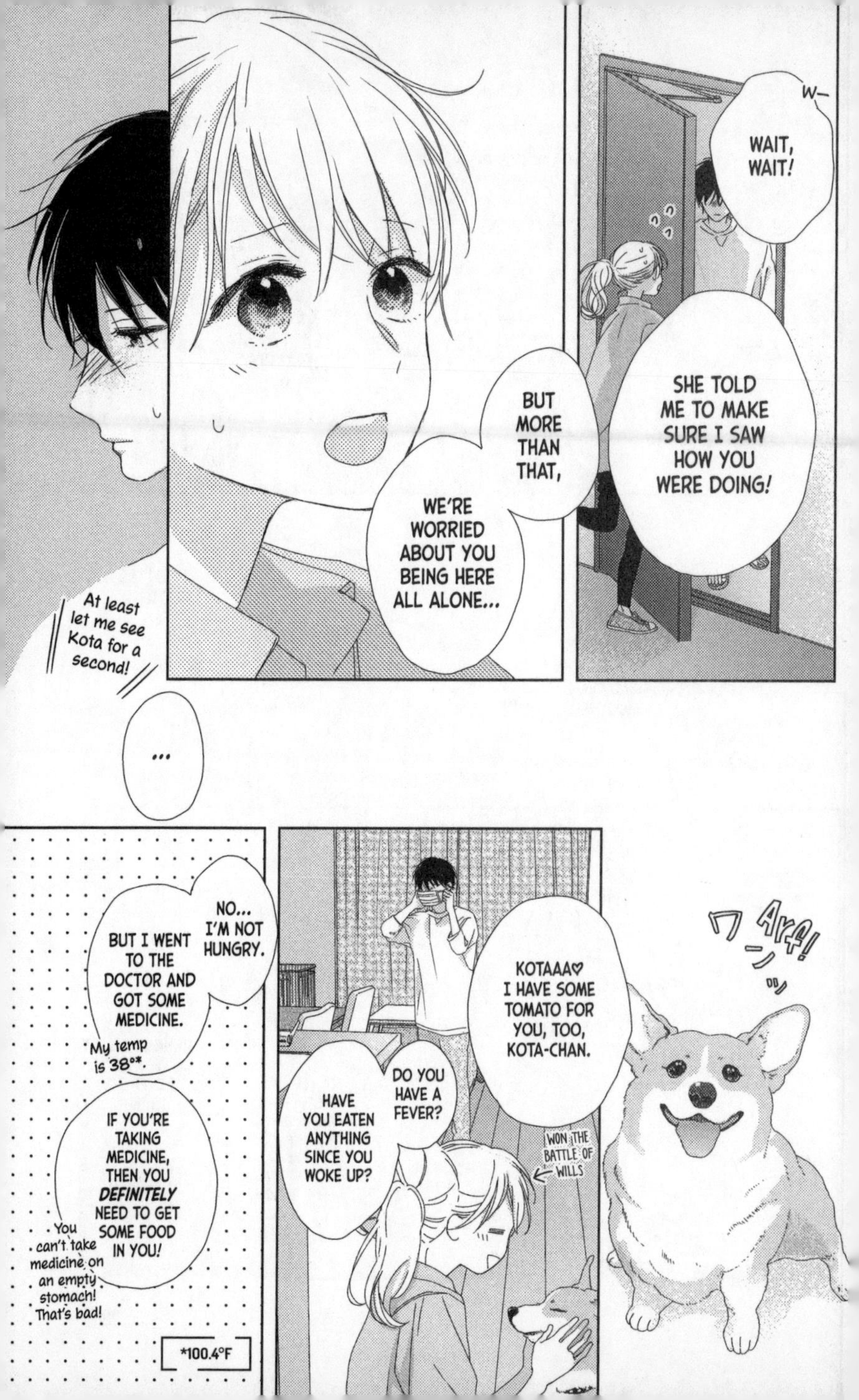
W—
WAIT, WAIT!
SHE TOLD ME TO MAKE SURE I SAW HOW YOU WERE DOING!
BUT MORE THAN THAT,
WE'RE WORRIED ABOUT YOU BEING HERE ALL ALONE...
At least let me see Kota for a second!
...
Arf!
KOTAAA♡ I HAVE SOME TOMATO FOR YOU, TOO, KOTA-CHAN.
WON THE BATTLE OF WILLS
DO YOU HAVE A FEVER?
HAVE YOU EATEN ANYTHING SINCE YOU WOKE UP?
NO... I'M NOT HUNGRY.
BUT I WENT TO THE DOCTOR AND GOT SOME MEDICINE.
My temp is 38°*.
IF YOU'RE TAKING MEDICINE, THEN YOU *DEFINITELY* NEED TO GET SOME FOOD IN YOU!
You can't take medicine on an empty stomach! That's bad!
*100.4°F

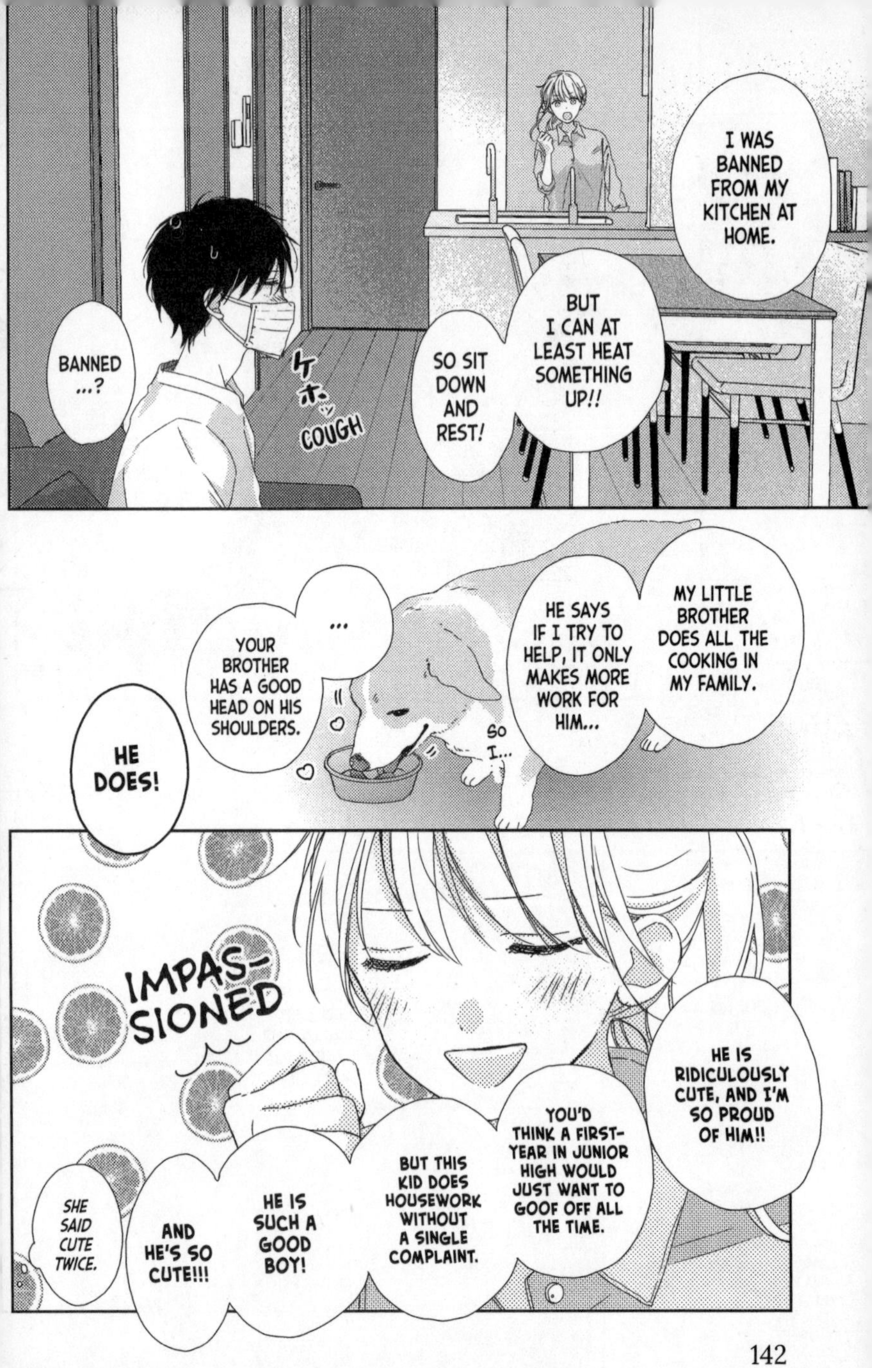
I WAS BANNED FROM MY KITCHEN AT HOME.
BUT I CAN AT LEAST HEAT SOMETHING UP!!
SO SIT DOWN AND REST!
ケホッ COUGH
BANNED ...?
MY LITTLE BROTHER DOES ALL THE COOKING IN MY FAMILY.
HE SAYS IF I TRY TO HELP, IT ONLY MAKES MORE WORK FOR HIM...
SO I...
...
YOUR BROTHER HAS A GOOD HEAD ON HIS SHOULDERS.
HE DOES!
HE IS RIDICULOUSLY CUTE, AND I'M SO PROUD OF HIM!!
YOU'D THINK A FIRST-YEAR IN JUNIOR HIGH WOULD JUST WANT TO GOOF OFF ALL THE TIME.
BUT THIS KID DOES HOUSEWORK WITHOUT A SINGLE COMPLAINT.
HE IS SUCH A GOOD BOY!
AND HE'S SO CUTE!!!
IMPAS-SIONED
SHE SAID CUTE TWICE.

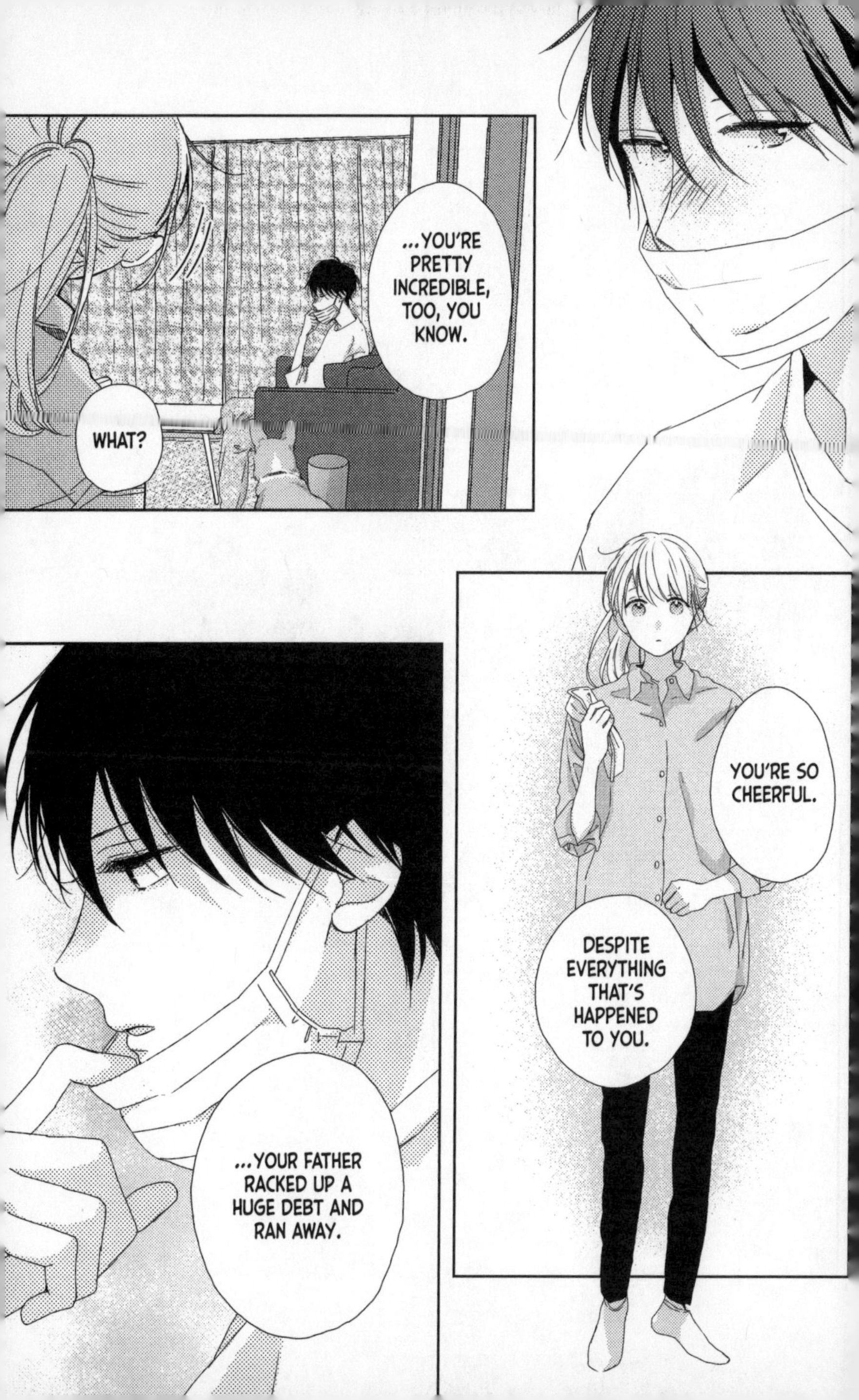
...YOU'RE PRETTY INCREDIBLE, TOO, YOU KNOW.
WHAT?
YOU'RE SO CHEERFUL.
DESPITE EVERYTHING THAT'S HAPPENED TO YOU.
...YOUR FATHER RACKED UP A HUGE DEBT AND RAN AWAY.

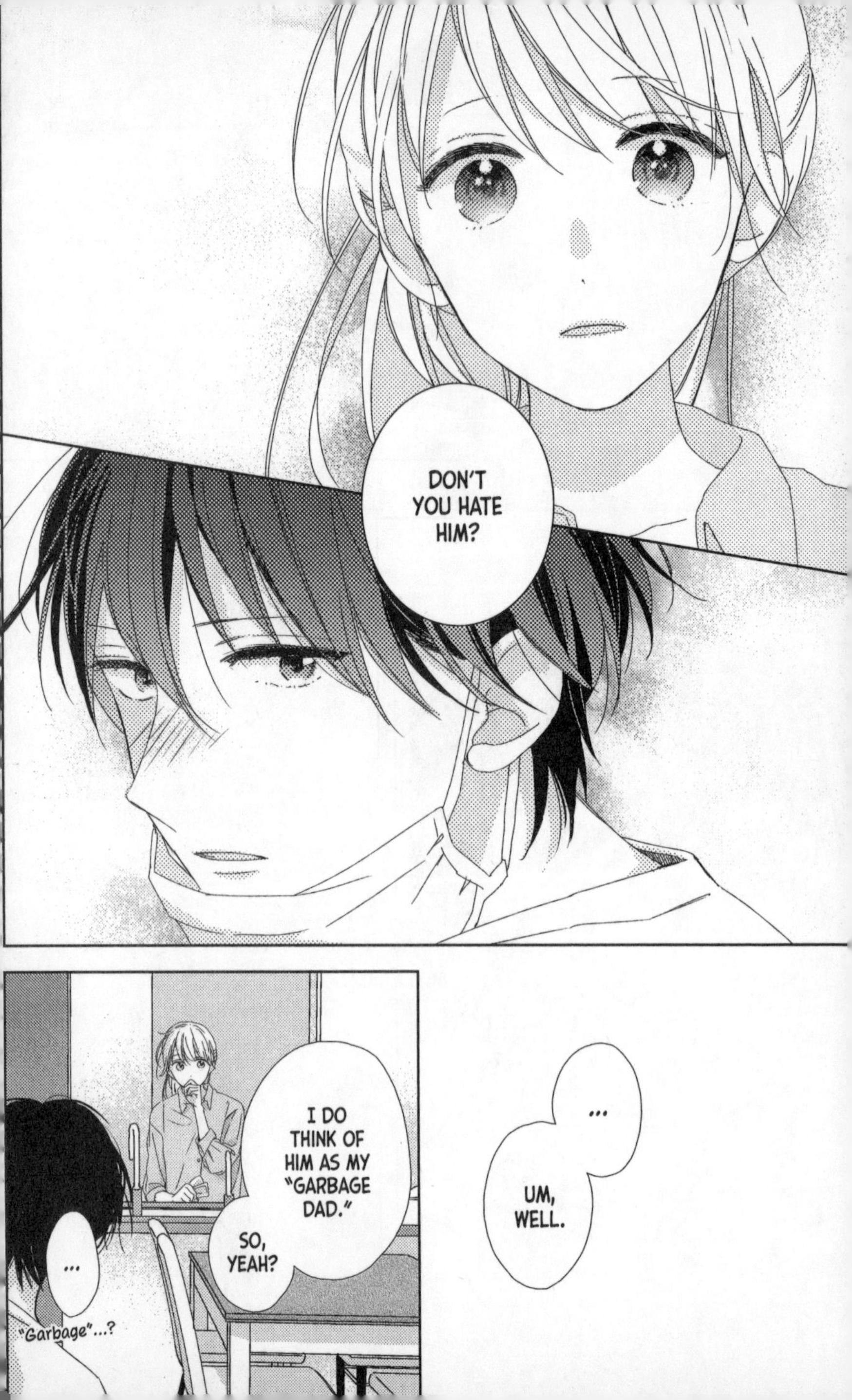
DON'T YOU HATE HIM?
...
UM, WELL.
I DO THINK OF HIM AS MY "GARBAGE DAD."
SO, YEAH?
...
"Garbage"...?

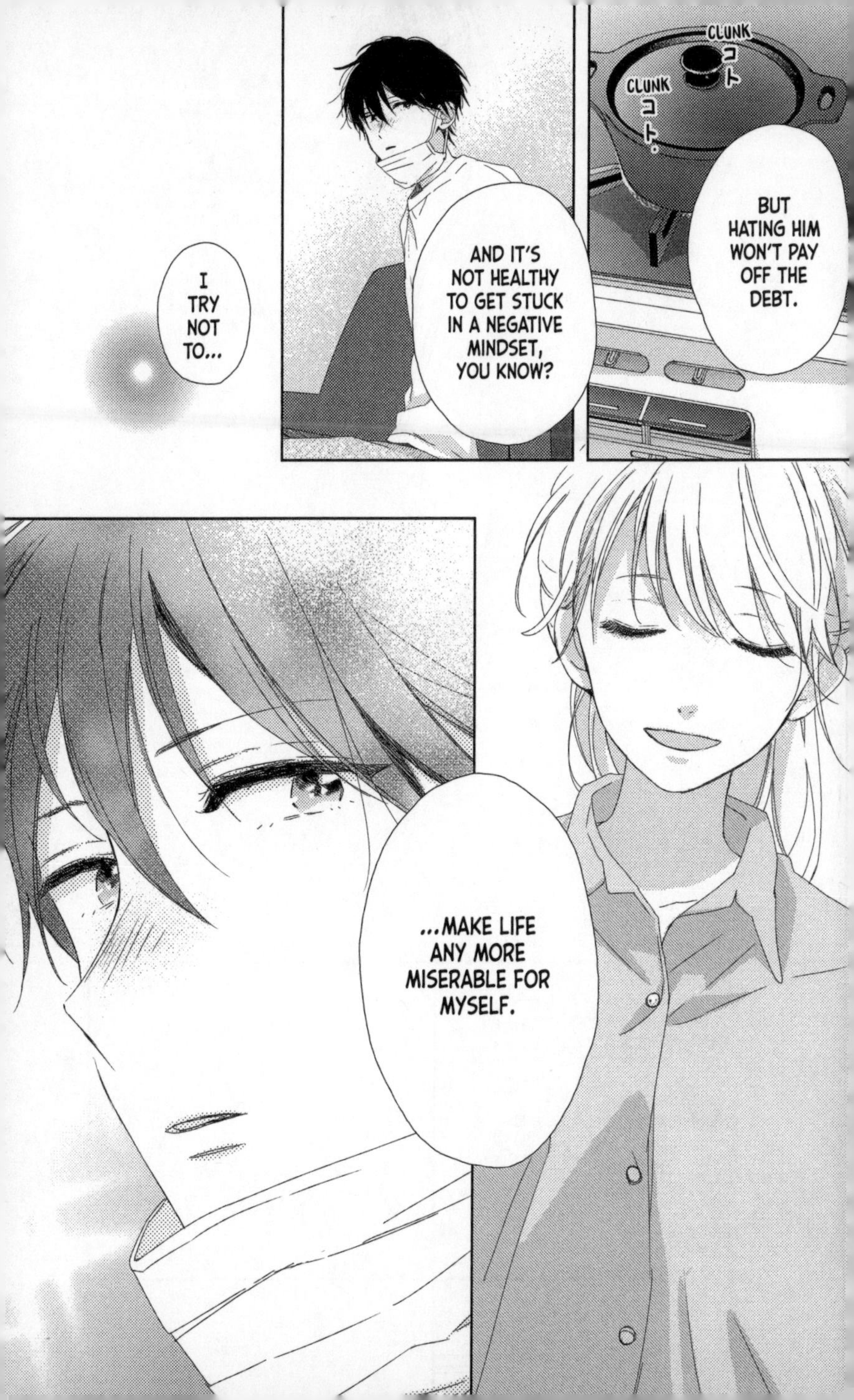
CLUNK
コト
CLUNK
コト.
BUT HATING HIM WON'T PAY OFF THE DEBT.
AND IT'S NOT HEALTHY TO GET STUCK IN A NEGATIVE MINDSET, YOU KNOW?
I TRY NOT TO...
...MAKE LIFE ANY MORE MISERABLE FOR MYSELF.

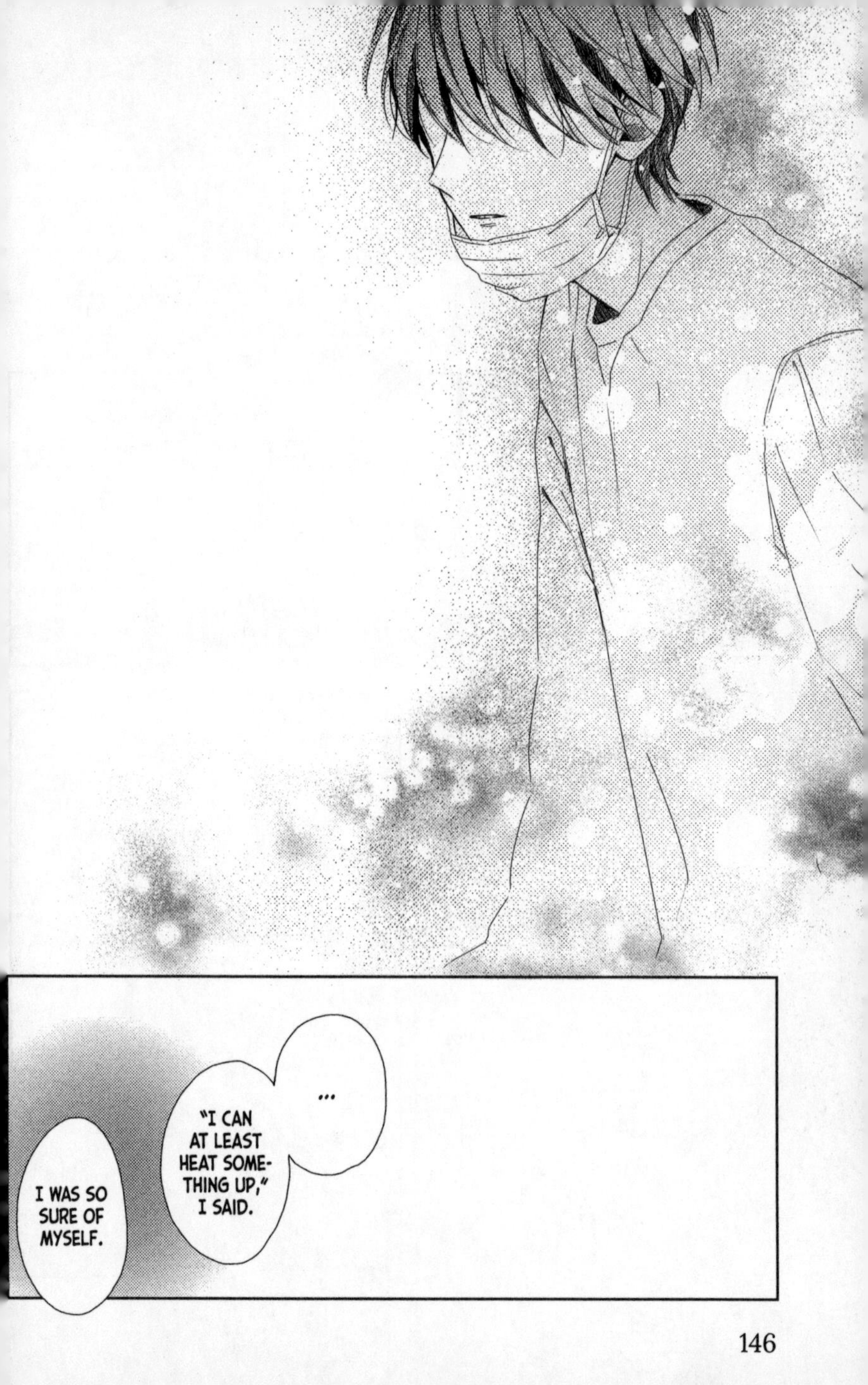
...
"I CAN AT LEAST HEAT SOMETHING UP," I SAID.
I WAS SO SURE OF MYSELF.

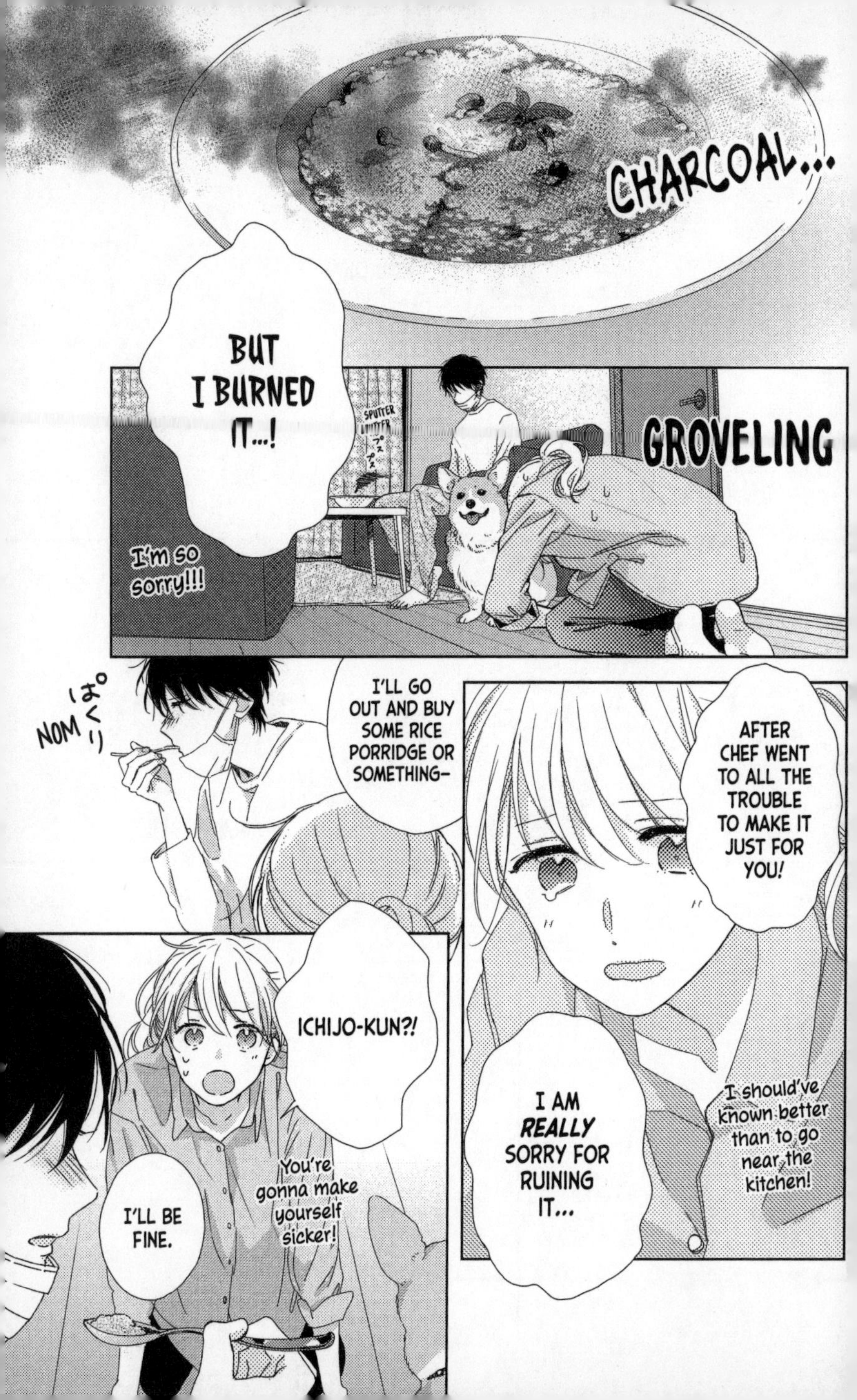
CHARCOAL...
BUT I BURNED IT...!
GROVELING
SPUTTER SPUTTER
プスプス
I'm so sorry!!!
AFTER CHEF WENT TO ALL THE TROUBLE TO MAKE IT JUST FOR YOU!
I should've known better than to go near the kitchen!
I AM REALLY SORRY FOR RUINING IT...
I'LL GO OUT AND BUY SOME RICE PORRIDGE OR SOMETHING–
NOM
ぱくり
ICHIJO-KUN?!
You're gonna make yourself sicker!
I'LL BE FINE.

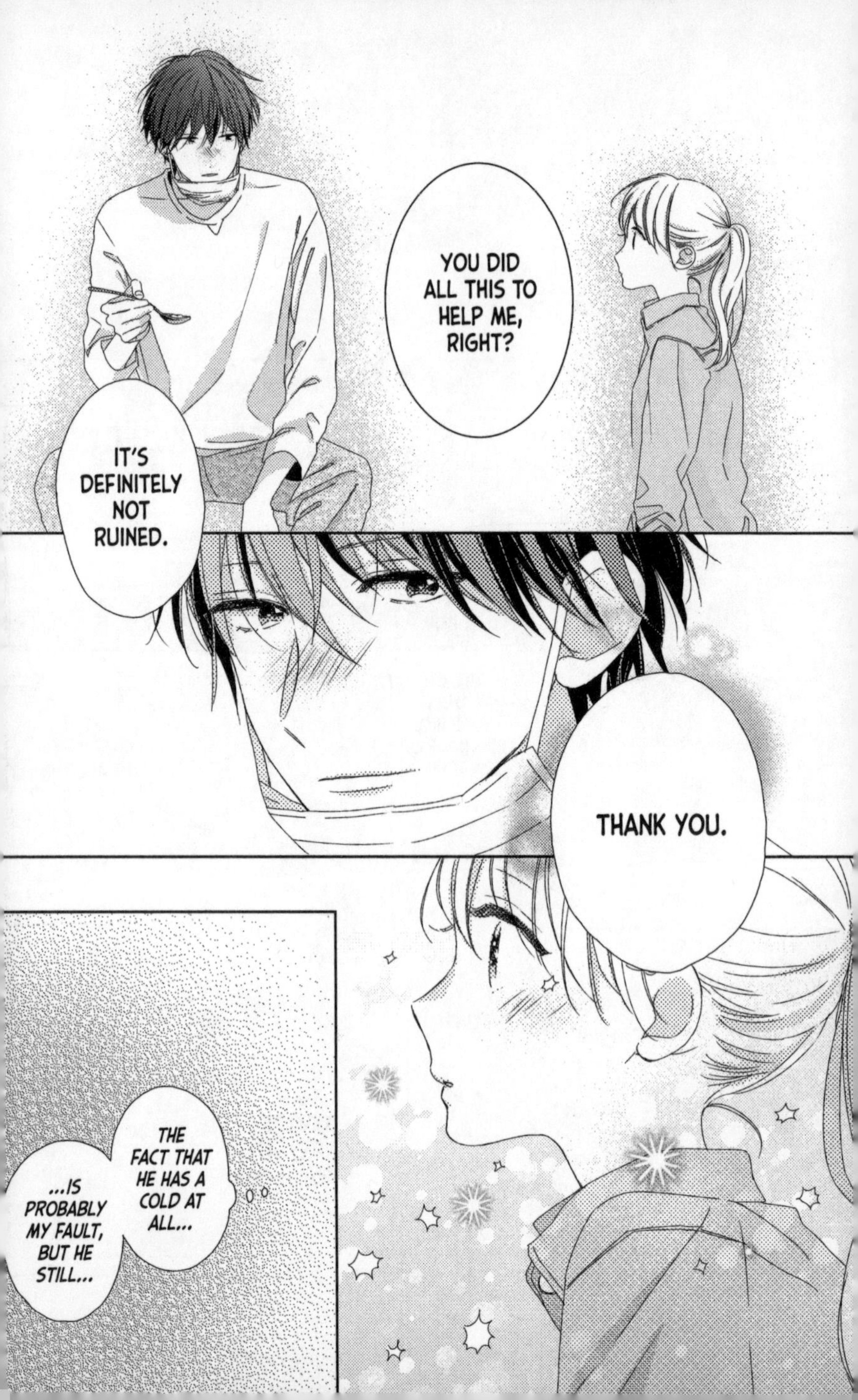
YOU DID ALL THIS TO HELP ME, RIGHT?
IT'S DEFINITELY NOT RUINED.
THANK YOU.
THE FACT THAT HE HAS A COLD AT ALL...
...IS PROBABLY MY FAULT, BUT HE STILL...

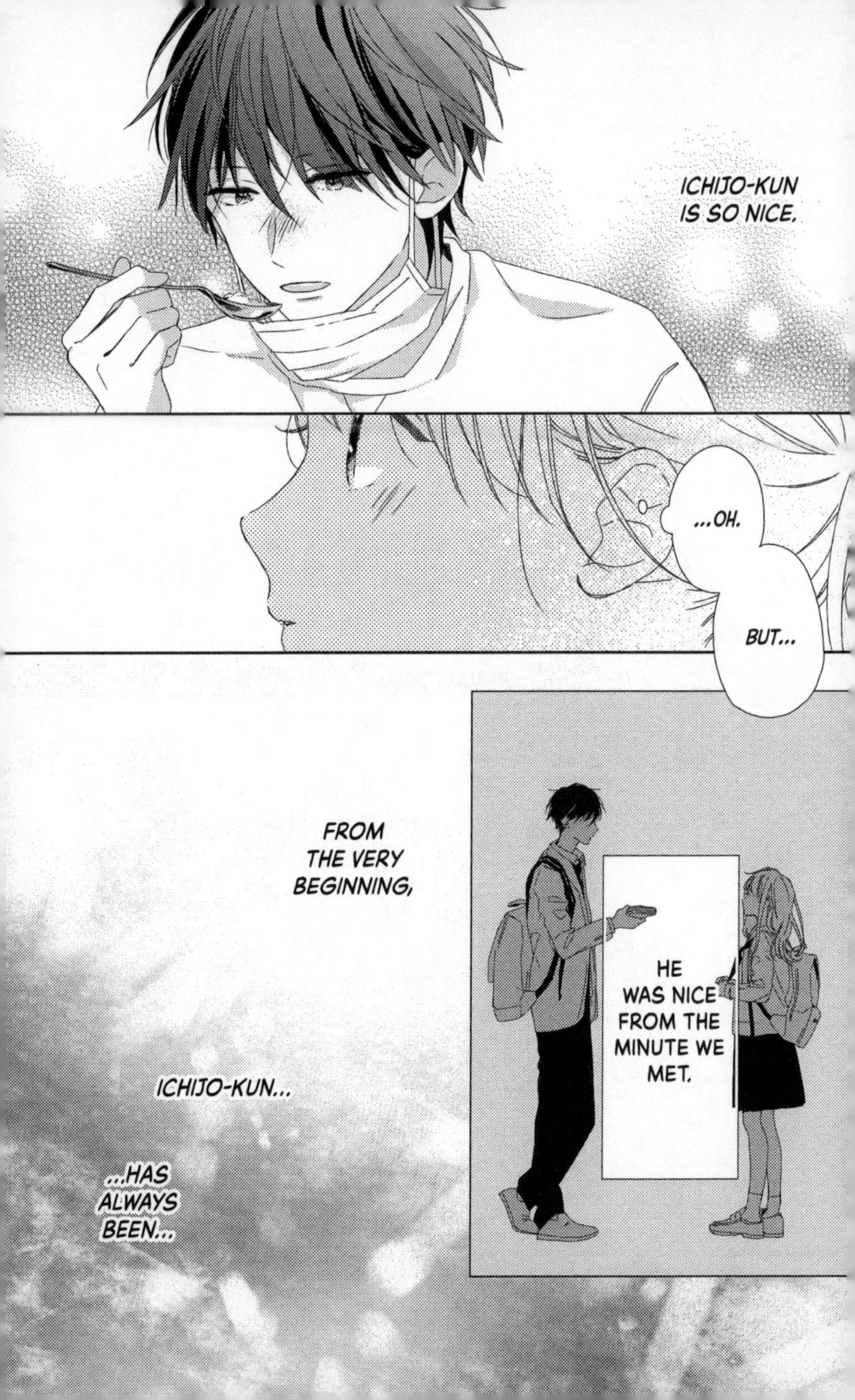
ICHIJO-KUN IS SO NICE.
...OH.
BUT...
HE WAS NICE FROM THE MINUTE WE MET.
FROM THE VERY BEGINNING,
ICHIJO-KUN...
...HAS ALWAYS BEEN...

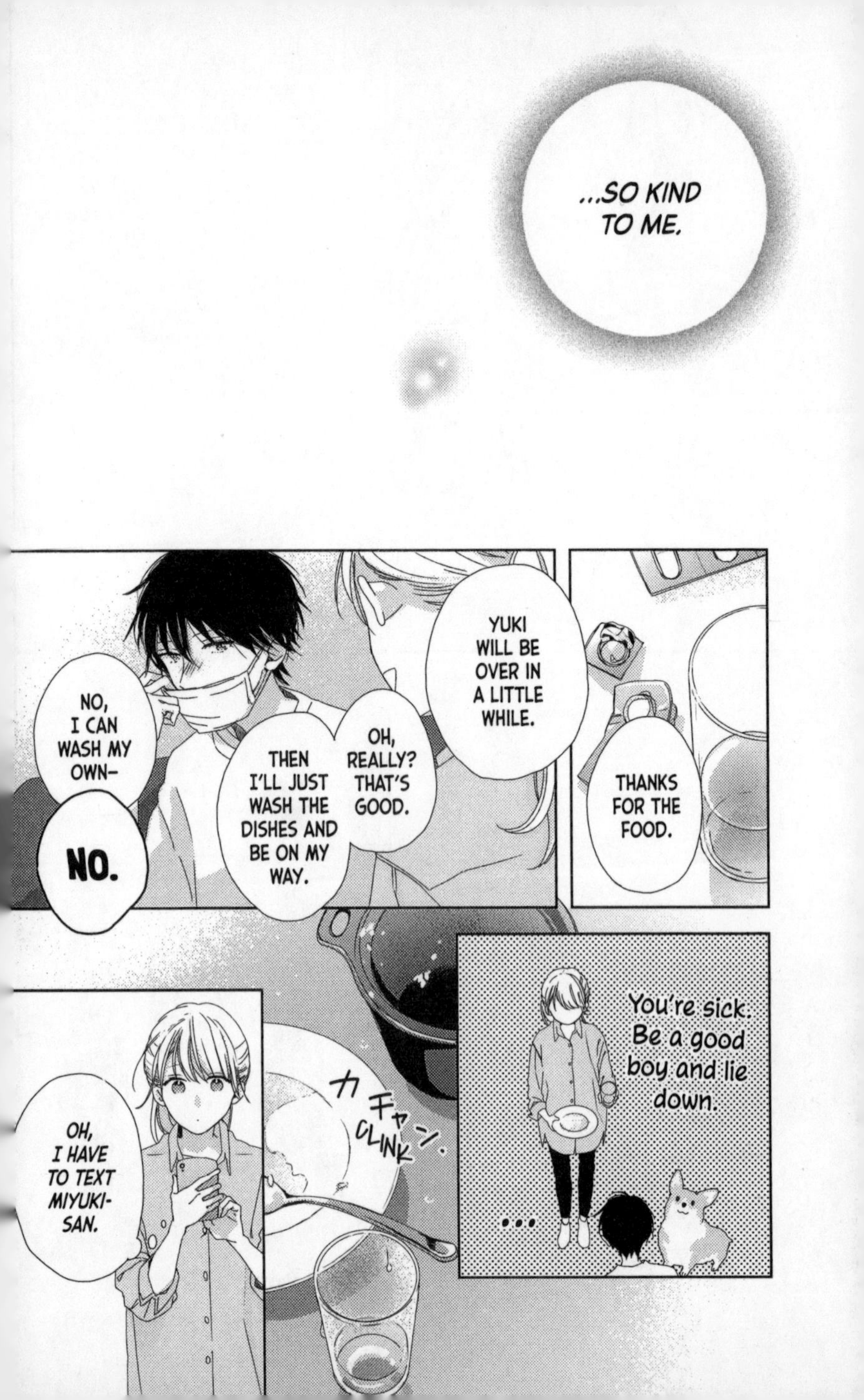
...SO KIND TO ME.
THANKS FOR THE FOOD.
YUKI WILL BE OVER IN A LITTLE WHILE.
OH, REALLY? THAT'S GOOD.
THEN I'LL JUST WASH THE DISHES AND BE ON MY WAY.
NO, I CAN WASH MY OWN–
NO.
You're sick. Be a good boy and lie down.
...
カチャン
CLINK
OH, I HAVE TO TEXT MIYUKI-SAN.

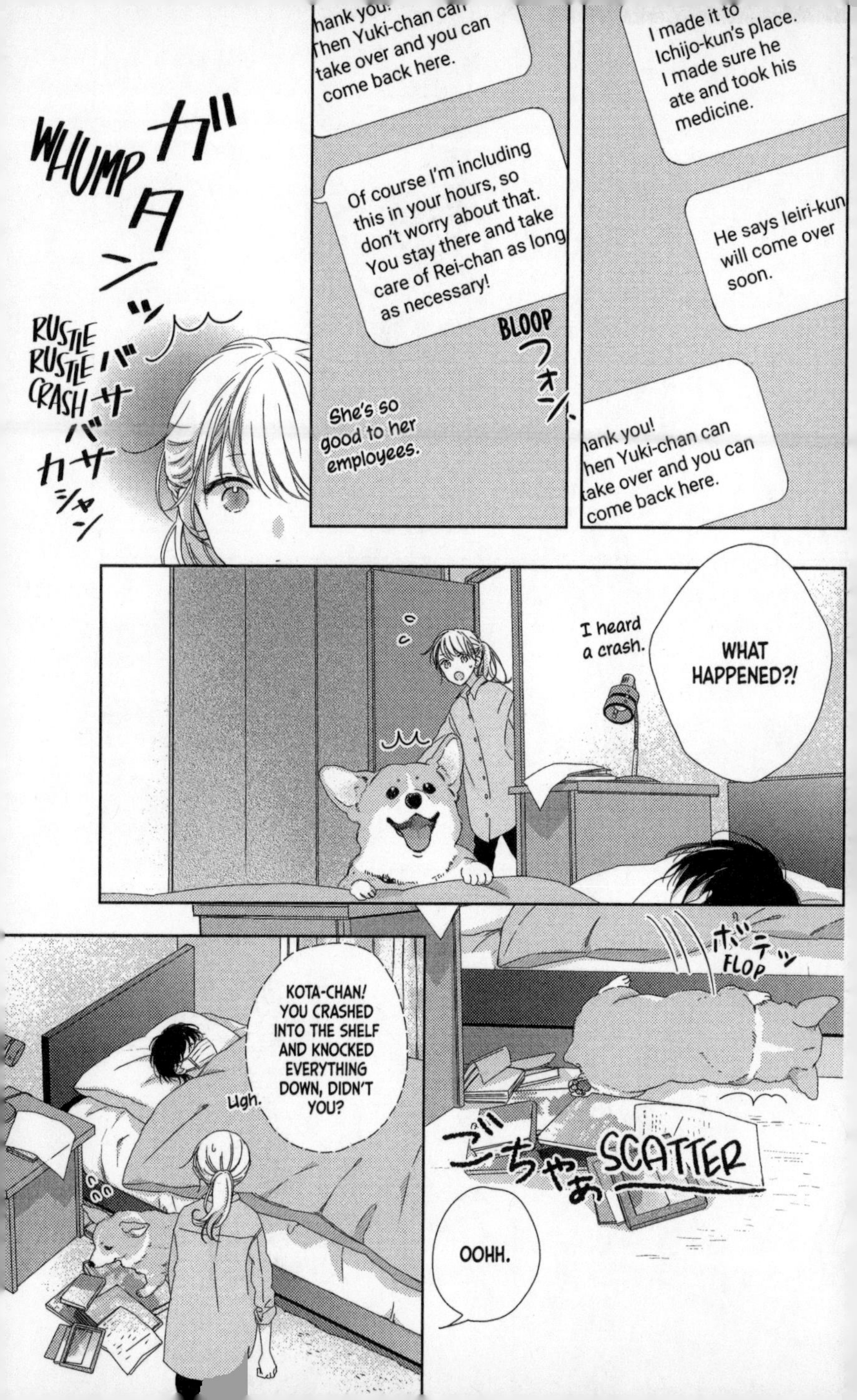
I made it to Ichijo-kun's place. I made sure he ate and took his medicine.
He says Ieiri-kun will come over soon.
hank you! hen Yuki-chan can ake over and you can come back here.
hank you! Then Yuki-chan can take over and you can come back here.
Of course I'm including this in your hours, so don't worry about that. You stay there and take care of Rei-chan as long as necessary!
BLOOP フォン
She's so good to her employees.
WHUMP ガタンッ
RUSTLE RUSTLE CRASH バサバサカシャン
WHAT HAPPENED?!
I heard a crash.
FLOP ボテッ
SCATTER ごちゃあ
OOHH.
KOTA-CHAN! YOU CRASHED INTO THE SHELF AND KNOCKED EVERYTHING DOWN, DIDN'T YOU?
Ugh.

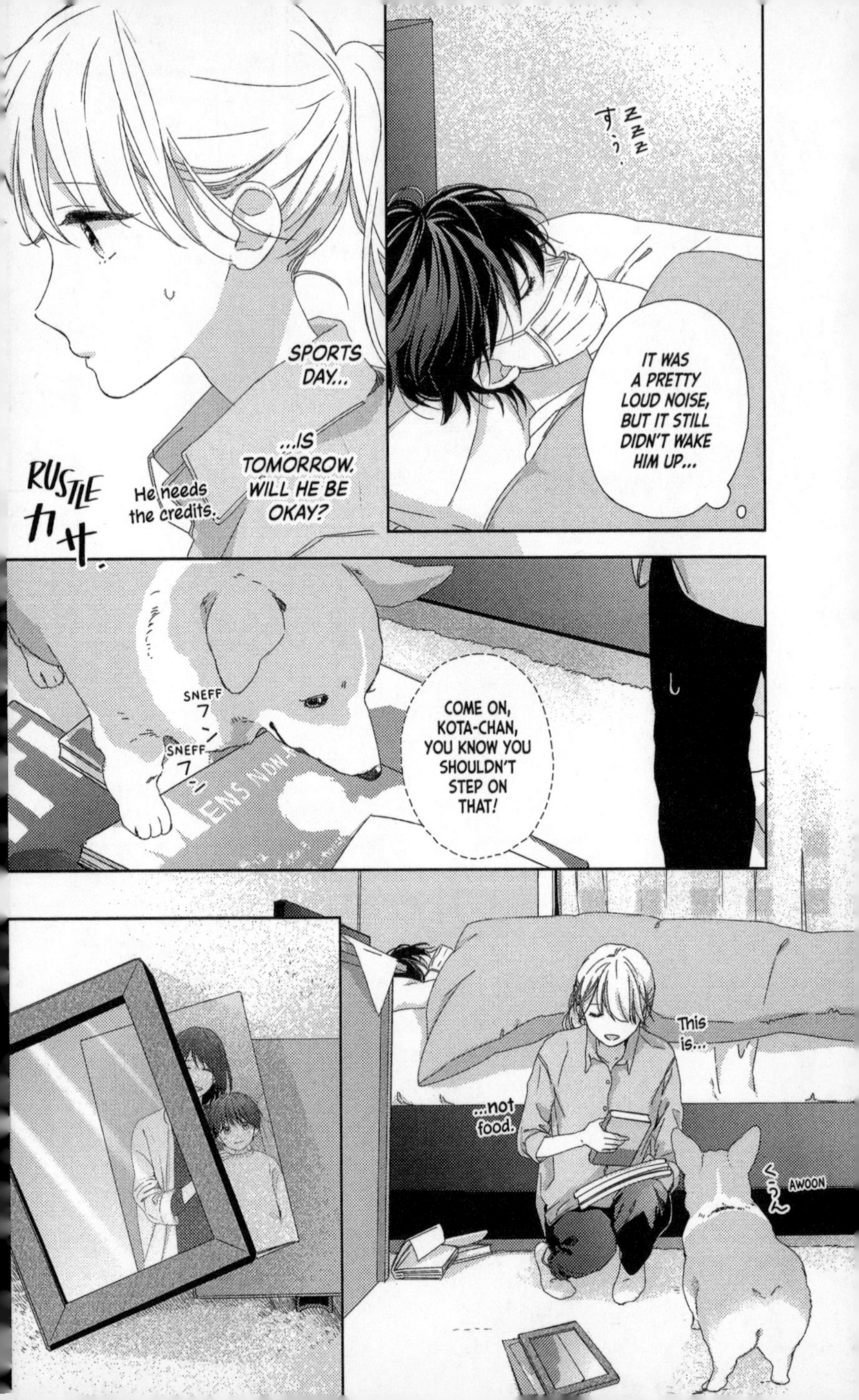
すぅ
ZZZ
IT WAS A PRETTY LOUD NOISE, BUT IT STILL DIDN'T WAKE HIM UP...
SPORTS DAY...
...IS TOMORROW. WILL HE BE OKAY?
He needs the credits.
RUSTLE
カサ
COME ON, KOTA-CHAN, YOU KNOW YOU SHOULDN'T STEP ON THAT!
SNEFF
フン
SNEFF
フン
くぅん
AWOON
This is...
...not food.

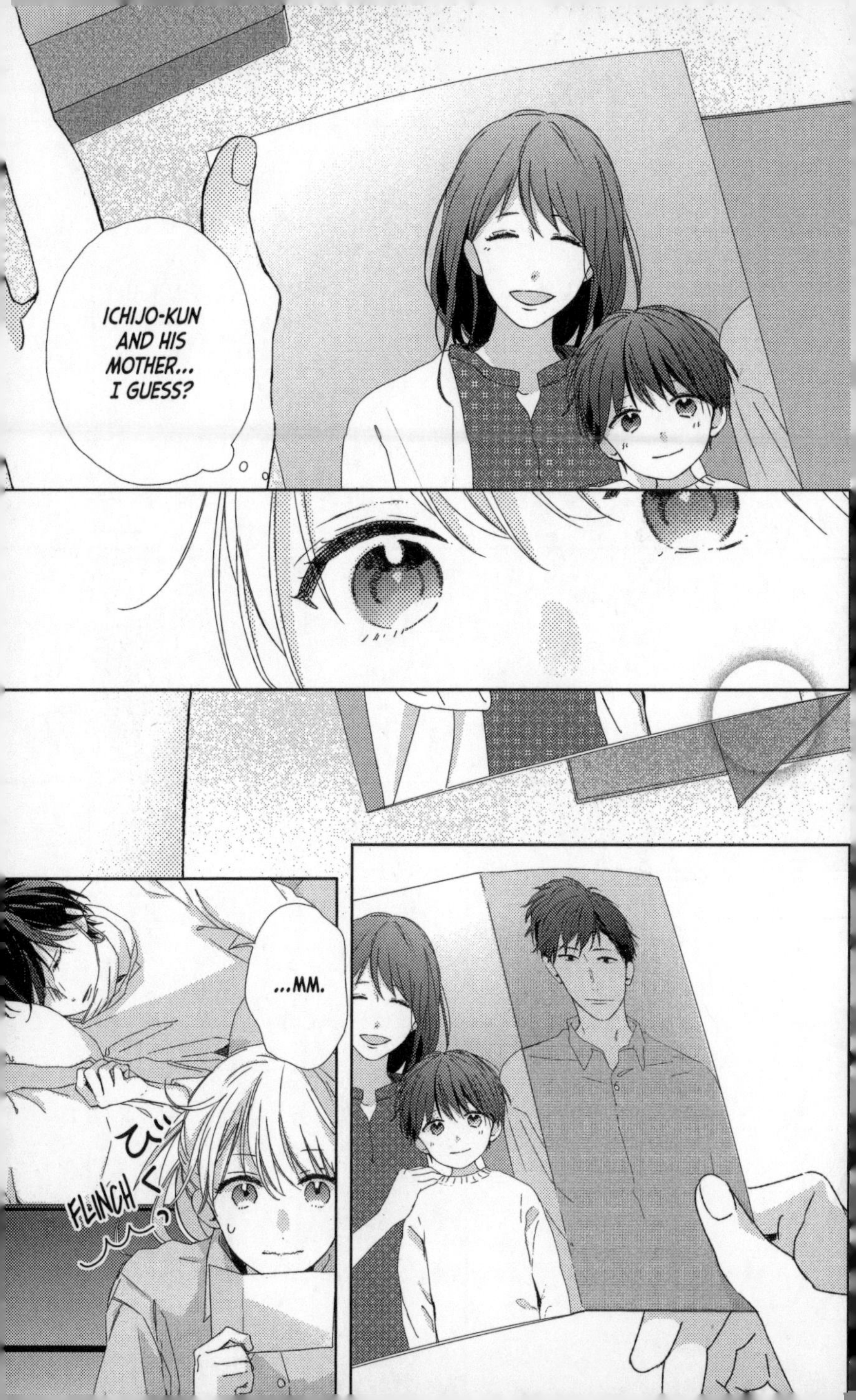
ICHIJO-KUN AND HIS MOTHER... I GUESS?
...MM.
ビくっ
FLINCH

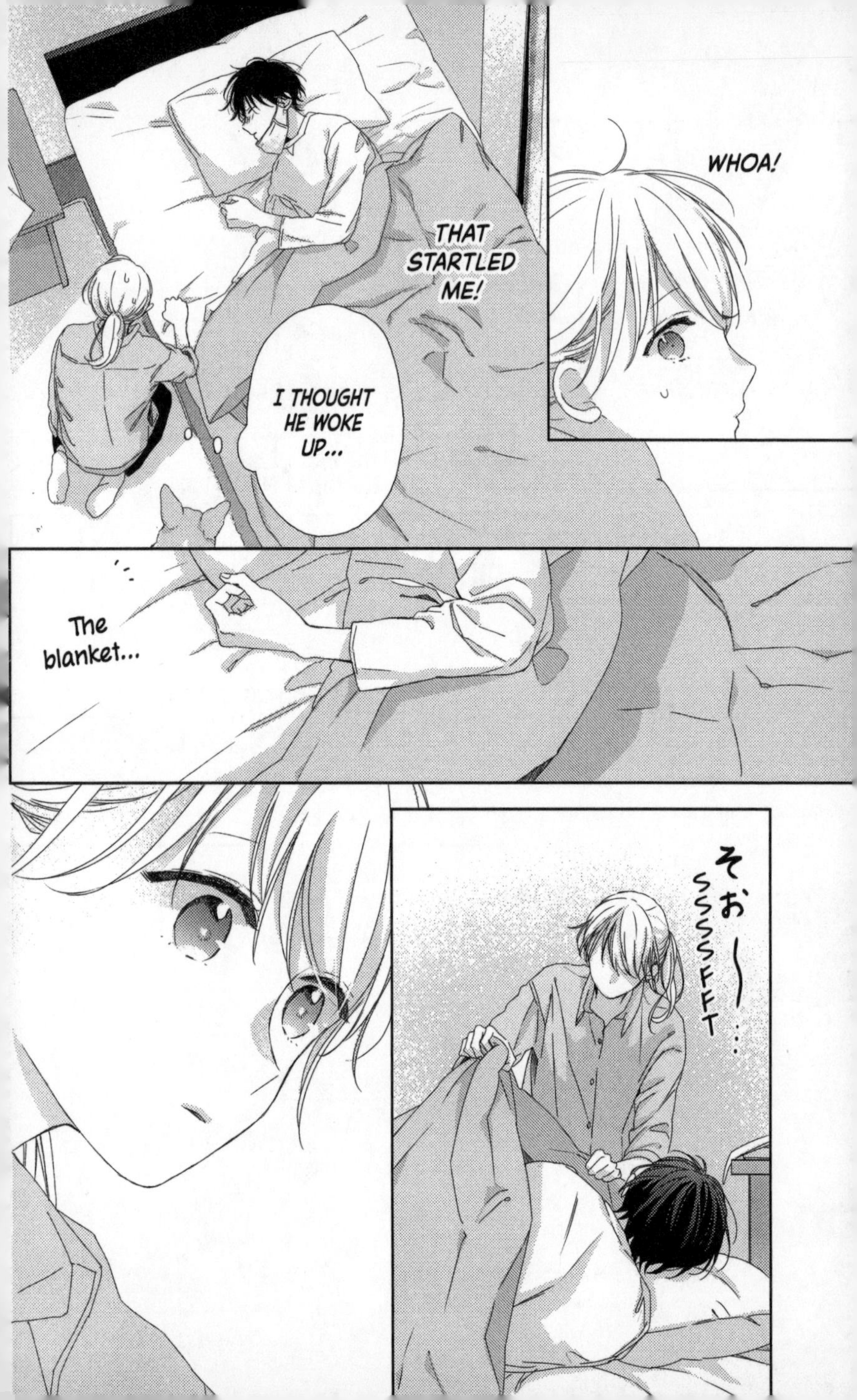
WHOA!
THAT STARTLED ME!
I THOUGHT HE WOKE UP...
The blanket...
そお〜…
SSSSFFT

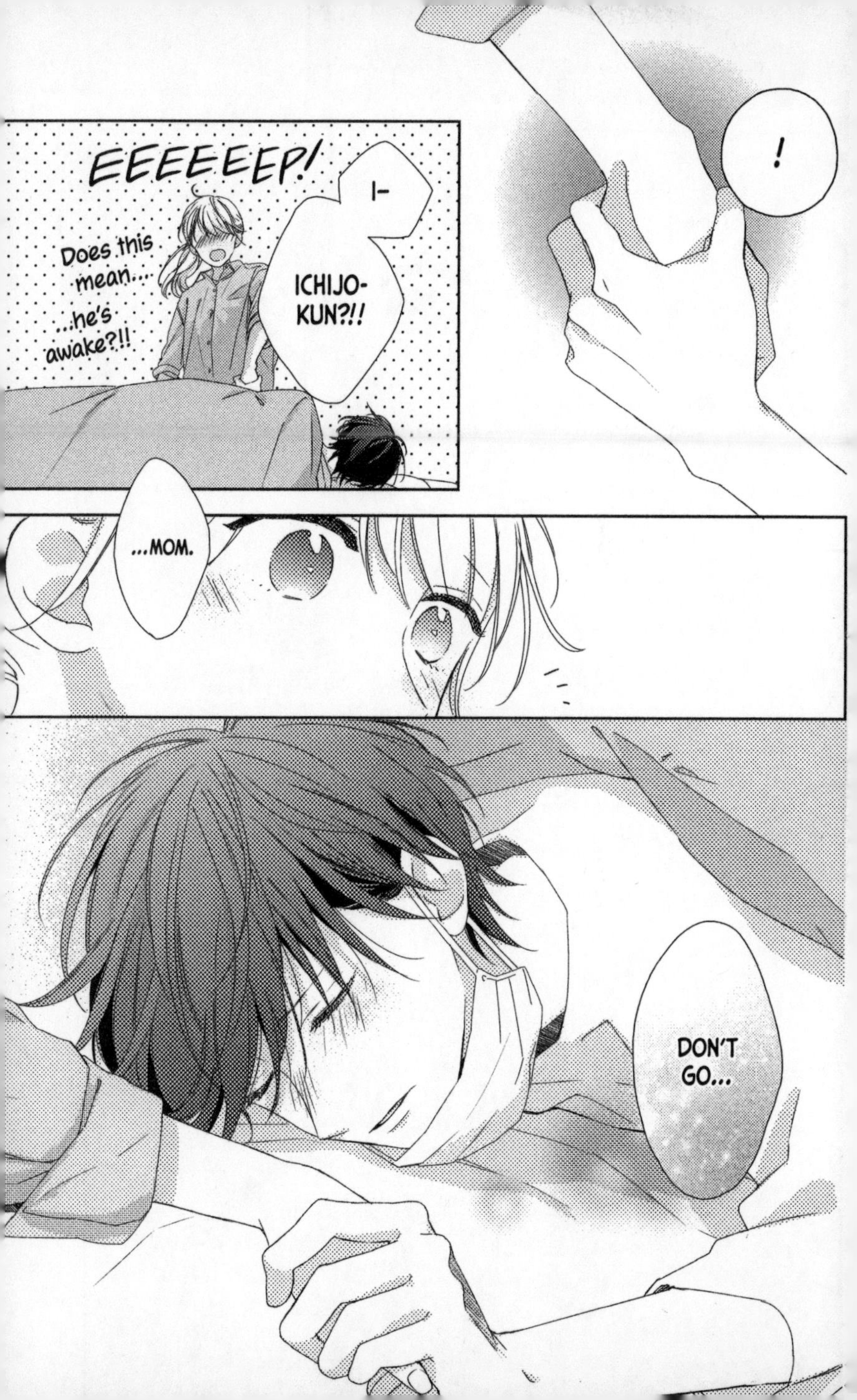
!
EEEEEEP!
I-
ICHIJO-KUN?!!
Does this mean...
...he's awake?!!
...MOM.
DON'T GO...

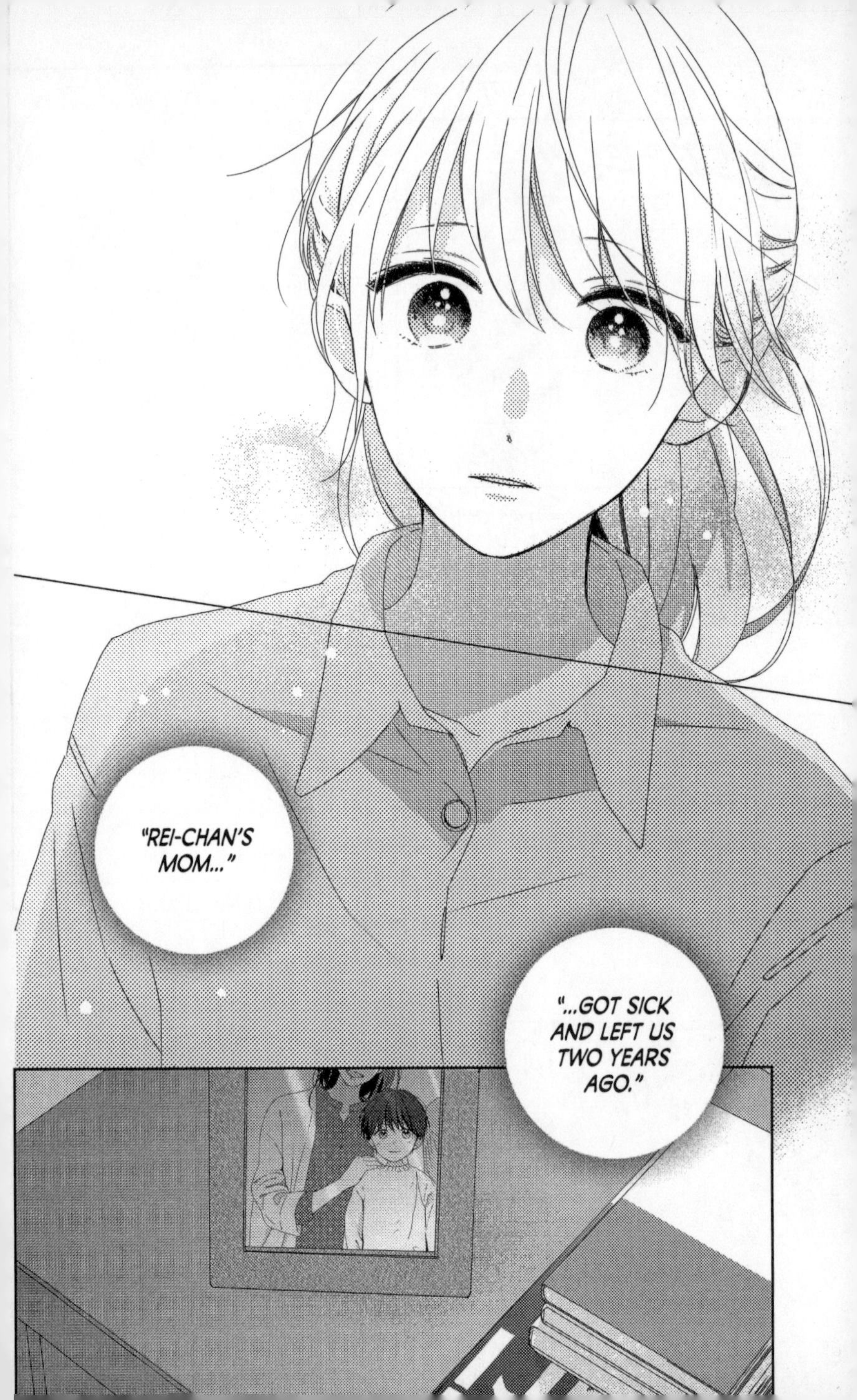
"REI-CHAN'S MOM..."
"...GOT SICK AND LEFT US TWO YEARS AGO."

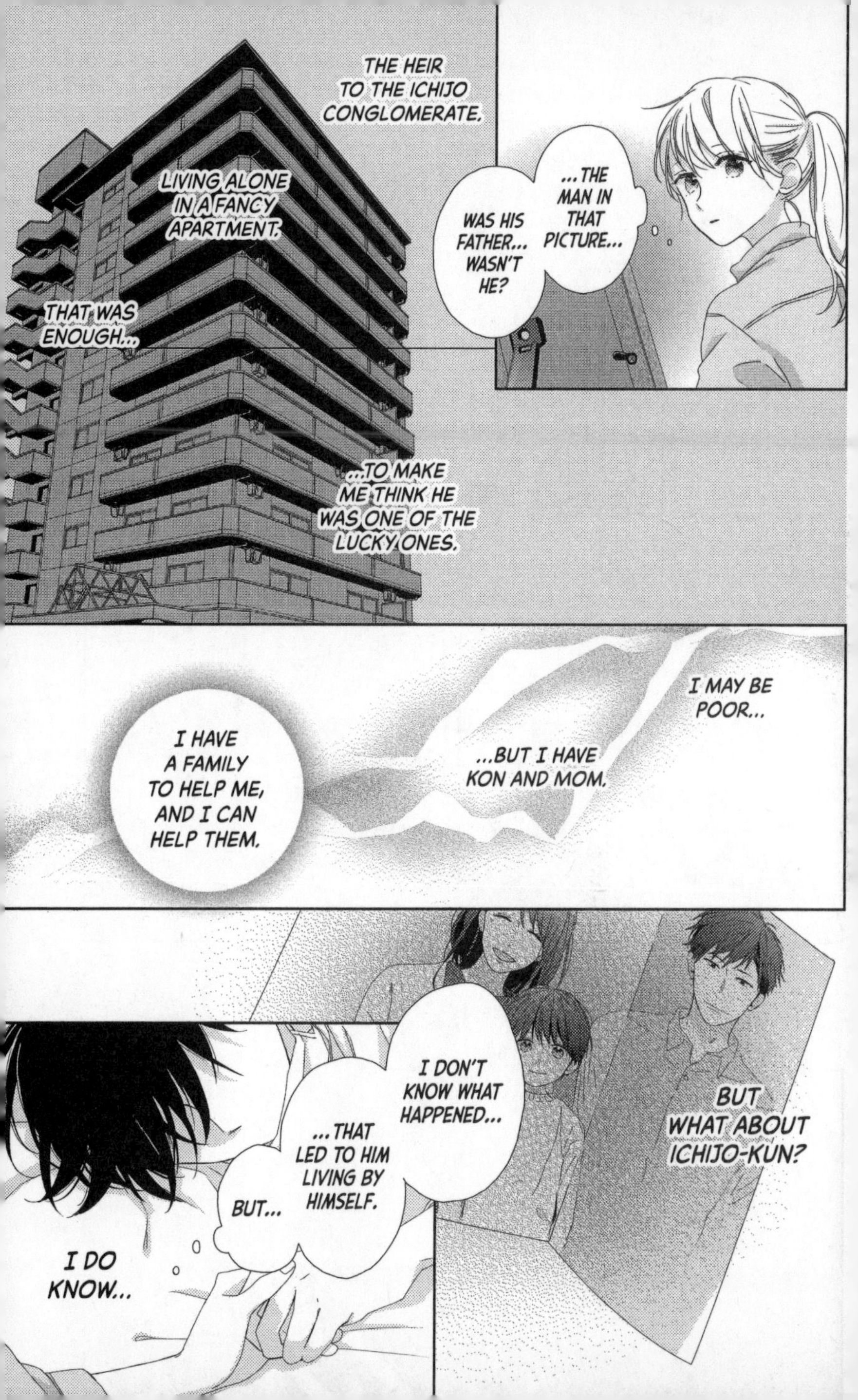
...THE MAN IN THAT PICTURE...
WAS HIS FATHER... WASN'T HE?
THE HEIR TO THE ICHIJO CONGLOMERATE.
LIVING ALONE IN A FANCY APARTMENT.
THAT WAS ENOUGH...
...TO MAKE ME THINK HE WAS ONE OF THE LUCKY ONES.
I MAY BE POOR...
...BUT I HAVE KON AND MOM.
I HAVE A FAMILY TO HELP ME, AND I CAN HELP THEM.
BUT WHAT ABOUT ICHIJO-KUN?
I DON'T KNOW WHAT HAPPENED...
...THAT LED TO HIM LIVING BY HIMSELF.
BUT...
I DO KNOW...

...THAT HE'S HERE,

IN THIS APARTMENT,

ALL ALONE,

...

HE DOES HAVE YOU, KOTARO.

AROON?

RIGHT, SORRY.

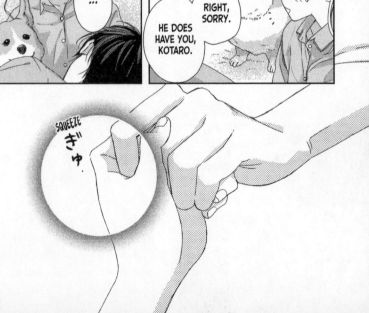

SQUEEZE

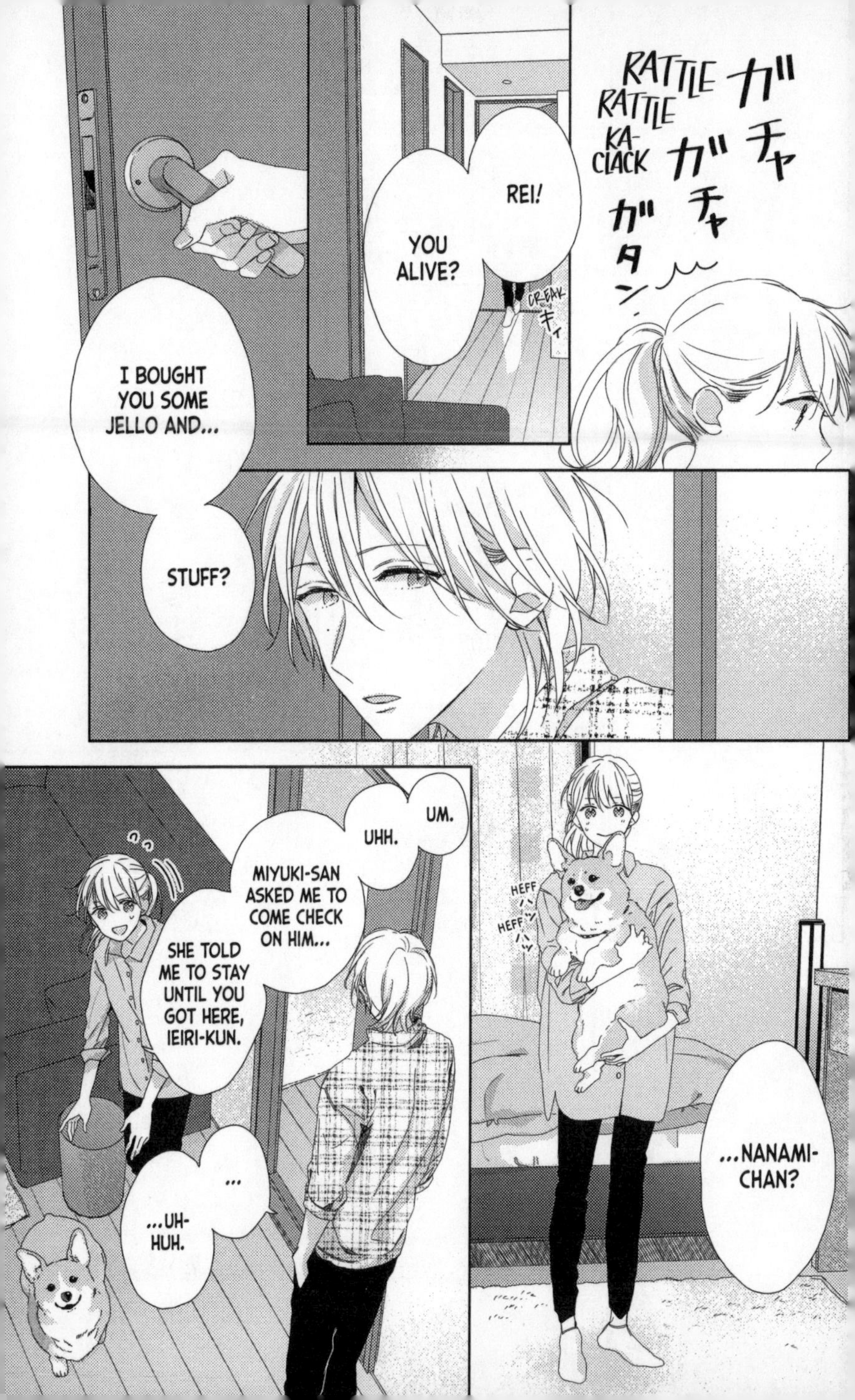
RATTLE RATTLE KA-CLACK
ガチャガチャガタン
REI!
YOU ALIVE?
CREAK
キィ
I BOUGHT YOU SOME JELLO AND...
STUFF?
...NANAMI-CHAN?
HEFF HEFF
ハッハッ
UM.
UHH.
MIYUKI-SAN ASKED ME TO COME CHECK ON HIM...
SHE TOLD ME TO STAY UNTIL YOU GOT HERE, IEIRI-KUN.
...
...UH-HUH.

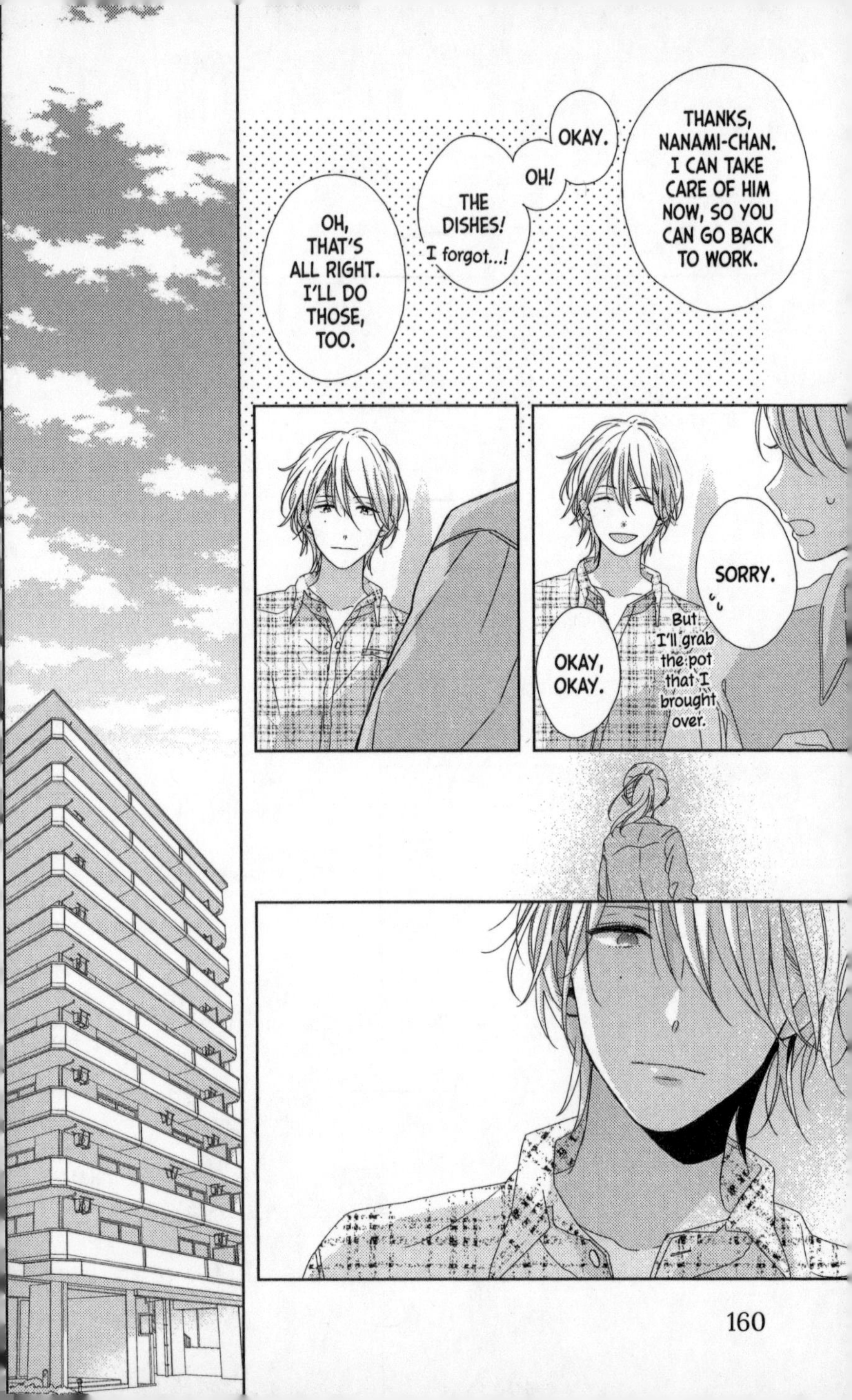
THANKS, NANAMI-CHAN. I CAN TAKE CARE OF HIM NOW, SO YOU CAN GO BACK TO WORK.
OKAY.
OH!
THE DISHES!
I forgot...!
OH, THAT'S ALL RIGHT. I'LL DO THOSE, TOO.
SORRY.
But I'll grab the pot that I brought over.
OKAY, OKAY.

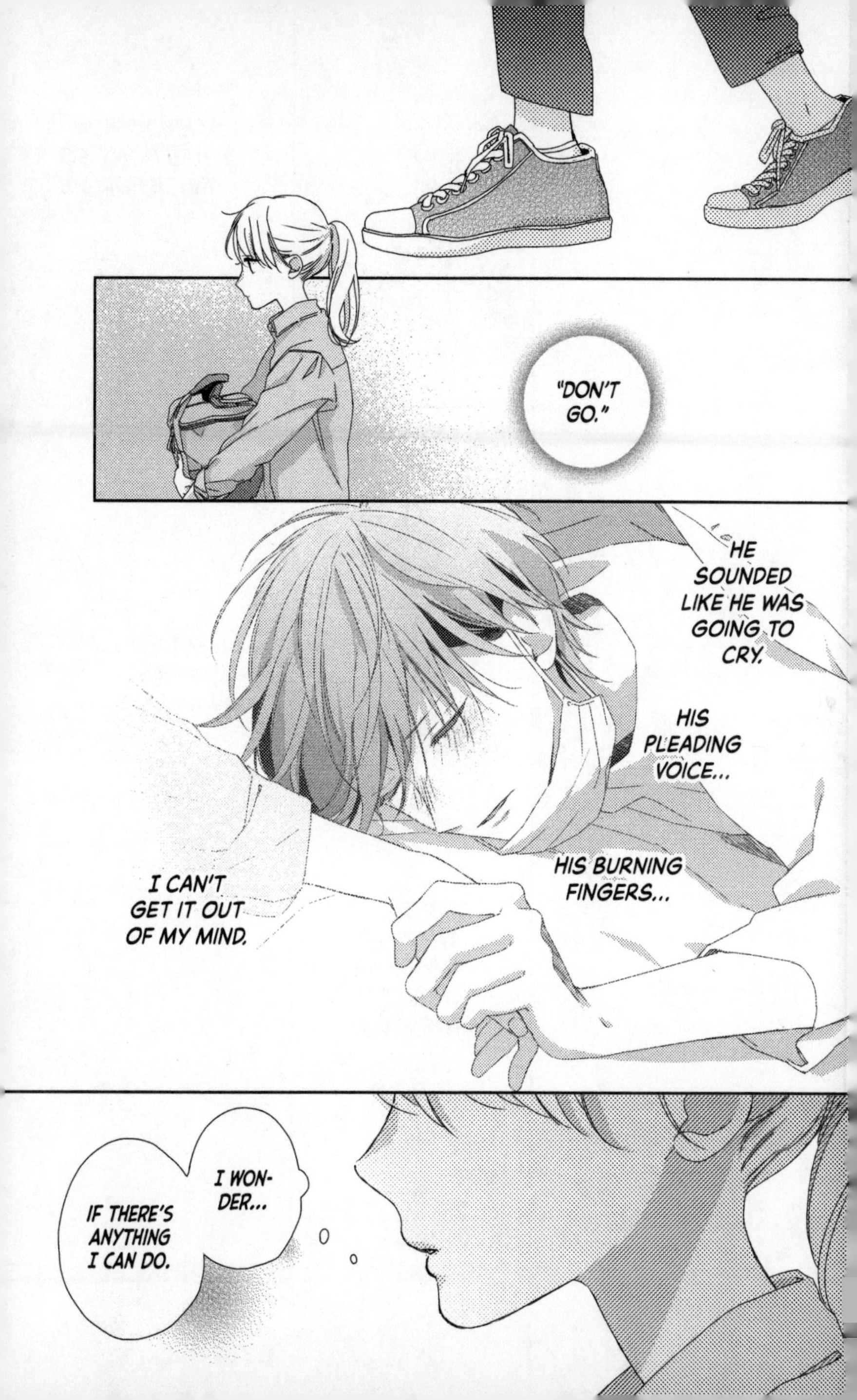
"DON'T GO."
HE SOUNDED LIKE HE WAS GOING TO CRY.
HIS PLEADING VOICE...
HIS BURNING FINGERS...
I CAN'T GET IT OUT OF MY MIND.
I WON-DER...
IF THERE'S ANYTHING I CAN DO.

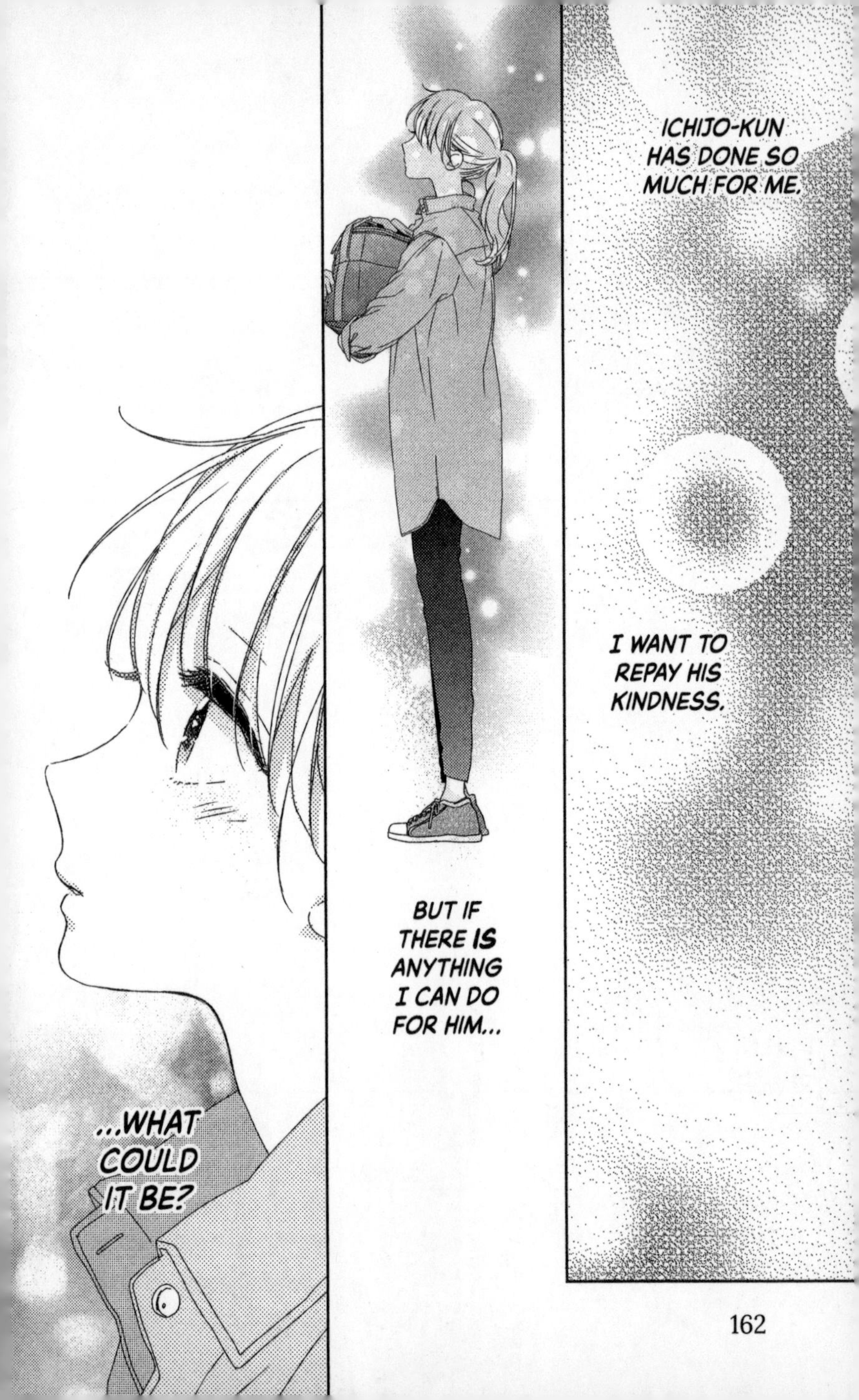
ICHIJO-KUN HAS DONE SO MUCH FOR ME.
I WANT TO REPAY HIS KINDNESS.
BUT IF THERE IS ANYTHING I CAN DO FOR HIM...
...WHAT COULD IT BE?

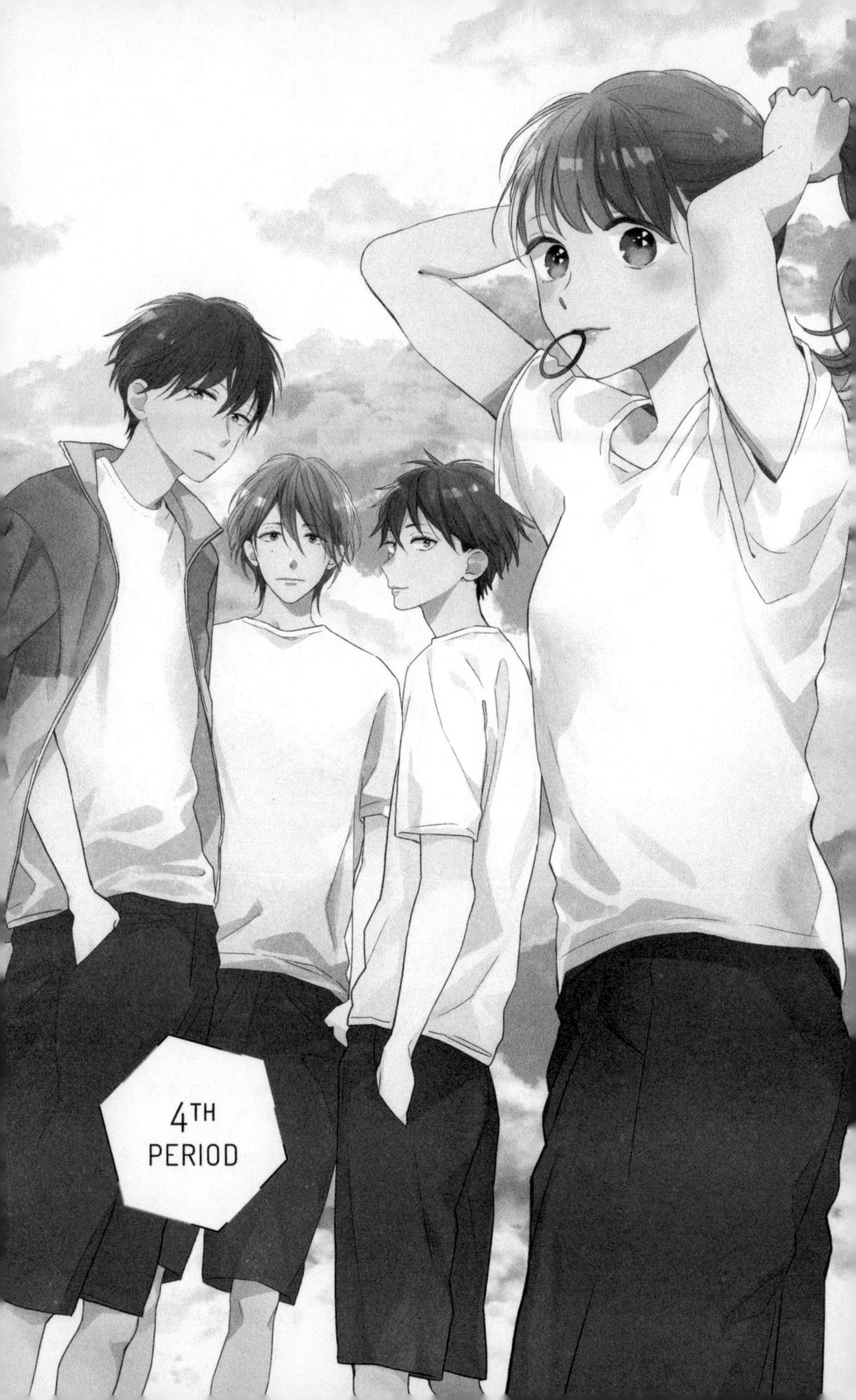
4TH PERIOD

AFTERWORD

THANK YOU VERY MUCH FOR PICKING UP VOLUME 1 OF *THOSE NOT-SO-SWEET BOYS!*

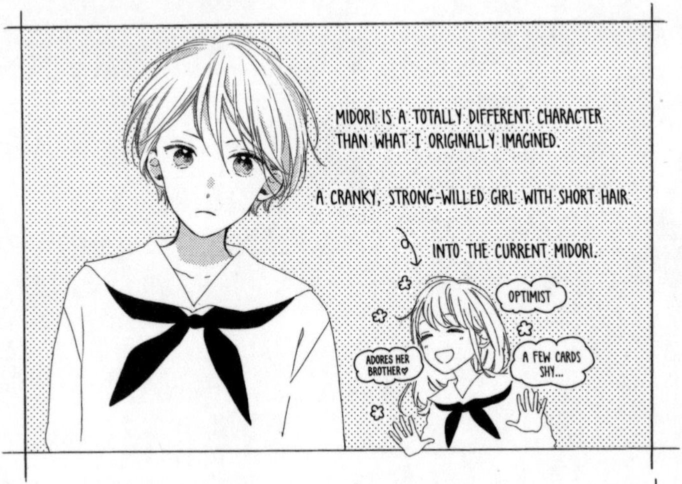
MIDORI IS A TOTALLY DIFFERENT CHARACTER THAN WHAT I ORIGINALLY IMAGINED.
A CRANKY, STRONG-WILLED GIRL WITH SHORT HAIR.
INTO THE CURRENT MIDORI.
OPTIMIST
ADORES HER BROTHER♡
A FEW CARDS SHY...

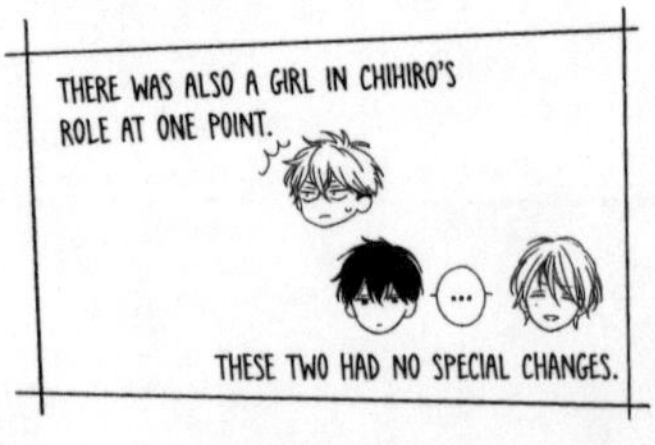
THERE WAS ALSO A GIRL IN CHIHIRO'S ROLE AT ONE POINT.
...
THESE TWO HAD NO SPECIAL CHANGES.

Special Thanks.

AKI NISHIHIRO-CHAN
FRIENDS, FAMILY
MY EDITOR
KODAMA-SAN
EVERYONE AT THE DESSERT EDITORIAL DEPARTMENT
ARCO INC.
EVERYONE WHO WAS INVOLVED IN THE CREATION AND SELLING OF THIS WORK.

I HOPE WE CAN MEET AGAIN IN VOLUME 2!

YOKO NOGIRI

IF THERE **IS** ANYTHING I CAN DO FOR ICHIJO-KUN...

...WHAT COULD IT BE?

BEFORE I COULD COME UP WITH A GOOD, SOLID ANSWER...

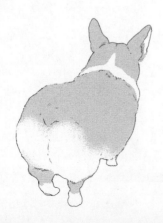

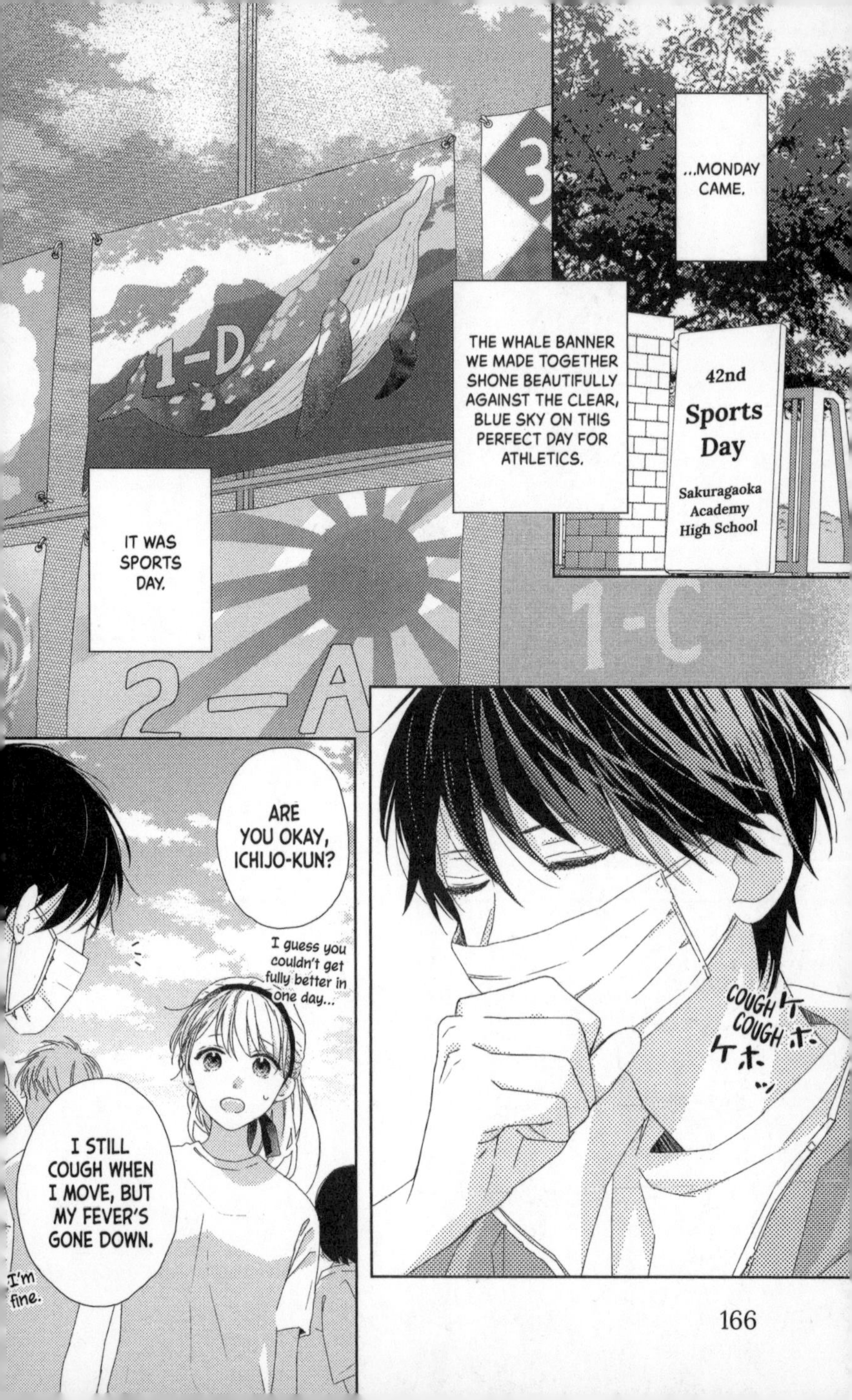
...MONDAY CAME.
42nd Sports Day Sakuragaoka Academy High School
THE WHALE BANNER WE MADE TOGETHER SHONE BEAUTIFULLY AGAINST THE CLEAR, BLUE SKY ON THIS PERFECT DAY FOR ATHLETICS.
3
1-D
IT WAS SPORTS DAY.
2-A
1-C
COUGH COUGH
ケホ ケホッ
ARE YOU OKAY, ICHIJO-KUN?
I guess you couldn't get fully better in one day...
I STILL COUGH WHEN I MOVE, BUT MY FEVER'S GONE DOWN.
I'm fine.

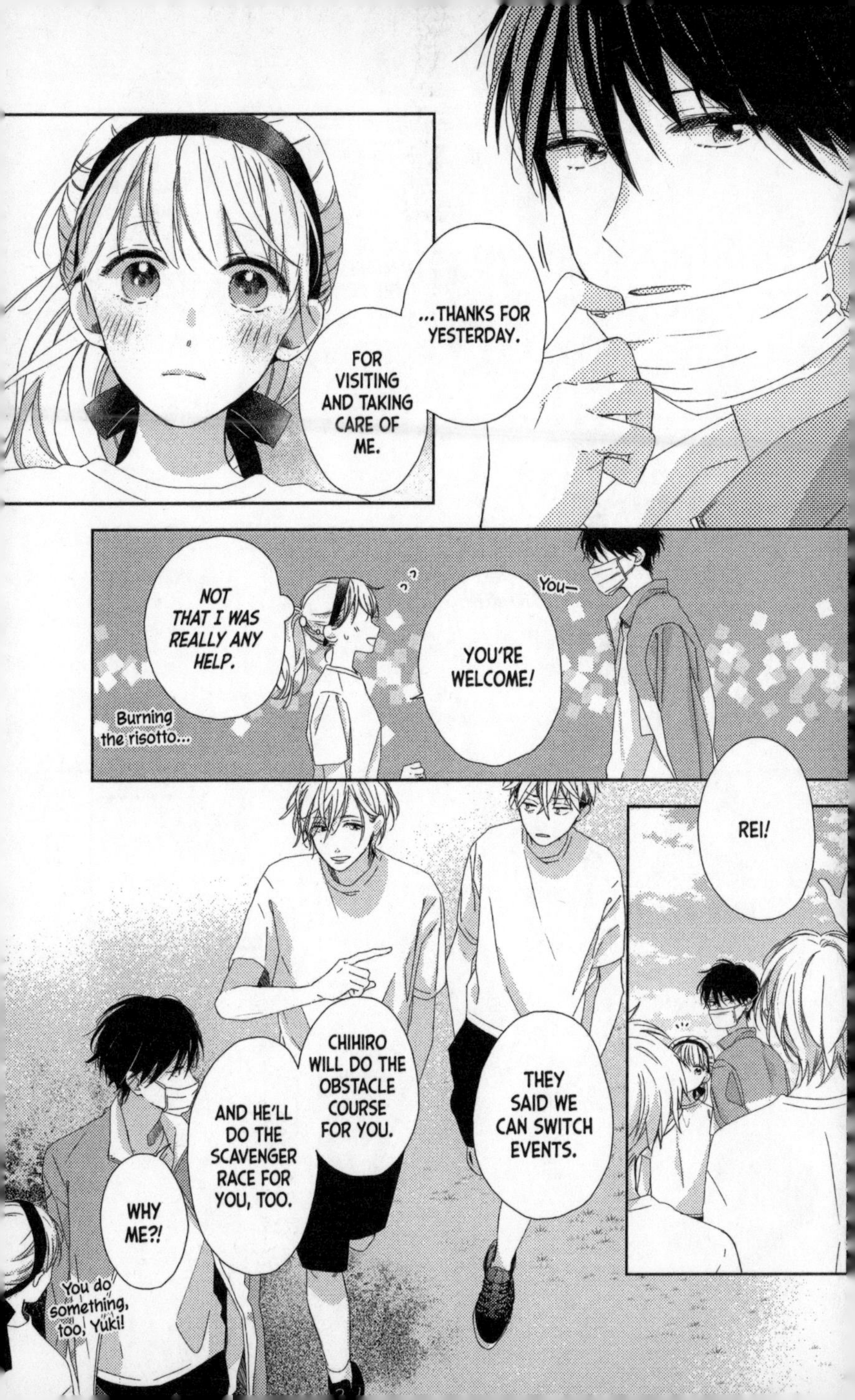
...THANKS FOR YESTERDAY.
FOR VISITING AND TAKING CARE OF ME.
You—
YOU'RE WELCOME!
NOT THAT I WAS REALLY ANY HELP.
Burning the risotto...
REI!
THEY SAID WE CAN SWITCH EVENTS.
CHIHIRO WILL DO THE OBSTACLE COURSE FOR YOU.
AND HE'LL DO THE SCAVENGER RACE FOR YOU, TOO.
WHY ME?!
You do something, too, Yuki!

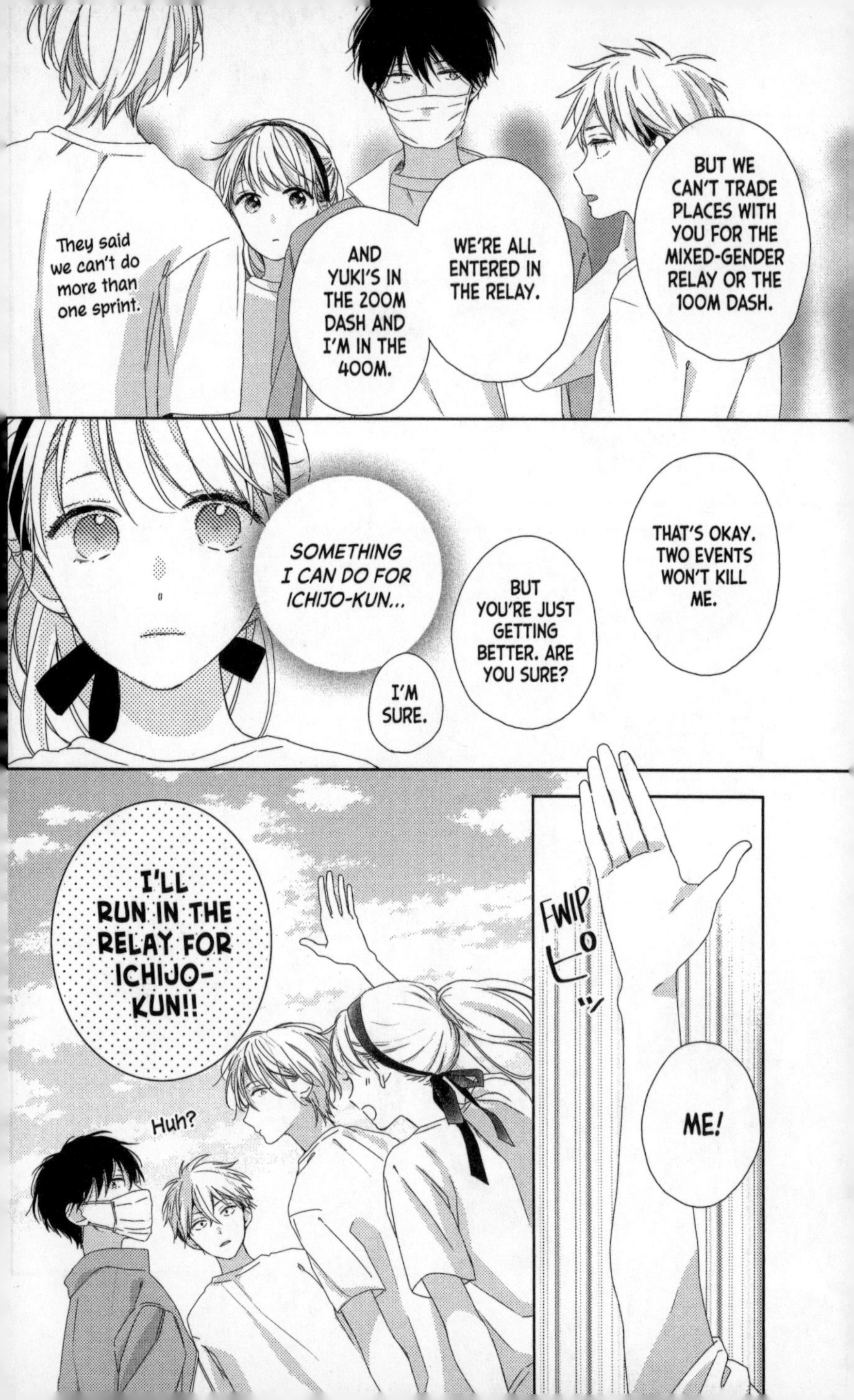
BUT WE CAN'T TRADE PLACES WITH YOU FOR THE MIXED-GENDER RELAY OR THE 100M DASH.
WE'RE ALL ENTERED IN THE RELAY.
AND YUKI'S IN THE 200M DASH AND I'M IN THE 400M.
They said we can't do more than one sprint.
THAT'S OKAY. TWO EVENTS WON'T KILL ME.
BUT YOU'RE JUST GETTING BETTER. ARE YOU SURE?
SOMETHING I CAN DO FOR ICHIJO-KUN...
I'M SURE.
FWIP
ME!
I'LL RUN IN THE RELAY FOR ICHIJO-KUN!!
Huh?

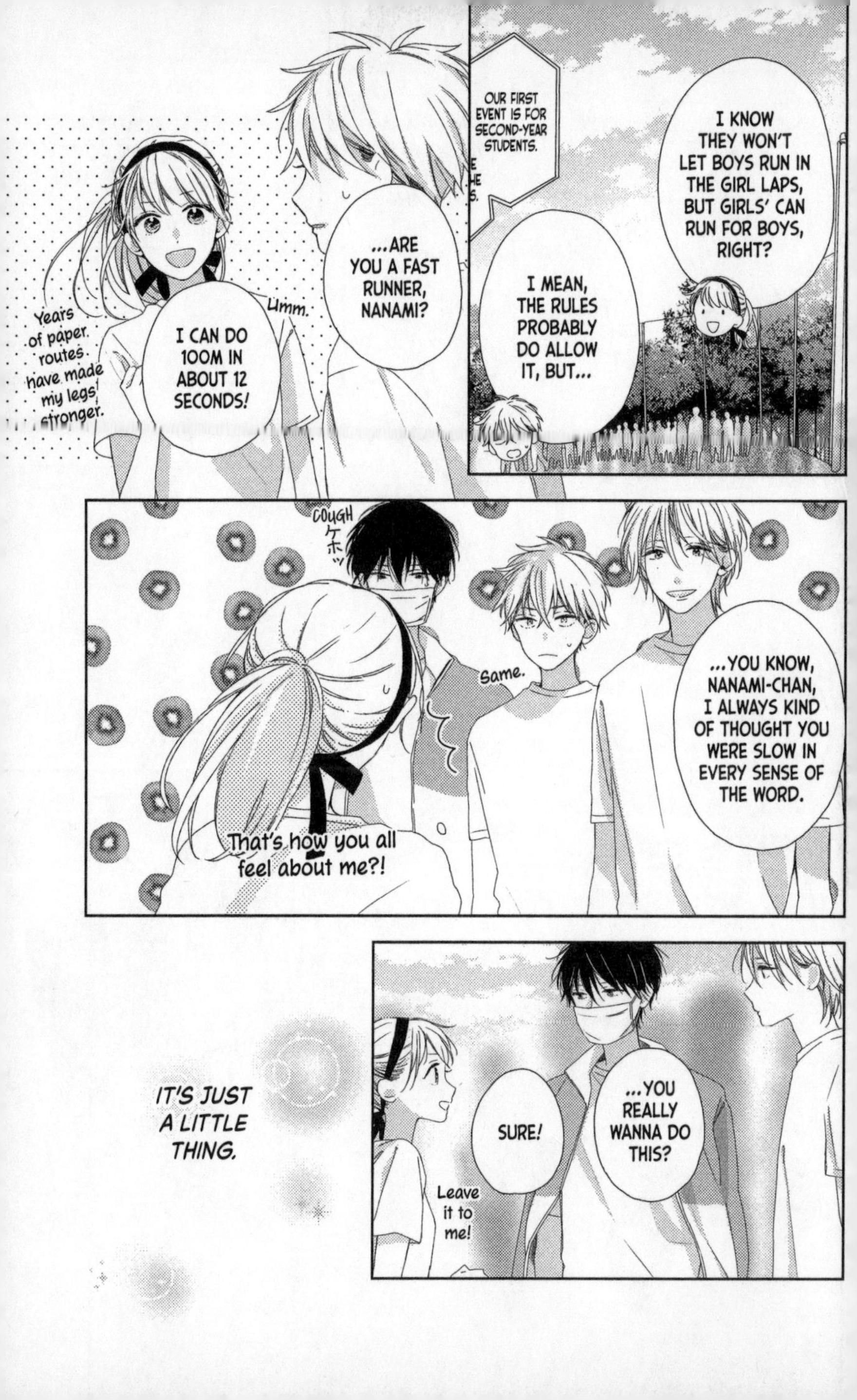
I KNOW THEY WON'T LET BOYS RUN IN THE GIRL LAPS, BUT GIRLS' CAN RUN FOR BOYS, RIGHT?
OUR FIRST EVENT IS FOR SECOND-YEAR STUDENTS.
I MEAN, THE RULES PROBABLY DO ALLOW IT, BUT...
...ARE YOU A FAST RUNNER, NANAMI?
Umm.
I CAN DO 100M IN ABOUT 12 SECONDS!
Years of paper routes have made my legs stronger.
...YOU KNOW, NANAMI-CHAN, I ALWAYS KIND OF THOUGHT YOU WERE SLOW IN EVERY SENSE OF THE WORD.
Same.
COUGH
ケホッ
That's how you all feel about me?!
...YOU REALLY WANNA DO THIS?
SURE!
Leave it to me!
IT'S JUST A LITTLE THING.

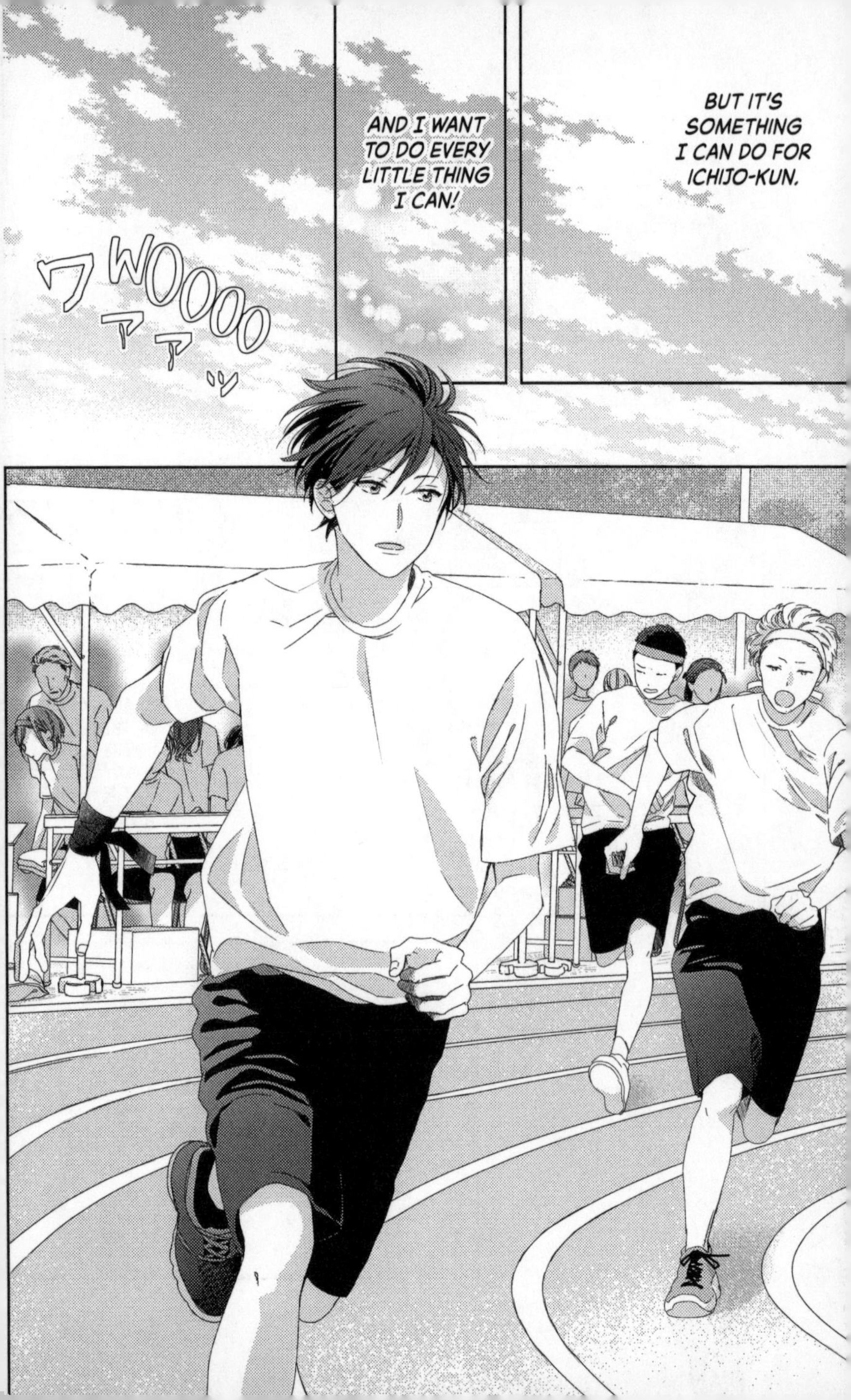
BUT IT'S SOMETHING I CAN DO FOR ICHIJO-KUN.
AND I WANT TO DO EVERY LITTLE THING I CAN!
WOOOOO
ワアアッ

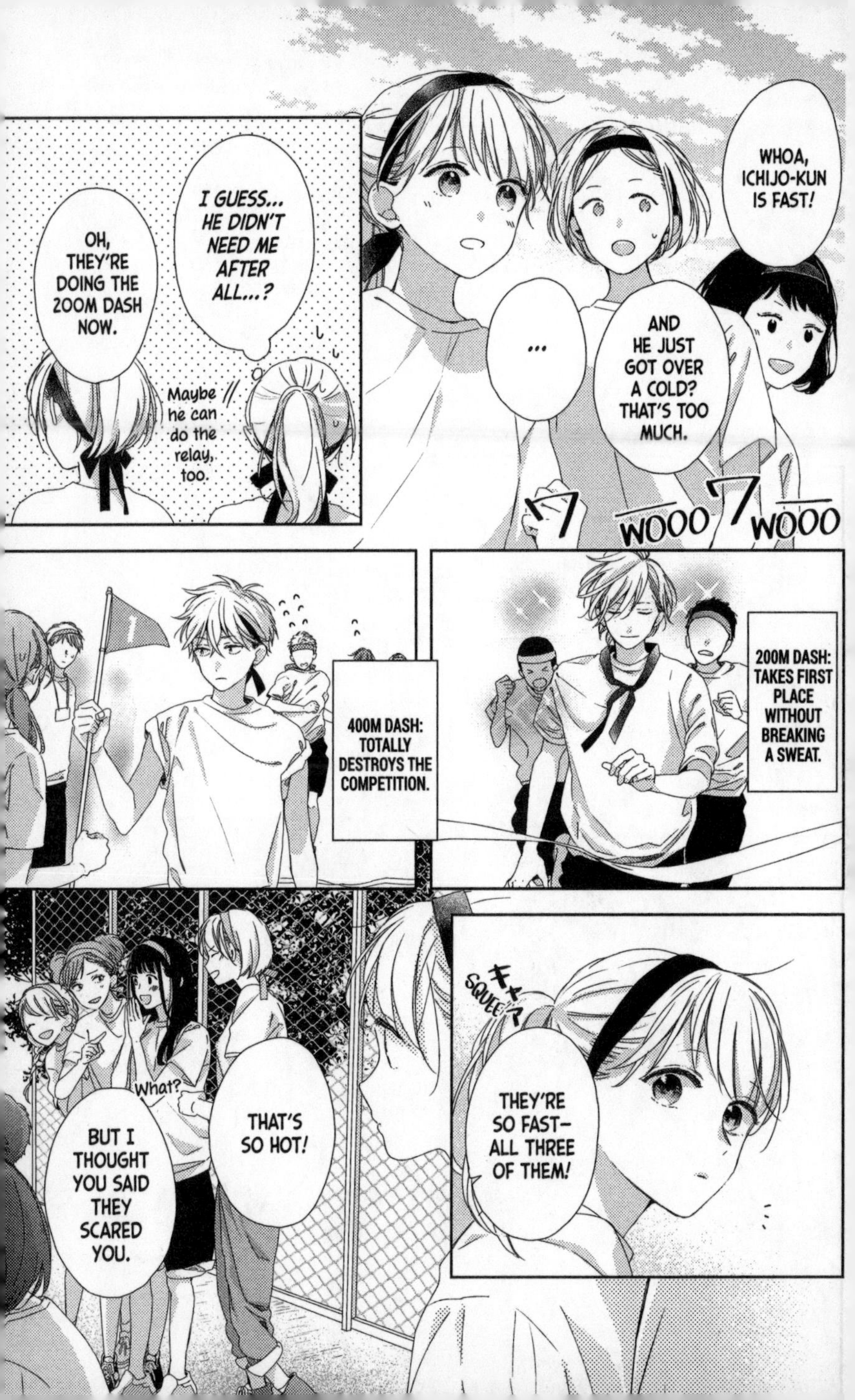
WHOA, ICHIJO-KUN IS FAST!
AND HE JUST GOT OVER A COLD? THAT'S TOO MUCH.
...
WOOO
WOOO
I GUESS... HE DIDN'T NEED ME AFTER ALL...?
OH, THEY'RE DOING THE 200M DASH NOW.
Maybe he can do the relay, too.
200M DASH: TAKES FIRST PLACE WITHOUT BREAKING A SWEAT.
400M DASH: TOTALLY DESTROYS THE COMPETITION.
キャア
SQUEE
THEY'RE SO FAST—ALL THREE OF THEM!
THAT'S SO HOT!
What?
BUT I THOUGHT YOU SAID THEY SCARED YOU.

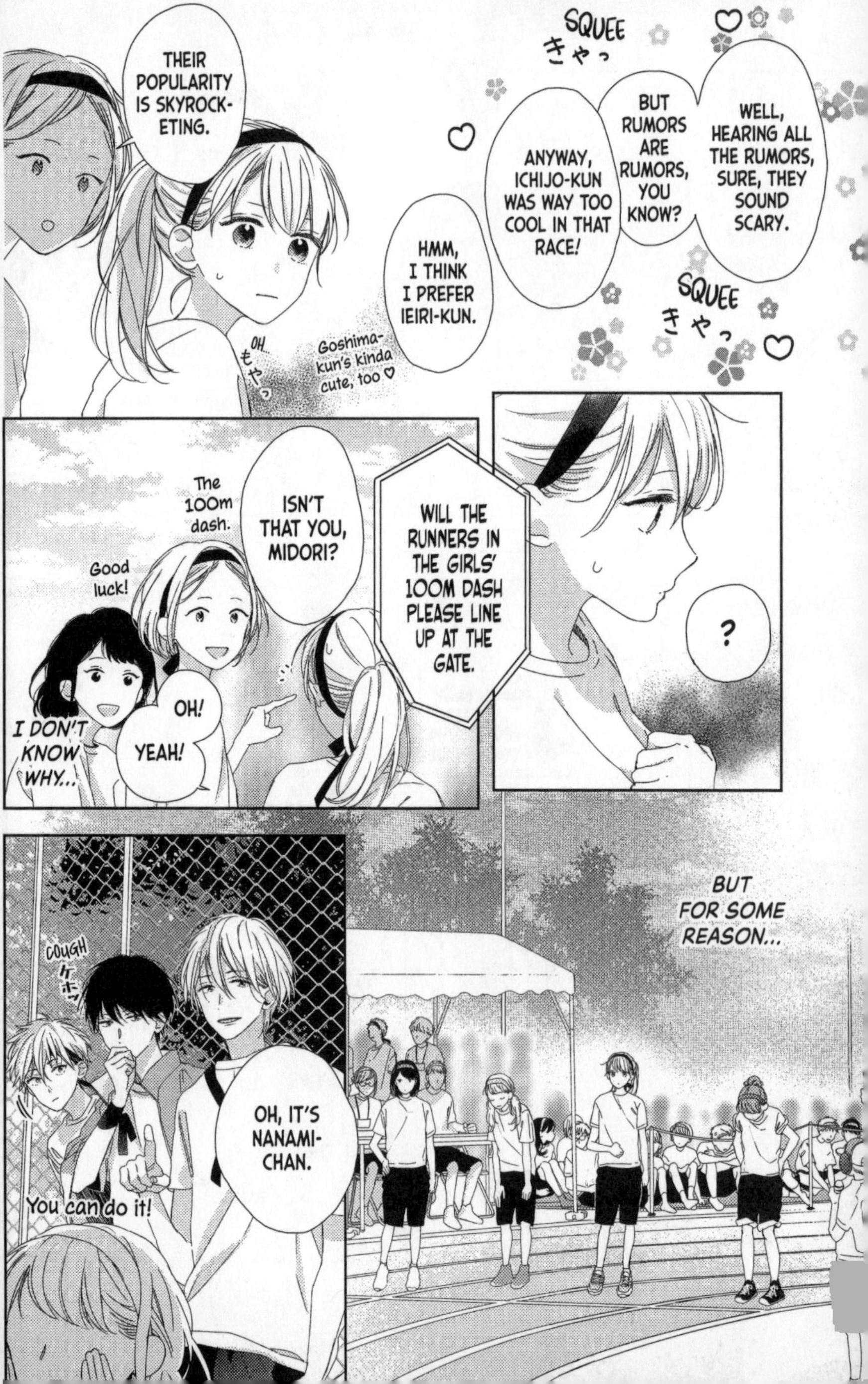
SQUEE
きゃっ
WELL, HEARING ALL THE RUMORS, SURE, THEY SOUND SCARY.
BUT RUMORS ARE RUMORS, YOU KNOW?
ANYWAY, ICHIJO-KUN WAS WAY TOO COOL IN THAT RACE!
SQUEE
きゃっ
HMM, I THINK I PREFER IEIRI-KUN.
Goshima-kun's kinda cute, too ♡
OH...
もやっ
THEIR POPULARITY IS SKYROCKETING.
?
WILL THE RUNNERS IN THE GIRLS' 100M DASH PLEASE LINE UP AT THE GATE.
ISN'T THAT YOU, MIDORI?
The 100m dash.
Good luck!
OH!
YEAH!
I DON'T KNOW WHY...
BUT FOR SOME REASON...
OH, IT'S NANAMI-CHAN.
COUGH
ケホッ
You can do it!

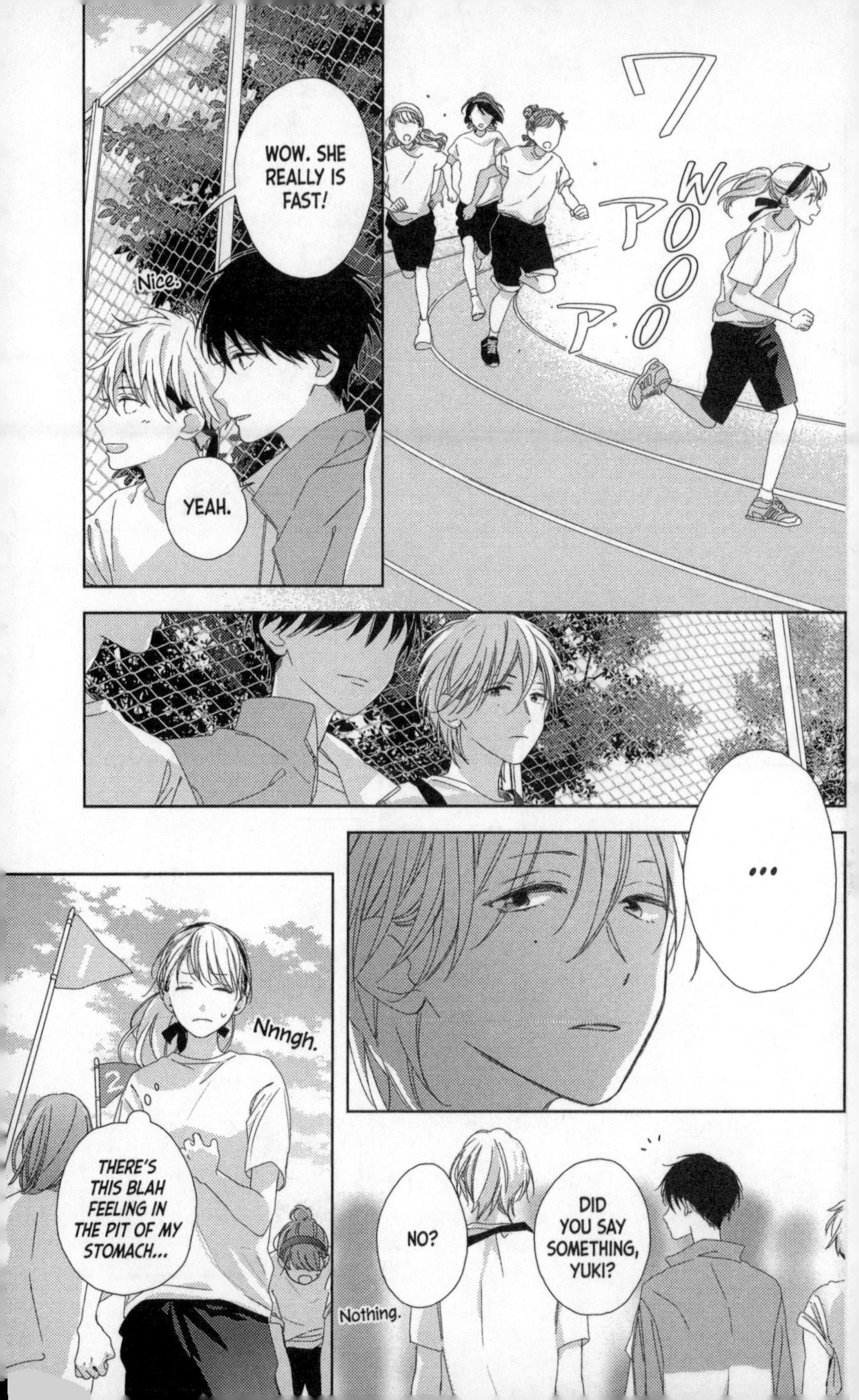
WOOOO
ワアア
WOW. SHE REALLY IS FAST!
Nice.
YEAH.
...
DID YOU SAY SOMETHING, YUKI?
NO?
Nothing.
Nnngh.
THERE'S THIS BLAH FEELING IN THE PIT OF MY STOMACH...

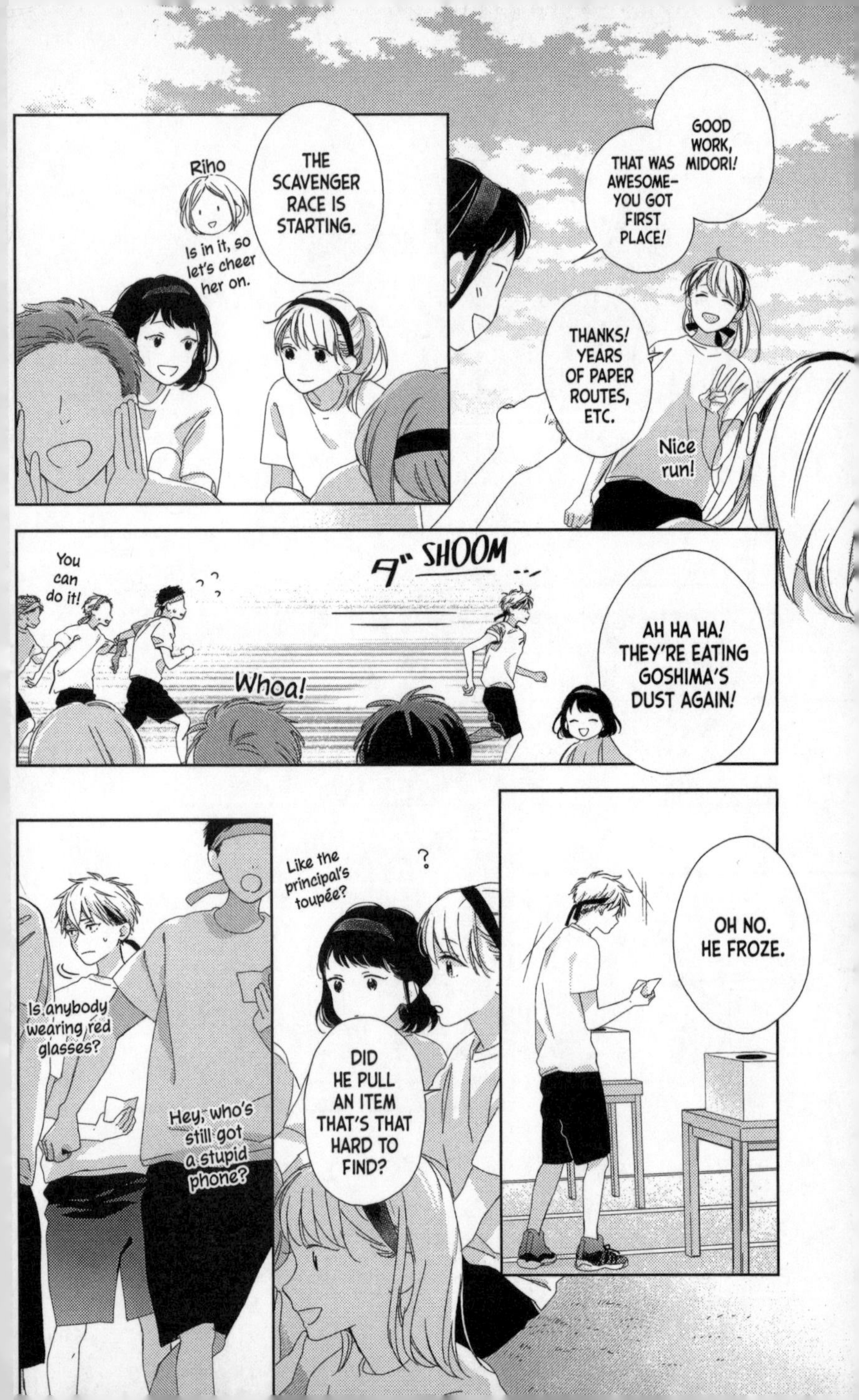
GOOD WORK, MIDORI!
THAT WAS AWESOME—YOU GOT FIRST PLACE!
THANKS! YEARS OF PAPER ROUTES, ETC.
Nice run!
THE SCAVENGER RACE IS STARTING.
Riho
Is in it, so let's cheer her on.
AH HA HA! THEY'RE EATING GOSHIMA'S DUST AGAIN!
ダ SHOOM
Whoa!
You can do it!
OH NO. HE FROZE.
?
Like the principal's toupée?
DID HE PULL AN ITEM THAT'S THAT HARD TO FIND?
Is anybody wearing red glasses?
Hey, who's still got a stupid phone?

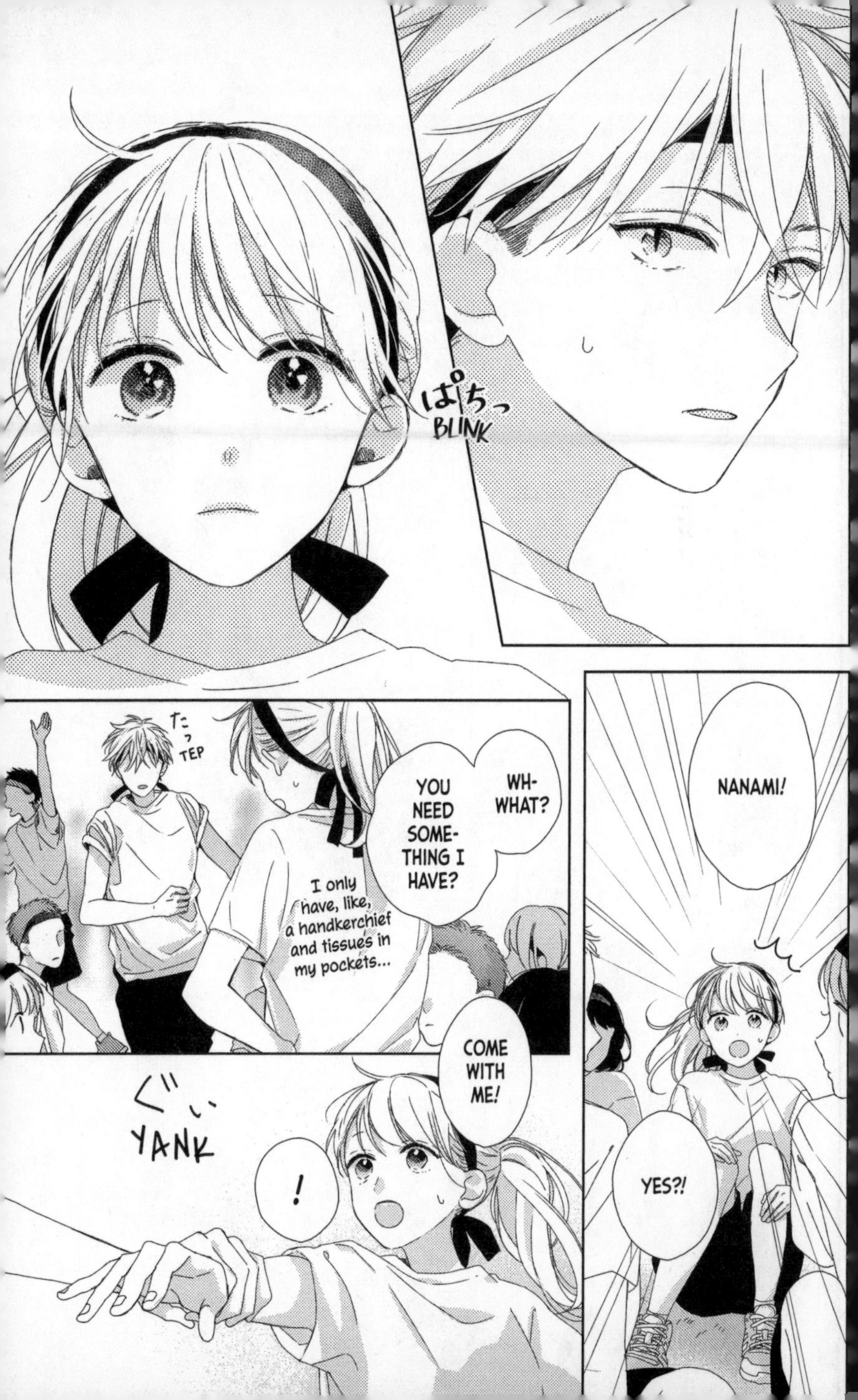
ぱちっ
BLINK
NANAMI!
YES?!
WH- WHAT?
YOU NEED SOME- THING I HAVE?
I only have, like, a handkerchief and tissues in my pockets...
たっ
TEP
COME WITH ME!
ぐい
YANK
!

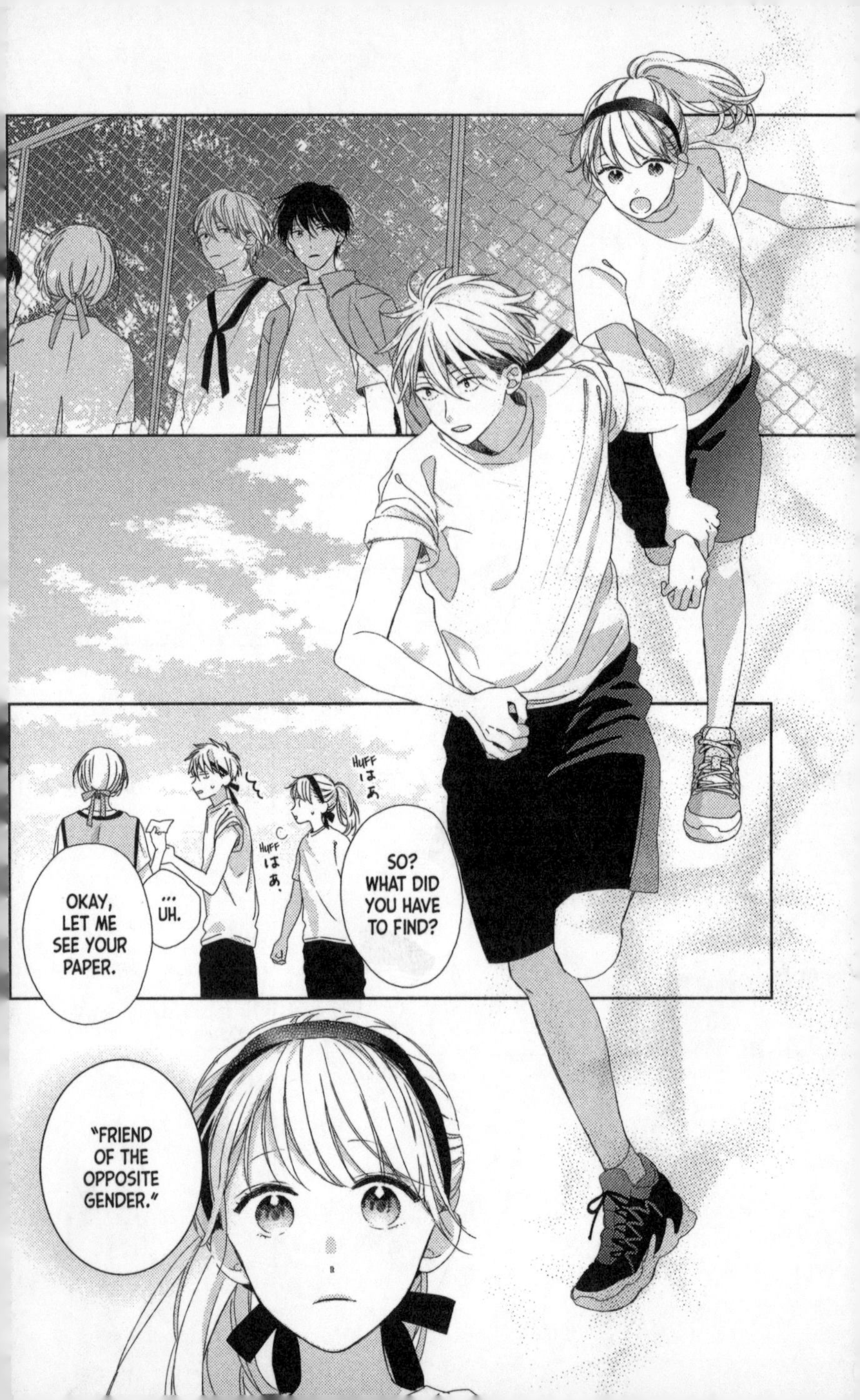
HUFF はあ
HUFF はあ、
SO? WHAT DID YOU HAVE TO FIND?
... UH.
OKAY, LET ME SEE YOUR PAPER.
"FRIEND OF THE OPPOSITE GENDER."

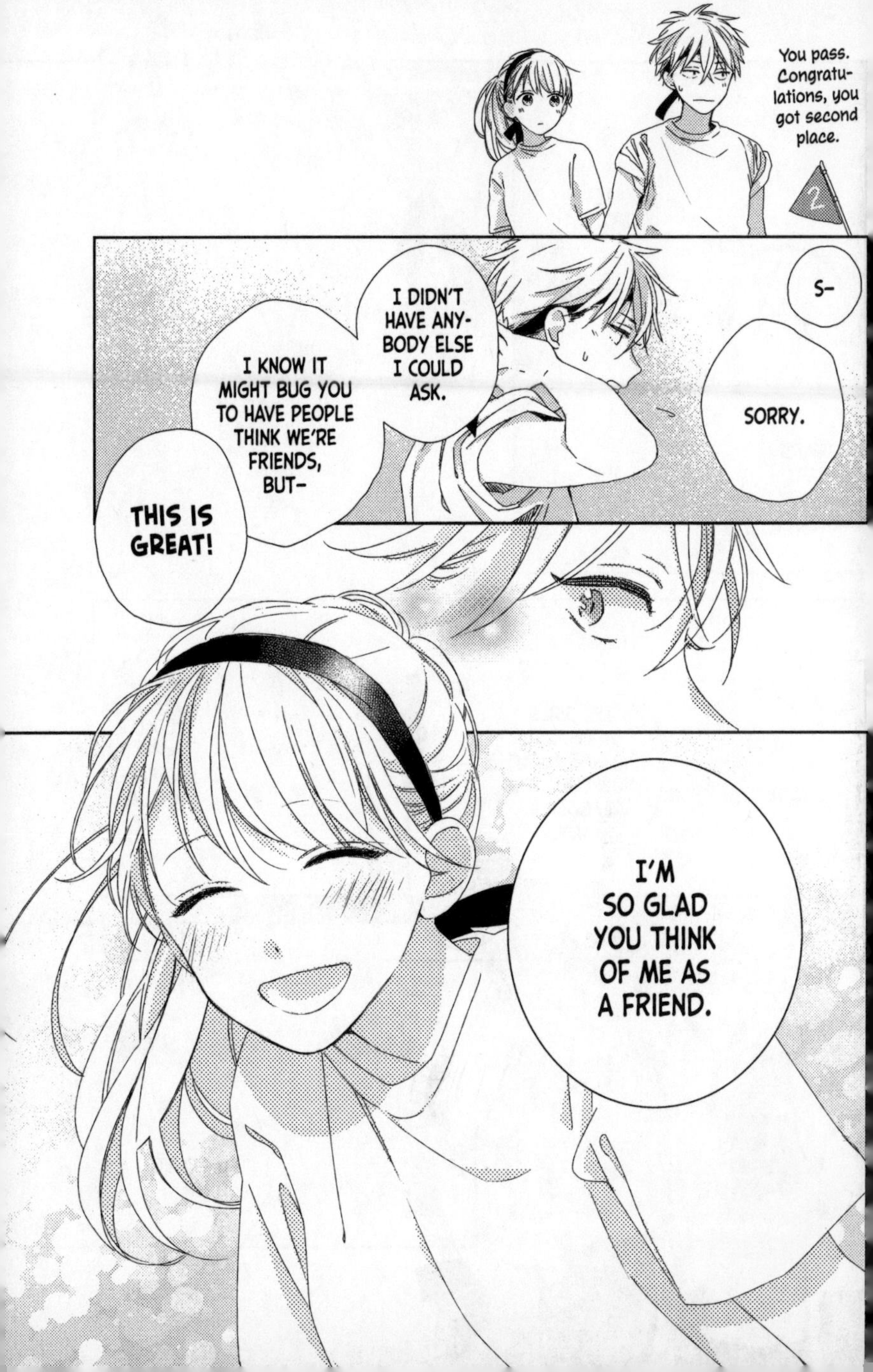
You pass. Congratulations, you got second place.
S-
SORRY.
I DIDN'T HAVE ANYBODY ELSE I COULD ASK.
I KNOW IT MIGHT BUG YOU TO HAVE PEOPLE THINK WE'RE FRIENDS, BUT-
THIS IS GREAT!
I'M SO GLAD YOU THINK OF ME AS A FRIEND.

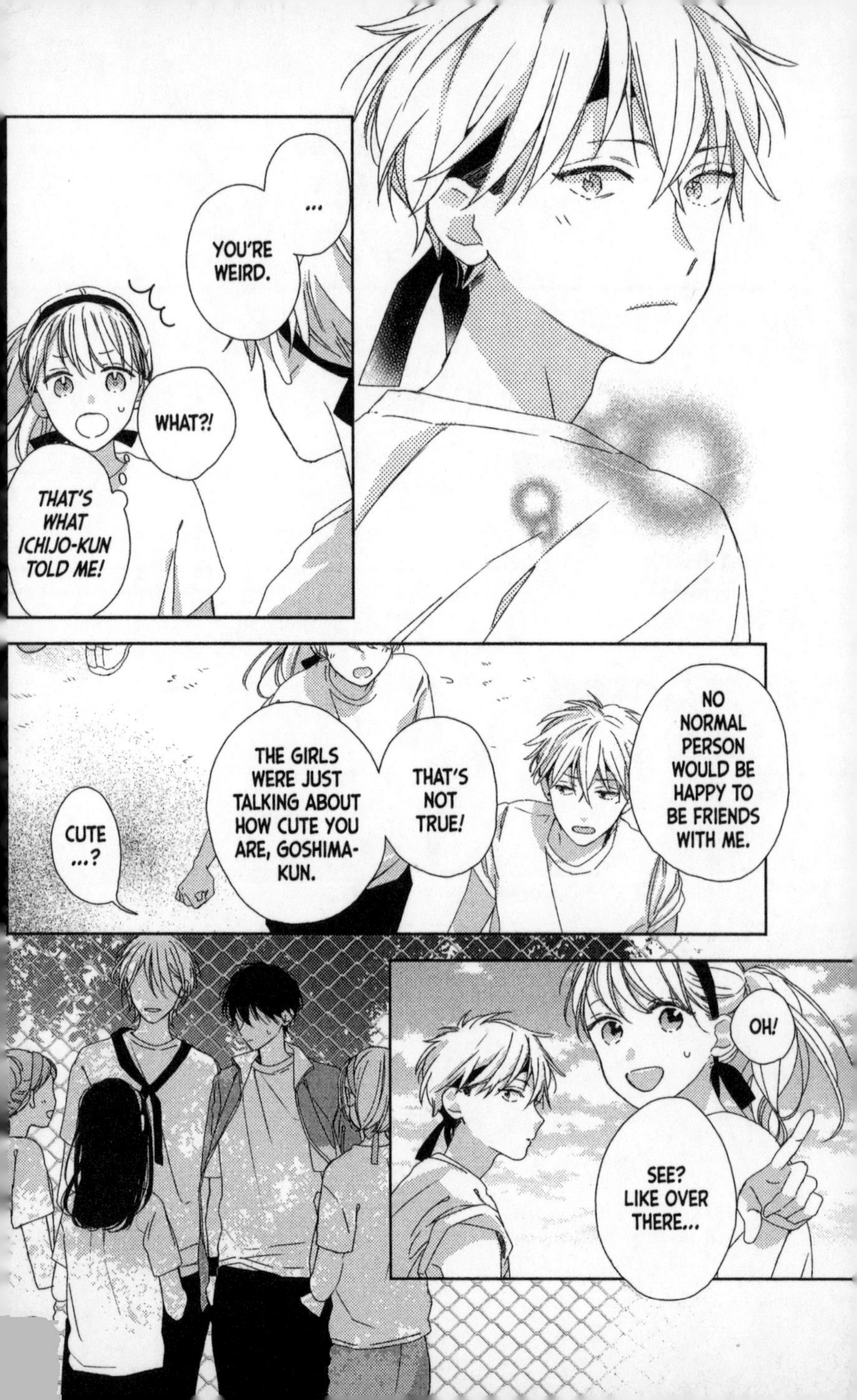
...
YOU'RE WEIRD.
WHAT?!
THAT'S WHAT ICHIJO-KUN TOLD ME!
NO NORMAL PERSON WOULD BE HAPPY TO BE FRIENDS WITH ME.
THAT'S NOT TRUE!
THE GIRLS WERE JUST TALKING ABOUT HOW CUTE YOU ARE, GOSHIMA-KUN.
CUTE ...?
OH!
SEE? LIKE OVER THERE...

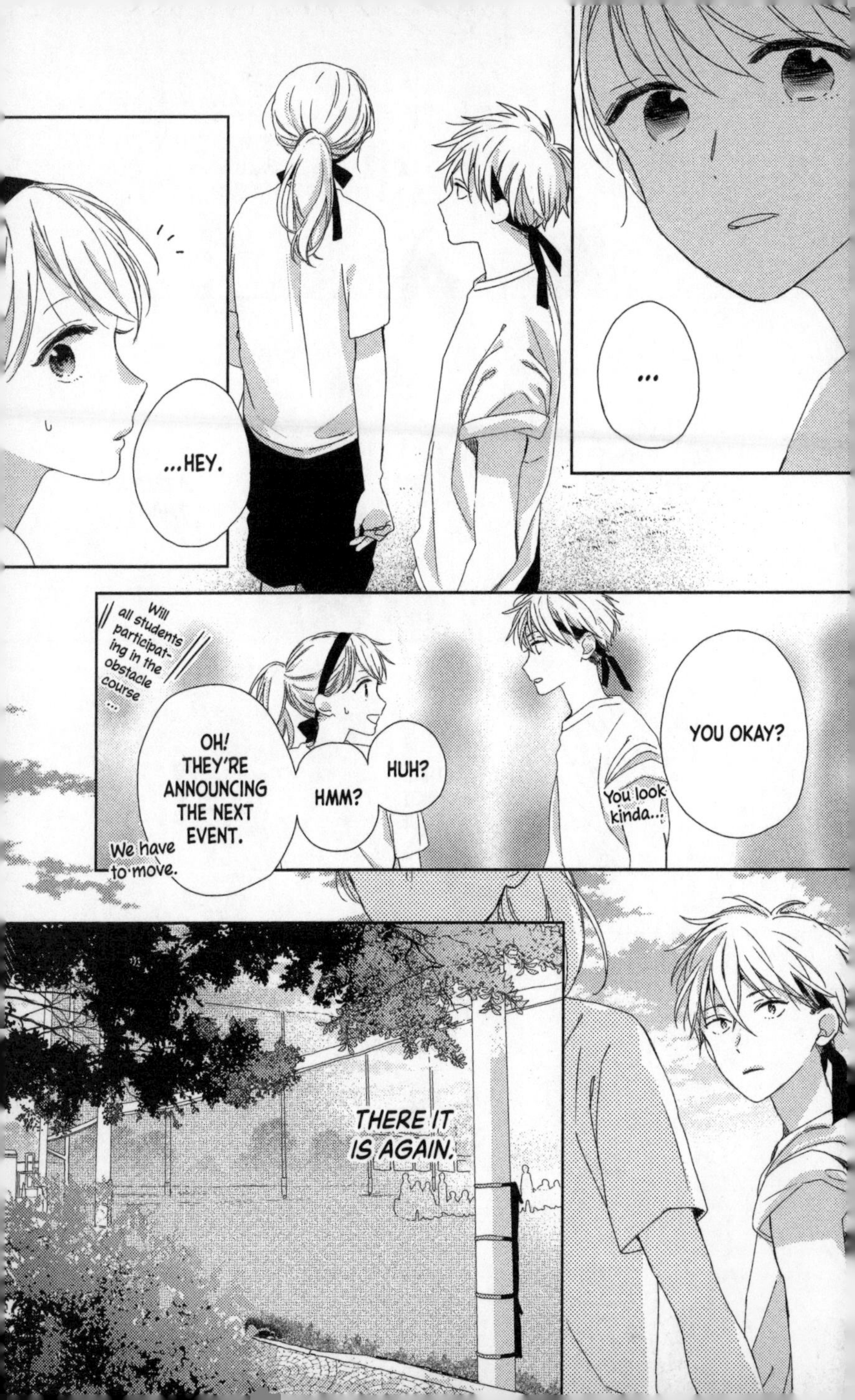
...
...HEY.
YOU OKAY?
You look kinda...
HUH?
HMM?
OH! THEY'RE ANNOUNCING THE NEXT EVENT.
We have to move.
Will all students participating in the obstacle course...
THERE IT IS AGAIN.

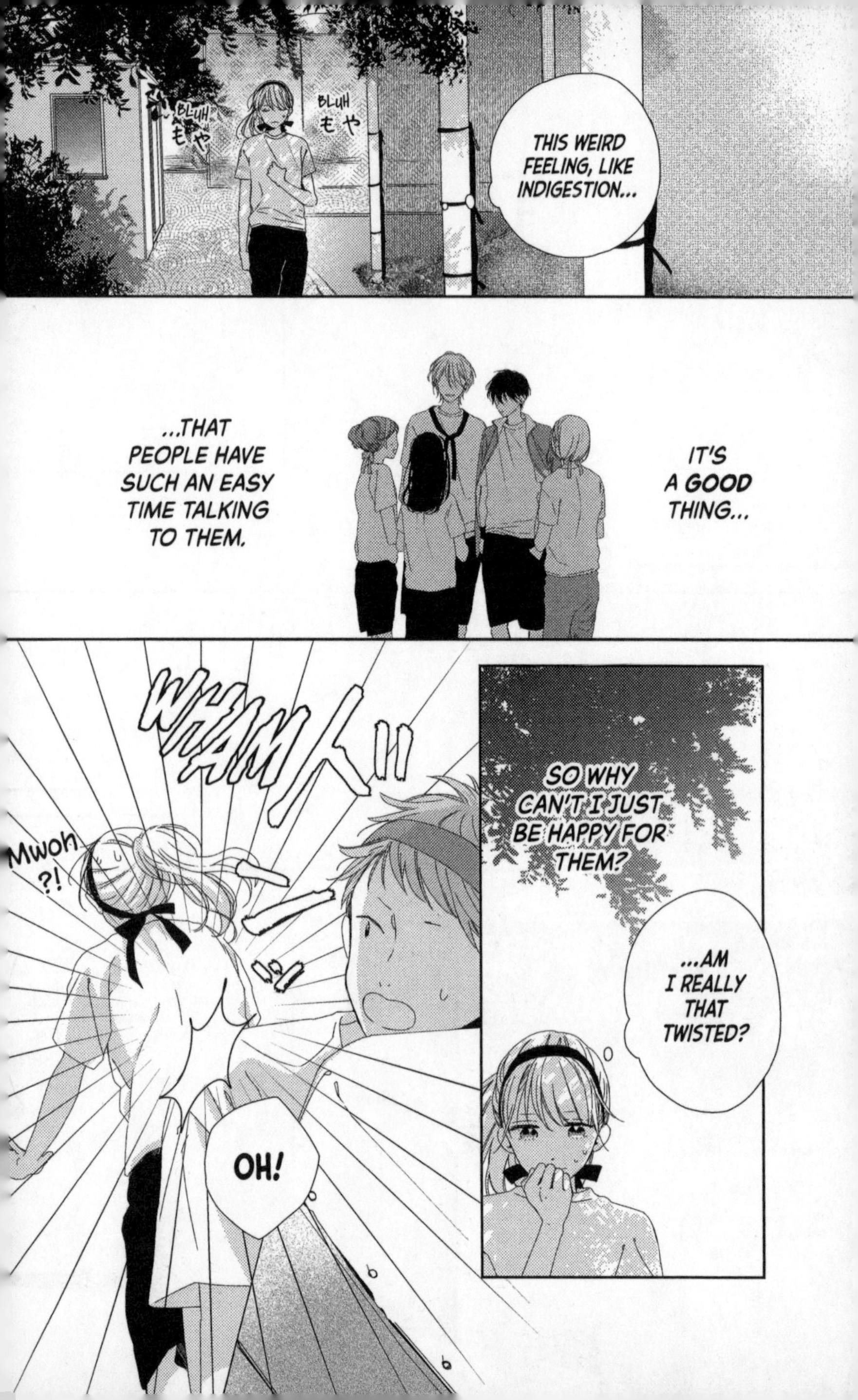
THIS WEIRD FEELING, LIKE INDIGESTION...
BLUH もや
BLUH もや
IT'S A GOOD THING...
...THAT PEOPLE HAVE SUCH AN EASY TIME TALKING TO THEM.
SO WHY CAN'T I JUST BE HAPPY FOR THEM?
...AM I REALLY THAT TWISTED?
WHAM
Mwoh ?!
OH!

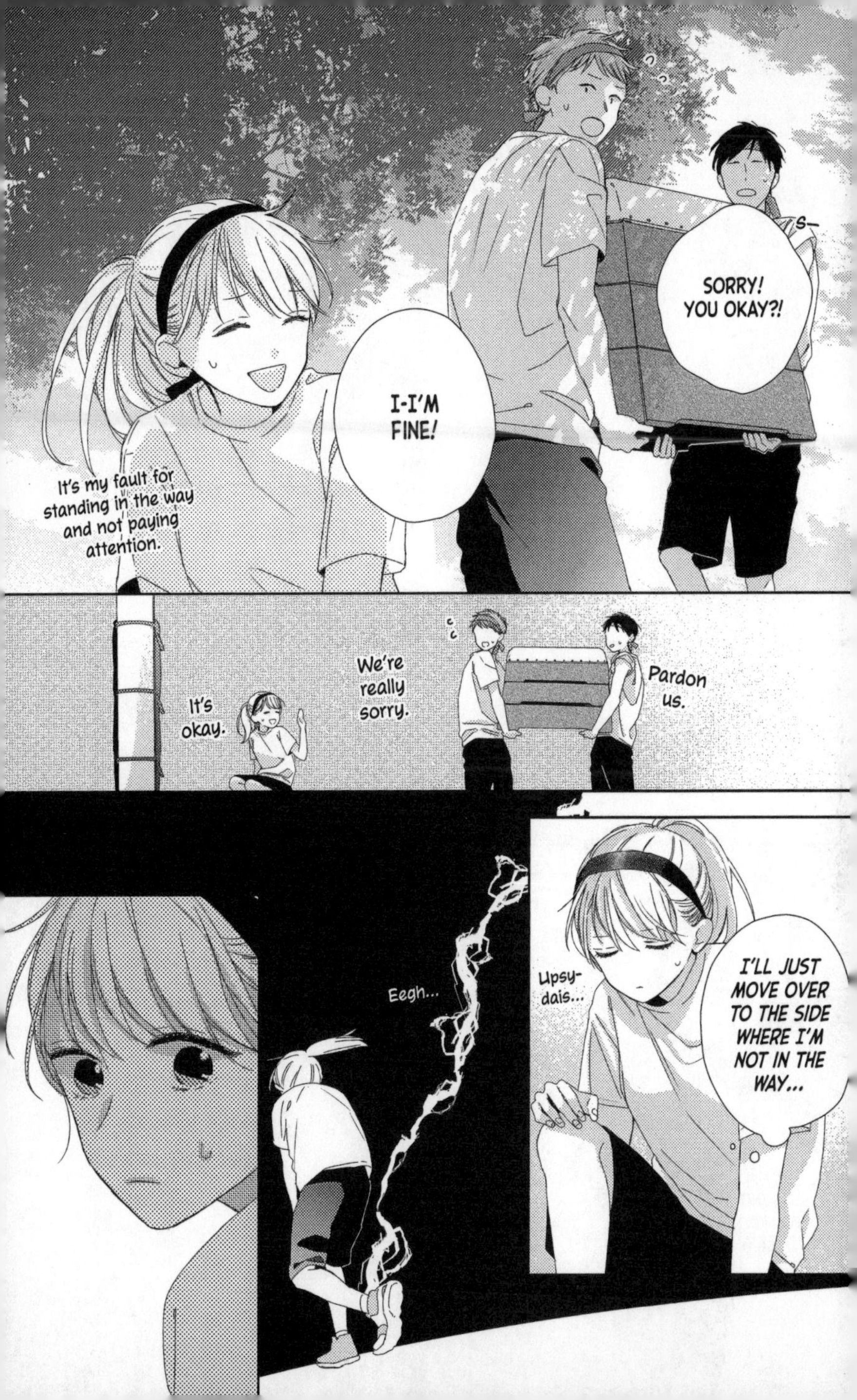
S—
SORRY! YOU OKAY?!
I-I'M FINE!
It's my fault for standing in the way and not paying attention.
Pardon us.
We're really sorry.
It's okay.
I'LL JUST MOVE OVER TO THE SIDE WHERE I'M NOT IN THE WAY...
Upsy-dais...
Eegh...

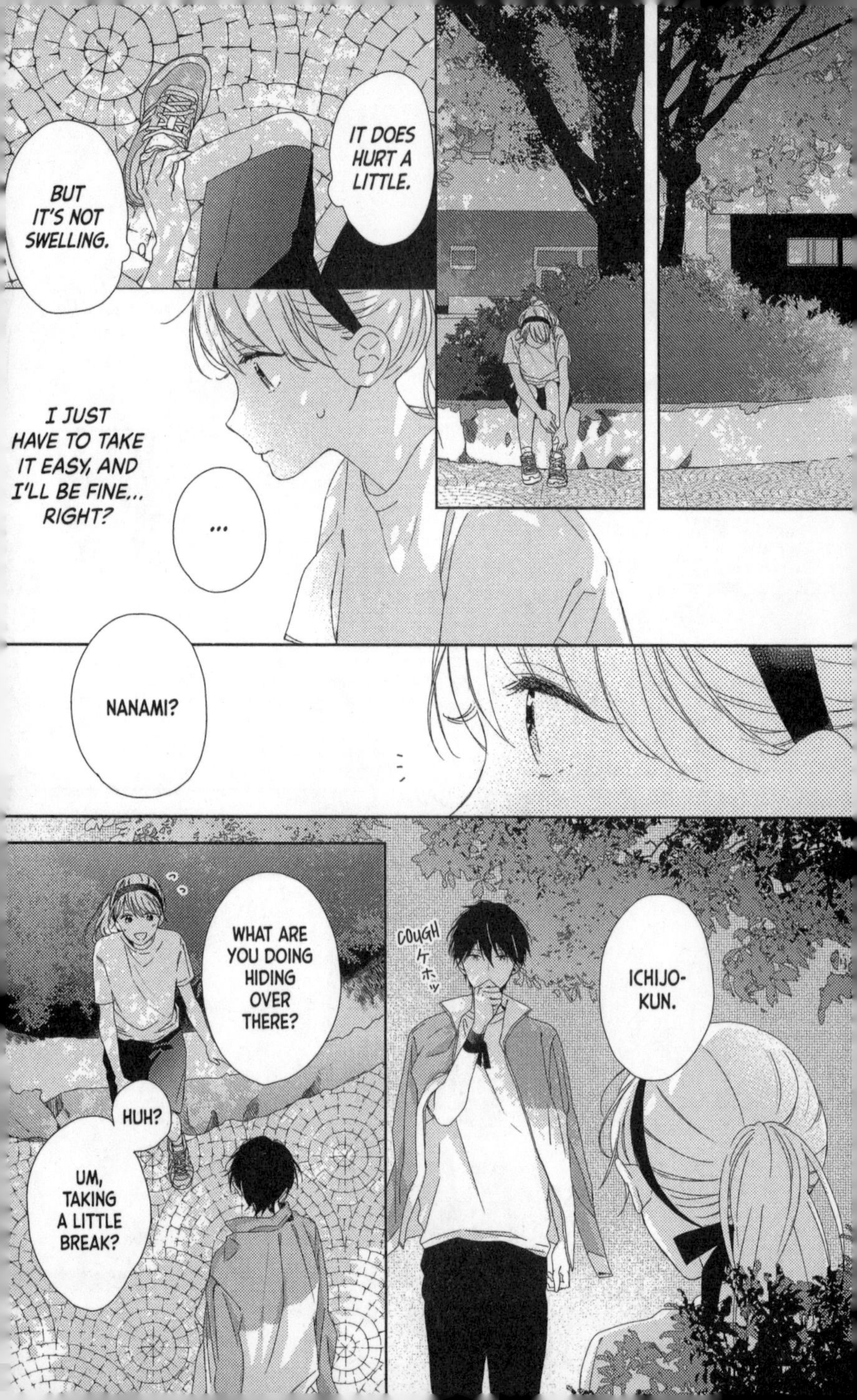
IT DOES HURT A LITTLE.
BUT IT'S NOT SWELLING.
I JUST HAVE TO TAKE IT EASY, AND I'LL BE FINE... RIGHT?
...
NANAMI?
ICHIJO-KUN.
COUGH
ケホッ
WHAT ARE YOU DOING HIDING OVER THERE?
HUH?
UM, TAKING A LITTLE BREAK?

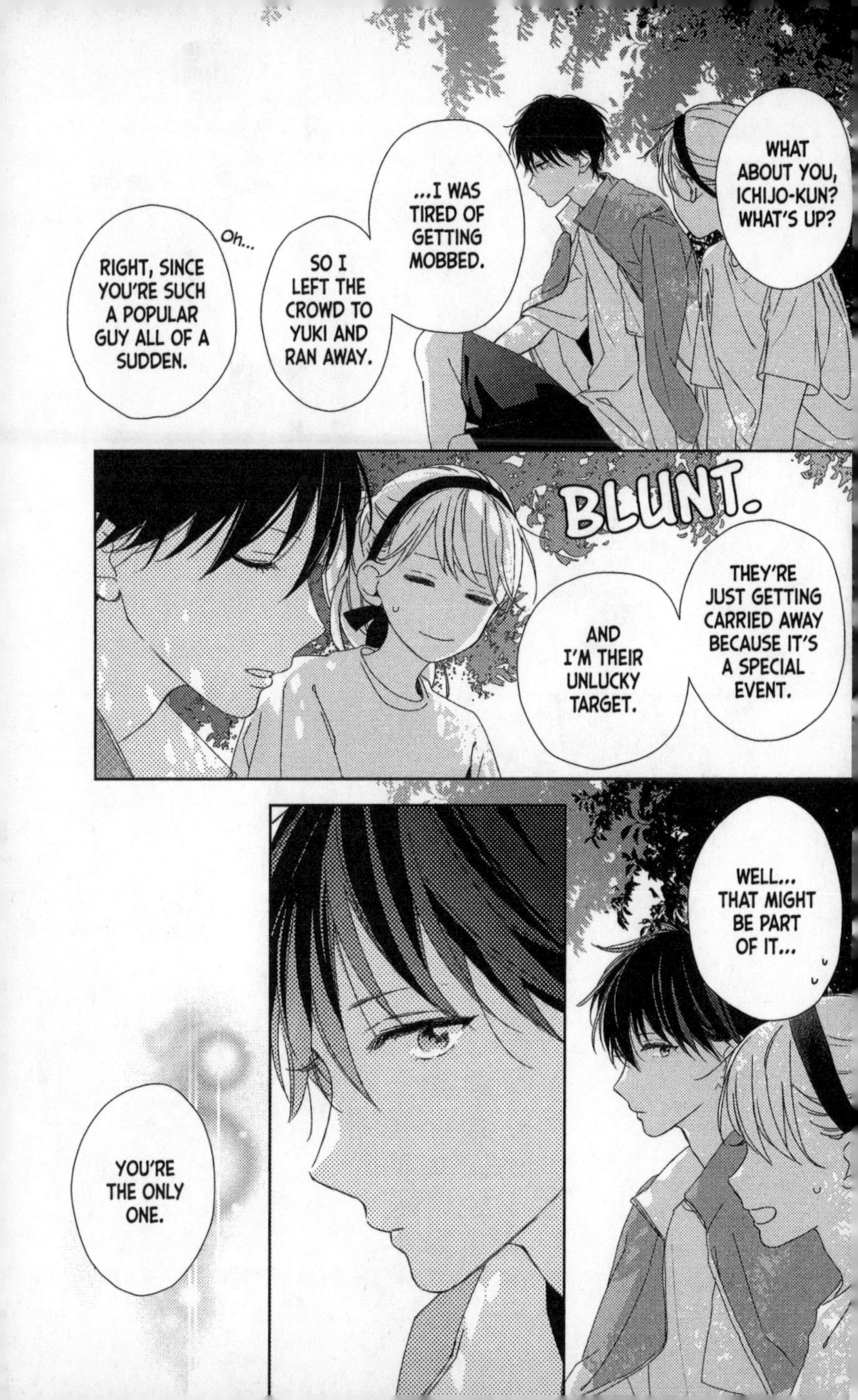
WHAT ABOUT YOU, ICHIJO-KUN? WHAT'S UP?
...I WAS TIRED OF GETTING MOBBED.
SO I LEFT THE CROWD TO YUKI AND RAN AWAY.
Oh...
RIGHT, SINCE YOU'RE SUCH A POPULAR GUY ALL OF A SUDDEN.
BLUNT.
THEY'RE JUST GETTING CARRIED AWAY BECAUSE IT'S A SPECIAL EVENT.
AND I'M THEIR UNLUCKY TARGET.
WELL... THAT MIGHT BE PART OF IT...
YOU'RE THE ONLY ONE.

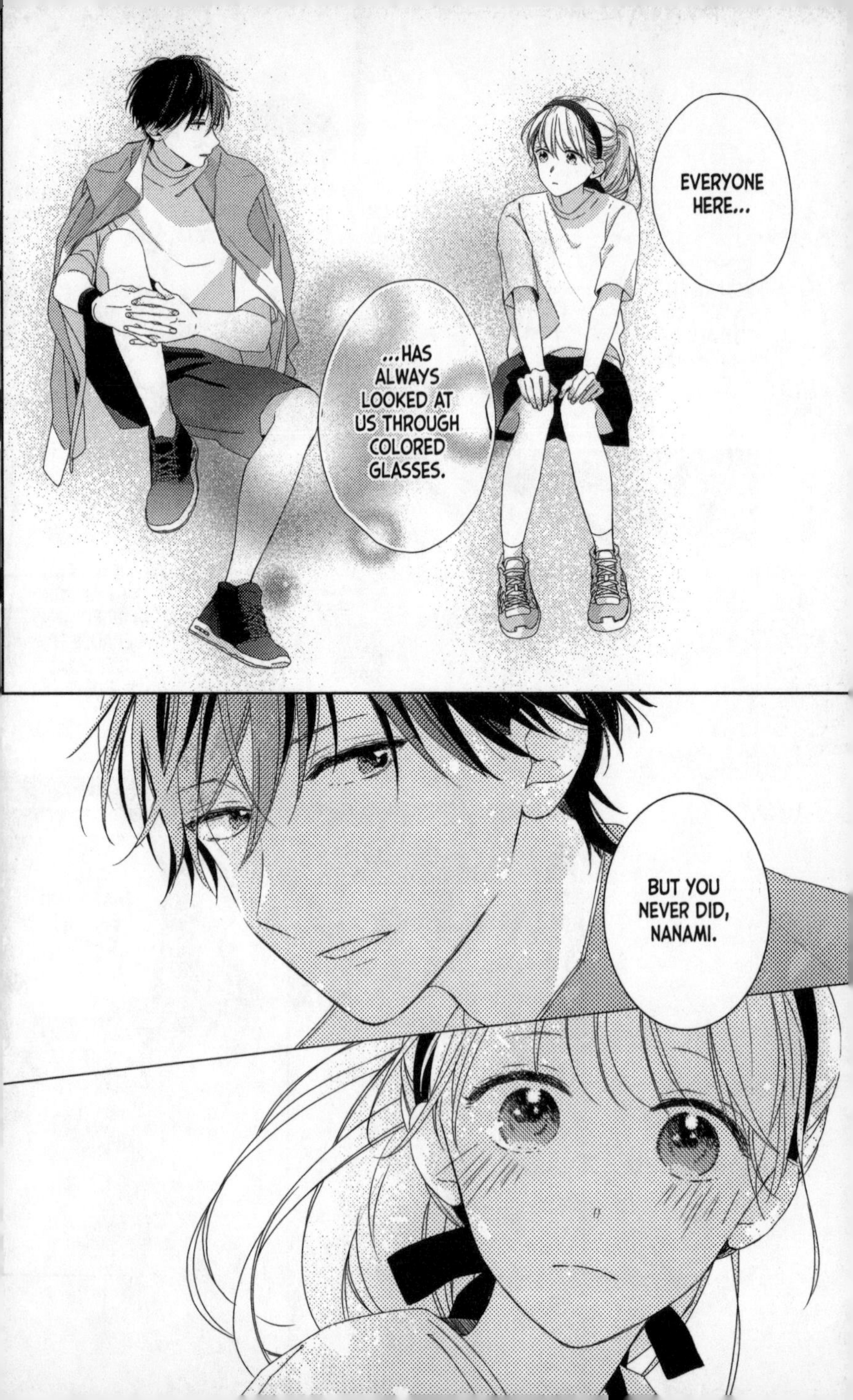
EVERYONE HERE...
...HAS ALWAYS LOOKED AT US THROUGH COLORED GLASSES.
BUT YOU NEVER DID, NANAMI.

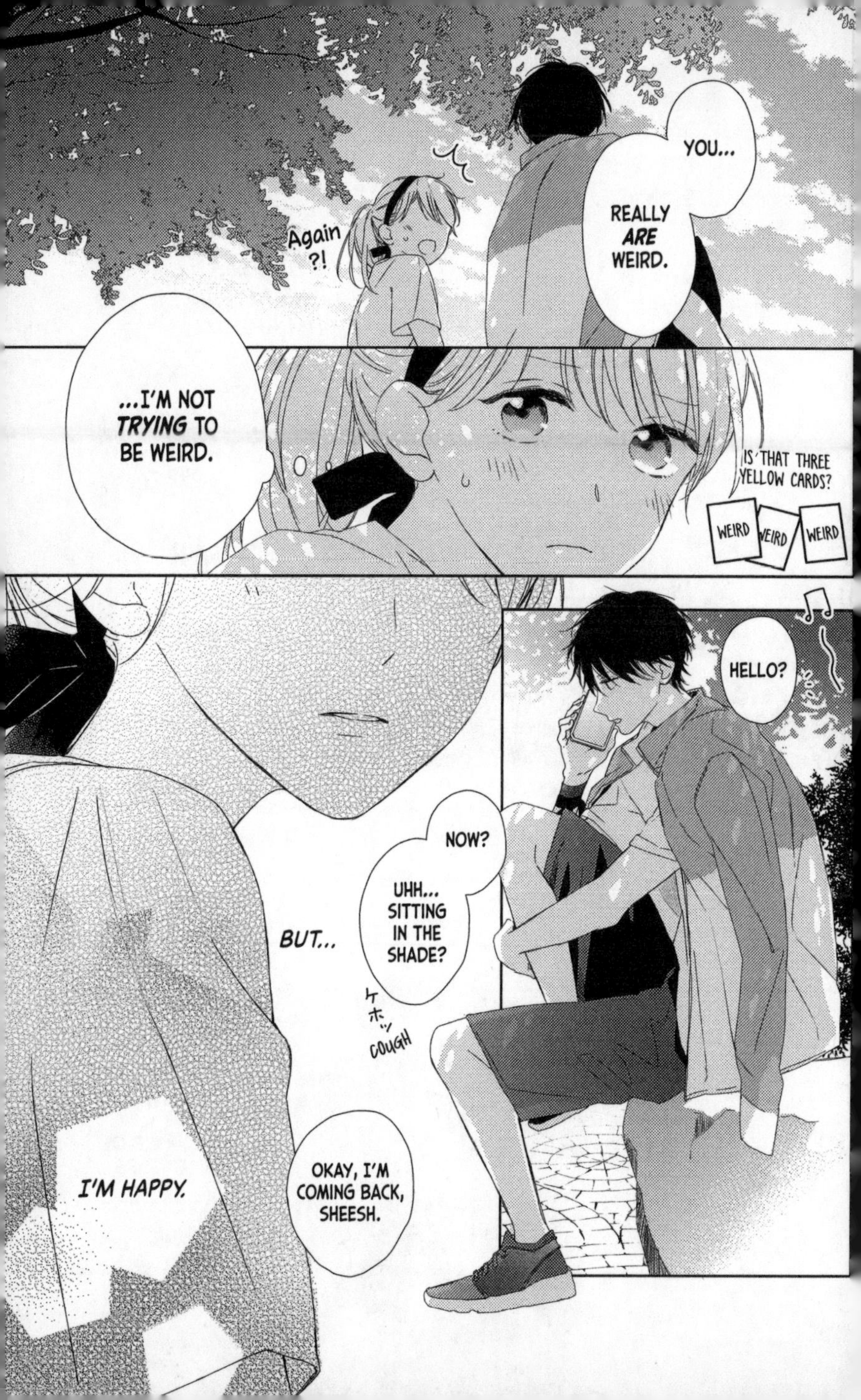
YOU...
REALLY ARE WEIRD.
Again ?!
...I'M NOT TRYING TO BE WEIRD.
IS THAT THREE YELLOW CARDS?
WEIRD
WEIRD
WEIRD
HELLO?
NOW?
UHH... SITTING IN THE SHADE?
ケホッ COUGH
OKAY, I'M COMING BACK, SHEESH.
BUT...
I'M HAPPY.

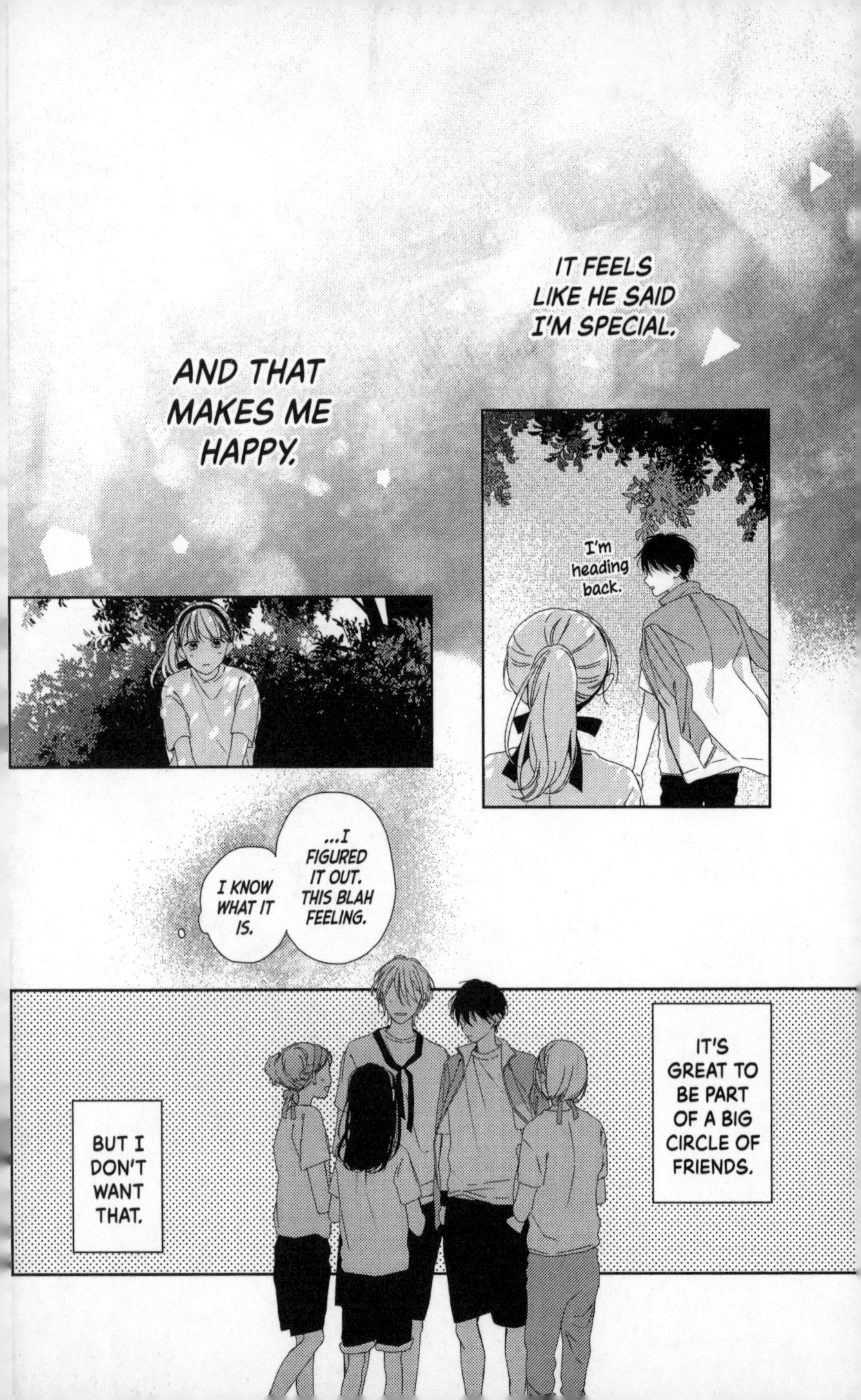
IT FEELS LIKE HE SAID I'M SPECIAL.
AND THAT MAKES ME HAPPY.
I'm heading back.
...I FIGURED IT OUT. THIS BLAH FEELING.
I KNOW WHAT IT IS.
IT'S GREAT TO BE PART OF A BIG CIRCLE OF FRIENDS.
BUT I DON'T WANT THAT.

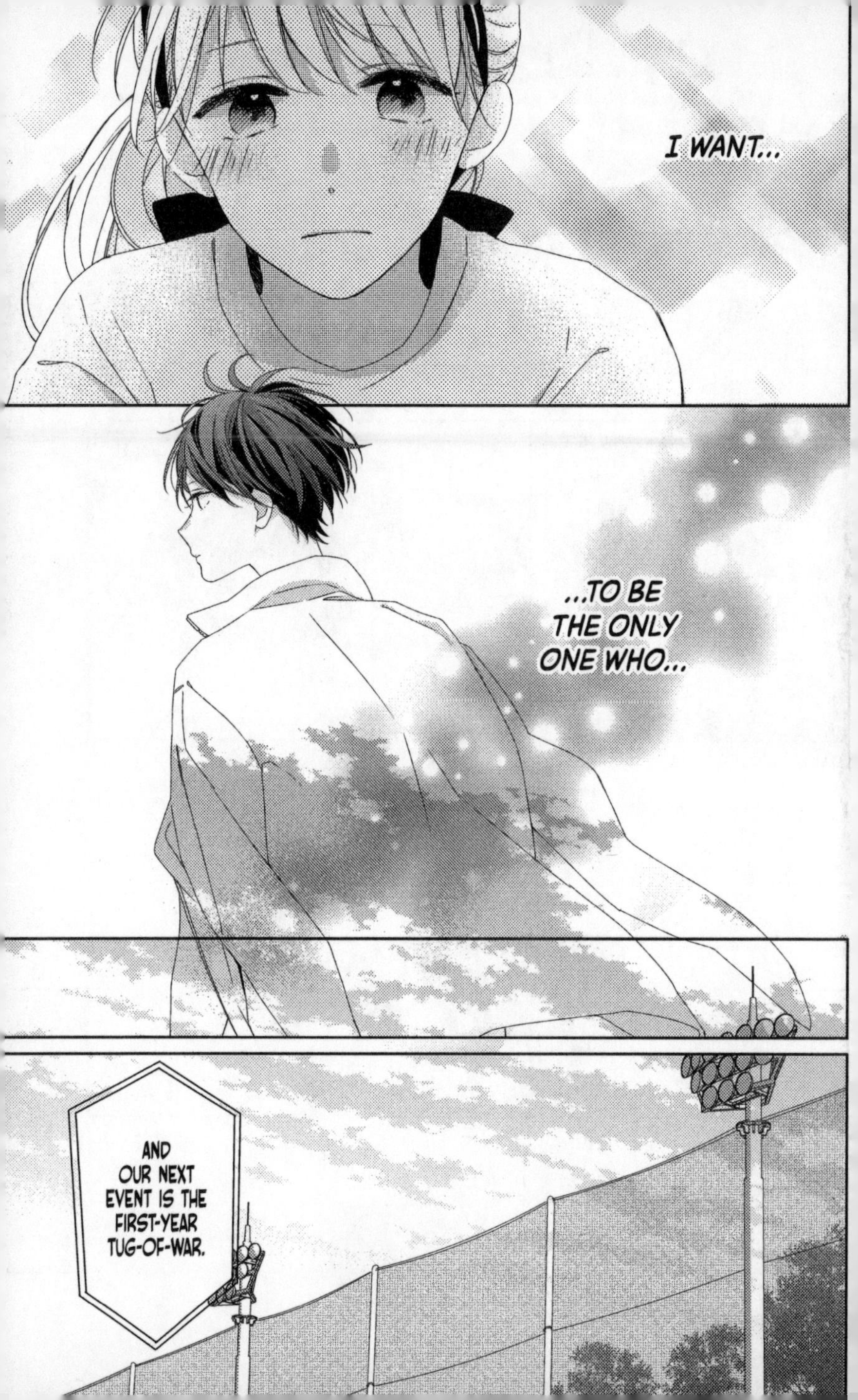
I WANT...
...TO BE THE ONLY ONE WHO...
AND OUR NEXT EVENT IS THE FIRST-YEAR TUG-OF-WAR.

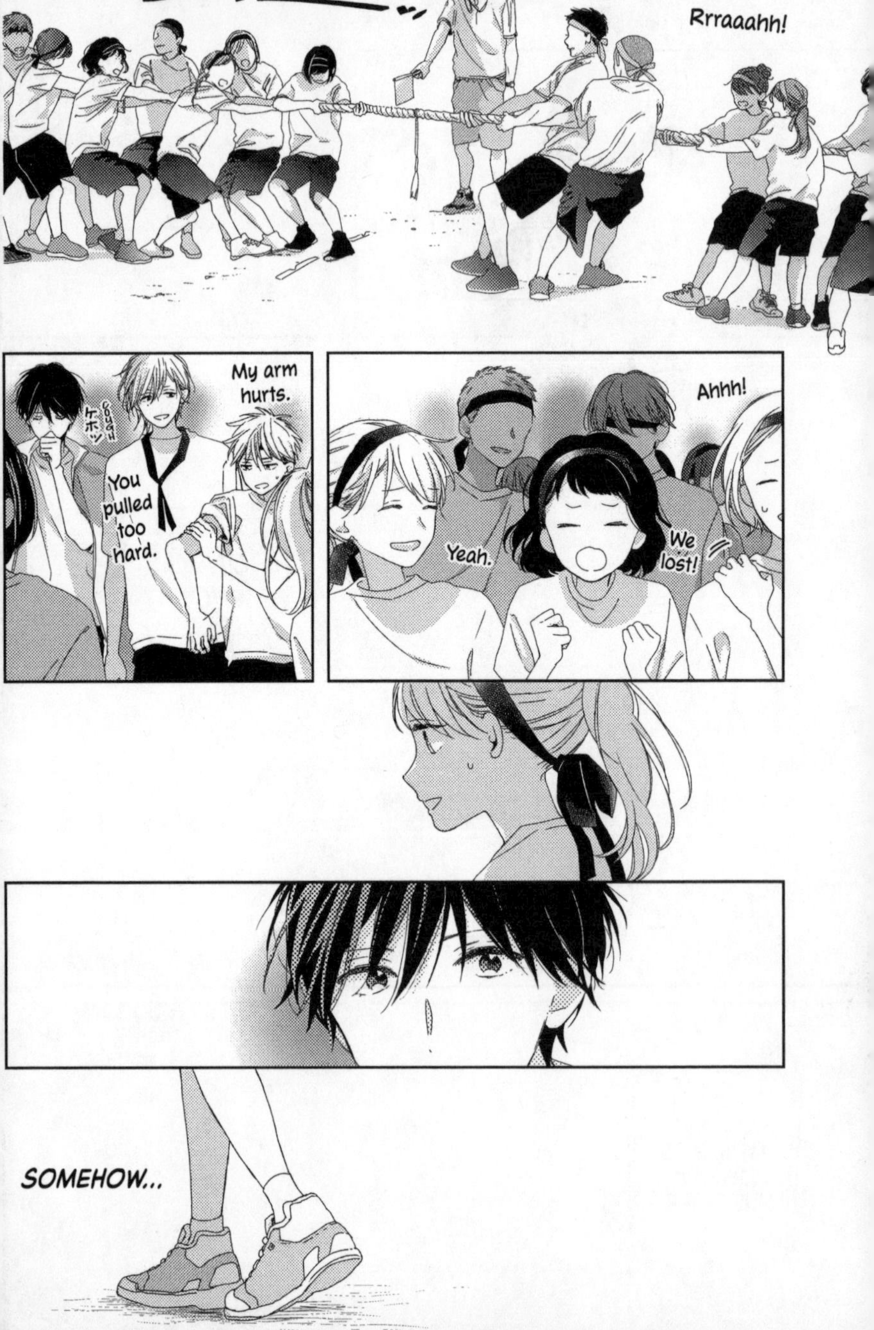
Rrraaahh!
ピピッ
FW-FWEEEEET
Ahhh!
We lost!
Yeah.
My arm hurts.
ケホッ COUGH
You pulled too hard.
SOMEHOW...

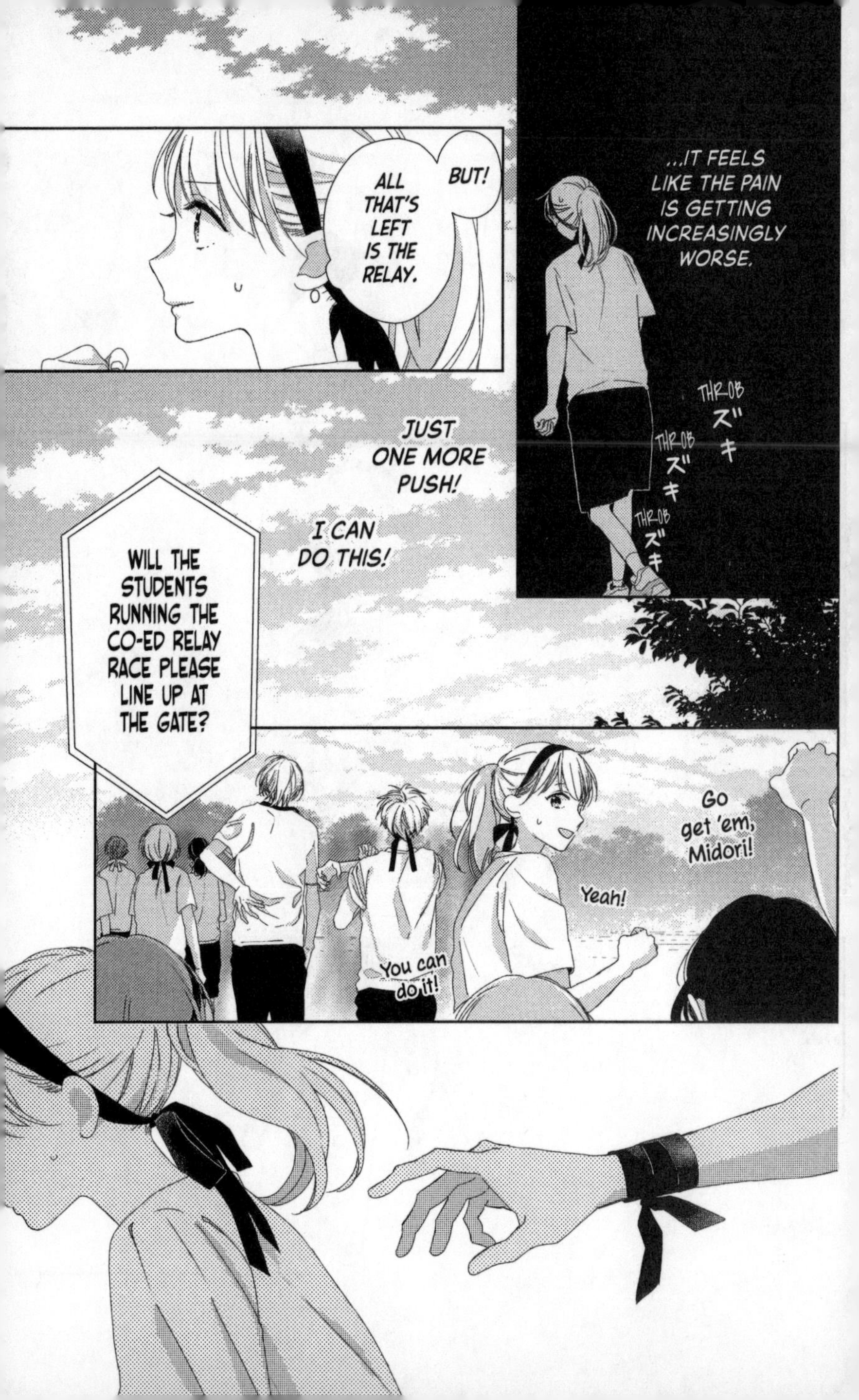
...IT FEELS LIKE THE PAIN IS GETTING INCREASINGLY WORSE.
THROB ズキ
THROB ズキ
THROB ズキ
BUT!
ALL THAT'S LEFT IS THE RELAY.
JUST ONE MORE PUSH!
I CAN DO THIS!
WILL THE STUDENTS RUNNING THE CO-ED RELAY RACE PLEASE LINE UP AT THE GATE?
Go get 'em, Midori!
Yeah!
You can do it!

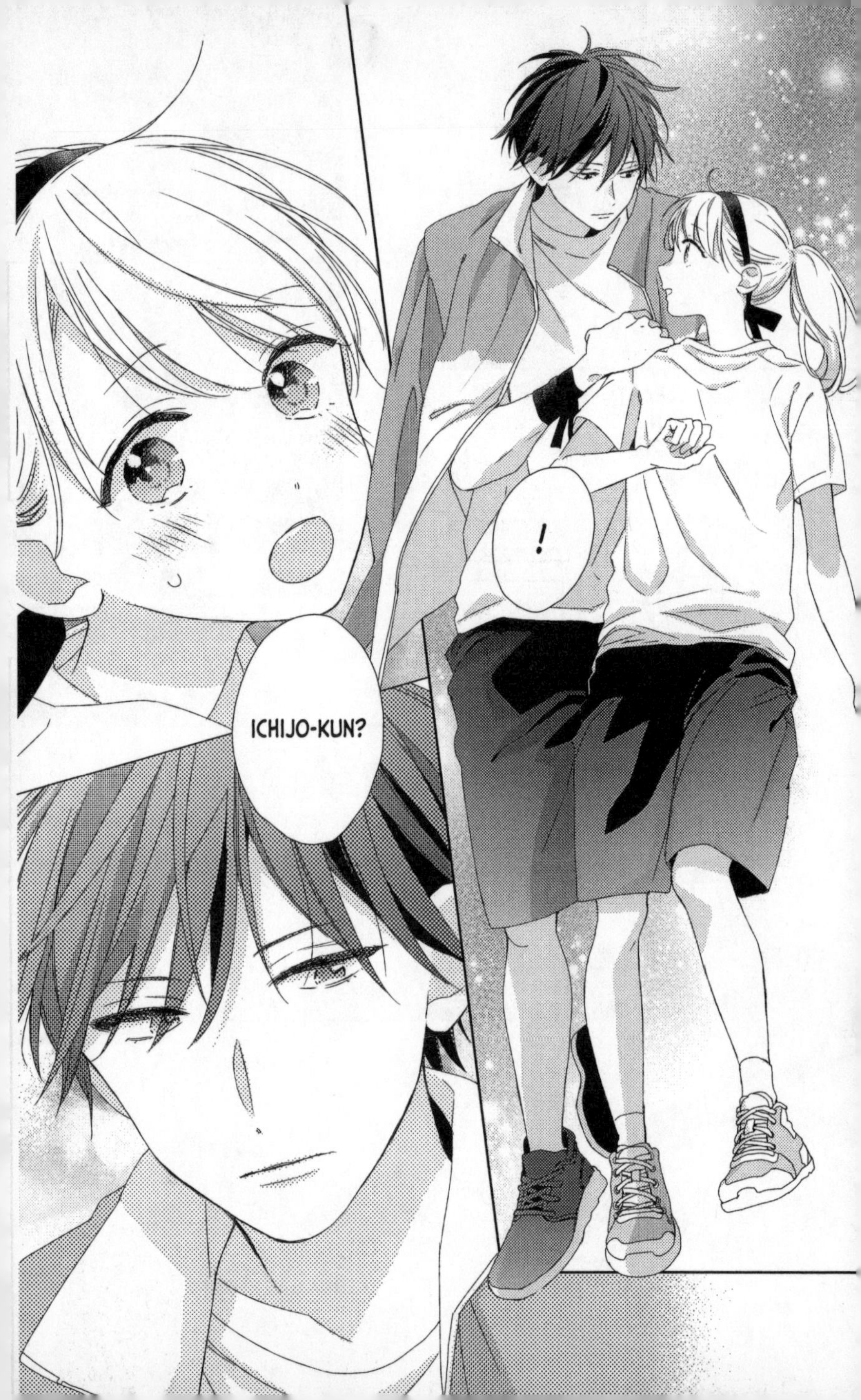
!
ICHIJO-KUN?

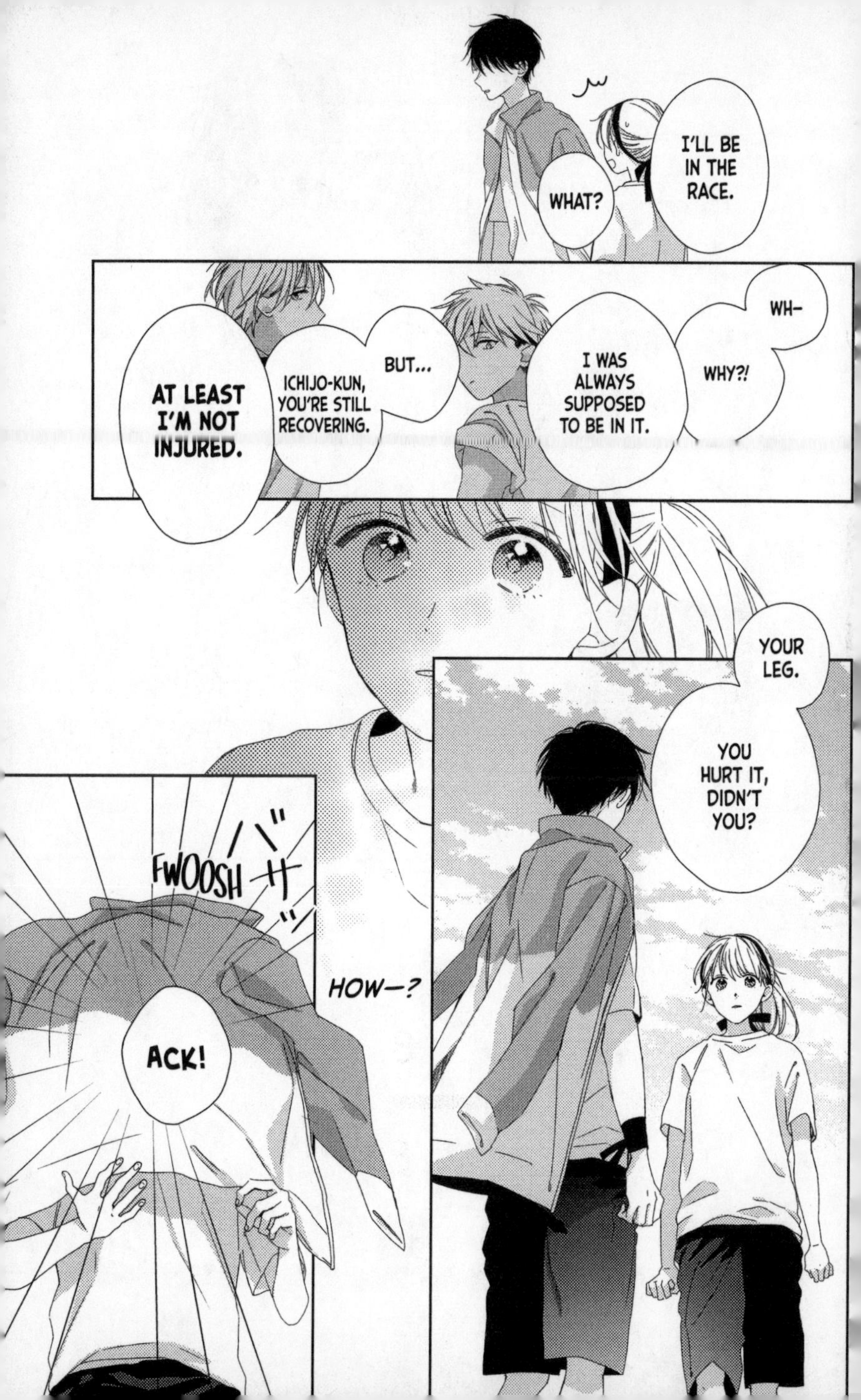

I'LL BE IN THE RACE.
WHAT?
WH-
WHY?!
I WAS ALWAYS SUPPOSED TO BE IN IT.
BUT...
ICHIJO-KUN, YOU'RE STILL RECOVERING.
AT LEAST I'M NOT INJURED.
YOUR LEG.
YOU HURT IT, DIDN'T YOU?
HOW—?
FWOOSH
バサッ
ACK!

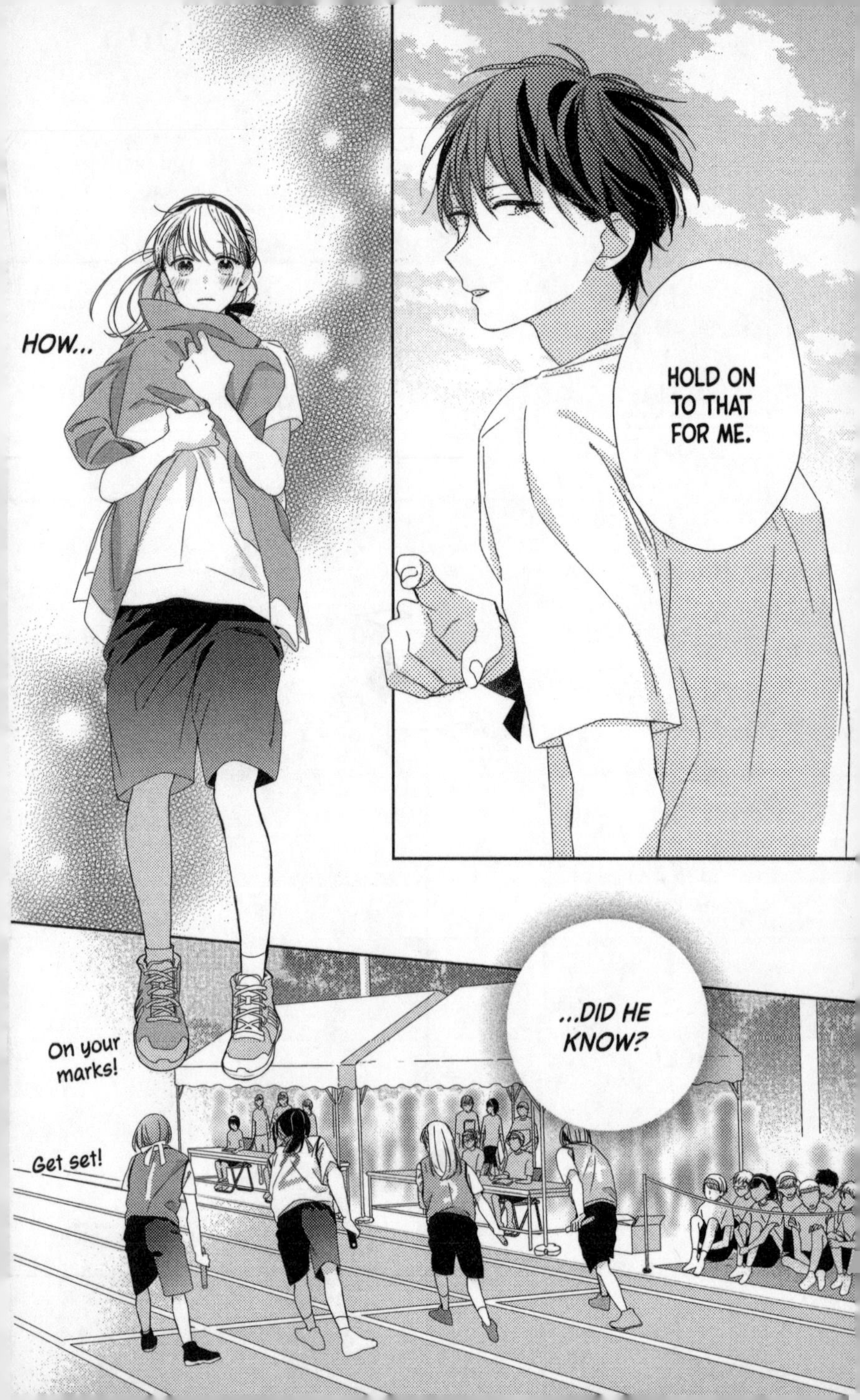
HOLD ON TO THAT FOR ME.
HOW...
...DID HE KNOW?
On your marks!
Get set!

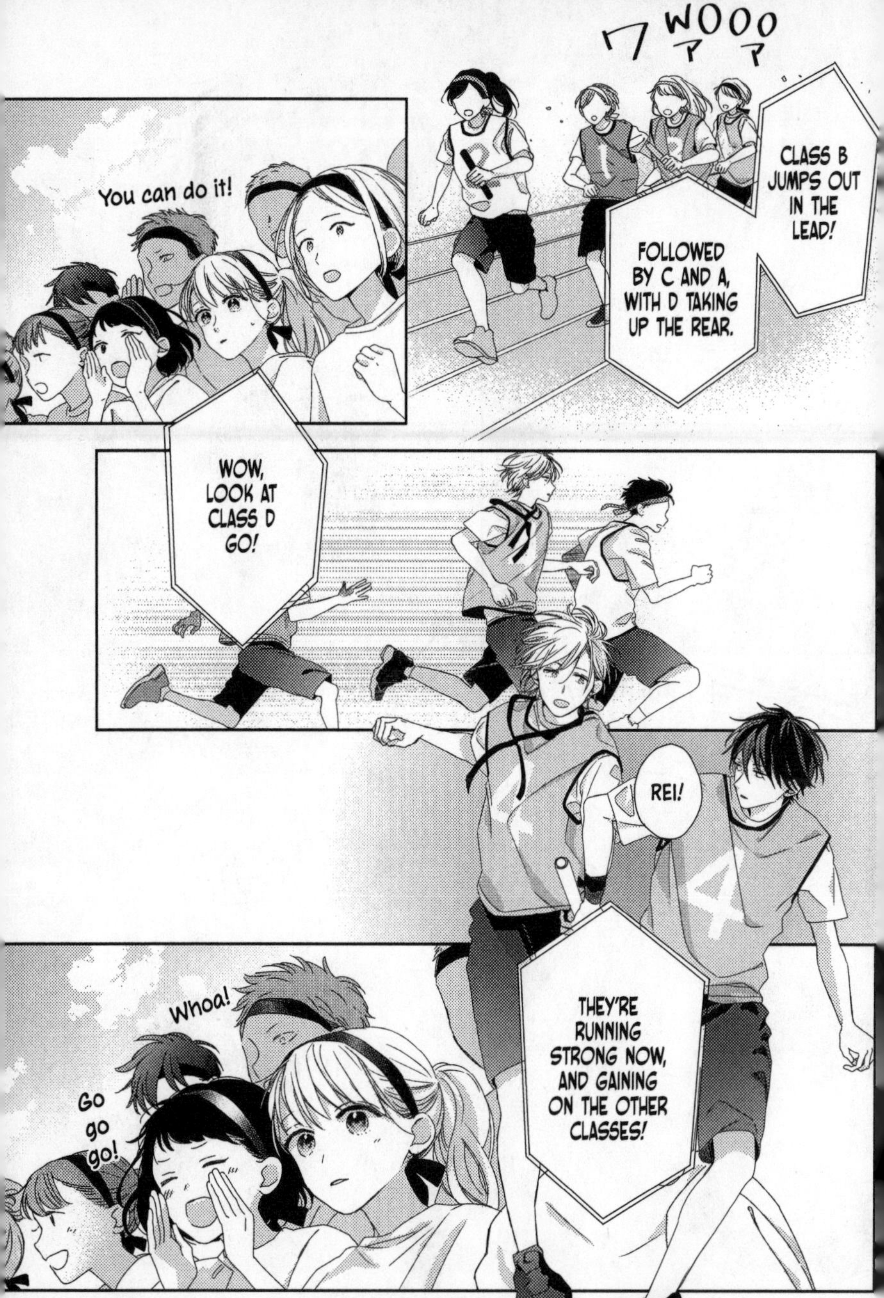
ワ WOOO アア
CLASS B JUMPS OUT IN THE LEAD!
FOLLOWED BY C AND A, WITH D TAKING UP THE REAR.
You can do it!
WOW, LOOK AT CLASS D GO!
REI!
THEY'RE RUNNING STRONG NOW, AND GAINING ON THE OTHER CLASSES!
Whoa!
Go go go!

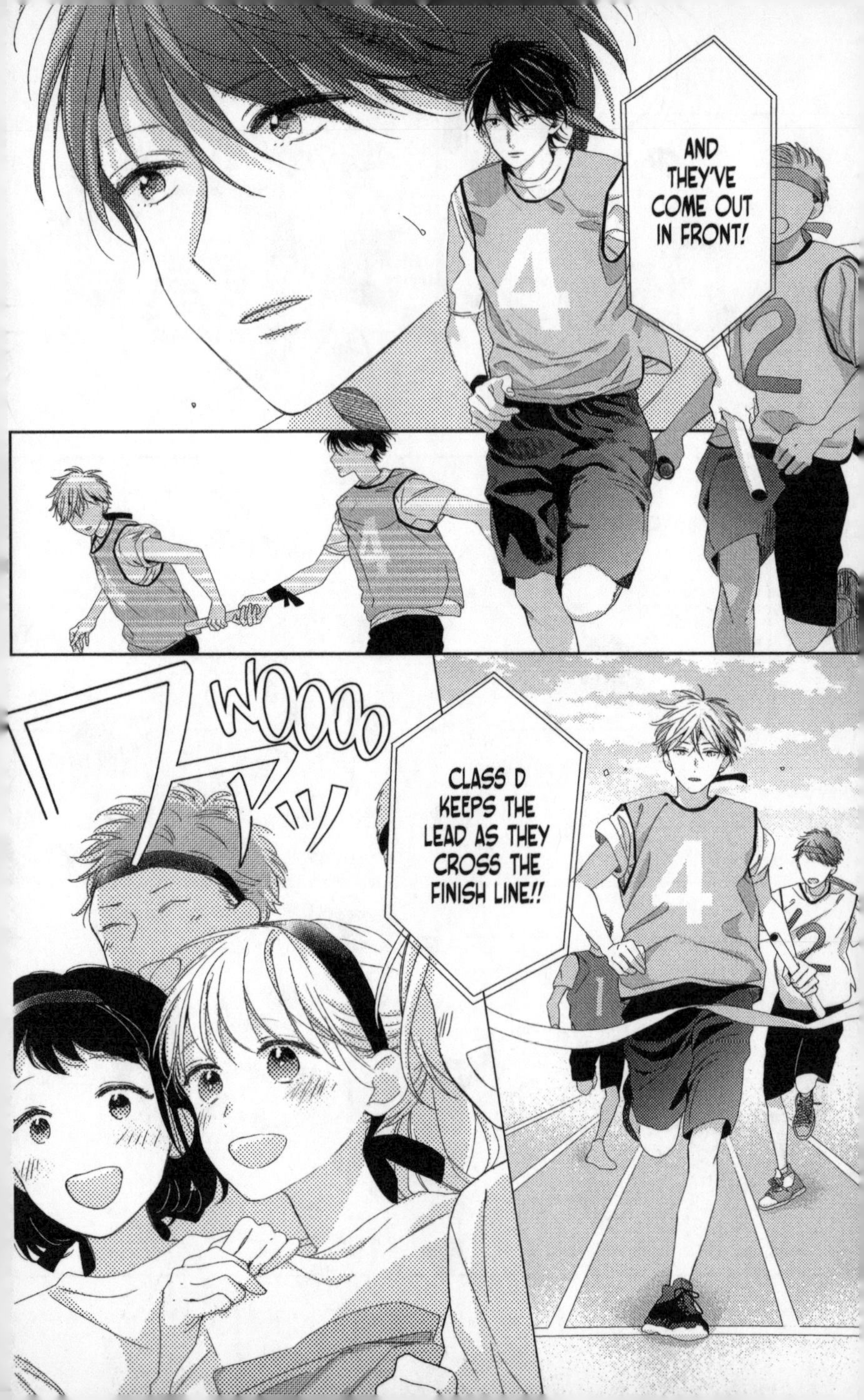
AND THEY'VE COME OUT IN FRONT!
CLASS D KEEPS THE LEAD AS THEY CROSS THE FINISH LINE!!
WOOOO

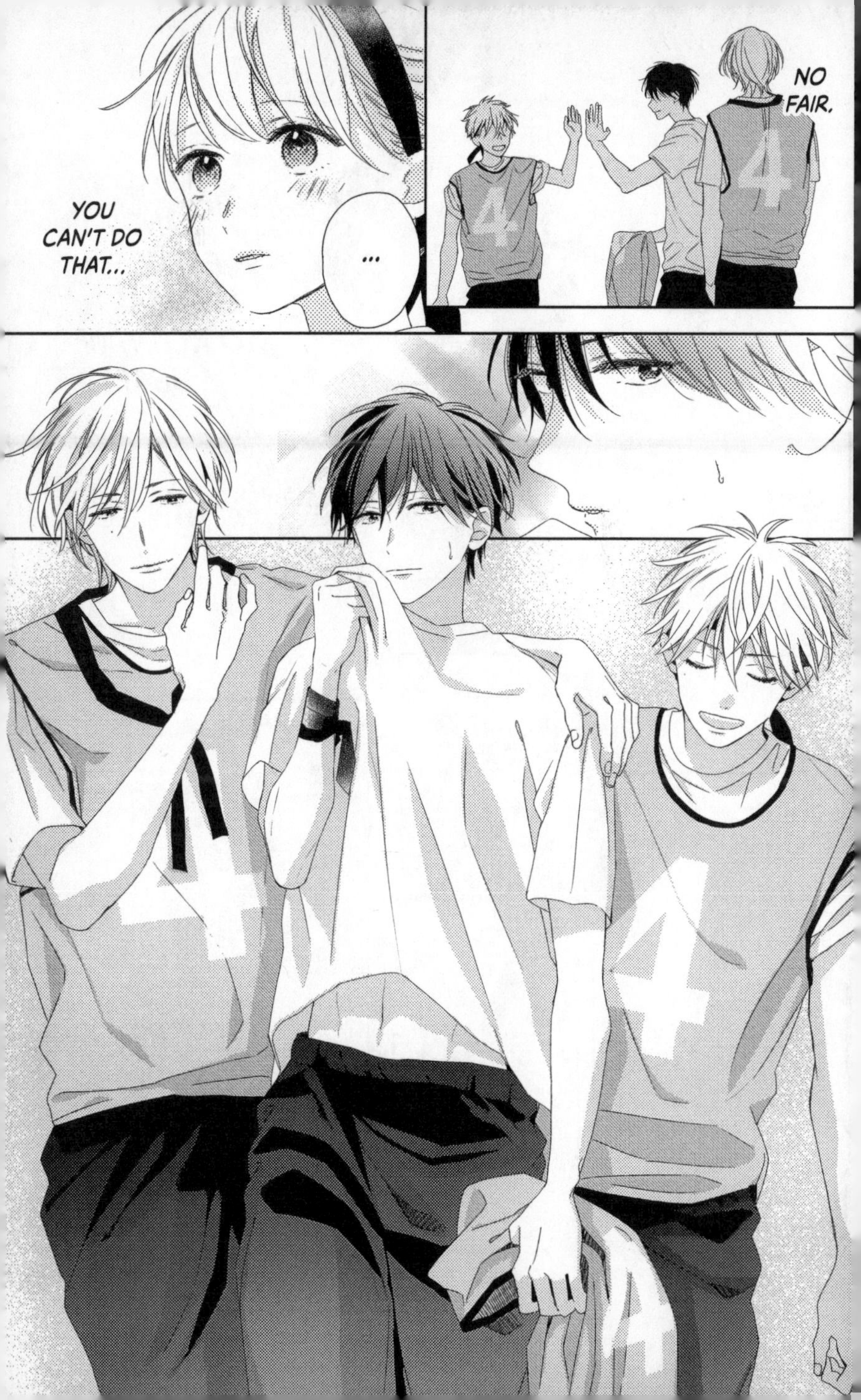
NO FAIR.
...
YOU CAN'T DO THAT...

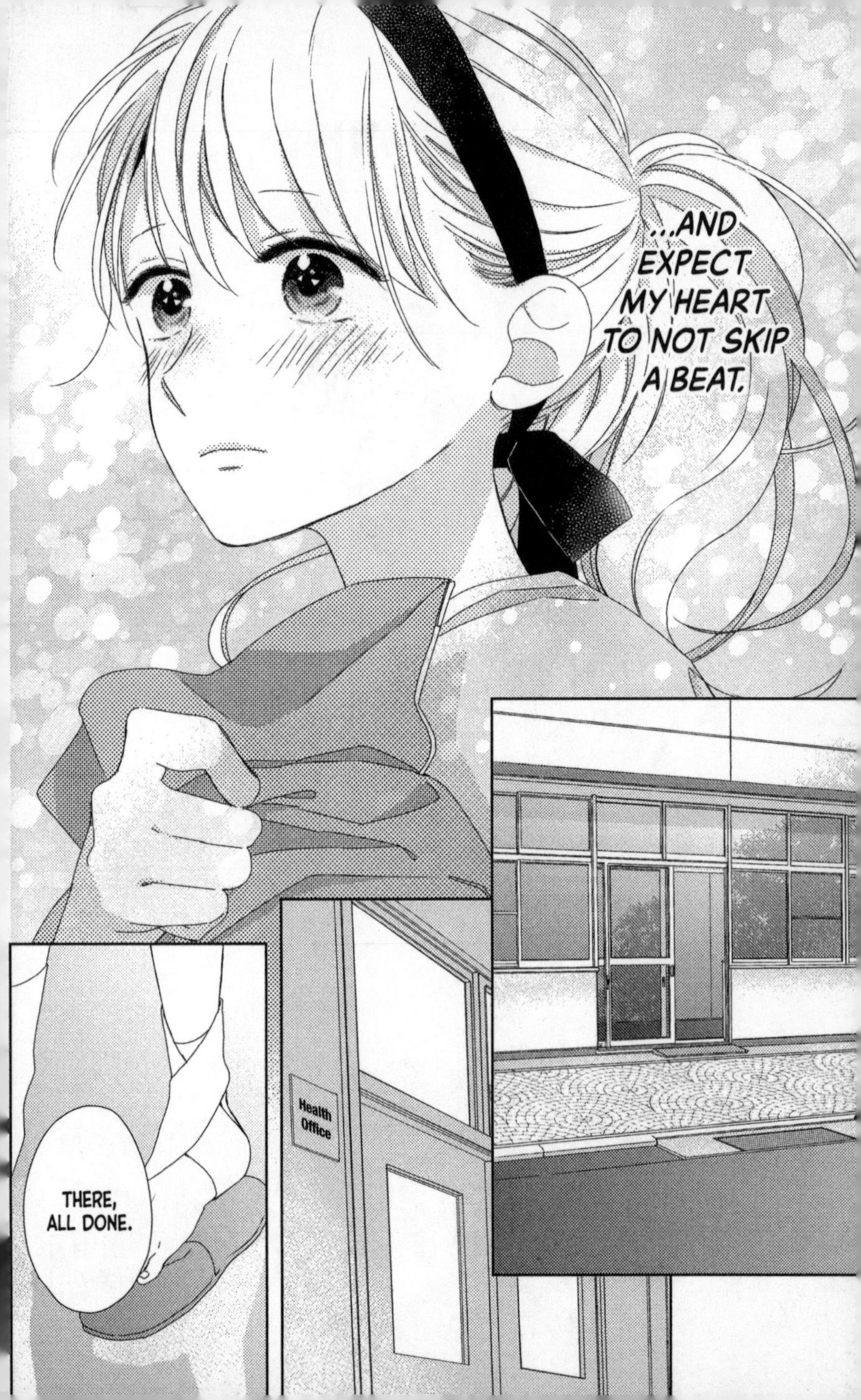
...AND EXPECT MY HEART TO NOT SKIP A BEAT.
Health Office
THERE, ALL DONE.

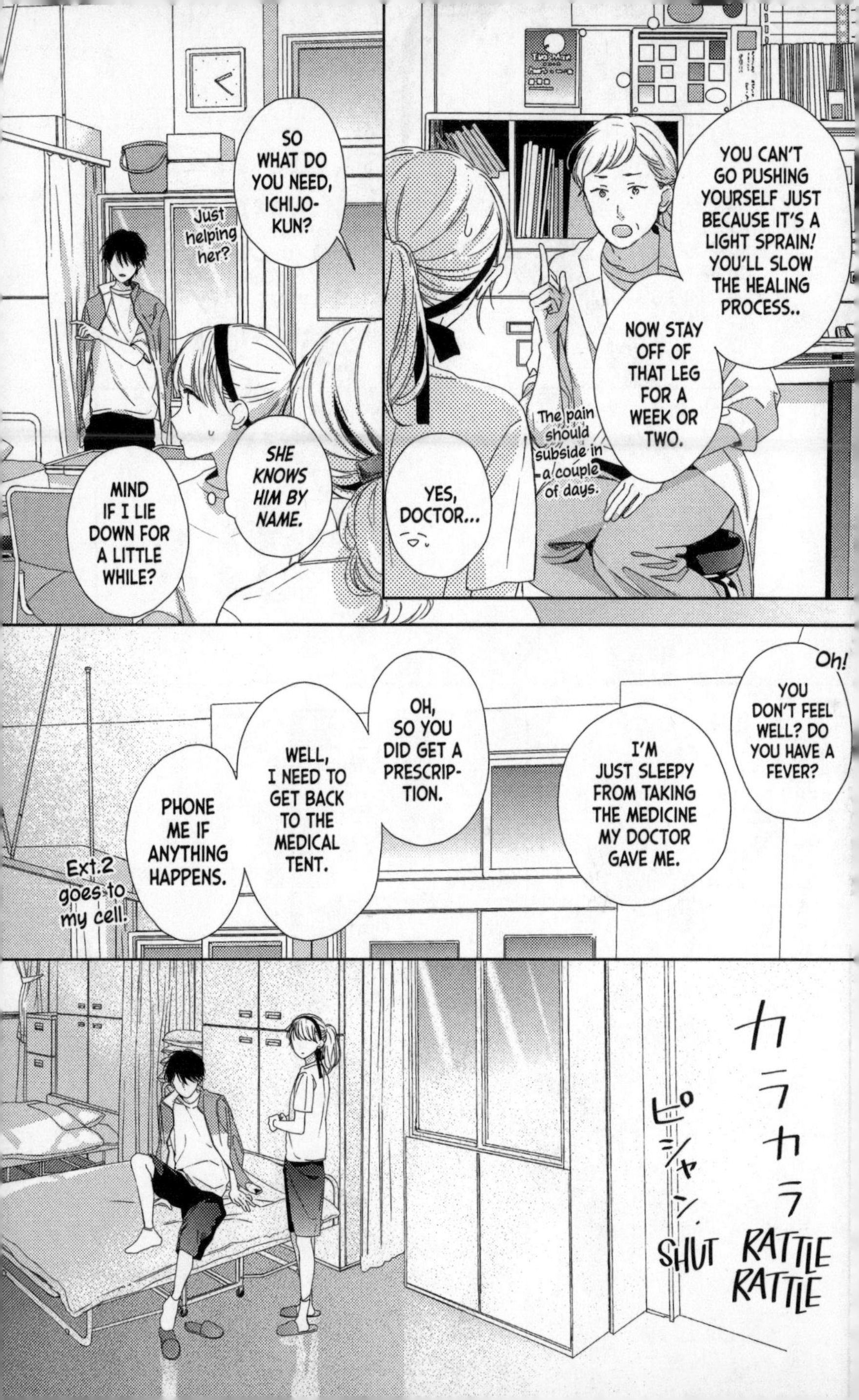
YOU CAN'T GO PUSHING YOURSELF JUST BECAUSE IT'S A LIGHT SPRAIN! YOU'LL SLOW THE HEALING PROCESS..
NOW STAY OFF OF THAT LEG FOR A WEEK OR TWO.
The pain should subside in a couple of days.
YES, DOCTOR...
SO WHAT DO YOU NEED, ICHIJO-KUN?
Just helping her?
SHE KNOWS HIM BY NAME.
MIND IF I LIE DOWN FOR A LITTLE WHILE?
Oh! YOU DON'T FEEL WELL? DO YOU HAVE A FEVER?
I'M JUST SLEEPY FROM TAKING THE MEDICINE MY DOCTOR GAVE ME.
OH, SO YOU DID GET A PRESCRIPTION.
WELL, I NEED TO GET BACK TO THE MEDICAL TENT.
PHONE ME IF ANYTHING HAPPENS.
Ext.2 goes to my cell.
カラカラ
RATTLE RATTLE
ピシャン
SHUT

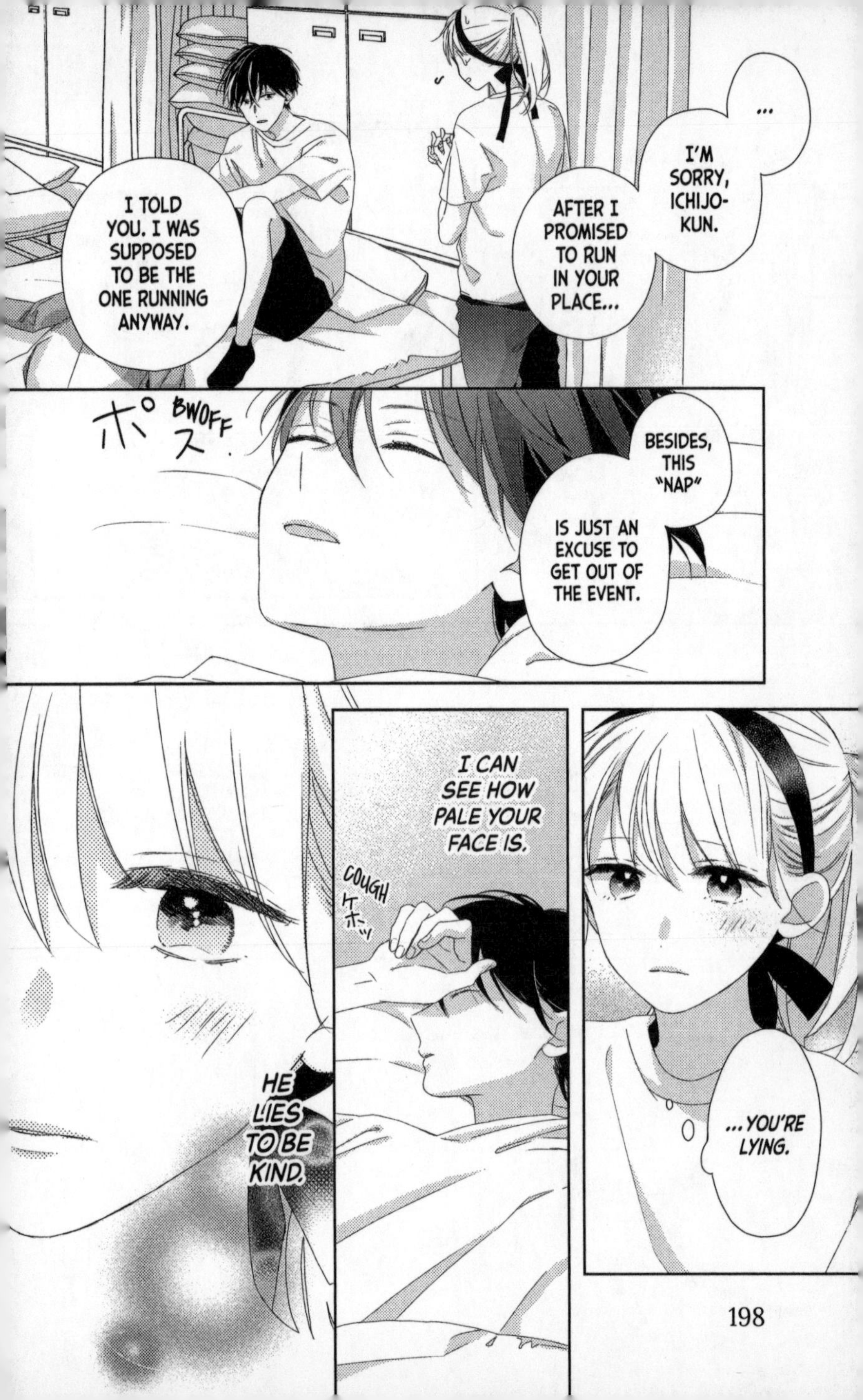
...
I'M SORRY, ICHIJO-KUN.
AFTER I PROMISED TO RUN IN YOUR PLACE...
I TOLD YOU. I WAS SUPPOSED TO BE THE ONE RUNNING ANYWAY.
BESIDES, THIS "NAP"
IS JUST AN EXCUSE TO GET OUT OF THE EVENT.
ポス BWOFF
...YOU'RE LYING.
I CAN SEE HOW PALE YOUR FACE IS.
ケホッ COUGH
HE LIES TO BE KIND.

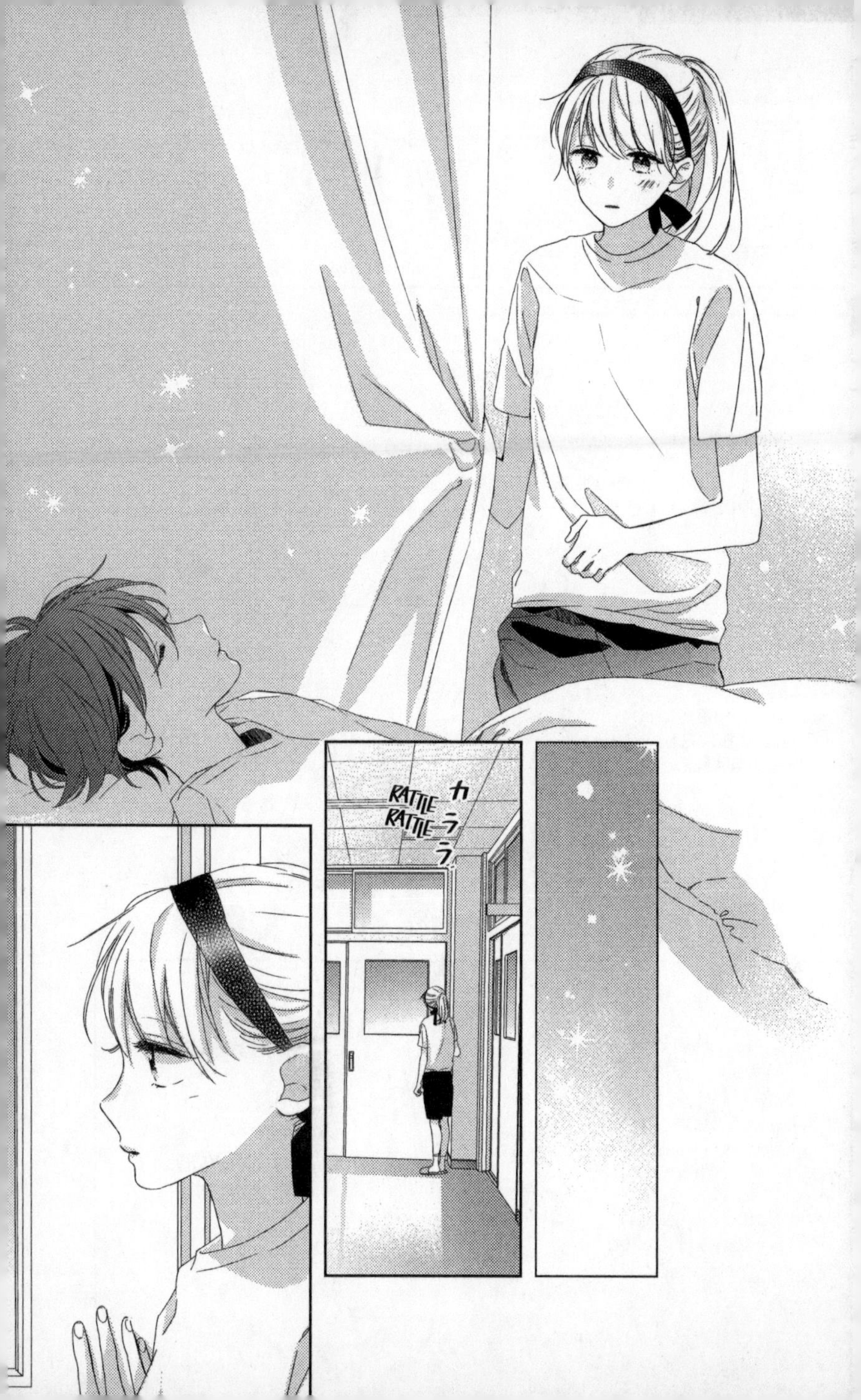
RATTLE RATTLE
カララ

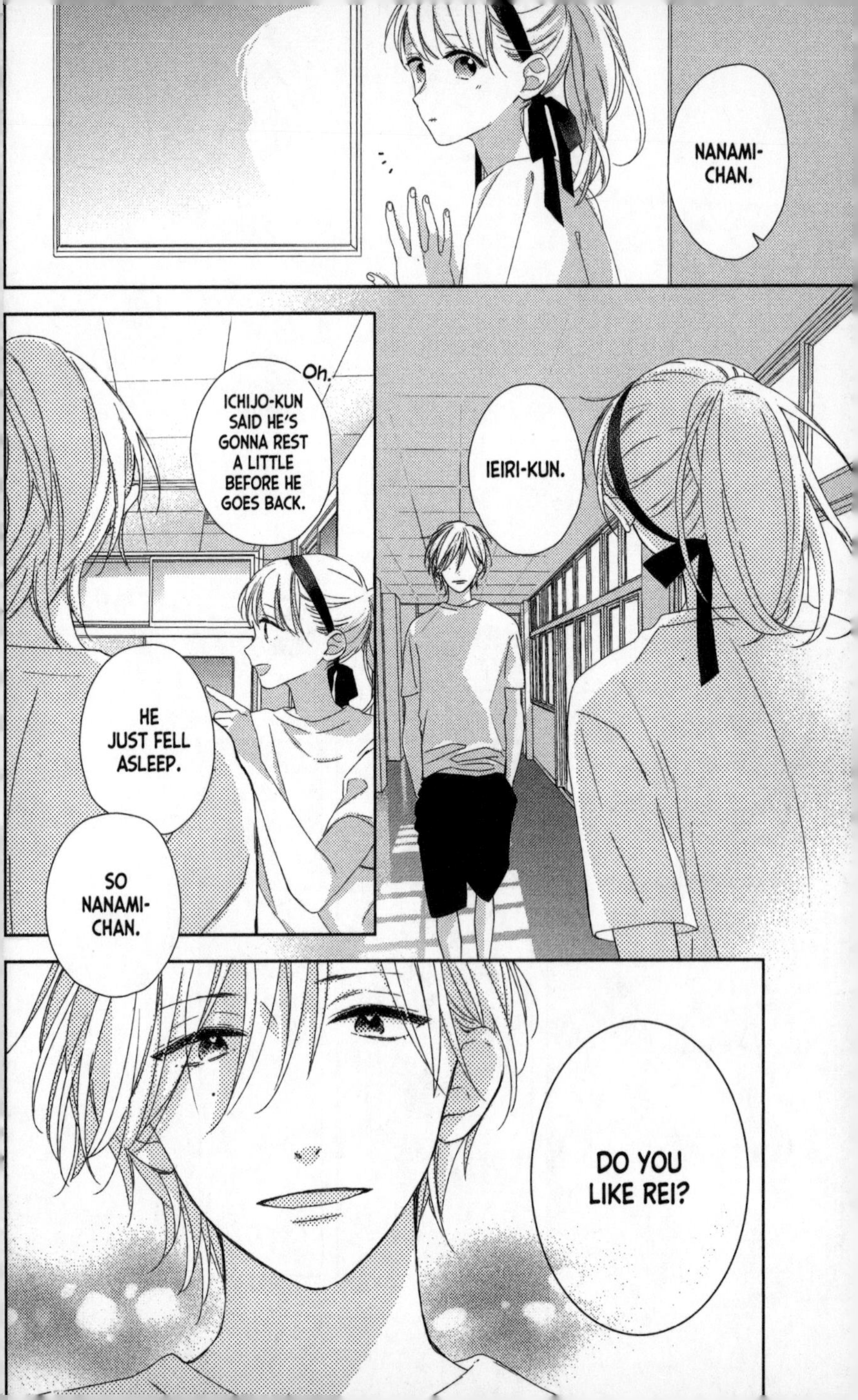
NANAMI-CHAN.
IEIRI-KUN.
Oh.
ICHIJO-KUN SAID HE'S GONNA REST A LITTLE BEFORE HE GOES BACK.
HE JUST FELL ASLEEP.
SO NANAMI-CHAN.
DO YOU LIKE REI?

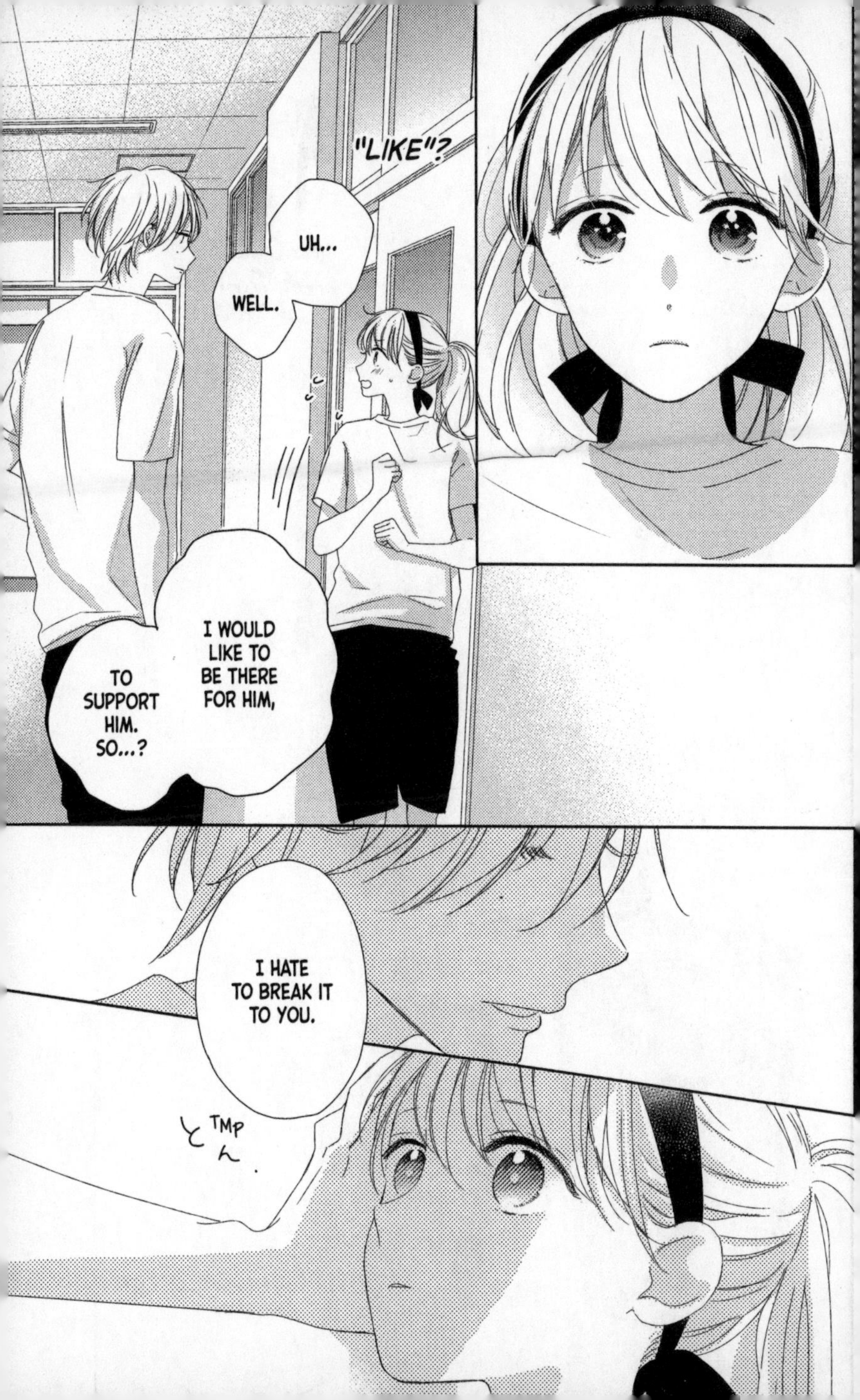
"LIKE"?
UH...
WELL.
I WOULD LIKE TO BE THERE FOR HIM,
TO SUPPORT HIM. SO...?
I HATE TO BREAK IT TO YOU.
とん TMP

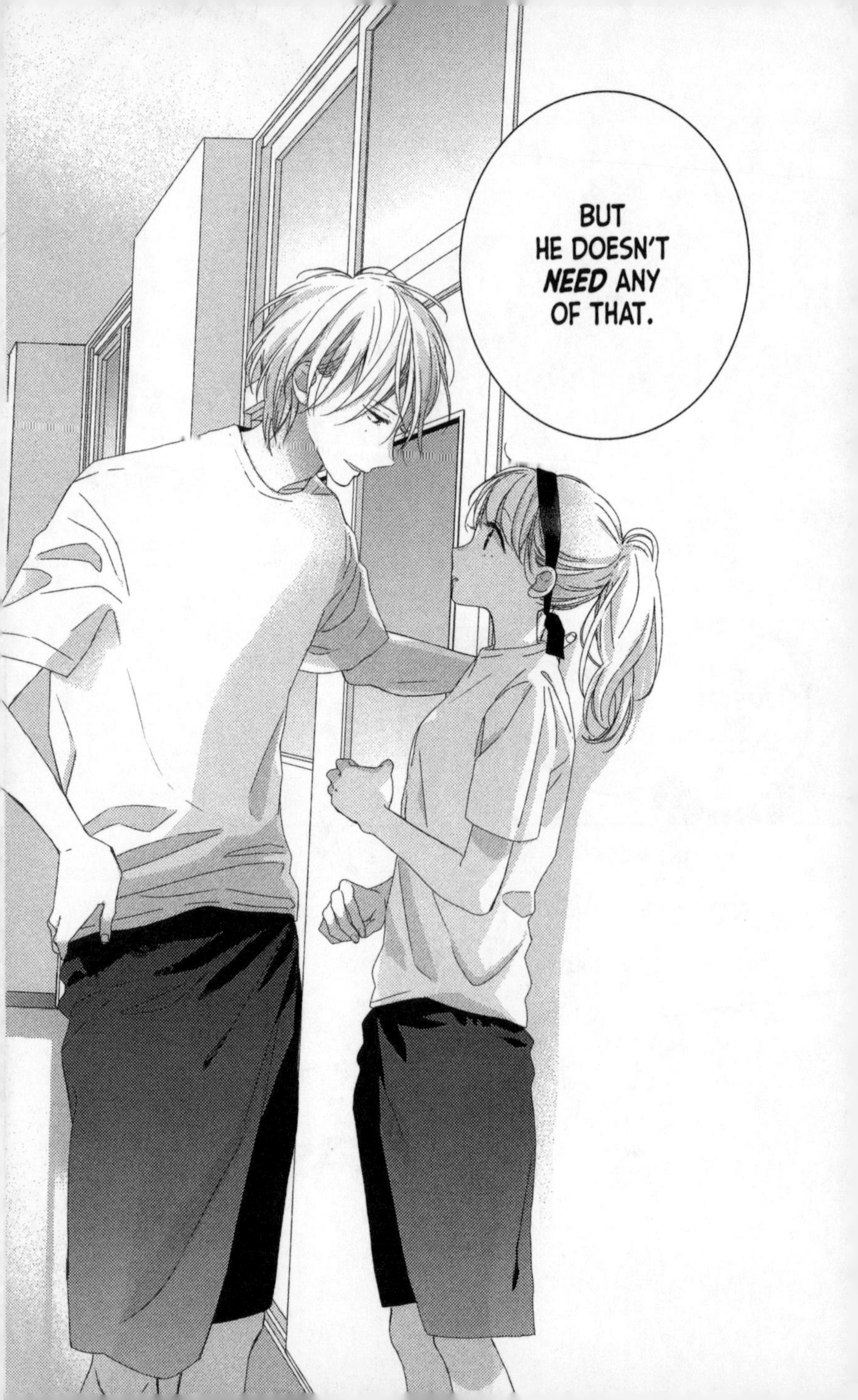
BUT HE DOESN'T *NEED* ANY OF THAT.

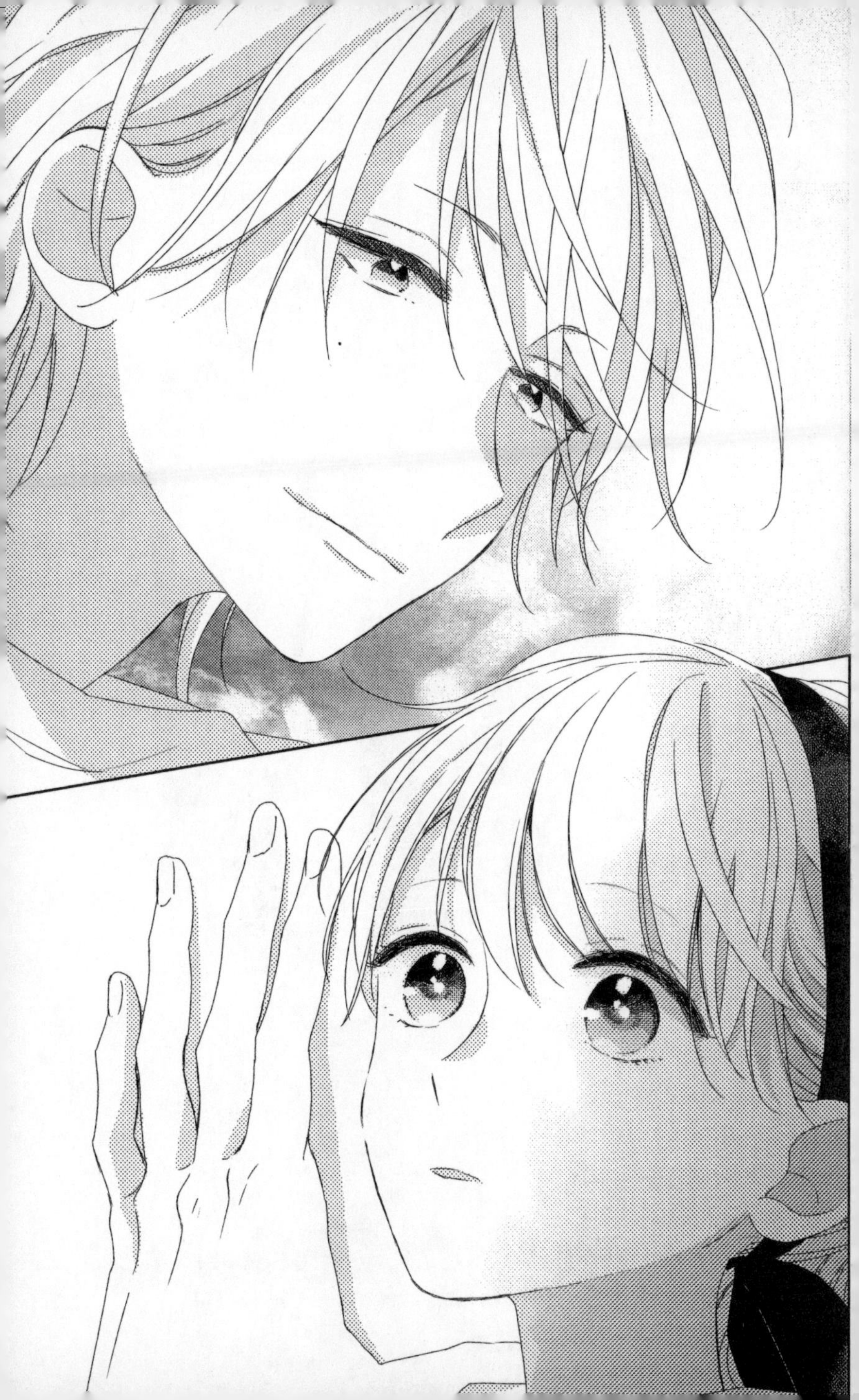

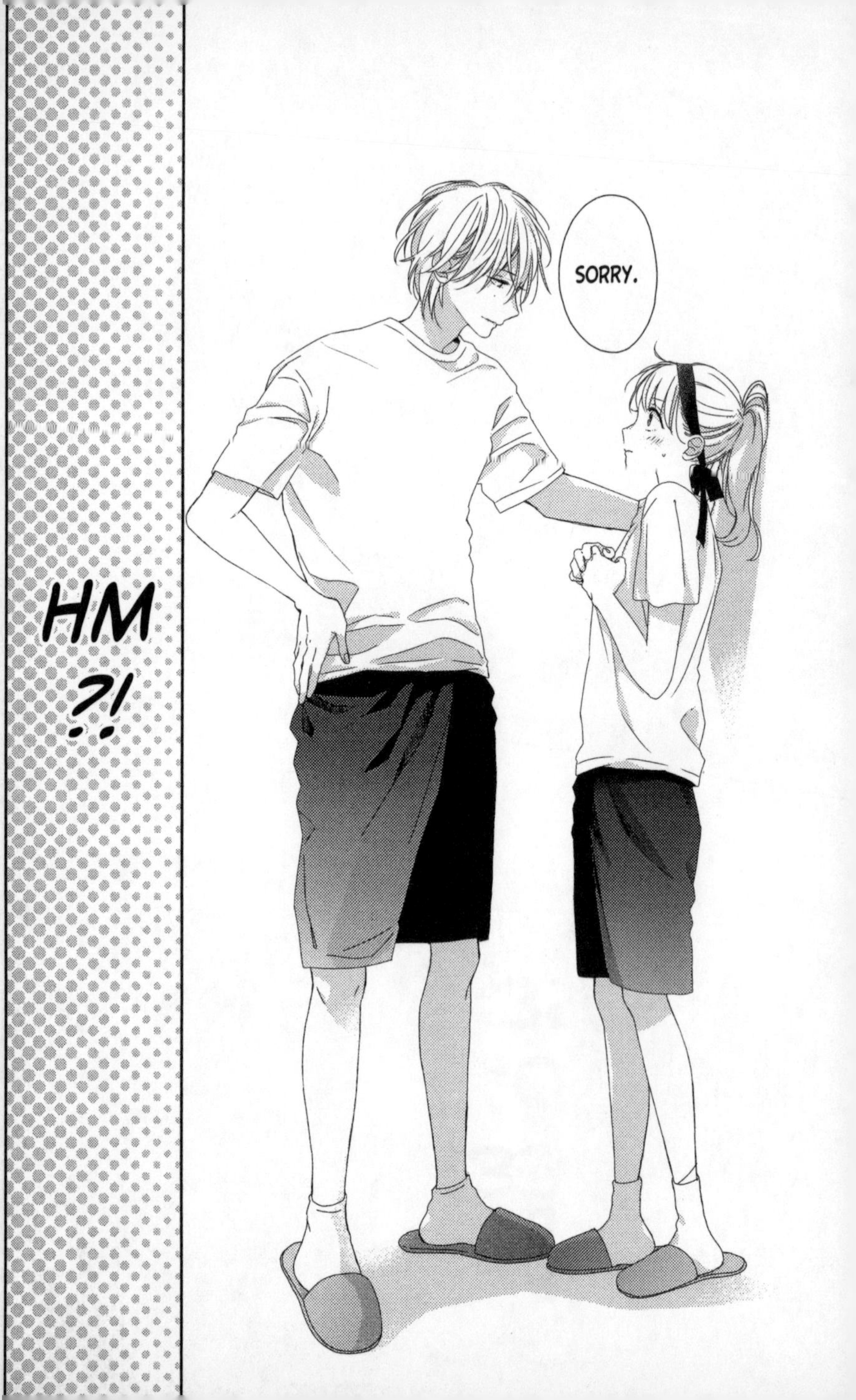
SORRY.
HM ?!

Those
Not-So-
Sweet
Boys

PART TIME AT A RESTAURANT

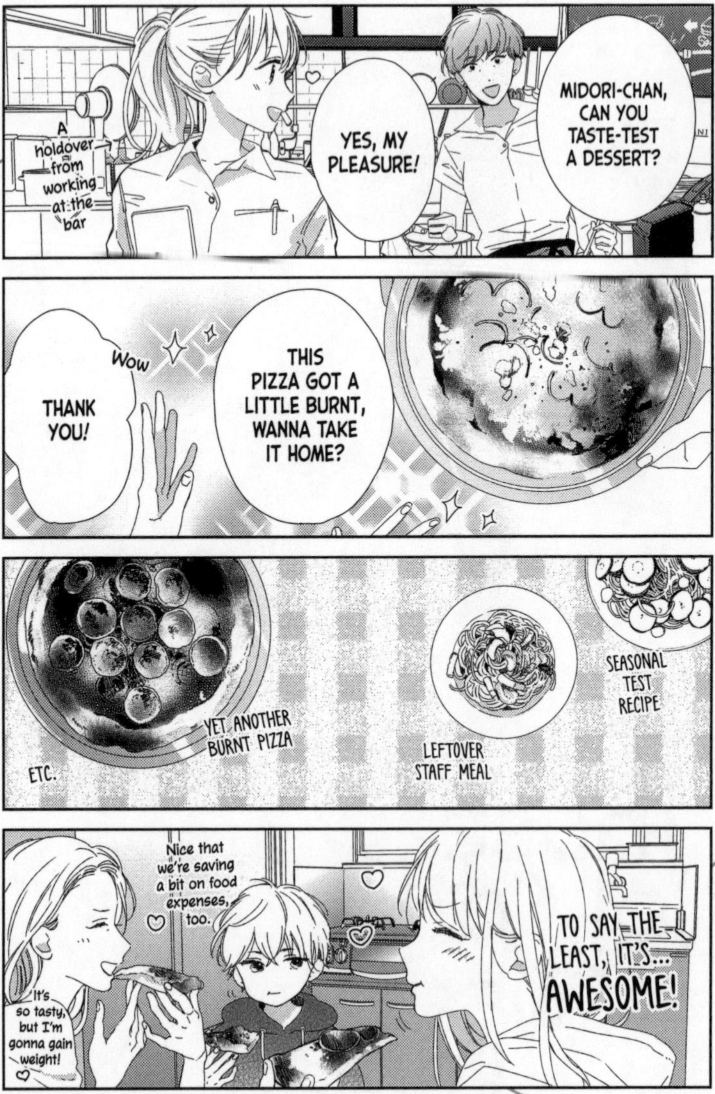
MIDORI-CHAN, CAN YOU TASTE-TEST A DESSERT?
YES, MY PLEASURE!
A holdover from working at the bar
THIS PIZZA GOT A LITTLE BURNT, WANNA TAKE IT HOME?
Wow
THANK YOU!
SEASONAL TEST RECIPE
LEFTOVER STAFF MEAL
YET ANOTHER BURNT PIZZA
ETC.
TO SAY THE LEAST, IT'S... AWESOME!
Nice that we're saving a bit on food expenses, too.
It's so tasty, but I'm gonna gain weight!

A PRESENT FOR KOTA
A SAMPLER SET FROM THE PET SUPPLY STORE
200 YEN (APPROX. $2)
SNACK SAMPLER SETS
NO ADDITIVES HEALTHY, DOG FRIENDLY, AND WALLET FRIENDLY!
PICK FOR YOUR PUP'S FAVES!
1 BAG 200 YEN

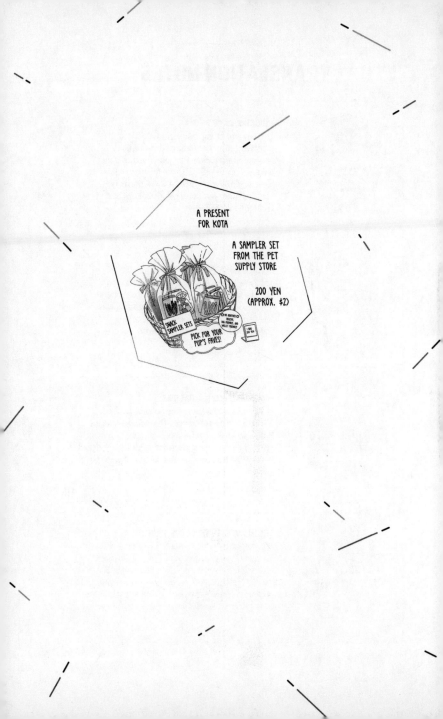

TRANSLATION NOTES

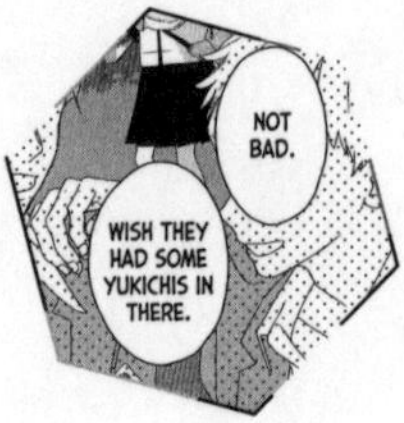
NOT BAD.
WISH THEY HAD SOME YUKICHIS IN THERE.

YUKICHIS, PAGE 7

This boy is referring to Fukuzawa Yukichi, a prominent Japanese historical figure who appears on the 10,000-yen note. The monetary amount is close to $100, so the American equivalent would be a Benjamin. A wallet that only contains 5,000 yen would not include any bills featuring Yukichi-san.

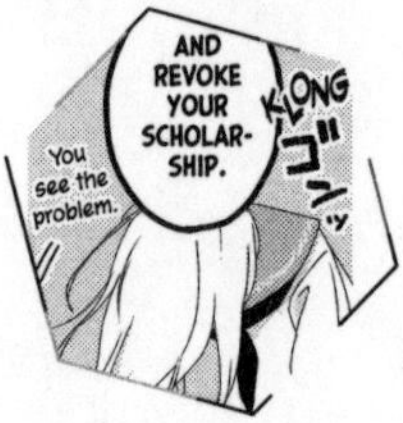
KLONG
AND REVOKE YOUR SCHOLARSHIP.
You see the problem.

SCHOLARSHIP, PAGE 17

To be more specific, this school offers a tuition exemption. This means that a student can attend the school without paying the normal admission fees and tuition if they meet specific criteria, usually involving academic excellence.

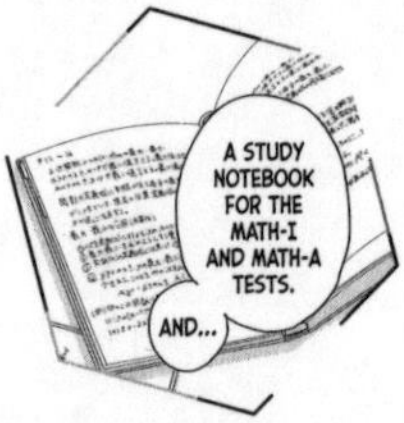
A STUDY NOTEBOOK FOR THE MATH-I AND MATH-A TESTS.
AND...

MATH I AND MATH A, PAGE 45

In Japanese education, mathematics as a subject is divided into different courses. The required course is Math-I, which teaches functions, formulas, trigonometry, etc. Math-A is mostly a supplementary course and teaches things such as statistics, probability, and properties of integers.

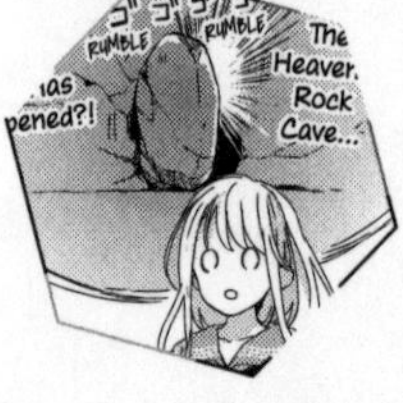
The Heaven. Rock Cave...
RUMBLE
RUMBLE

THE HEAVENLY ROCK CAVE, PAGE 51

Amano-Iwato, or "the Heavenly Rock Cave," is a traditional tale from Japanese mythology. According to legend, Amaterasu, the sun goddess, was harassed by Susano-o, the god of storms, until she hid in a rock cave and refused to come out, leaving the world in darkness. It took the other gods much persuading to get her to emerge.

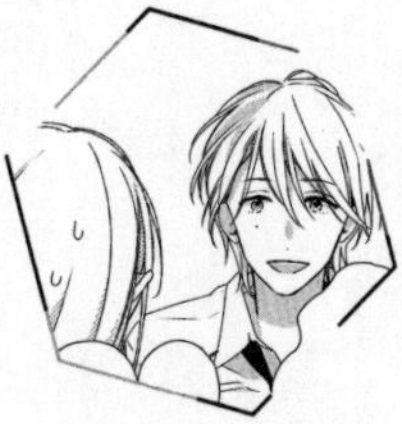

5 IN ART, PAGE 105
In Japan, the grading system is based on numbers instead of letters. A 5 is the equivalent of an A.

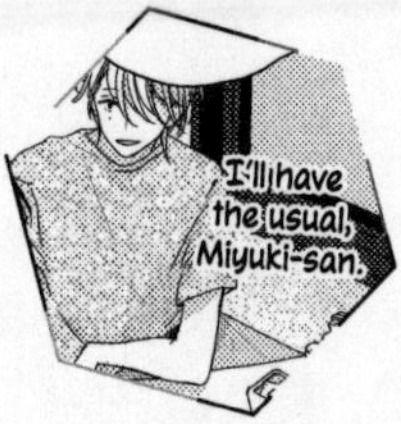

I'll have the usual, Miyuki-san.

REI-CHAN, PAGE 129
The suffix *-chan* is attached to someone's name to indicate closeness and friendship on behalf of the speaker. However, it is mostly often applied to women, girls, and young children. It is not very common for a speaker to use *-chan* on boys Rei's age unless they are very close.

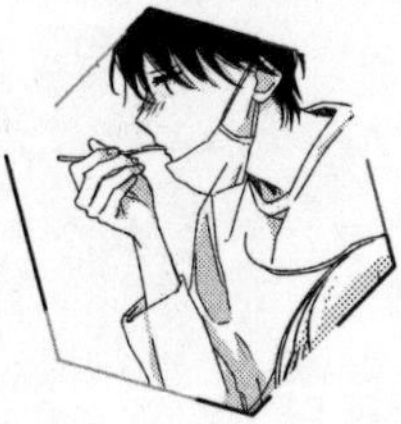

RICE PORRIDGE, PAGE 147
Rice porridge, or *okayu*, is a common dish served to people who are ill, because it is so easy to digest. It is made of mostly rice and water, possibly with some toppings, such as green onions or ginger, to add flavor.

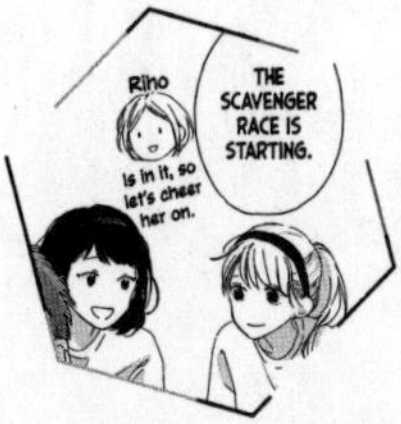

THE SCAVENGER RACE IS STARTING.
Rino is in it, so let's cheer her on.

THE SCAVENGER RACE, PAGE 174
A common event in Japanese sports days is the scavenger race, which is similar to, but not exactly like, a scavenger hunt. When the race starts, the competitors run to a table where they pick up a piece of paper telling them one item they must find. In normal circumstances, the items assigned are something that would commonly be on hand, and the participants are allowed to ask the spectators if anyone has it. They must be the first to the finish line carrying their assigned item.

A picture-perfect shojo series from Yoko Nogiri, creator of the hit *That Wolf-Boy is Mine!*

Mako's always had a passion for photography. When she loses someone dear to her, she clings onto her art as a relic of the close relationship she once had... Luckily, her childhood best friend Kei encourages her to come to his high school and join their prestigious photo club. With nothing to lose, Mako grabs her camera and moves into the dorm where Kei and his classmates live. Soon, a fresh take on life, along with a mysterious new muse, begin to come into focus!

LOVE IN FOCUS

Love in Focus © Yoko Nogiri/Kodansha Ltd.

Praise for Yoko Nogiri's *That Wolf-Boy is Mine!*

"Emotional squees...will-they-won't-they plot...[and a] pleasantly quick pace."
—Otaku USA Magazine

"A series that is pure shojo sugar—a cute love story about two nice people looking for their places in the world, and finding them with each other." —Anime News Network

A SMART, NEW ROMANTIC COMEDY FOR FANS OF *SHORTCAKE CAKE* AND *TERRACE HOUSE*!

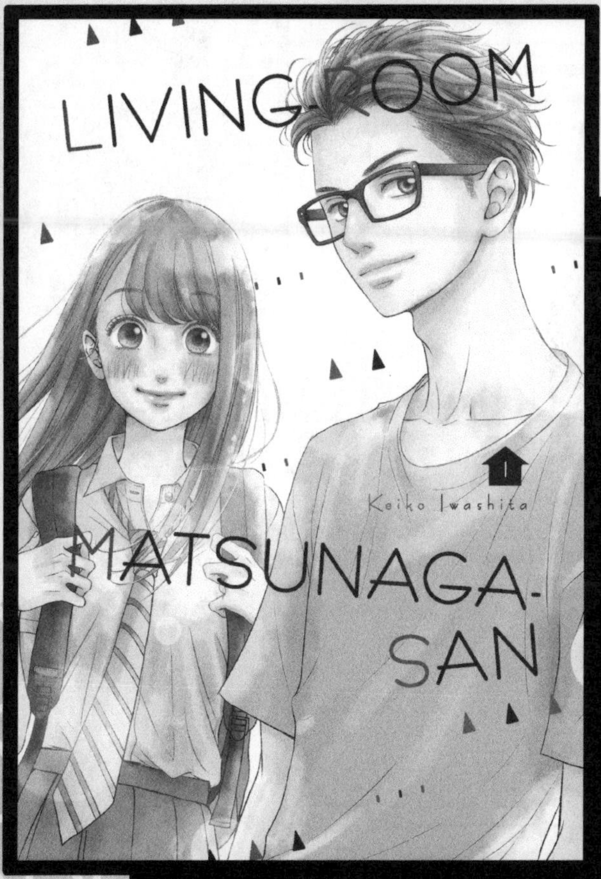
LIVING-ROOM
MATSUNAGA-SAN
1
Keiko Iwashita

KC KODANSHA COMICS

A romance manga starring high school girl Meeko, who learns to live on her own in a boarding house whose living room is home to the odd (but handsome) Matsunaga-san. She begins to adjust to her new life away from her parents, but Meeko soon learns that no matter how far away from home she is, she's still a young girl at heart — especially when she finds herself falling for Matsunaga-san.

WAITING FOR SPRING

A sweet romantic story of a soft-spoken high school freshman and her quest to make friends. For fans of earnest, fun, and dramatic shojo like *Kimi ni Todoke* and *Say I Love You*.

KISS ME AT THE STROKE OF MIDNIGHT

An all-new Cinderella comedy perfect for fans of *My Little Monster* and *Say I Love You*!

LOVE AND LIES

Love is forbidden. When you turn 16, the government will assign you your marriage partner. This dystopian manga about teen love and defiance is a sexy, funny, and dramatic new hit! Anime now streaming on Anime Strike!

YOUR NEW FAVORITE ROMANCE MANGA IS WAITING FOR YOU!

THAT WOLF-BOY IS MINE!

A beast-boy comedy and drama perfect for fans of *Fruits Basket*!

"A tantalizing, understated slice-of-life romance with an interesting supernatural twist."

- Taykobon

WAKE UP, SLEEPING BEAUTY

This heartrending romantic manga is not the fairy tale you remember! This time, Prince Charming is a teenage housekeeper, and Sleeping Beauty's curse threatens to pull them both into deep trouble.

A Kodansha Comics Trade Paperback Original
Those Not-So-Sweet Boys 1 copyright © 2019 Yoko Nogiri
English translation copyright © 2021 Yoko Nogiri

Published in the United States by Kodansha Comics, an imprint of
Kodansha USA Publishing, LLC, New York.

Publication rights for this English edition arranged through
Kodansha Ltd., Tokyo.

First published in Japan in 2019 by Kodansha Ltd., Tokyo
as *Amakunai Karera no Nichijo wa.*, volume 1.

ISBN 978-1-64651-174-7

Original cover design by Tomohiro Kusume + Sayaka Nagai (arcoinc)

Printed in the United States of America.

www.kodanshacomics.com

9 8 7 6 5 4 3 2 1
Translation: Alethea Nibley & Athena Nibley
Lettering: Sara Linsley
Editing: Haruko Hashimoto
Kodansha Comics edition cover design by Phil Balsman

Publisher: Kiichiro Sugawara

Director of publishing services: Ben Applegate
Associate director of operations: Stephen Pakula
Publishing services managing editor: Noelle Webster
Assistant production manager: Emi Lotto, Angela Zurlo
Logo and character art ©Kodansha USA Publishing, LLC